CONFUCIAN TRADITIONS
IN EAST ASIAN MODERNITY

CONFUCIAN TRADITIONS
IN EAST ASIAN MODERNITY

*Moral Education and
Economic Culture in Japan and the
Four Mini-Dragons*

EDITED BY
Tu Wei-ming

HARVARD UNIVERSITY PRESS
Cambridge, Massachusetts
London, England   1996

This collection of essays was prepared under the auspices of the
American Academy of Arts and Sciences.

Library of Congress Cataloging-in-Publication Data

Confucian traditions in east Asian modernity : moral education and economic
  culture in Japan and the four mini-dragons / edited by Tu Wei-ming.
      p.   cm.
  "Essays were prepared under the auspices of the Academy of Arts and
Sciences."
  Includes index.
  ISBN 0-674-16086-X (cloth : alk. paper)
  ISBN 0-674-16087-8 (paper : alk. paper)
  1. East Asia—Civilization—Confucian influences. I. Tu, Wei-ming.
DS509.3.C67   1996
950—dc20   95-30852

CONTENTS

PREFACE

This conference volume grew out of a meeting funded by the Luce Foundation at the home of the American Academy of Arts and Sciences (AAAS), May 15–18, 1991. More than twenty scholars from Japan, South Korea, Hong Kong, Singapore, Israel, and North America took part in an intense discussion of papers circulated beforehand. These were subsequently revised by the authors and edited for publication. This book is the work of seventeen scholars in their respective fields offering different perspectives on the Confucian role in industrial East Asia. Strictly speaking, however, this collaborative effort in its current form is no more than proceedings of an international conversation which continues to generate new dynamism and create new possibilities. As such, it has all the trappings of an interim report: tentativeness, conflicting interpretations, and divergent perspectives. Its heuristic value, however, is immense, for it represents the current thinking of some of the most sophisticated minds on this vital and intriguing subject.

The question of whether the Confucian ethic has contributed to the rise of industrial East Asia has attracted much public attention and generated a great deal of scholarly inquiry since the 1970s. The issue is significant not only for academicians working on East Asia and nonspecialists engaged in or interested in East Asian affairs, but also for journalists, business executives, and policymakers. The region's ability to sustain the world's highest growth rate since the 1950s has merited serious attention by developmental economists, comparative sociologists, and political scientists. It is not the growth rate itself, however, but the various structural and functional reasons underlying this "economic miracle" and the emerging form of life it engenders that present a particularly thought-provoking challenge to the intellectual community.

When in 1987 a small coterie of Harvard colleagues, at the suggestion of the AAAS, gathered in the Cambridge home of the Academy to explore ways of understanding and studying this phenomenon, the plan was first to assess the overall impact of the rise of industrial East Asia by focusing on Japan in areas such as industry, international trade, global finance, foreign aid, science, technology, art, and literature. The second step was to consider the implications of the rise of industrial East Asia for mainland China, and eventually to comment on its significance for western Europe and North America. A line of exploration that would run parallel to this overall plan was for studying the Confucian role in industrial East Asia, involving scholars in the humanities as well as social scientists. The justification was the felt need to appreciate the role of culture, not only as a background to but also as a constitutive part of economic dynamics. We assumed that any sophisticated analysis of the rise of industrial East Asia must wrestle with issues of moral education, political authority, social solidarity, and religious beliefs.

A generous grant from the Luce Foundation enabled us to launch the Confucian project in 1989 by organizing a workshop to discuss a variety of perspectives on the role of Confucian culture in industrial East Asia. Focusing on topics such as Confucian ethics as a common discourse, cultural identity and social implications, gender and family, community and education, political culture and economic ethics, and popular thought and religion, twenty-seven participants from the fields of anthropology, economics, history, philosophy, political science, religion, and sociology engaged in an intense and provocative exchange of views on the Confucian *Problematik*. The discussions were published in *The Confucian World Observed: A Contemporary Discussion of Confucian Humanism in East Asia*.[1]

Rarely has there been such an opportunity to engage scholars working in many different fields in the kind of interdisciplinary and cross-cultural joint venture undertaken by the AAAS. Before the Academy's project was launched, a concerted effort had been made to wrestle with the mode of questioning based on Max Weber's classic study of the interaction between ethicoreligious values and economic behavior. Under the sponsorship of the Institute of East Asian Philosophies in Singapore, a series of international meetings was organized to explore ways of addressing Weber's thesis, with particular attention to the East Asian experience.[2] Several of the participants in the Academy's project were present at these meetings.[3]

While remaining true to the spirit of the Academy in associating many specialized lines of concentration by gathering the individuals in whom they are embodied so that the group as a whole is enriched, we were critically aware of the danger that, since each of us is narrowed by our area of specialization, the results of our conversation might lack the coherence needed to set a new agenda for furthering productive scholarship. In retrospect, our sense of the precariousness of the enterprise was not at all exaggerated. The asymmetry between social scientists and humanities scholars, between Japanologists and Sinologists, between economists and culturalists, and between idealists and realists was blatantly clear.

Fortunately, all the participants had a genuine desire for interdisciplinary and cross-cultural communication, a strong commitment to work toward a common agenda, and, perhaps most significant, a shared concern for the basic issues involved and a tacitly agreed upon methodological orientation. Benjamin Schwartz of Harvard University, Peter Berger of Boston University, and Edward Tiryakian of Duke University, the three senior scholars who did not contribute papers but who were enormously helpful in shaping the character of the May 1991 conference, set the tone for the conversation.

The arduous task of transforming the papers into a conference volume, however, required not only the collaboration of the authors but also the painstaking efforts of two friends and fellow students of East Asian culture. Brian Hoffert, a graduate student at Harvard, ably edited all the papers and then stored the entire manuscript in the computer while he was finishing his M.A. in philosophy at the University of Hawaii; and Nancy Hearst, librarian of the John King Fairbank Center for East Asian Research, scrupulously went over the manuscript before it was submitted to the press for copyediting. I am indebted to them for their thoroughness and professionalism. I also thank Corinne Shilling of the Academy and Terry Lautz of the Luce Foundation for their continuous support. David Xiaokang Chu of the Cultural China Program at the East-West Center, under a generous grant from Lawrance and Mary Rockefeller, Henry Rosemont of St. Mary's University, and Rossanne Vaugh Hall of Cambridge have spent inordinate amounts of time and energy helping to shape the manuscript. I gratefully acknowledge their friendship and encouragement. Finally, I am saddened to report that one of our contributors, Edward Shils, passed away on January 23, 1995. The *New York Times*'s obituary, with extensive information on his brilliant career, appeared the next day. His piece for our volume, a major effort to learn from the Confucian tradition, reflects his lifelong commitment to understanding the social role of the intellectual in a comparative perspective. As his assistant, Christine C. Schusenberg, notes, "Confucianism and civil society in the tradition of Chinese intellectuals"[4] became one of Professor Shils's consuming scholarly preoccupations toward the end of his life. We are in his debt.

CONFUCIAN TRADITIONS
IN EAST ASIAN MODERNITY

INTRODUCTION

This is not a book on Confucianism—Confucian thought, Confucian ethics, or Confucian theory in practice. Nor is it a book on the defining characteristics of the Confucian tradition and its modern transformation. Rather, it is an inquiry into the dynamic interplay of intellectual, social, political, and economic currents in Japan and the Four Mini-Dragons (South Korea, Taiwan, Hong Kong, and Singapore), with particular attention to the cultural implications of the rise of industrial East Asia. The contributors take the Confucian dimension as the point of entry for our inquiry. Confucian concerns (i.e., self-cultivation, regulation of the family, social civility, moral education, well-being of the people, governance of the state, and universal peace) provide a general framework for our joint venture. The Confucian *Problematik*—how a fiduciary community can come into being through exemplary teaching and moral transformation—underlies much of the discussion.

Our inquiry is guided by a critical consciousness that leads us to question all unexamined assumptions about the rise of industrial East Asia. We do not as a group subscribe to any one thesis or hypothesis as the best way to understand its cultural implications. Since our primary purpose is to comprehend, we hope collectively to bring new insights to this multifaceted phenomenon through our varying interpretations. Our strategy, then, is not to seek consensus but to provide an open forum to accommodate several seemingly conflicting lines of thought. While we are acutely aware of the need for significantly different perspectives, our intent is to explore those ideas, norms, and values that underlie the moral fabric of East Asian societies. It is certainly advisable, at this early stage, not to tie up loose ends prematurely in studying such an immensely complex phenomenon as the rise of industrial East Asia, an area that continues to undergo unprecedented transformation. By characterizing our endeavor as an attempt to probe the Confucian traditions of East Asian modernity, we mean to show that there are different ways to conceptualize the Confucian heritage of modern East Asia, and that this points toward the need for reexamining the whole idea of modernity.

As this digested conversation indicates, there is as much contested interpretation as there is "fusion of horizons" on virtually all aspects of the Confucian thesis. For instance, is Confucian ethics a common discourse in industrial East Asia? We find that the answer varies according to academic discipline, regional specialization, and personal judgment. Historians, especially intellectual historians, tend to stress the common heritage and shared spiritual orientation, whereas anthropologists are wary about making broad generalizations and prefer to offer "thick descriptions" of the local scene. Japanologists, while acknowledging the ubiquitous presence of the Confucian pattern of behavior, tend to minimize the prominence of Confucian thought in Japan's modern transformation. The relevance of Confucian ethics in the economic ethos and political culture of Taiwan, Hong Kong, Singapore, and overseas Chinese communities is taken for granted by Sinologists, but there is no consensus on the role and function of the Confucian ethic in the modern transformation of these societies.

It ought to be noted, however, that it was the towering figure of American Japanology, Edwin Reischauer, who, in his seminal essay "The Sinic World in Perspective," first emphasized the pervasiveness of the Confucian mentality in contemporary East Asia, including Japan.[1] Though mindful of Japan's uniqueness,[2] Reischauer insisted on situating Japan in the East Asian cultural universe to show that its economic dynamism indicates not merely exceptionalism but a pattern of modern transformation encompassing the whole of East Asia. Putting the Sinic world in perspective thus provides a proper context for understanding Japan, the Four Mini-Dragons, overseas Chinese communities, and, eventually, socialist East Asia (mainland China, North Korea, and Vietnam).

Surely "the claim that Confucian ethics, as reflected in government leadership, competitive education, a disciplined work force, principles of equality and self-reliance, and self-cultivation, provides a necessary background and powerful motivating force for the rise of industrial East Asia"[3] has yet to be substantiated. Nevertheless, the benefit of addressing the issue is obvious. The difficulty of confronting the role of culture in industrial East Asia is, of course, enormous, but by focusing our attention on the Confucian role, we are compelled to wrestle with the question instead of relegating it to the background or to a residual category. Already this "Confucian hypothesis" has stimulated an impressive array of productive research and will continue to challenge us to formulate more comprehensive and refined interpretations.

Among the conceptual resources widely tapped for this kind of inquiry, the Weberian mode of questioning, as demonstrated in Max Weber's *Protestant Ethic and the Spirit of Capitalism,* looms large in our discussion. But the method of finding the functional equivalent of the Protestant ethic in the "modernized" or "vulgarized" Confucian ethic is too facile, simpleminded, and mechanistic to merit serious attention. This observation is not meant to downplay the importance of a work ethic in East Asian productivity. In fact, several significant empirical studies have helped us to understand the correlation between value orientation, attitude, and performance in East Asian industry, and the Confucian ethic is often identified as a positive factor in these studies. Nevertheless, the inadequacy of regarding the Confucian ethic in East Asia as the functional equivalent of the Protestant ethic is obvious: what it manages to reveal may turn out to be misleading, but what it inadvertently conceals is at times vitally important. After all, Weber's brilliant study of the psychocultural conditions that made possible the development of the spirit of capitalism was, in his view, only a preliminary step toward estimating "the quantitative cultural significance of ascetic Protestantism in its relation to the other plastic elements of modern culture."[4]

In *The Protestant Ethic and the Spirit of Capitalism* Weber indicates that he is critically aware of the requisite intermediate steps involved in the kind of cultural study for which his was a mere beginning:

> The next task would be rather to show the significance of ascetic rationalism, which has only been touched in the foregoing sketch, for the content of practical social ethics, thus for the types of organization and the functions of social groups from conventicle to the State. Then its relation to humanistic rationalism, its ideal of life and cultural influence; further to the development of philosophical and scientific empiricism, to technical development and to spiritual ideals would have to be analyzed. Then its historical development from the mediaeval beginnings of worldly asceticism to its dissolution into pure utilitarianism would have to be traced out through all the areas of ascetic religion.[5]

What Weber outlined was his vision of the rise of the modern West, a vision pregnant with fruitful ambiguities and far-reaching implications for comparative civilizational studies.

Understandably, Weber's well-known interpretive stance on Confucianism served as a point of departure for the entire discussion, notwithstanding the obsolescence of many of his empirical observations. For example, Weber's concluding remark in *The Religion of China* is still highly suggestive:

> The Chinese in all probability would be quite capable . . . of assimilating capitalism which has technically and economically been fully developed in the modern culture area. It is obviously not a question of deeming the Chinese "naturally ungifted" for the demands of capitalism. But compared to the Occident, the varied conditions which externally favored the origin of capitalism in China did not suffice to create it. Likewise capitalism did not originate in occidental or oriental Antiquity, or in India, or where Islamism held sway. Yet in each of these areas different and favorable circumstances seemed to facilitate its rise. Many of the circumstances which could or had to hinder capitalism in China similarly existed in the Occident and assumed definite shape in the period of modern capitalism.[6]

Evidently there is fluidity in Weber's characterization of the genetic reasons for the development of capitalism. As Wolfgang Schluchter notes, since Weber was mainly concerned with a specific historical question—namely, why industrial capitalism emerged in the Protestant West—his interpretation leaves open the possibility that different forms of capitalism might grow out of a variety of cultural traditions in response to the challenge of the modern West.[7] This may be what prompted Peter Berger to characterize industrial East Asian capitalism as a "second case."[8]

Our venture to explore the Confucian influence in Japan and the Four Mini-Dragons is part of this international collaborative effort to come to terms with the rise of industrial East Asia as a cultural phenomenon as well as an economic and political process. Our decision to involve scholars from different academic disciplines, with different regional specializations and working at different levels of generalization and in different styles of explanation, was predicated on the assumption that, since the subject has attracted much attention from policymakers, the mass media, and the general public, it is imperative that we continue our brainstorming to raise thought-provoking questions. Our purpose, then, is to achieve a broad grasp of the interplay between cultural values and the economic, political, social, and ethical life of East Asian peoples.

The underlying assumption that culture matters and that economic facts and political institutions are laden with cultural values was neither trivialized nor relegated to a residual category. While opinions varied in assigning specific weight to the Confucian factor in explaining the dynamic transformation of industrial East Asia, there was a remarkable convergence of views on the need to problematize the Confucian hypothesis and to provide sophisticated cultural and historical background to the Confucian thesis in current interpretive literature on East Asia in the English-speaking community. Imagine a reporter from Beijing who intended to write a series of articles on the American economy, polity, and society during the highly energized 1994 election season, yet who not only was unfamiliar with Christian symbols but insisted on the irrelevance of the Protestant tradition to his journalistic task. Would we have much faith in his ability to present culturally sophisticated reports on the current American scene, including the presidential debates?

Surely, just as it is conceptually vague and misleading to label American society Christian, it is neither instructive nor correct to characterize any East Asian society as Confucian. Still, cultural sensitivity and cultural competence, as reflected in either a general theory or an empirical investigation, are desirable and often necessary. I mention this, of course, not to conflate knowledge about Confucian ethics with sensitivity to and competence in East Asian culture, but to acknowledge that familiarity with Confucian ethics can serve as a litmus test for judging intellectual seriousness in approaching East Asia as a subject in comparative civilizational studies.

We must not underestimate the complexity of the methodological issues involved in addressing the Confucian role in East Asian societies, itself a fine art, because that role is both elusive and pervasive. We are, on the one hand, at a loss to identify and define how the Confucian ethic actually works in economic organization, political ideology, and social behavior. And yet, on the other hand, we are impressed by its presence in virtually every aspect of interpersonal relations in East Asian life. Understandably, the authors of this volume have chosen a variety of methods to investigate the phenomenon. The range of options includes the core curriculum in moral education, ancestral veneration in family ritual, styles of protest among the intelligentsia, symbolic resources in the development of a civil society, the formation of a political ideology, and networking in economic behavior and organization.

If we try to look for an integrated pattern to tell us the precise boundaries and significance of the Confucian influence in industrial East Asia, we are most likely to be disappointed. At the same time, while we frankly admit to an asymmetry in style, method, and level of analysis, we maintain that *Confucian Traditions in East Asian Modernity* offers a many-faceted conversation rather than discrete monologues. Indeed, there are so many points of convergence and intersections of communication that it is not farfetched to claim that this book represents a new attempt by like-minded scholars to come to grips with moral education and economic culture in contemporary East Asia. The broad picture that emerges from the contributors' focused, sometimes highly specialized studies is, in Jürgen Habermas's expression, a lifeworld, significantly different from our own in the West (specifically western Europe and North America) and yet modern in every sense of the word.

Two implications are worth mentioning. First, there is the fascinating phenomenon of traditions in modernity. The question in what sense has the Confucian ethic contributed to the economic dynamics of industrial East Asia seems less interesting than a much more profound subject of investigation: How does the Confucian tradition, in belief, attitude, and practice, continue to impede, facilitate, and guide the modern transformation in East Asia, and, in the process, how is it being rejected, revitalized, and fundamentally restructured? The limited Weberian project of searching for the functional equivalent of the Protestant ethic must be subsumed under Weber's general comparative civilizational perspective—namely, given the vital importance of the value orientation in economic development, what can the Confucian influence in industrial East Asia tell us about the relation between tradition and modernity?

Weber's assertion that since "the impediments to the development of capitalism must be sought primarily in the domain of religion,"[9] Confucianism, Hinduism, Islam, Buddhism, and, by implication, all indigenous religious traditions, unlike Protestantism, are detrimental to the modernizing process initiated in western Europe and must therefore be thoroughly revised. A more reasonable position is to argue for the transformative potential of all these major ethicoreligious traditions. What the experience of development in industrial East Asia suggests is not the passing of a traditional society but the continuing role of tradition in providing the rich texture of an evolving modernity. Confucianism—and, presumably, Hinduism, Islam, Buddhism, and indigenous religious traditions (for instance, those of the Maori)—may have impeded the modernization of a traditional Oriental society in the Occidental sense. But the modernization of a Confucian society—or, for that matter, a Hindu, Islamic, Buddhist, or Maori society—requires the continuous participation and creative transformation of its ethicoreligious traditions. Since the rise of industrial East Asia indicates the authentic possibility of a Confucian spirit of capitalism, it may not be outrageous to imagine a Hindu, Islamic, Buddhist, or Maori spirit of capitalism.

This inevitably leads to the second implication: Can the modernization process assume cultural forms different from those identified as characteristically Western since the period of the Enlightenment? In other words, are market economy, democratic polity, and individualism so essential to the modernist project and so integrated as three inseparable dimensions of modernity that no society can ever become modernized without simultaneously being Westernized? The rise of industrial East Asia, at a minimum, has significantly complicated the Weberian picture of modernization as rationalization, a sort of unfolding of the Enlightenment mentality. Indeed, no matter how diverse and complex we imagine the West to be (Weber's concept is certainly sophisticated enough to accommodate many conflicting trends), the inclusion of the East Asian experience in the picture of modernity makes it extremely difficult to interpret modernization in light of exclusively Western symbolic resources. Once we begin to acknowledge the compatibility of a market economy and an authoritarian state, recognize the centrality of family virtues to social solidarity, appreciate the fruitful interplay between group consensus and personal independence, construct ideas of civil society based on indigenous categories, and employ new conceptual apparatuses such as network capitalism to understand a different kind of economic dynamics, we are well on our way to an alternative vision of modernity.

In the East Asian cultural context, government leadership is deemed indispensable for a smooth functioning of the domestic market economy and vital for enhancing national comparative advantage in international competition. The central government is expected to have a holistic vision of the well-being of the nation and a long-term plan to help people maintain an adequate livelihood so that they can attain their aspirations of human flourishing. Strong government with moral authority, a sort of ritualized symbolic power fully accepted by the overwhelming majority, is acclaimed as a blessing, for it is the responsibility of the ruling minority to translate the general will of the people into reasonable policies on security, health care, economic growth, social welfare, and education. Indeed, political leaders (including civil servants) in East Asia often possess a commanding influence in the public sphere. They may not be able to dictate the agenda or control the outcome of a public debate, but their voice normally overpowers the voices of other sectors in the society, such as the mass media, the business community, and the intelligentsia. Either in self-understanding or in public image, the political leader ought to be a teacher as well as an exemplar and a public servant. Indeed, scholars, journalists, and entrepreneurs often cultivate their most cherished and coveted personal ties with members of officialdom. The Confucian scholar-official mentality still functions in the psychocultural construct of East Asian societies. The best minds in business, the media, and the academic community are often readily available for political appointments.

The lack of clear boundaries between public and private in East Asian societies, occasioned by the pervasive influence of politics in all segments of the lifeworld, may not conform to the Western model of modernity, with its highly differentiated spheres of interest. It is, however, wholly commensurate with the centrality of the family in East Asia, not only as a basic social unit but as a metaphor for political culture. The structure and function of the family varies substantially among Chinese, Japanese, and Korean societies, but the family's supreme role in capital formation, power politics, social stability, and moral education is comparable in all East Asian communities. The classic Confucian vision that "only when families are regulated are states governed" (stated in the opening passage of the *Great Learning*) is still taken absolutely seriously in East Asian political culture. The idea of the state as an enlarged family may have lost much of its persuasiveness, but the metaphor of the family is widely present in all forms of social organization. Moreover, family-style connectedness is characteristic of many prominent modes of interpersonal communication based on educational, territorial, and religious ties. The lack of development of Western-style civil society rooted in voluntary associations is clearly attributable to the saliency of this noncontractual, extralegal, and ascriptive networking.

Implicit in the significance of the family for social intercourse is the idea of duty. The sense that one is obligated to, and responsible for, an ever-expanding network of human relatedness may not be a constraint on one's independence and autonomy. On the contrary, since personal dignity is predicated on one's ability not only to establish oneself but also to take care of others, one's level of independence and autonomy is measurable in terms of the degree to which one fulfills obligations and discharges responsibilities to family, community, state, the world, and Heaven. The psychological mechanism reflected in the fear of losing face in public, which is often accompanied by a profound sense of personal guilt, is deduced from this. As the eminent New Confucian thinker Tang Junyi (T'ang Chün-i, 1909–1978) perceptively notes, duty consciousness prompts East Asian moral and political leaders to act so as to enhance the public good. The difficulty East Asian societies have in developing a sophisticated legal system based on human rights lies not only in the absence of a juridical tradition but also in the strong presence of a different style of moral reasoning.

A significant and captivating aspect of this alternative East Asian vision of modernity is the communal spirit. Although, as many observers of the industrial East Asian scene have noted, "individualism has flourished as growth has occurred; [and] hedonism has also increased, in the sense of viewing happiness not as a reward for hard work but as a natural right that is also a goal in itself"[10] in Japan and elsewhere, the trends that were expected to change the social structure of the East Asian workplace do not seem to have fundamentally undermined the power of the communal spirit. Consensus as a preferred way of decision making, negotiation as a conventional method of resolving conflict, informal arbitration as a frequent substitute for formal legal procedures, and, as a last resort, the common practice of mediation through third parties rather than direct confrontation between rivals are all symptomatic of an overriding concern for group solidarity in politics, business, and society at large in East Asia. In this particular connection what Japan and the Four Mini-Dragons symbolize is a less adversarial, less individualistic, and less self-interested but highly energized and fiercely competitive approach to modernization.

It is vitally important to note that the East Asian form of modernity is in a substantial way "Western." After all, it has been the result of a conscious response to the challenge of the modern West since the mid-nineteenth century. Without the Western model, including the Dutch, British, French, German, and more recently American examples, East Asian societies would not have embarked on a restless march toward modernization. What would East Asia have become had the imperialist powers never imposed their way of life on the Land of the Rising Sun, the Hermit Kingdom, and the Middle Country? Although the region most likely would not have developed the "capitalist spirit" as Weber understood it, the overwhelming presence of the modern West for more than a century makes this kind of counterfactual supposition historically insignificant, if not theoretically inconceivable. Indeed, East Asian intellectuals have reluctantly but thoroughly accepted modern Western nations as the initiators, executors, and judges of the international rules of the game in foreign trade, diplomacy, power politics, military confrontation, and transnational communication for so long that they themselves have taken it for granted that modernization, in theory and practice, is synonymous with Westernization. The record number of industrial East Asian leaders in academia, politics, business, the mass media, and the military who were educated in the United States since the end of the Second World War further enhances the impression that Westernization is, by and large, Americanization.

The rise of industrial East Asia, paradoxically, signifies the continuous vitality and dynamism of modernization as Westernization. This is clearly evidenced in the persuasive power of market economy and democratic polity and the attendant Enlightenment values, such as progress, equality, liberty, human rights, individual dignity, and due process of law, in the psychocultural construct of the East Asian intelligentsia. Modernization as Americanization is perhaps most obviously demonstrated in the receptivity of East Asian youth to American popular culture and the susceptibility of the East Asian general public to American consumerism. The commanding influence of American higher education, however, especially research universities, on the East Asian natural sciences, social sciences, and humanities may have been the single most important factor in perpetuating the image of the United States as a future-oriented global intellectual leader in East Asian minds.

Nevertheless, the modernizing experience in industrial East Asia seriously challenges all the conceptual apparatuses that have been used to characterize Western-style modernity. The modern West may have prompted East Asia to modernize in the initial stages, but as the process gathered momentum, a variety of indigenous resources were mobilized. The structures that emerged, therefore, appear significantly different from those in western Europe and North America. It seems that the social and cultural capital that has sustained the economic dynamism of Japan and the Four Mini-Dragons has been at least commensurate with Confucian ethics, if not thoroughly Confucian in nature. Even if Weber was correct in assuming that Confucianism had impeded the development of modern industrial capitalism in traditional East Asia, the thesis that the Confucian ethic is incompatible with the spirit of capitalism is untenable. On the contrary, it has been shown that the Confucian ethic is not only compatible with the capitalist spirit but may actually have helped industrial East Asia to develop a different form of modern industrial capitalism. Indeed, attempts have been made to argue a much stronger hypothesis—namely, that the capitalism rooted in Confucian ethics may turn out to be more consequential for the twenty-first century than the classic capitalism fashioned by the inner-worldly asceticism of the Puritan ethic. The implications are profound and far-reaching. The contributors to *Confucian Traditions in East Asian Modernity* are particularly interested in two of these implications: the role of tradition in modernity and the ways in which the modernizing process may assume several different cultural forms.

In our conference we did not intend to cover, even in bold outline, all the salient features of East Asian modernity. By focusing our attention on the Confucian dimension, we wanted to probe the cultural resources that made modern industrial East Asia distinctive. We are admittedly far from able to make any definitive statements about either the modern transformation of Confucian humanism or the nature of East Asian modernity as shaped by Confucian traditions. As part of an ongoing international conversation, we have nevertheless taken an important step toward setting up a long-term comprehensive agenda for a systematic inquiry into the cultural significance of the rise of industrial East Asia for comparative civilizational studies. Especially noteworthy is our pioneering attempt to formulate a method of interdisciplinary and cross-cultural communication so that the kinds of issues mentioned herein may be addressed appropriately and persistently.

PART I

INTELLECTUAL AND INSTITUTIONAL RESOURCES

This volume begins with four essays exploring the symbolic resources of the Confucian heritage most relevant to East Asian modernity. They are highly selective in a rich repertoire of subject matter for focused investigation. Although the authors do not intend to present either a comprehensive or a fully integrated approach, they do address some of the crucial issues in understanding the modernization of East Asian society. The essays raise fundamental questions about the transformation of the Confucian tradition and offer fresh insights into a sustained Confucian characterization of East Asia today. Whether from the stance of an inside participant or an outside observer, in the style of sympathetic appreciation or critical reflection, or for the sake of opening up the field for further questioning or bringing the discussion to a tentative conclusion, the authors' perspectives are captivating and challenging. They compel us to regard the Confucian influence as requisite "social and cultural capital" rather than as desirable but dispensable background in vital areas such as moral education, cultural identity, the art of government, and the development of civil society in industrial East Asia.

Wm. Theodore de Bary, in "Confucian Education in Premodern East Asia," engages us in a reflection on moral education, a defining characteristic of Confucian learning and teaching. Intent on showing the complex relationship between Confucianism and modernization in East Asia, he rejects outright the simplistic attempt to establish any monocausal connection between the Confucian work ethic and economic development. Instead, by focusing on the perennial humanistic concern for self-cultivation and social responsibility—or, in Confucian terminology, "self-discipline for the governance of men"—he calls attention to both the strengths and the limitations of the core curriculum in Confucian moral education and identifies the critical programmatic and institutional issues.

In de Bary's bold strokes the Confucian curriculum, as embodied primarily in Chu Hsi's Four Books, stands out in sharp relief against the background of modern Western learning, with its emphasis on diversity. While affirming the general impression that the cultural base for such a curriculum was too narrow to accommodate the educational mission of modernization, de Bary underscores the value of "learning for one's self" as dictated by the *Analects, Mencius,* the *Great Learning,* and the *Doctrine of the Mean* and reiterates the argument that the Confucian pattern of moral education that persisted in school after school and age after age in China proper, and was even upheld in the radically different social and political circumstances of Korea and Japan (we may also add Mongolia, Manchuria, and Vietnam), cannot be explained in political, ideological, or utilitarian terms alone. "Cultural merits," to borrow a term used by de Bary, also enabled Confucian learning to influence family, society, and politics profoundly in premodern East Asia. Actually, as de Bary notes, individual, family, and local initiatives, rather than the actions of the state, were often instrumental in spreading the Confucian message.

The educational pattern that provided generation after generation of East Asian students with a basic orientation toward life and learning may not be compatible with the intellectual demands of a modern multicultural world, but it seems that a modified and expanded core curriculum rooted in the Confucian concern for character building can be designed and developed, or at least imagined, in the current discussion about moral education. De Bary does not address this hypothetical question. Rather, in his study *The Trouble with Confucianism* he has identified an inherent structural weakness of the Confucian educational project prior to the impact of the West as a way of addressing the issue from an internalist perspective. In his view the difficulty lies in the classical vision, as exemplified in the *Great Learning* that self-cultivation is a precondition for regulating the family, which in turn is the necessary condition for governing the state. The vision of linking the self through the family to the state may have the advantage of overcoming the unresolvable tension between self and society, but its fatal flaw is its total inattention to society with all of its mediating intermediary institutions. The lack of continuity and staying power of community compacts, community schools, and mutual aid associations in premodern China was symptomatic of this social lacuna.

An obvious implication of this absence for education is the gap between the personality ideal and the actual social and political conditions for its realization. If the infrastructure necessary for the implementation of the Confucian core curriculum was not properly developed in traditional East Asia, were Confucian ideas and values merely floating resources without a social base? While de Bary criticizes the Confucian elite for placing too much emphasis on self-sufficiency and autonomy at the expense of developing a sustained institutional mechanism to deal with the fiscal realities of universal education, he fully acknowledges that Confucian moral education, as promoted by families and local schools, was pervasive enough to touch the hearts and minds of the general public. For it was not only the privileged domain of the cultural elite but also a constitutive part of popular thought. It is in this sense that de Bary believes that the questions Confucians raised about learning to be human, "this essential personal dimension of life," have yet to be answered, and that all of us, individually and communally, are answerable for them.

Edward Shils's comparative study "Reflections on Civil Society and Civility in the Chinese Intellectual Tradition" addresses a timely issue. The lack of a fully articulated social vision between the family and the state in the Confucian tradition, which prompted de Bary to offer his sympathetic yet critical reflection on the typically Confucian version of "weakness of the will" in institution building, seems to suggest the inherent difficulties Confucian countries confront in allowing a civil society to flourish. Shils may agree with this prognosis, but in terms of symbolic resources, he sees significant points of convergence between classic Confucian humanism and the values necessary for laying the intellectual foundation of civil society. Although, as he notes, ideas of civil society do not feature prominently in the Confucian intellectual orientation, some of the Confucian core values are not only compatible with but indispensable to the development of such a society.

His method of analysis as well as the content of his observations significantly expand the intellectual horizon defining the current discussion of civil society in cultural China. Acknowledging that both the ideological argument for and the historical reality of civil society are Western, he nonetheless assumes that, given an ideal type, there are necessary and conducive conditions for new civil societies to emerge and for existing ones to endure. This deceptively simple approach enables him to offer a masterly narrative explaining how the idea of civil society evolved in the modern West, who shaped its usage in Western political discussion, and why it has assumed a renewed saliency in the contemporary discourse on democracy. His immersion in both the historical background and modern relevance of the concept as a perennial human concern as well as a unique Western experience empowers him to take a panoramic view of the commensurability of Confucian thought to the essential values embodied in any healthy civil society.

Two observations in Shils's account are particularly noteworthy for our purpose. First, as an established idea in Western traditions of thought, civil society may have its deepest roots in ancient Greece and the European Middle Ages, but not until the nineteenth century, when Hegel defined it as the sector of society beyond the family and short of the state, did it assume a distinctive meaning in modern consciousness. The cluster of interrelated structures such as the market, private ownership and control of the instruments of production, an independent judiciary and public opinion, rule of law, and a moderately centralized mechanism of governance congenial to the functioning of a civil society came into being rather recently in the West. But, Shils writes, Karl Marx's deliberate attempt to appropriate the Hegelian conception of civil society in his formulation of the capitalist stage of human development made the term almost disappear from usage in English-speaking countries. Instead, "bourgeois society," encompassing both the family and the state, gradually gained prominence in public parlance as well as in technical sociological literature. The notion of civil society as a focus of international intellectual discussion, referring either to the "civil part" (as contrasted with the state, military, police, or family) of society or to an open, pluralist societal ideal has been the result of democratic movements in eastern Europe, notably Poland and Czechoslovakia.

The second observation is that civil society entails the participation of individuals in the civil collective self-consciousness of the society as a whole. It is not only a matter of organized institutions such as political parties, legislative bodies, the separation of governmental powers, voluntary associations, the institution of private property, private business firms and markets, and so on. This is perhaps the main reason why Shils calls attention to civility as a motive force underlying all the institutional structures of civil society.

Prompted by the question of whether Confucian teaching as part of ancient Chinese philosophy contains any elements of civil society, Shils examines a wide range of relevant institutional and intellectual issues. His preliminary finding that Confucius was not concerned with critical dimensions of a civil society such as the market, private property, public debate, political contention, and human rights does not deter him from exploring salient features of the Confucian tradition that would contribute to the workings of civil society. Although he concludes that Confucianism does not have a concept of civil society as a complex of institutions and patterns of activities different from the family and the state, he notes that it provides accounts of certain attitudes of civil society. By implication, the Confucian tradition may not have developed a civil society from within, but it can become a motive force for cultivating attitudes that are compatible with and necessary to civil society, and can therefore serve as a resource for facilitating the growth of such a society in East Asia.

Shils's interpretive position is not necessarily in conflict with Samuel Huntington's observation that "Confucian democracy" is an oxymoron; but, by addressing the issue from a broadly conceived comparative civilizational perspective, Shils allows flexibility and openness in dealing with such an immensely complex phenomenon. His insistence that a civil society must "contain a considerable element of traditionality" and that "the traditionality is inherent in collective self-consciousness, which refers not only to the society of the immediate present but also to that of the past, both recent and remote," counsels receptivity and sensitivity in probing subtle relationships between tradition and its modern transformation in any culture. Understandably, he underscores sharable values and commensurability in spirit between classical Confucian humanism and modern Western concepts of civility and civil society.

The list of topics that Shils scrutinizes is extensive. Subjects relevant to the institutional apparatuses of a civil society include rule of law, legislation, the market, the public sphere, public opinion, and measures dealing with the common people. Under the rubric of civility, core values such as trustworthiness, respect, flexibility, breadth, and tolerance are singled out for focused investigation. He also thoughtfully discusses government, intellectuals, and politics in the Confucian tradition.

Shils identifies the center of Chinese imperial society as the most fundamental barrier to civil society. This center, consisting of "those who are intensely in contact with the Way," is occupied by "the emperor as the ritual head of Chinese society and those who are learned in the classics from which the Way is to be apprehended and understood." Nevertheless, he asserts that the extension of the barrier that "would bring the center and the periphery nearer to each other in a common moral order" has potential for the realization of civil society in China. This paradox seems to sum up the main purpose of our collaborative intellectual enterprise: exploring the creative transformative potential of those thoughts and institutions in East Asian

Confucian traditions which are believed to be inimical to modernization defined in Western terms.

Following a different but compatible line of thinking, in "The Intellectual Heritage of the Confucian Ideal of *Ching-shih*," Chang Hao grounds his discussion of the Confucian theory and practice of "ordering the world" on the moral idealism that underlies the Confucian sense of vocation for the cultural elite. De Bary's concern about Confucian institution building, Shils's observations on the Confucian transformative potential for civil society, and Chang's analysis of the Confucian idea of *ching-shih* belong to the same political-cultural discourse characterized by an intense moral overtone. Evoking Eric Voegelin's notion of "the order of soul," Chang brings to the fore the tension between the "transmission of the Way" and the "transmission of rulership" in Confucian political culture. Consequently, according to the Confucian cultural ideal the dynastic state is not a terminal community for the political order. Yet a Herculean commitment to transform the world from within compels the Confucians to become embedded in the social and political reality of their times. As a result, their transcendent vision does not involve a fundamental break with the cumulative institutional tradition in which they define their vocational niche. To illustrate this point, Chang shows that in Neo-Confucian thought a future-oriented utopian vision is not necessarily incompatible with a firm determination to maintain the present political order.

The Confucian vision of the political order as a moral gemeinschaft may set an idealist tone for any discussion of the art of government, but realism and pragmatism also characterize the Confucian discourse on statecraft. The ethic of "an unvarnished, raw utilitarianism," Chang writes, was rejected by mainstream Confucian thinkers, but the ethics of social consequence rather than the ethics of absolute ends features prominently in the Confucian way of governance. He observes that the cultural ideal that affirms the primacy of an ethical center, emerging as "the result of a radiation of moral-spiritual influences from the exemplary character of an elite headed by the emperor," does not undermine the development of sophisticated theories and practices of "the institutional measures of government."

In examining the divergent trends within the statecraft school, Chang sketches an extensive repertoire of institutional and intellectual resources in the Confucian tradition in dealing with political issues such as kingship, feudalism, bureaucracy, and lineage. Especially noteworthy is the Confucian proclivity to take seriously the "soft," nonbureaucratic structures, such as ritual (*li*), in a discourse on governance. The political debates, often with far-reaching policy implications, centered on questions of moral ideals versus political expedience, public-mindedness versus self-interest, righteousness versus profit, and long-term principles versus short-term utilities. The willingness of some of the most prominent and articulate statecraft thinkers and practitioners to transcend these seemingly incompatible dichotomies and explore concrete measures to reconcile and combine them gives a rich texture to what may be called the Confucian reflection on political economy.

As Chang notes, however, conspicuously absent from virtually all the recurrent trends of statecraft thought is the repudiation of kingship as an institution. With the possible exception of the great Ming intellectual historian Huang Tsung-hsi, no traditional Confucian thinker ever challenged the legitimacy of the imperial system. Of course there were powerful anti-despotic protests against individual rulers or dynastic regimes, but the underlying institution seems to have been taken for granted. This does not mean that the Confucian tradition lacks transformative potential for restructuring the polity. In fact, the followers of the statecraft school were instrumental in establishing the ideal of collective wealth and power in nineteenth-century China as a response to the challenge of the modern West. Indeed, Chang maintains that the new conceptual resources (for example, nation-state or democracy) for institutional organization were "as much a function of the shift of internal balance in the Confucian heritage as of new models introduced from the West."

Chang's essay concludes with a thought-provoking idea. The concerted effort of modern Chinese intellectuals to repossess the inner dynamics of Confucian statecraft thinking may have prompted China's receptivity to and understanding of liberal-democratic ideas from the West, but the truly challenging task ahead is to give a more complex and nuanced picture of the interplay between the Confucian heritage and the modern transformation. Implicit in this idea is a shift of emphasis. Although the role and function of the Confucian tradition in East Asian modernization will continue to be questioned, the time is also ripe to assess and evaluate the modernizing process as a global phenomenon in the Confucian perspective.

Liu Shu-hsien's essay, "Confucian Ideals and the Real World: A Critical Review of Contemporary Neo-Confucian Thought," underscores the point that Confucianism as the symbol of a cultural ideal ought to be clearly differentiated from its actual embeddedness in social and political ideologies, institutions, and practices. He maintains that, as an ideal, the Confucian tradition is characterized by moral perfectionism and an "anthropocosmic vision" of mutuality between Heaven and the human world. This has served as a source of inspiration for Confucians from Mencius to Chu Hsi. Indeed, throughout Chinese history the Confucians have demonstrated a critical consciousness and a spirit of protest precisely because as followers of the cultural ideal they could not but detach themselves from the status quo and commit themselves to a fundamental transformation of the existing society and polity. Implicit in this tension between what the Confucians realistically perceive the world to be and what they idealistically desire the world to become is the great transformative potential linking the cultural ideal with social and political realities.

Diametrically opposed to the Weberian interpretation of Confucian ethics as "adjustment to the world," Liu's thesis poses a challenging question to those who subscribe to the idea of the Confucian state and, by implication, the entire discourse on Confucian China. Actually, Liu's intention is to demythologize these convenient labels, which in his view are dangerously misleading and densely concealing. They mislead because the politicization of Confucian values as a mechanism of ideological control, as in the case of the Han dynasty, is a profound distortion rather than a fulfillment of the moral ideals of Confucian and Mencian teachings; they conceal because the authentic manifestation of the Mencian line of the Confucian humanist spirit, as revealed time and again in the political protest and social criticism of principled scholar-officials throughout Chinese history, is never fully acknowledged.

Liu further asserts that, although deeply rooted in the Confucian cultural ideal, "inner sageliness and outer kingliness" as the highest moral standard for self-cultivation and political responsibility is neither realizable nor practicable in the lifeworld. It serves, however, as a source of inspiration or, in de Bary's words, a direction of life. Although the Confucians are thoroughly committed to the transformation of the world and, therefore, fully aware of the inevitability of being-in-the-world, their worldliness is anchored in a transcendent dimension that enables them to distance themselves from the corrupting influence of the existing society and polity and empowers them to criticize and improve the status quo. The lack of differentiation between church and state in the Confucian tradition must not be interpreted as the sacralization of political power. In fact, as guardians of the "transmission of the Way" *(tao-t'ung)*, the Confucian intellectuals have generated much symbolic power and moral authority beyond the control of the ruling minority.

The apparent successes of so-called Confucian pragmatism in developing bureaucratic structures (e.g., the examination system), creating social organizations (e.g., family rituals), and enhancing economic productivity (e.g., network capitalism) must not blind us to the obvious failures of the Confucian tradition to develop democratic institutions, to create a civil society, and to enhance the capitalist entrepreneurial spirit. Yet, if we follow Liu's argument, underlying the apparent and obvious is a much more subtle and significant Confucian *Problematik:* Fully acknowledging that I am in but not of the world, how can I exert the utmost to attain the cultural ideal which

I know can never be realized in practical terms? This is in full accord with de Bary's insistence on the "essential personal dimension of life" as the most enduring and relevant aspect of the Confucian heritage.

Against this background Liu's review of New Confucian thought is predicated on the emergence of a communal critical self-consciousness among the most brilliant contemporary Confucian thinkers. Their intellectual and spiritual self-definition, indubitably rooted in the Confucian tradition, is primarily a deliberate response to the modern West. What they perceive as the Confucian presence in East Asian modernity is a philosophical argument, an existential commitment, and indeed, in Paul Tillich's sense, an ultimate concern. Whether or not they have actually extended their influence beyond the ivory tower, they have, with profound self-reflectiveness, already created a cultural space and an authentic possibility for the creative transformation of Confucian humanism as a living tradition in modern East Asia.

1

CONFUCIAN EDUCATION IN
PREMODERN EAST ASIA

Wm. Theodore de Bary

EDUCATION IN PREMODERN EAST ASIA

Education, essential to civilized life in any age, has acquired a new importance for the study of premodern East Asia. Much of this interest comes from recent reevaluations of the role of Confucianism in the modernization of the area, and especially of its formative influence on what is now often referred to as post-Confucian East Asia. Earlier in the twentieth century Confucianism was apt to be seen as an obstacle to modernization; more recently the Confucian work ethic and encouragement of learning have been credited with giving East Asian peoples the motivation, discipline, and skills necessary to engage in many essential processes of modernization. Changing political perceptions have also had an effect. Revolutionary movements were once bent on removing conservative Confucian influences from education. Today the same elements, now well established in power and inclined to emphasize stability as the key to economic progress, are hoping a revival of traditional Confucian values will contribute to self-discipline and social order.

Modernization is still the avowed aim of the People's Republic of China, but now this aim is qualified by deep reservations about the alleged effects of Westernization on the moral fabric of society; efforts are being made to revive Confucian moral teachings as a corrective to "bourgeois liberal" influences. The special blessing given by Jiang Zemin, general secretary of the Chinese Communist party (CCP), to the Confucian Conference in Beijing in October 1989 is a striking confirmation of a trend seen much earlier in the noncommunist states of Taiwan, South Korea, and Singapore. Nor can we ignore similar reactions against modernizing trends expressed in fundamentalist movements elsewhere, especially in the Islamic world, but even in the heart of Western societies.

In these circumstances modernization ceases to be a simple, unquestioned value, and the character of traditional education in premodern East Asia is also subject to reexamination. Although Confucianism has often been identified with traditional elites, the values most often credited with helping East Asians to modernize rapidly are generalized ones, assumed to be widely shared and not just the property of the elite. If formal education was indeed limited to the few, by what means did these values become so widely diffused? If these are shared values, what do we make of the conventional distinction between elite and popular culture or of the sharp differentiation between literate leaders and illiterate masses? In recent scholarly studies of popular culture in China, distinctions between elite and nonelite have tended to become blurred. This, in turn, leaves us with the question of how much weight should be assigned to informal education compared to formal instruction, to semiliterate or nondiscursive means of communication compared to schools in the process of transmitting a common set of values. In this respect family and community rituals in many forms and on different levels of society assume greater importance as a nonliterate means of inculcating traditional attitudes and values.

To recognize the complexity of factors at work is to imply not that earlier studies of traditional thought and education were misconceived, but only that they may have fallen short insofar as intellectual history and studies of popular thought were assumed to be dealing with antithetical and mutually exclusive rather than correlative factors. Studies of so-called elite versus popular thought may have their own significance on their proper level of historical development or social action, but significance also is attached to whatever educational infrastructure may or may not have linked the two.

It has become fashionable to downplay the role of formal thought in history in favor of popular consciousness or *mentalité,* but it can be shown that key *thinkers* actually did have an influence on the ideas and action of key *players* in both the Japanese and the Chinese reform movements of the nineteenth century. This was possible insofar as both thinkers and players operated in the same intellectual milieu, and it can be demonstrated from the writings of certain political activists that they were inspired by specific thinkers. To be effective, political or economic leaders must act in close concert with others. They are nothing without collaborators, and in this sense all are members of a group, acting together on the basis of shared values, customs, and practices which are acquired through common educational influences or other patterns of socialization. Among the elite in premodern East Asia, this common culture often came from schooling; but the crucial point would seem to be whether, as a group, members of the educated classes studied a common curriculum and engaged in a common discourse, not whether they necessarily studied under the same teachers or at the same schools (i.e., wore the same school tie as in England).

From this point of view, it is important to know on an intellectual level whether a prominent thinker, striking perhaps for his originality or independent views, was also able to exert a significant educational influence through the translation of his ideas into widely read texts, especially books with a place in the school curriculum or even primers used in the home. Here the schools that must be considered significant are not only schools of thought in the scholarly or intellectual sense, remarkable for their originality or distinguishable by an affinity of ideas, but also institutions that provide basic education to large numbers of people. Scholars today, and especially intellectual historians, may be struck by thinkers of intrinsic philosophic interest or others who are impressive for their singular erudition, but these may be types that attract only the learned few without necessarily moving either active leaders or their larger followings. Much of twentieth-century East Asian scholarship has been devoted to the rediscovery of neglected thinkers of interest primarily because in some way they resemble prominent thinkers in the West. For all their distinction as scholars, the exponents of the Han Learning (Han-hsüeh) in Ch'ing China, or of the roughly comparable *Soraigaku* in Tokugawa Japan, or those identified with the so-called *Sirhak* ("substantial learning") of late Choson Korea probably made an impression on only a few of the sophisticated, scholarly elite, and had little influence on the shared discourse of educated persons in general, among whom the vocabulary in Chu Hsi's Four Books continued to have wide currency, despite all the philosophical critiques and philological attacks leveled against Neo-Confucianism in the late seventeenth and eighteenth centuries.

In the same vein, a contrast is often drawn between Chinese education, strongly oriented toward preparation for the civil service examinations, and Japanese education, which may have been more liberal, less career oriented, and more diversified. This is no doubt an oversimplification, since the Han Learning itself could not have developed as vigorously as it did in Ch'ing China if scholars had been exclusively preoccupied with meeting examination requirements and conforming to official orthodoxy, or if their intellectual formation had actually produced such a deformation or constriction of outlook as to handicap them in the pursuit of critical scholarship.

As a general contrast on the level of scholarly thought and inquiry, one could probably make a case for a greater intellectual diversity in the late Tokugawa as compared to nineteenth-century China. Yet whether one accepts this or not, the question remains whether a similar contrast can be drawn on the level of general education. Following the same reasoning as in the earlier comparison of Han Learning in Ch'ing China, *Sorai-gaku* in eighteenth-century Japan, or *Sirhak* in late Chosŏn Korea, one could allow for greater or less diversification of thought in the higher reaches of learning without its necessarily affecting more basic levels of education. On the level of primary and secondary education, introductory primers and intermediate instruction may well have been quite similar in both cases, with basic Neo-Confucian texts, especially Chu Hsi's Four Books, as the common denominator. From this point of view, more attention should be given to widely available textbooks and actual curricula than to the writings of famous scholars, and especially to manuals, encyclopedias, and other popular reference works intended for daily use in the household or office.

Yet other levels of education may also be involved. Apart from persons with some degree of formal learning, there were large numbers of people reached by less formal processes—in schools, guilds, workshops, clubs, cultural and religious associations, and so on—which transmitted skills, techniques, and general know-how in ways perhaps more generally thought of as training or apprenticeship than as education, but no less significant as a contribution to the processes of modernization in the form of creating a skilled or semiskilled work force. These are to be found not solely in the more obvious public forms, but also in domestic arts and crafts, which often reached a high level of refinement and complexity. Nor, if social discipline is also considered vital to sustaining social peace, stability, and continuity of life amidst the inevitable dislocations of rapid economic change, should traditional community rituals be overlooked.

Thus, although factors such as rates of literacy, the relative availability of public print media, and the accessibility of schooling are important indices of educational level, one must consider less formal, nondiscursive means of communication as no less significant.

At any rate, the foregoing are some of the considerations that seem to me relevant to any comparative discussion of education in premodern East Asia, if modern East Asia is to be considered in any sense post-Confucian.

EDUCATION IN PREMODERN CHINA

The longstanding view of premodern education in China as dominated by the state and official orthodoxy is at best a half-truth that needs substantial qualification. In what follows the matter is treated first under its institutional and systemic aspects, next in terms of educational content, and third in relation to larger intellectual trends and the broader East Asian scene.

Institutional Patterns

Chinese education tended to be elitist in that at its upper levels it was increasingly channeled toward official recruitment, with limited opportunities at the top, and on the lower levels it was dominated by local elites (i.e., gentry families and local officials). This was so in spite of the fact that many scholars and officials in both the Ming and Ch'ing believed in universal access to education and subscribed to the classic Confucian model of "public" schools at all levels of society, an ideal of universal schooling promoted by Chu Hsi in his preface to the *Great Learning*. Notwithstanding repeated formal pronouncements in favor of establishing such a system, and even some official initiatives from Yüan times to the late Ch'ing period, little came of these initiatives, either for lack of adequate material provision from the government or because of disappointment with the routinization of learning that accompanied the bureaucratization of education.

Learning on the lower level was mostly carried out within the home or in local schools (*she-hsüeh* or *i-hsüeh*), dependent on the support of the local gentry, drawing on local resources, and thus subject to some vicissitudes and variations. On the level of intermediate and higher learning, local academies served some educational functions, but too often they led a precarious existence, being similarly dependent on gentry support and the patronage of individual officials, both of which were uncertain and subject to changing economic and political fortunes. The life of most academies was marked by a recurrent pattern of establishment, short-term growth, decline, neglect, revival, decline, and so on. In the Ch'ing period, to the extent that some academies enjoyed the patronage of the court or of high government officials, their importance as centers of independent intellectual discourse tended to be compromised.

Nevertheless, however much in theory the state claimed ultimate authority and reserved for itself supreme control over education, in practice it rarely asserted these powers. Although it had a major role in setting the criteria for official recruitment which served as a magnet for participants in the educational system, generally it left to local elites the responsibility for both the support and the direction of education, which varied greatly with the quality of individual leadership in local and regional affairs. Neo-Confucians often deplored the failure of the court to commit resources to the maintenance of a universal school program and complained about the distorting effect on education of the official recruitment system; but it must be said that, as things stood, the existing situation corresponded in important respects to the Neo-Confucian perception of a proper human order, grounded in values such as self-reliance, individual responsibility, family cooperation, and local self-governance. The overarching ideal, accepted throughout East Asia wherever the Neo-Confucian curriculum became established, is expressed in Chu Hsi's succinct formulation: self-discipline for the governance of men *(hsiu-chi chih-jen)*. In principle this voluntaristic approach applied to everyone, from the ruler down to the common man, with the ruler obliged to set an example for all men of self-restraint, self-correction, and self-improvement.

Given this dominant model in both thought and social organization, it is not surprising that the central government only sporadically provided either positive material support or active intervention in the educational process on the local level. It is also significant that religious or quasi-religious organizations played little or no part in the schools, as compared to the situation in the West (and apparently also in Japan) during these same years. Community compacts, community granaries, and scholarly academies served something of an organizing function on the local level, but on the whole one would have to question whether they demonstrated sustained institutional effectiveness, continuity, or survival power sufficient for them to assume a significant educational burden. (By "one would have to question" I mean that the evidence thus far puts the matter in great doubt, but only so much as to prompt further study, not to dispose of the issue.) At any rate, in the local community and even on the regional level—where there were few institutions of a higher order or of a more public character serving as an infrastructure between family and state administration—the pattern of individual, family, and clan initiative still largely prevailed.

In these circumstances the universalistic tendency in Confucian thought, symbolized by the overarching concepts of Heaven *(t'ien)* and All-Under-Heaven *(t'ien-hsia),* and expressed in the Neo-Confucian aim of achieving universal schooling, did not necessarily work to close the gap between self and state. Although there is evidence of communitarian activity arising in certain local settings during the nineteenth and early twentieth centuries—activity focusing on a public sphere *(kung)* as distinct from a state or official sphere *(kuan)*—it seems to have had little effect in generating new educational initiatives with a substantial impact on the curriculum. Nor have we reason to assume that such an expectation would have been warranted.

At this point it may be in order to ask whether the sense of crisis in education that developed in nineteenth-century China was to any degree generated from within—perhaps even derived in part from the perennial Neo-Confucian complaint about the inadequacy of court support for school-ing in general—no less than by external influences from the West. The chal-lenge of the latter was, of course, very real: pressures for the expansion of education and for radical change in the curriculum both occurred in Japan in the 1870s and the 1880s. If, however, we do not assume that Westerni-zation was inevitable or that it constituted the only option in *all* respects, it becomes pertinent to ask whether certain kinds of change or reform in ed-ucation might have occurred without Western intervention—a possibility to be considered not only on the level of influential thinkers but also in terms of infrastructure, local organization, and community activity. Whatever the difficulties and limitations of Chinese education, one cannot assume that it had no natural growth of its own and that it was simply standing stock-still, waiting for the West to break in and start something.

True enough, by the mid-nineteenth century it is difficult to draw a clear line between indigenous developments and foreign influences. Yet if one takes for purposes of illustration the case of Fang Tung-shu (1772–1851), an orthodox Neo-Confucian about whom I have written in *The Trouble with Confucianism,* one finds a powerful argument for the reform and re-vival of the academies stated entirely on grounds of tradition and China's past experience; indeed, Fang's argument stands in sharp contrast to those made by reformers at the end of the century, who were more likely to cite the successful experience of foreign nations than Chinese precedents. Fang's argument was couched in terms of the need for schools and academies to serve as centers for the informed discussion of public issues, which seemed to him sorely lacking in his time. He, however, drew on no foreign models but only on Confucian examples from the past, when such informal discus-sion of public issues was, he claimed, considered indispensable to the for-mulation of sound policy decisions.[1]

Undeniably, however, the most momentous changes that did in fact occur in the late nineteenth century arose from external pressures and were in-spired by non-Chinese examples. By 1898 the sense of crisis had become so intense that many reformers felt an urgent need to do something drastic about education. China's defeat in the Sino-Japanese War and Japan's rapid success in modernization impressed K'ang Yu-wei and his colleagues in the Reform Movement of 1898, who undertook radical steps toward creating a national school system based on the Prussian and Japanese models, but with little apparent understanding of why earlier Chinese efforts had failed. I have discussed this failure in *East Asian Civilizations* (Chapter 4) and further in *The Trouble with Confucianism,* and shall not go into it at any length here. But when K'ang tried to expedite the development of such a school system, the best he could do was try to convert the existing local academies into middle schools, with a Western curriculum, and to convert the buildings known as "illicit shrines" *(yin-ssu)* into elementary schools. Although K'ang's reforms foundered for reasons of his own political weakness and personal inadequacies as a statesman, it is apparent that he could not call upon an institutional infrastructure adequate to shoulder the burden being placed on it by decree from above. This in turn reflected a persistent disinclination of Neo-Confucian scholar-officials to address in any systematic way the actual problem of resource allocation in support of such a major undertaking. As I have said elsewhere: "This indisposition was nourished by Neo-Confucian habits of mind favoring self-sufficiency and autonomy. These in turn justified a laissez-faire policy at court, leaving local government on its own to mobilize resources for local needs, while licensing the court to promulgate ideal prescriptions and rationalistic plans that often failed to come to terms with fiscal realities on the local level."[2]

Educational Content and Practice in the Premodern Period

Instruction on the primary level appears to have been aimed at two main goals, basic literacy and socialization, both involving the use of standard texts such as *Three Character Classic (San-tzu ching), Thousand Character Text (Ch'ien-tzu wen), Classic of Filial Piety (Hsiao-ching),* and Chu Hsi's *Elementary Learning (Hsiao-hsüeh).* One exception might be observed in the declining use of *Elementary Learning* as a basic primer. This work proved increasingly difficult to use because, as an anthology made up of classical texts, it could not be easily understood by beginning students, while its contents, providing a ritual for the home and primary school, no longer had much relevance for those advanced students better able to read the classic texts. Chu's *Elementary Learning* thus served more as a teacher's manual than as a primer for the young.

This is not to deny the significance of ritual practice in the school as an instrument of socialization alongside texts read for basic literacy. Indeed, with the recent heightening of Western scholarly interest in ritual and symbolic thought, indications of a renewed emphasis on Confucian ritual among some Ch'ing scholars may attract our attention. Nevertheless, the question remains how we should interpret this renewed advocacy of the rites. The possibility cannot be discounted that expressions of Confucian concern for them may reflect more a sense of alarm than a realistic hope of reinstituting the rites; that is, instead of actually marking a strong revival of Confucian ritual, this advocacy may have been prompted by worries over a continuing decline in the observance of traditional rites as Confucians proved unable to adapt classic models to contemporary society or to contest the hold of "vulgar" Buddhist and Taoist rituals on the popular mind. And if this was so on the local or popular level, it was hardly less so on the level of the imperial court itself. Even during the Ming dynasty, when Neo-Confucian texts and teachings were supposedly ensconced as official state orthodoxy, the court engaged in many unorthodox rites—occult, illicit, and superstitious from the Confucian point of view—and even such a prominent Confucian statesman as Ch'iu Chün (1420–1495) felt that reform of court practice in this respect was, if anything, more urgent than the improvement of popular customs.[3]

On the next level of education it is remarkable how much continuity and homogeneity is found in the core texts, which, whatever the individual local variations in curricula, tended to center on the Four Books, the Five Classics, standard histories (especially the *Shih-chi* and *Han-shu*), the literary anthology *Wen-hsüan*, and masters of poetry and prose in the T'ang and Sung. In the absence of any direction from above, there appears to have been a continuing consensus on the kind of basic curriculum outlined early in Ch'eng Tuan-li's *Ch'eng-shih chia-shu tu-shu fen-nien jih-ch'eng*.[4] The same curriculum, which gave a high priority to Chu Hsi's version of the Four Books, seems to have maintained its dominance in age after age, school after school, without any central direction to account for this considerable homogeneity (other than the powerful magnet represented by the civil service exams and the students' hopes of competing in them). The fact that this pattern largely held true even in the different social and political circumstances of Korea and Japan raises a fundamental question as to whether these classic texts might not have survived on their own cultural merits, quite apart from utilitarian purposes or ideological uses. Yet consideration of this question would also have to deal with the issue of available alternatives. Had better and more practicable proposals for school curricula been put forward and successfully tested anywhere? Can we assume that systemic inertia alone accounts for the persistence of this standard Neo-Confucian curriculum throughout East Asia? Is it not striking that so radical a reformer in seventeenth-century China as Huang Tsung-hsi (1610–1695), who called for substantial institutional changes in education and who had his philosophical differences with the Ch'eng-Chu school, seemed content to leave Chu Hsi's curriculum largely in place?[5]

On the higher level of elite culture, academies served a variety of functions: promoting scholarly research and discussion, preparing candidates for examinations, providing meeting places for the local elite or centers for Confucian ritual, and so on. Ch'ing academies were much less active as centers for public discussion than those of the late Ming, but they were perhaps more closely identified with classical research.

Han learning (historical, philological, and text-centered studies) was the dominant form of research scholarship, to such an extent that Liang Ch'i-ch'ao referred to it as the "Ch'ing orthodoxy." Actually, it coexisted with the Chu Hsi orthodoxy still regnant in the examination system. One had relatively little effect on the content or direction of the other. They were parallel, and not necessarily mutually exclusive, modes of scholarly activity, involving critical inquiry and evidential (k'ao-cheng) research, attracting some "private" scholars who turned away from the examination business and the writing of eight-legged essays. High officials patronized k'ao-cheng projects, sometimes on a grand scale, in the midst of their continuing involvement with official recruitment and examination on several levels. Given the paucity of official posts in contrast to the number of trained scholars, it is not surprising that many unsuccessful candidates turned to scholarly research as an outlet for their talents.

The persistence of a Neo-Confucian core curriculum in education while Han learning dominated advanced research corresponded in some degree to a well-established dichotomy in Neo-Confucian education between a core of classical studies and specialized technical studies. Contrary to a widespread modern myth concerning Confucianism as dominated by an "amateur ideal," as early as in the Sung dynasty Hu Yüan (993–1059) had recognized the need for specialization in certain practical fields (hydraulic engineering, military tactics, mathematics, law) alongside the humanistic study of the classics. The latter itself, however, had by now developed into fields of specialized research. Even traditionalists, such as Tseng Kuo-fan in the mid-nineteenth century, not only tolerated but actually insisted on specialization ("concentration") in scholarship, along with general education in the classics and the cultivation of literary skills.

In this symbiotic relationship between an educational core curriculum and advanced scholarly research, it was possible for the one to be relatively insulated from the other and to proceed in parallel not only in China but in Japan, where no "examination orthodoxy" prevailed. The work of scholars on the leading edge of classical research had little effect on the core curriculum, and the latter, as conducted on the lower level, was determined pretty much by local options in the absence of any clear signal from above—options exercised more on the basis of cultural preferences than of political alignments.

Finally, among the choices available it is questionable whether any of the scholarly specialists or independent critics in China or Japan had come up with a more satisfactory set of basic texts than those of Chu Hsi. Who else had a more coherent and systematic core curriculum to offer, with a set of classical humanistic readings comparable in clarity, precision, and conciseness of expression, to say nothing of philosophic depth and subtlety?

The curriculum of Chu Hsi and Ch'eng Tuan-li has perhaps been underestimated simply because it was narrowly and rigorously defined at its base. This was a matter of setting priorities in a proper educational sequence, not of excluding further possibilities at the upper end of the learning process. If in both China and Japan mature Confucian scholarship in the early nineteenth century exhibits a marked eclecticism and contributes to a diversity of research orientations on the advanced level, it could suggest that a spirit of liberal intellectual inquiry was actually nourished by this core curriculum rather than stunted by it. Moreover, the relative ease with which many young Chinese and Japanese of the late nineteenth and early twentieth centuries made the transition to Western education suggests that the Four Books, with Chu Hsi's commentary, were anything but a fatal handicap in preparing them for entry into the modern world.

Admittedly the traditional curriculum was highly focused on humanistic learning, which remained narrowly based on Chinese texts. Within this limited educational program there was no place even for the learning of China's Asian neighbors Japan and Korea, to say nothing of India. In this respect, then, one can easily conclude from hindsight that the traditional Neo-Confucian curriculum could not possibly have survived unmodified and unexpanded in a modern multicultural world.

We must remember, however, that it was conceived as a *core* curriculum— that is, it was intended to establish a center and a starting point from which the student would work outward by degrees, in ever-expanding concentric circles, to embrace All-Under-Heaven. Though a defined program with limits at each stage, it did not set fixed boundaries on one's intellectual horizons. As a scholar grew to greater maturity of mind, his reach would extend beyond what was nearest at hand. Even within the Chinese context this outreach of scholarly inquiry was able to carry well beyond the traditional curriculum and produce the new evidential research of the Ch'ing period, which stood in some contrast to the traditional learning. Indeed, even "orthodox" Neo-Confucians loyal to Chu Hsi and the Four Books did not find that such loyalty precluded an interest in Western learning. Similarly, scholars in Korea and Japan with the same Neo-Confucian intellectual formation developed their interest in "practical learning" (*sirhak* or *jitsugaku*) to include Western studies in the eighteenth and nineteenth centuries. One cannot conclude, then, that Neo-Confucian education imposed inherent, rigid limits on the intellectual curiosity of premodern East Asians, nor should one assume that the defined form of the Neo-Confucian core curriculum also fixed forever the boundaries of intellectual inquiry.

To say this is by no means to retract what I said earlier—that the Neo-Confucians worked out of too narrow a cultural base, which would need to be expanded as Confucians entered the modern world, and which, indeed, even had its limitations in the Chinese setting itself. We have seen this in the case of *Elementary Learning,* supposedly a basic primer but one so tied to difficult classical texts that it could at best serve as a teacher's guide and not as introductory reading at all, except among a limited number of privileged students. Yet the very fact that this text, so influential in the early Neo-Confucian movement, had been superseded by less difficult texts in the nineteenth century tells us that a change was taking place in Chinese education. The core was still there in the Four Books, but adjustments were being made around it which, to me at least, suggest a continuing need to make learning somewhat more accessible. Although that learning was still for the most part classical and "traditional," a closer examination of the most widely used texts in the nineteenth century might reveal trends of significance for understanding the changes taking place within the tradition—a possibility that has not been seriously explored as long as the presumption was that the tradition had become exhausted and we had nothing to learn from it in any case.

A more prejudicial assumption, however, has been that traditional Neo-Confucian education, on account of its being so narrowly based and centered on a core, could only yield in its entirety to a completely open and unrestricted type of education. This has been accompanied by other modern Western assumptions about the unlimited value of science, technology, and industrialization, and it has led to the almost total predominance of specialized training in technical disciplines in the twentieth century. In the process, centrifugal forces have created a vacuum in educated public discourse, a vacuum into which have rushed liberationist ideologies. Thus China, destabilized by repeated revolutions and almost completely disconnected from any traditional values on the intellectual level, saw an imposed uniformity and conformity of doctrine as the only alternative to an anarchy of individual choices and technical specializations. Marxist scriptures—the writings of Marx, Engels, Lenin, Stalin, and Mao—took the place of Confucian texts as the required core in higher education, except when, during the extremes of the Cultural Revolution, virtually all learning was set aside in favor of the single authoritative guide for all "proletarians": the Little Red Book. The dead end of this process we have seen at T'ien-an-men. Students could no longer tolerate life in an ideological straitjacket; they realized that a vocational specialization bound up tightly with political indoctrination was still morally and spiritually suffocating. After the crackdown the ruling regime, for its part, had nothing better to offer than compulsory reeducation in the same worn-out dogmas.

Athough the Neo-Confucian core program had been limited and narrowly defined, it at least provided the individual with a basic orientation to life and learning—"Learning for One's Self," according to Confucius and Chu Hsi. The Four Books with Chu Hsi's commentary gave the individual a sense of self-worth and self-respect not to be sacrificed to any short-term utilitarian purpose; a sense of place in the world not to be surrendered to any state or party; a sense of how one could cultivate one's individual powers to meet the social responsibilities that the enjoyment of learning always brought with it—powers and responsibilities not to be defaulted on. Moreover, it gave a sense of educational process through discursive learning *(chiang-hsüeh)* in dialogue among teachers and students which allowed different understandings of traditional teachings to emerge.

Whatever else becomes of education in the future, whether in China or elsewhere in the world, one would hope that something of these values might survive. Modernization would not then be seen as taking place at their expense. Yet in the discussion of "post-Confucian" East Asia the emphasis is usually put on the economic advantages of shared social values, group discipline, and subordination to established authority—in short, to a kind of social conformism. If anything is said about the traditional conception of the individual, it is mostly in terms of being deeply imbued with a sense of duty or responsibility to others, not with any sense of individual rights or one's own self-worth.

Much of my discussion rests on dubious modern Western antitheses between the individual and the group, between rights and duties. In the Confucian case one cannot assume that these values are incompatible or necessarily in opposition; they are best understood as reciprocal and mutually reinforcing. Confucian ethics, instead of being primarily a social or group ethic, as it is often referred to, starts with self-cultivation, and works outward from a proper sense of self to the acceptance of reciprocal responsibilities with others in widening circles of personal relationship concentric with that self.

Insofar as family relations have served as the paradigm for such a system and have been conceived primarily as affective, emotional ties rather than as legalistic and contractual ones, the language of rights or of legal entitlements does not fit the case well. Forms of mutual respect, rooted in a deep reverence for life and for all life-generating or life-sustaining forces, were thought of by the Confucians as shared *rites,* possessing a religious aura but resting in practice on a voluntary or consensual basis instead of on the co-ercive threat implied in the legal enforcement of *rights*.

To the extent that these customary observances and consensual modes of conduct were traditionally nurtured in the family and the authority of the family continued to be upheld, Confucian values may have been sustained even in developing societies, although adapting well in other respects to modernizing trends. But even so it may still not be adequate to think of this survival in the twentieth century simply as a Confucian form of work ethic; it is only one manifestation of what is more truly a family ethic, ideally built on mutually supportive and emotionally satisfying personal relations. One might well doubt whether, in the longer view, any such work ethic could survive the eclipse of the family system itself, or whether it could be called Confucian if, instead of centering on an organic conception of the self in relation to one's social and natural environment, it were oriented more to the modern Western sense of the individual as almost completely indepen-dent.

Yet even to reaffirm this underlying organic and familial basis of the so-called work ethic may not be enough to justify calling it Confucian. For Confucius himself, important though the family was, it did not constitute the prime focus of his teaching but was only the main context in which to understand the nature of the self, and especially the person, as providing leadership to the group (most notably in the form of the noble man, or *chün-tzu*). Certainly the basic Neo-Confucian texts, the Four Books (*Great Learn-ing, The Mean, Analects*, and *Mencius*), are centrally concerned with self-cultivation of the person as the prospective bearer of leadership responsibilities. And though this capacity was engendered and nourished in both primary and essential respects within the family, in all of the Four Books the process culminates in education or training that goes beyond the home and family, most notably in schools and academies.

This being so, it poses a fundamental question for anyone who would think that Confucianism, as a form of self-cultivation, may still exert any influence in twentieth-century East Asia. Since there has been no Confucian schooling for most of the past century, what grounds are there for supposing that Confucianism exists in any form which addresses this central concern of the traditional teaching? And in the absence of such, is it any wonder that most people who write about Confucian or post-Confucian East Asia have the greatest difficulty defining what it is they are talking about? To go on about the family ethic is one thing, since even though that notion may be somewhat elusive, implicit understandings of particular family relations, ob-ligations, and ritual practices give some experiential meaning or substance to the discussion. But it is another thing when one tries to move beyond this limited sphere to the larger arena of social and political responsibility. The answers here cannot be found in family life alone, absent the scholarly or intellectual discussion that normally would take place in the school.

Nor does it really address the problem to say that, after all, there are some so-called New Confucian scholars speculating about these matters today who write and teach as professors in modern universities. All well and good; but in these cases the problem has to be confronted in a new and quite different form from the traditional one. The New Confucian scholars cannot assume that there is much carryover from the past or that they are building on a living awareness of Confucian tradition in the minds of educated young people today. That awareness has to be re-created, if it still can be, almost wholly anew. I say "if it still can be" because it is not at all clear that even where such "New Confucians" can be found they have any influence on existing school curricula or educational programs.

Let me conclude with a personal anecdote that may illustrate the point. Not long ago, when I was doing research at Kyoto University, I was asked to give a talk at the nearby Ritsumeikan University on the occasion of the inauguration of a new program of international studies intended to give a new direction to the undergraduate curriculum. Ritsumeikan, in the post–World War II era, had had a reputation as a hotbed of radicalism, but apparently in recognition of Japan's growing international involvements, no doubt as well as from some awareness of Marxism's fading importance in the world, it was considered time for a new educational start.

As one who believes that internationalism should begin at home and not from the kind of high-flying global perspective that leaves the student in effect "spaced out," I thought it would be appropriate to recall something of the earlier, prewar origins of the school, before Ritsumeikan joined the ranks of supposedly full-fledged universities. An original sponsor of the Ritsumeikan was Prince Saionji Kimmochi (1849–1940), a distinguished elder statesman of the old court aristocracy whose role in the Meiji renovation had generally been considered liberal and progressive. In this respect he exemplified the "enlightenment" that was a keynote of the era, *Meiji* signifying "enlightened rule."

Shortly after the establishment of Kyoto Imperial University as the local counterpart of Tokyo Imperial University—that is, as the premier Western-style institution of learning in the old capital—Saionji helped to found the Ritsumeikan as a school that would supplement the specialized, technically oriented programs of Kyoto University by providing a kind of extracurricular academy for the study and discussion of Confucian-style humanistic learning. Apparently he did not see the two—Confucian and Western learning—as antithetical, but regretted that with the wholesale shift to the latter, something valuable in the old-style classical humanistic formation was being lost.

Saionji was not alone in this; similar sentiments were being expressed in the early decades of this century by scholars who felt that a new generation of Japanese unable to read classical Chinese, an integral part of the old curriculum, would be cut off from the classics and their humanizing influence. Indeed, such sentiments were not unlike those of Western educators in roughly the same era who feared that the increasing abandonment of classical language study in Greek, Latin, and sometimes Hebrew would leave a new generation of Americans impoverished in the same way, without direct access to the classics and to a liberal education in the traditional learning of the West.

At any rate, in adopting the name Ritsumeikan, Saionji and the scholars associated with him in this enterprise were drawing on a rich concept in Confucian thought. The expression *ritsumei,* or *li-ming* in Chinese, comes from Mencius, for whom it means literally "to establish one's own destiny," or more freely "to take one's destiny into one's own hands." Several connotations of the term are relevant here: *li (ritsu)* means "to take one's stand" or "to establish oneself in life," and *ming (mei)* means one's "ordained destiny." The idea is that one must accept the defining circumstances of one's life situation (destiny) while also recognizing their moral implications, and in that context decide what is to be one's calling, vocation, or life's commitment. This calls for active self-definition, not passive acquiescence in the fulfilling of social roles (as is so often supposed by those who regard the Confucian concept of moral responsibility as no more than obedience to assigned social roles and duties). In short, it provides the primary basis for self-cultivation: accepting responsibility oneself for establishing one's own commitments and shaping one's own life within certain inescapable limits.

It would not be difficult to elaborate further on the concept. Even a cursory look at the language of the original Ritsumeikan school anthem or the idealistic statement of purpose in the university bulletin reveals overtones of Chu Hsi's commentary on the passage in *Mencius,* with the deeper philosophical nuances of Neo-Confucian teaching that must still have meant something to the school's founders. But to raise them here would be pointless. When I put the question to my student and faculty audience, only one professor of Chinese classical literature had any notion of where the name Ritsumeikan came from or what it meant. The students themselves had no idea, and though they seemed genuinely interested and eager to learn, the concept was no longer a part of their mental furniture, as it had been for Saionji's generation.

By my own estimate this would largely be true of students throughout

East Asia today, and not just of the Japanese. It is one of the hard facts of life that would-be Confucians must be aware of. But if this speaks to one meaning of "post" in the expression "post-Confucian East Asia," it is still not the whole story. For if "post" here means "past," the past of a people is never completely done for, never something wholly dispensable to them. If they are to understand who they are and where they have come from, the recollection of this idea may tell them and us something else of importance: that in the discussion of Confucianism and modernization, it is not enough simply to ask what the former may have contributed to the latter as a process of economic development. The question is also one of what Confucianism can still contribute to education in the modern world, reminding us that this essential personal dimension of life—the shaping of a self, the making of a life, the qualitative, direct process by which the self matures into a responsible person or, as Mencius put it, "takes charge of one's own destiny"—all this, and not the mere ingesting of information or indiscriminate acquiring of new experiences, has rarely been dealt with, but only bypassed, in modern education. The question posed by Mencius, Chu Hsi, and Saionji remains to be answered, and we are, one and all, answerable for it.

2

REFLECTIONS ON CIVIL SOCIETY
AND CIVILITY IN THE CHINESE
INTELLECTUAL TRADITION

Edward Shils

The term *civil society* is well established in Western tradition of thought about politics, government, and society. In antiquity, civil society was conceived of as the antithesis of the state of nature whereby human beings lived as solitary individuals or families or clans which were in violent conflict, and lacked any authority other than patriarchal authority with overwhelming internal jurisdiction. Civil society, by contrast, was a society larger than a clan, with orderly government, internally at peace, and with a "magistrate," monarch, or the like who could adjudicate disputes peacefully between individual clans or families. Then, in the European Middle Ages, civil society acquired the added meaning derived from its contrast with ecclesiastical society: the civil as distinguished from the divine. It also, somewhat later, came to include the more explicitly peaceful activities and institutions of society in contrast with military activities and institutions. Still later was commerce added as a notable feature of a society where manners had become refined and discriminating, and where modes of life had become more pacific.

The idea of civil society was given a more specific sense by Hegel. Hegel's idea of civil society referred to the sector of society beyond the family and short of the state, beyond the primordial patriarch or father and short of the territorial sovereign. It was the sphere of private interest, in other words, the market. As

Adam Smith had done for the market, Hegel placed the self-regulating civil society within the setting of a larger, territorially bounded society ruled by the state and sustained by the family.

Hegel's delineation of civil society was not entirely confined to market relations. He included associations, guilds, and corporations, which are involved with market activities. These both furthered and limited the activities of the individual meant to gain benefits for himself and his immediate family. Nevertheless, the main feature of civil society as understood by Hegel was the prevalence of actions aimed at realizing private benefits through exchange and at the same time conferring benefits on the society as a whole. The state, according to Hegel, was the supreme power, but it did not regulate everything. Families had their own sphere, as did civil society.

Karl Marx, despite his criticism of Hegel, adopted his idea of civil society, regarding it as the decisive sector of society as a whole, dominant even over the state. Marx transformed Hegel's view of the relationship between state and society, calling the society as a whole "bourgeois society" *(bürgerliche Gesellschaft)*, which in German refers simultaneously to civil society. Marx thus made the part stand for the whole, both terminologically and substantively, by making the bourgeois aspect of society ascendant over all the other aspects of society and over all of culture.

CIVIL SOCIETY AND COLLECTIVE SELF-CONSCIOUSNESS

After Marx, the term *civil society* almost disappeared from use in English-speaking countries. In Germany, as we have seen, it came to be synonymous with "bourgeois society," that is, a society distinguished by the predominance of the bourgeoisie in all spheres of life; it practically ceased to refer to the part of society that was distinct from the state and the family.

In eastern Europe, where communism had triumphed after the Second World War and had obliterated—at least in public—all traces of civil society, both the term and the idea underwent a revival and further development. The spuriousness of the communist declaration of the superiority of communist society over bourgeois society became more and more apparent. Critics of the regimes in practically all the European communist societies demanded the establishment of a "civil society."

True to their Marxist heritage, but insistent on the establishment of a liberal order, the eastern European thinkers used the term "civil society" to refer to a society in which the civil element prevailed. They conceived of it as a society in which there was private ownership of the instruments of production and a competitive market. But the eastern European political reformers went far beyond this. A civil society was one in which the state was entirely subordinate to the civil part of society. Civil society was not just the market for exchanges between economically interested individuals or firms; it also encompassed a complex of institutions for influencing the scale and substance of government activities and for performing various important social functions, a mode for conducting public life. The government was to be subordinated in a civil manner—that is, openly and peacefully.

Divergent interests and ideals had to confront one another rationally: they had to be the objects of bargaining, discussion, persuasion, and compromise. A society of divergent interests, pursued without constraint, had the potential to become a war of each against all. Therefore, there had to be some effective limits to the range and intensity of the pursuit of conflicting ends. Exchange in the competitive market is one such arrangement for bridling divergent interests. Traditionality is another, though it is certainly no guarantee of harmony. Indeed, it might have the opposite effect of making disagreements more rigid. The prospects for coercion have a restraining effect as well, but also may aggravate tension, creating greater disorder.[1]

The east European proponents of civil society have sought to establish a society in which the executive branch of the state is controlled by representative institutions, particularly through a legislature that is elected through the competition of political parties and is under the scrutiny of an independent judiciary and an independent public opinion. Public opinion is formed through exposure to a free press and intellectual institutions in which the freedom of belief, expression, assembly, association, and representation by petition, manifestation, and so on are guaranteed by a constitution. "Civil society" also refers to a mode of interaction between differing opinions about matters that are of concern to a large part of the population and that are affected by the decisions of government authority. This interaction should be public or open to more of the population than just those who participate directly in the interaction or confrontation.

The civil society these reformers seek is thus an open society in which governmental secrecy is kept to the minimum necessary for effective action. Secrecy is to be applied in only a very limited way, primarily in the military sphere. But the principle of the openness of civil society does not obliterate privacy in familial and personal relations or in voluntary associations which are not conspiratorial or subversive. In this view civil society comprises three equally legitimate sectors—the family, the market economy, including the political and cultural spheres, and the government—each of which enjoys some measure of autonomy, influences the others and is influenced by them, but none is supreme over the others.

In recent discussions the term "civil society" means both a pluralistic and a unitary society. The pluralism of outlooks, interests, and associations comes from the freedom to pursue individual and group objectives, within the limits set by the need to maintain peace and order. Its unitary character comes from the nature of the society, the members of which must participate in a collective self-consciousness. A civil society exists within territorial boundaries; citizenship becomes accessible through birth to parents who live in that society or through long residence within its territory. Citizenship is tantamount to full membership in the society, which entails both rights and obligations, the exercise of which entails participation in the collective activities of the society, including participation in politics by contention for public office; by voting in local, regional, and national elections; by free expression of ideals and interests through the organs of public opinion and through freedom of association, assembly, and petition.

Civil society also entails the participation of individuals in the collective self-consciousness of the society as a whole. This collective self-consciousness is the image of the civil society concurrently experienced by most of the members of the society. Being a citizen means being part of the society and being, moreover, entitled to the same respect or deference as any other, regardless of wealth, ancestry, or occupation. In principle, no member of the civil society is simply an external object to the others, each acting in his own self-interest. Participation in the collective self-consciousness of a civil society requires that each member have in mind an image of the others as participants in the same collective self-consciousness. These others are not only particular individuals whom he knows by name or whom he sees or with whom he is in direct interaction. The vast majority of others in any territorially extensive society are anonymous to the acting individual, although they are known to exist within the territorial bounds of his society. In a vague way the individual perceives that he is one with them in a larger translocal or national unity.

A subject or actor is not merely an object of the actions of others, however benevolently intended and however beneficial the effect. He is a "co-actor," acting either in concert with others, or against them, but usually with some measure of participation in the collective self-consciousness. They are all equally active and dignified parts of the society. Participation in the collective self-consciousness thus entails a certain measure of solidarity with all other members of the society. This means each has a desire to maintain the society against disintegrative tendencies and a solicitude not only for the society as a whole but for other individuals and groups regardless of their social status or wealth, the religious community to which they belong, their ethnic connections, and so on.

The civil society is also in part a national society. A national society might not be a civil society, although it may have a tendency in that direction. The reason for the affinity between the two is that both have a reference to territoriality as a criterion for membership. However desirable and necessary it might be for a multinational society to be a civil society, the obstacles are great and only rarely overcome. A nationality often seeks to be a full society and even a state; it can also become a civil society, although this is not inevitable. A civil society may contain several nationalities, but it will tend to be a national society at the same time. The collective consciousness of a civil society tends to become a national civil collective self-consciousness. Indeed, to the extent that a multinational society approximates a civil society, it moves toward becoming a national society, weakening the attachment of its members to their original nationality.

Nevertheless, nationality is not a constitutive property of civil society. It is, however, a very important factor in the formation of civil society. Nationality has a similar bearing on tradition and civility. A multinational society in which nationality has turned to nationalism is inimical to civil society; even in a nationally homogenous society extreme nationalism which demands uniformity and which is intolerant of differences is injurious to civil society. This nationalism is antithetical to civility. Nationality is *traditional* in that it accepts and esteems what has been transmitted from the past. But nationalism is *traditionalistic* in that it rejects what has been transmitted and alleges the superiority of the remoter past from which the recent past is alleged to have fallen away.

The collective self-consciousness of a civil society is reinforced by its traditionality, which refers not only to the society of the immediate present but also to that of the past, both recent and remote. The belief that one's society was civil in the past—that is, its particular institutions embody patterns that were valid in the past—adds to the normative authority of civil society as a whole and of its particular institutions. The First Amendment to the United States Constitution, for example, is not just a legal norm or set of norms contained in an existing document; its long endurance gives it sanctity. This is what I mean when I say that traditionality, while not being part of the abstract definition of civil society, is an important reinforcement of such a society.

The civil society is a society of the rule of law. Its laws are a complex of obligatory and prohibitive norms which are promulgated publicly and legitimately and usually apply throughout the society. Laws that restrict governments, guarantee the liberties of individuals and groups, and hold uncivil actions in check are a defining characteristic of civil society. It is these laws that hold individuals to their obligations and help individuals to fulfill additional obligations not required by law. The stability of these laws, institutions, and patterns is strengthened by their traditionality. This reinforces a sense of oneness with earlier phases of the society and with its heroic figures. Where the past actions and actors of a society become objects of collective self-consciousness, there is a strengthening effect that renders each acting subject more aware of properties which are perceived as common and valuable.

A civil society has internal tendencies both toward self-strengthening and toward self-weakening. Its mere existence as a going concern weighs on the minds of its members. It is what they have experienced, and so they regard its sheer existence as normative. Its existence compels them to act with civility—up to a point, for individual and pluralistic freedom can also lead to conflict and disruptions.

Underlying the institutional apparatus of civil society is the virtue of civility, which provides its motivating force. By civility I mean more than etiquette and courtesy. The whole complex of civility resembles what were called in the eighteenth century "polished" or "refined" manners. Now, in themselves, refined manners do not make a civil society. Politeness, etiquette, and so on are not integral to civil society, although they contribute to it by their mollifying effects, and by holding in check the rancor and aggressiveness that arise in the course of contention. There is, however, one feature of civility that embraces politeness but is fundamental to civil society. That is its concern for the common good. This is inherent in the collective self-consciousness of society. The "common good" of society is a manifestation of the individual's absorption into the collectivity to the point where he acts on behalf of the collectivity. It is the acceptance by the individual self-consciousness of the dictation of the collective self-consciousness in which the individual participates that makes him act toward others in his society with selfless solicitude.

Societies that are extremely inegalitarian in the distribution of status or deference are unlikely to be civil societies. The belief on the part of some members or strata of a society that others are of a much lower order of dignity is inimical to civil society. Religious sectarianism of an acute sort, like political sectarianism, is also inimical to civil society.

I do not think that, beyond a certain point, the size of the population or the geographic area makes a great deal of difference to the internal strength or weakness of the civil element or to the existence of a civil society as a whole. Except for rather small societies in which individuals know one another—Aristotle's idea of the ideal size for any society—the majority of the members are known to only a very few other members. They are largely anonymous to one another, whether they live only a half mile apart or a thousand miles away.

Moderately central rule is more congenial to the functioning of a civil society than is a high degree of centralization on the one hand or, on the other, a situation in which the loci of authority are so dispersed that there is scarcely a visible center at all. The attachment to society which is a vital product of the collective self-consciousness becomes too attenuated if the manifestations of the center are invisible at the peripheries. Hence a weak or invisible center has a negative effect on civil society because it diminishes the perception of inclusion within a common center.

ELEMENTS OF CIVIL SOCIETY IN CHINESE CLASSICAL TRADITIONS

This image of civil society (without my own sociological elaborations) is approximately the ideal that some eastern European politicians, scholars, and thinkers would like to see realized in their respective countries. The movement of thought in eastern Europe has had a certain echo in western Europe and the United States, where it has in turn sounded an echo in the minds of Chinese students from the People's Republic of China and the Republic of China in Taiwan and perhaps also among students from other Chinese communities in Asia and from Korea. It may also be found among younger teachers and students in the People's Republic. It has been with the interests in mind of some of these excellent young men and women who have attended my seminars in recent years that I have undertaken to explore the extent to which the prospects for civil society in China can be strengthened by drawing on Chinese classical traditions, most notably the Confucian tradition. In my seminars I have also considered the rudimentary presence of elements of the ideas of civil society in Taoism, Buddhism, and legalism.

I refer here not to the traditions of Chinese society or of Chinese institutions in the practical affairs of life but rather to intellectual traditions. The two areas are certainly not completely separate, but they are also not identical. The intellectual traditions may well espouse ideas that have some affinity with the idea of civil society, although they may never have been even approximately realized in China. My concern here is to see what the classical traditions contain of the idea of a civil society.

To attempt to account for the present political situation in China by exclusive reference to traditions established more than two millennia ago is no less unrealistic than it would be to explain the present state of Europe exclusively from the Aristotelian and Platonic traditions. Of course, these two Western traditions continue to live on in present-day institutions and beliefs. But they are not the only Western traditions, and moreover they have undergone changes which have been greatly influential. Not everything that happens in human societies is the product of intellectual traditions, however.

Adaptation to necessity in order to retain or increase benefits or to avoid or limit losses in changing circumstances has also left enduring marks on Western societies and has made them quite different from what they would have been had they been ruled exclusively by certain intellectual traditions. Nevertheless, it is not totally unrealistic to find some persistent influence, even if very general or attenuated, to fundamental traditions over a very extended period.

If we grant the efficacy of intellectual traditions, however attenuated or partial, in having certain effects on conditions separated by millennia, then it may be admitted that the Chinese classical tradition has probably had a similar enduring effect. The fact that the existing political regime has tried to extirpate the study of the sources of that tradition may indeed be regarded as rendering plausible the assertion that the Confucian tradition has persisted into communist China in the second half of the twentieth century. That tradition, or parts of it, might be nurtured and strengthened to the point where they may have some influence on future developments in Chinese society. This is not, however, the question I deal with here. My approach is a somewhat different one. The question I ask is whether there are any elements of civil society in the tradition of ancient Chinese philosophy. In the observations that follow, I examine a small selection of classical Chinese works and authors—Confucius, Mencius, Lao Tzu, Mo Tzu, Chuang Tzu, and Lord Shang—to discover the extent to which their ideas of political order approximate the idea of a civil society.

I begin my inquiry by reviewing the extent to which the political institutions and the patterns of conduct praised in Confucian political thought correspond to the idea of a civil society. Of the three components of civil society, Confucius surely was acutely aware of and solicitous toward the family and the state or government. If society is not made up only of family and state, then there is clearly a place for civil society in Confucian philosophy. The question is whether Confucius or his followers discerned that place.

In other words, does Confucius concern himself with the market and the use of private property, or what Hegel regards as complementary to the market, namely, associations of merchants and craftsmen? Does he provide a place for public discussion about the affairs of state? Does he think that individuals have a right to be protected from the state? Very preliminarily I would answer that he does not deal with any of these subjects. The functioning of the market and the processes of exchange and trade do not concern Confucius. Nor does he provide a place for political life around the ruler. He envisions advisers chosen by the ruler, sometimes from among those who put themselves forward; but there is no place in Confucianism for public political contention. And it is not so clear whether individuals, according to Confucius, have rights vis-à-vis their rulers.

The political order has always been distinguished from the family. The criteria by which members of a family distinguish their kinsmen from those who are not kinsmen (i.e., differences in their biological ancestry) are different from those by which they distinguish themselves from individuals who are not members of the same political order (i.e., differences in the territorial-political community to which they belong). Confucius does have a concept of the subject: a subject is determined by residence in a territory with a specific ruler. A civil society, however, is not the same as a political order, and a citizen is not the same as a subject. A political order may include a civil society, but for much of the history of mankind this has not been the case. And the political order as conceived by Confucius does not include a civil society. Confucianism, then, does not have a concept of civil society as a complex of institutions and patterns of activities different from those of the family and the state. Nevertheless, it does provide certain features that would contribute to the working of a civil society.

Limited Government

Civil society is founded on a dual attitude toward governmental authority. On one side is the belief that the powers of government are limited by constitution, law, and tradition and kept under the scrutiny of citizens; on the other is the belief that citizens are entitled, and even have a duty, to participate in political activities in a critical and affirmative manner.

Confucian thought has taken a fairly strong position—although not always free from ambiguity or ambivalence—on these topics. Confucianism declares that the powers of government must be limited to actions permitted by the Way. Confucius never recommended that the government take over or regulate the work of merchants, peasants, or craftsmen. They were to be left on their own, but they—especially the peasants—were to be treated with disinterest. Positive action is less important than adherence to the Way; Confucius praises one ruler (Shun) "who achieved order without taking any action."[2]

The obligation of a government to conform with the Way is basic to the pattern of a good society. It is difficult to say much about the substance of the Way, but it certainly seems to counsel restraint on governmental action. It is conducive to social peace and order, and it entails consideration for the well-being of the ordinary people, that is, the peasantry. This is to be achieved mainly by forbearing from certain actions rather than by active or positive performance.

The Way is a variant of natural law which imposes certain obligations on the ruler. His primary obligation is to perform the imperial rites regularly and meticulously. He also is obliged to adhere to the traditions embodied in the examples of the sage-kings. There is little said in either Confucius or Mencius regarding the political bearing of the performance of rites other than the maintenance of right relations and harmony with the Spirit of the Heavens.[3] Nevertheless, it may be said strict performance of the rites that affirm the Way heightens the likelihood that the ruler will conform with it. This performance affirms the validity of tradition. Another obligation imposed on the ruler is that he rule by benevolence. These concomitants of the performance of the rites place constraints on the expansion and arbitrariness of the ruler's exercise of power.

Confucius does not enter into detail about what is meant by benevolence. I take it to mean, in the common sense, a concern for the well-being of others, a desire for them to be happy or contented, and a generally sympathetic attitude toward them. To rule by benevolence is thus to be concerned with the well-being of those over whom one rules. This seems to be close to the idea of the benevolent ruler in civil society, who exercises his authority with good will toward and consideration of the happiness and contentment of the ruled, mainly the peasantry. During the period of the Warring States, the largest part of the Chinese population was made up of the peasantry. Rule by benevolence was therefore tantamount to royal civility.

This does not mean that Confucius thereby envisaged a civil society in either the narrow or the broad sense. A civil society is one in which individuals pursue ends in the public or civic sphere which they themselves choose and it is the obligation of the government to maintain such a situation. In Confucius—and in Mencius—ordinary individuals are seen as pursuing ends in the public sphere only when they are rebelling, burning, and looting, or when they are working poorly as a result of resentment, undernourishment, or feebleness, or when labor power is insufficient because too many have been taken into military service. Under ordinary circumstances the mass of the population is properly engaged in hard work on the land, obedience to the ruler, and deference and service to parents and ancestors. There is an economic sphere, but there is no market, for there is no freedom in the sale of one's labor. Neither is there a political sphere except for negative actions. There is indeed no public sphere even for the ruling houses. Such political activity as existed arose only through intrigue in the palace or court. And it was secret, not only from the wider public but from those against whom it was directed. Yet there is the fact of the benevolence of the ruler. This is a necessary component of civil society. Hence, there may be a place for Confucius in civil society.

Confucian Intellectuals and Public Office

The belief that the highly educated should take on responsibilities entailing critical and positive participation in the exercise of governmental authority is central to Confucianism. Confucius and Mencius both asserted the obligation of the educated to offer counsel and service to the ruler. Education is a means of comprehending the Way. Those who have studied the classics are therefore the best qualified to guide the ruler in actions in accordance with the Way. Indeed, Tzu-hsia intimates that one indication that "a man has received instruction" lies in the fact that he "offers his person to the service of his lord."[4]

Nevertheless, there are two limits to the obligations of the educated in their service to the ruler. Both are related to the dangers inherent to serving the state. There is first a danger that proximity to the exercise of high authority will be so attractive that the educated will disregard the moral substance of their official activity and will instead pursue wealth and status, thinking little about the Way. Confucians censured those scholars who became officials solely for the financial emoluments. They in turn were aware of the dangers of temptation to large remunerations, and they saw virtue in spurning them.[5] The only justification for accepting an appointment to a high office in government service was to aid the ruler in governing in accordance with the Way. Anything less amounted to corrupt exploitation of office for private gain.

Second, a scholar's efforts in public service may amount to nothing if his advice is disregarded. The ruler's refusal to follow the scholar's advice may be grounds for the latter's resignation.[6] Confucius said that the only persons who can be called "great ministers . . . [are] those who serve their lord according to the Way and who, when this is no longer possible, relinquish office."[7] Elsewhere he said, "Show yourself when the Way prevails in the Empire, but hide yourself when it does not."[8]

Despite these dangers, service to the empire is an obligation of the educated. "Tzu-Lu commented: 'Not to enter public life is to ignore one's duty . . . How . . . can the duty between ruler and subject be set aside? This is to cause confusion in the most important of human relationships, simply because one desires to keep unsullied one's character. The gentleman takes office in order to do his duty. As for putting the Way into practice, he knows all along that it is hopeless.' "[9] Tzu-Lu's position on the obligation to serve a ruler who does not put the Way into practice is somewhat different from that of Confucius, who asserts that a scholar should not serve a ruler who does not govern in accordance with the Way. But Confucians were not in perfect agreement on this matter, partly because it was a question of individual judgment to decide whether the ruler had departed so far from the Way that resignation was absolutely obligatory.

Confucius himself on at least one occasion thought that the obligation for an intellectual to be a civil servant was so strong that he must not be discouraged by the fact that the ruler did not always accept his advice.[10] Confucius' proposal was twice rejected, but he did not resign.

The Confucian view on the obligation of service to the ruler by the educated certainly approximates the requirements of a civil society because it is seen as a fulfillment of the obligation of responsible, critical participation. It places a special duty on those who, as an outcome of their studies, know the proper way to govern. Yet the Confucian view is not unequivocal. It also counsels abstention from sharing in the tasks of ruling on a moral and ultimately religious ground if the ruler or government does not behave properly—but again not entirely so. Confucius says that even for one who abstains from holding office, it is still possible to participate in government. A scholar who does not aspire to follow an official career can "take part in government . . . Simply by being a good son and friendly to his brothers . . . a man is, in fact, taking part in government. How can there be any question of his having actively to 'take part in government'?"[11] This appears at first sight to contradict what has just been said. Yet it may not. Perhaps Confucius means that maintaining the family is a contribution to maintaining public order or social harmony and hence is a contribution to the work of the government. The family has its place in the Way, and whatever sustains the family is an act of adherence to the Way. This in turn fortifies adherence to the Way in the realm. Thus, withdrawing into privacy might also be an act of service to the realm. Service to the state does not exhaust the performance of obligations of the gentleman-scholar in relation to the state. The gentleman-scholar "cultivates himself and thereby brings peace and security to his fellow men . . . He cultivates himself and thereby brings peace and security to the people."[12]

These references in the *Analects* to the political significance of actions that are not specifically or intentionally political (i.e., which are not aimed at influencing decisions made by persons in positions of government authority) raises interesting questions about the place of an idea of civil society in Confucius' writings. If this interpretation of *Analects* 2.21 and 14.42 is reasonable, there does seem to be a field of action outside the state proper and outside the family in which the actions of those who are not serving the state as civil servants and those who have withdrawn into their families have consequences for the political realm. These consequences occur in what in modern civil societies would be called the sphere of public opinion. It is a sphere in which attitudes toward the state, toward the incumbents of the roles of highest authority, are expressed. It is a sphere that is public but not yet political; we may tentatively call it the *prepolitical* sphere because actions here have political consequences. These are the actions and attitudes mainly of the ordinary, uneducated masses whose daily life does not entail any attitudes toward the government but who, if they become unruly, recalcitrant, or disobedient to their masters or "employers," can disturb public peace and order, culminating in rebellion and the expulsion of the ruler from his throne.

It is difficult to describe the nature of the private gentleman's influence on public order. His function in this respect is to maintain a state of public peace by providing an example to ordinary people. This example does not entail any overtly political attitudes or actions. It is an example of private, family piety, respect for ancestors and traditions, and respect for rulers. It is primarily as an example of a political attitude that social peace and order are maintained.

This is one plausible interpretation of these passages. It would indicate that the civil sphere has no positive content; it acquires content only when it is filled with a negative, destructive attitude. The alternative interpretation of these passages is that the private gentleman who is not a civil servant but who lives in the society of his family includes among the objects of his piety the king and his kingdom and that this attitude flows into the lower strata and inculcates into them a positively deferential attitude toward the ruler himself, and not just toward their immediate masters. If this second interpretation is accepted, then it must be said that there is a place for some elements of civil society in Confucius' thought.

In modern Western civilization, in which the tradition of incivility among intellectuals has acquired very widespread adherence, the self-evidentness with which Confucius and his disciples regard service to the ruler by intellectuals is notable. The concern for the good of the kingdom, ruled in accordance with the Way, is a concern for the good of society. A well-ruled kingdom must be one in which the ruler has the well-being of his subjects at heart. This is one important part of civil society, but it can also exist in the context of a society that is scarcely civil. Civility must be fairly dispersed throughout a society for it to be a civil society, quite apart from the institutions that are specific components of civil society as such. Confucius made no provision for such institutions. Nevertheless, the essential element of civility was fairly clearly enunciated. The imposition of the obligation of civility on intellectuals is a subtle achievement of Confucius in contributing to the idea of a civil society. At the same time, however, the justification he repeatedly gives for intellectuals to refuse to serve a prince who does not rule in accordance with the Way has an affinity with the abstention of intellectuals from the politics of civil society in western societies over the past two centuries.[13] Here, as in other respects, Confucius grasped a phenomenon that was essential to civil society: the willingness to renounce power or high office without bitterness. If a political sphere were to exist, though Confucius did not envisage it, his counsel about not clinging to office would be fully in accord with the pattern of a civil society.

Politics and Political Institutions

Confucius' discussion of proper conduct in politics and government for the gentleman-scholar or the educated man—in our contemporary vocabulary, the intellectual—goes a considerable distance toward the ideal of a civil society. But because he did not conceive of a political public sphere—civil society in the narrow sense—intellectuals who in modern societies might be active as publicists and the like had no such possibilities open to them, to say nothing of obligations. Confucius was quite explicit in rejecting the possibility of intellectuals' participating in public discussions and in the formation of public opinion. Indeed, intellectuals are expressly warned against voicing opinions about the affairs of government if they did not hold office. Twice in the *Analects* Confucius said, "Do not concern yourself with matters of government unless they are the responsibility of your office."[14] Politics as the public contention of rivals for political office is scarcely present in Confucius' mind, perhaps because there was in fact no such activity in China in his lifetime. Yet the idea of public political activity is not totally absent from his thought either, although the only form of contention for public office that he considered was the competition for appointment as a minister or counselor.

His praise of piety and learning had important implications which are potentially congenial to the idea of a civil society. The concept of civil society, with its emphasis on limited government, on private activities by businesses and voluntary associations, and on plurality, removes politics and political activities from the position of supreme value and chief means to all other values. In a civil society politics is only one among many fields of action, and political office only one among many prized roles. Confucius' views are very close to this. Confucius was of the belief that politics and public office should not be regarded as all that counts in human life. "To bring peace to the old, to have trust in my friends, and to cherish the young"[15]—that is what Confucius set his heart on. "Eagerness to learn" was placed above the potential civil virtue of persons "doing their best for others and . . . being trustworthy in what they say."[16] Such pluralism of values is also appropriate to a civil society. It provides a curb on political fanaticism, which is inimical to civil society. Confucius spoke of rulers and of rulers' officials and urged restraints on both. This is a fundamental principle. Nevertheless, the restraints on the ruler, as Confucius conceived them, were not realized through institutions, as they are in civil society.

The Rule of Law

The rule of the Way is not exactly like the rule of law, but it is not entirely dissimilar either. Confucian writers, most prominently Confucius and Mencius, seldom refer to laws, to legal codes, or to the judiciary. Confucius scarcely speaks of legislation. Perhaps he connected law with coercive sanctions, for he thought that "punishments" and "edicts" were not the means to ensure an orderly, harmonious society. If society were guided by virtuous rulers—rulers who perform the rites, respect their ancestors, conduct themselves with restraint, and do not engage in activities that cause distress among the common people—society would be peaceful and orderly. That is, there would be an absence of audible and physically violent public contention.

Departure from the Way is not assessed by the decision of a parliamentary body or a supreme court or controller general. It is not responded to by the displeasure of the electorate or the organs of public opinion. Rather, the ruler's departure from the Way precipitates disorder in the kingdom. Confucius does not, however, specify whether the common people become troublesome because they perceive that the ruler has disrespected the Way or because their living conditions have fallen below the level they think should have been assured to them by the stipulations of the Way. Could it be that the Way of natural law (or custom) is tacitly accepted by the ruler, and that the common people are vaguely aware that natural law (or customary law) requires that they should live in a certain way and with a certain standard of living? Could it be that they think that if the actions of the ruler prevent them from living in that certain way and from enjoying that standard of living then the ruler has offended against the Way (or against natural and customary law) and that they no longer owe him obedience? This would imply that the common people have a sense of the legitimacy of authority constituted by adherence to the Way.

Alternatively, Confucius' view about the Way in its relation to disorder in the realm might be interpreted to mean that the Mandate of Heaven itself intervenes in earthly affairs in order to show its displeasure with the ruler's departure from the Way by inducing a degree of disorder in the realm to the point where the ruler is overthrown or even the point where his dynasty is broken. When the Way is observed, the public or civil sphere does not exist. Disorder in the empire primarily refers to the restiveness, recalcitrance, or rebelliousness of the lower classes. It is not just that the Way is the protector of the common people—though it is indeed that—but rather that the common people are the device whereby the emperor's departure from the Way is made manifest. This gives the common people a special function: their restiveness is evidence of deviance from the Way.

In the former interpretation there is an incipient civil sphere, for the common people have a sense of their rights under the auspices of the Way and under the eye of Heaven. They are ordinarily dutiful (and publicly inert) when the Way is observed and become recalcitrant and even violent only when their "rights" under the Way are infringed. Both interpretations are problematic, however. In neither is the civil sphere an established and legitimate field of action for the common people so long as the Way is respected by the ruler. The common people have no proper part in enforcing adherence. All they can do is protest, in the first interpretation against departures from the Way (or natural or customary law), and in the second in response to the deprivations they are subjected to, thereby manifesting the displeasure of the Spirit of the Heavens.

Confucius made no provision for a constitution other than the Way and the traditions of the sage-kings. The latter, like the Way, are never substantively depicted, apart from their examples of benevolence, courtesy, respect, solicitude for the peaceful ordering of society, and avoidance of military adventures. Confucius never refers to any laws as binding on the ruler other than the Way and the traditions of the sage-kings. Civil servants, by contrast, were intermittently under very stringent control and were subject to harsh sanctions. Nothing of this is spoken of by Confucius or his disciples. Neither does he provide the common people with any right or institutional arrangement to remonstrate against the conduct of an official. In short, Confucius made no provision for the rule of law. It could be said, however, that if the Way is interpreted as the equivalent of natural law, then it may be elaborated into a body of laws. But this possibility is not envisioned by Confucius.

Legislation and Legislature

Confucianism also makes no provision for legislation or a legislature. The monarch is the legislator who acts on the advice of his ministers or counselors, who are themselves guided only by the Way, custom, the principle of benevolence (and cognate virtues), and calculations of expediency. Although it could be said that the Way—the cosmic order as it is manifested in the conduct of the realm—is a form of natural law, it is a form of natural law that is silent about the natural rights of individuals or collectivities. (The family in its various guises is the only collectivity mentioned, and the only right the family enjoys is the right to act in a ritually correct manner toward its ancestors in the male line.)

Individuals have many obligations toward ancestors, parents, the older generation, and the ruler. Confucius lays much stress on these obligations, but he does not refer to their enactment in legislation or their enforcement by officials and judges. Since individuals have no rights, it is entirely consistent for Confucian thought not to mention the panoply of institutions that now promulgate and protect the rights of individuals, institutions, and collectivities. Since sovereign power rests entirely on the monarch, it would be inconsistent to recommend the creation of a legislature, for such a legislature could have only advisory functions, which were already being performed by scholarly advisers to the ruler.

There being no legislature, there is no need for a process of selecting legislators. Elections are not the only means of selecting legislators, but since the sovereign does not need them, and the persons who might be their electors have no rights to have their interests represented, no approximation to a concept of representative institutions is to be found in Confucian writings. The mass of the population, or even a small, rather narrowly circumscribed minority, having no legitimate demands to be represented, either in an elected legislature or before the ruler, have no need for representative institutions. In its treatment of the relation between legitimate demands or desires and the ruler's decisions, Confucian thought is perfectly consistent. The common people may have legitimate demands, but they are not expressed, and there are in Confucian writings no clear references to any way in which they can be made known to the ruler and the officials, except by recalcitrance, rebellion, or flight. (I deal with this somewhat more fully under the heading "The Common People.")

Confucianism does not envisage a legal order, that is, an order of general, abstract laws interpreted by judges and applied to particular cases. It conceives, rather, of a moral, ultimately metaphysical order—the Way—which limits the mode and range of the exercise of governmental powers. Confucius must have known about laws, but he does not refer to them. It is interesting to speculate why this is so. Did he deem them an unworthy means of controlling the actions of individual subjects? Did he regard moral convictions with respect to the worthiness of government authority as the only valid norms for restraining the behavior of subjects?

Neither does Confucius conceive of a judiciary that analyzes facts, determines what the law bearing on the facts is, and hands down decisions. He says nothing about the independence of judges or magistrates, or even about their existence.

Interests and the Market

A ruler has an interest in continuing to rule; an ordinary man has an interest in having sufficient food and in working within the limits of his physical capacities; a parent has an interest in being respected; a scholar has an interest in being appointed to public office. In Confucian thought these are all legitimate interests. Confucius does not acknowledge a conflict of legitimate interests. He accepts that there are desires, those that are proper (i.e., in accordance with the Way) and those that are improper. The latter give rise to conflicts of interest between individuals and between different sectors of society, between rulers and scholars, and between rulers and ordinary people. Parochial or sectoral interests exist only when the Way is not followed. Failure to follow the Way reduces men to a state of animality. In this animal state there are conflicts. Among human beings these conflicts are factitious. Adherence to the Way avoids them.

Rulers who depart from the Way may exploit and maltreat their subjects, creating what would now be thought of as a conflict of interest between rulers and subjects. But the conflict is inadmissible and illegitimate, and so is the divergence of interests through which the conflict emerged. There is no place in the Confucian view for the entire institutional paraphernalia which has developed in modern liberal democratic societies for allowing divergent interests to be represented and pursued, and for protecting their pursuit while at the same time limiting it. Confucius did not imagine conflict over incompatible interests within the framework of adherence to the Way, and he did not devote himself to imagining institutions for containing the conflicts of interests within the limits of social peace and order. Hence he foresaw no problem of preventing those conflicts from becoming too acute for the maintenance of the necessary minimum of social order; adherence to the Way would inhibit such conflicts.

Neither was Confucius concerned with the private ownership of property. He did not disapprove of it, but he made no argument for it; he merely accepted it as given. He did not disapprove of wealth so long as it had not been "attained through immoral means."[17] But he certainly did not regard the acquisition of wealth through commerce as meritorious: "It is a shameful matter to be rich and noble when the Way falls into disuse in the state."[18] Seeking profit, although tolerable, was not estimable. In short, he did not have a high opinion of commerce, but he seems to have accepted its functional utility. In a civil society, by contrast, commerce has an honorable place. I would infer that for Confucius the only proper way to acquire wealth was to inherit it or to have it bestowed by the ruler. Commerce was characteristic of "the small man." Being in favor of the division of labor, Confucius must have allowed a place for the exchange of products, but he never went as far as Hegel did in defining civil society as the realm of production and exchange.

Openness and the Conflict of Interests and Ideals

A civil society requires publicity about the actions of government, for if the ruler's benevolence were not visible to his subjects, how could he influence them? The charismatic influence of the gentleman also requires that it be seen by those who are under his influence. How and where do the different classes meet? Confucius is silent on this point, in marked contrast with the legalistic view that people must not be allowed to share in "the thoughts about the beginning of an affair."[19] And yet for the legalists, concerned with applying stern laws, the promulgated laws and penalties must be made known to the ruler's subjects. Confucius says nothing on this matter.

Confucius also had little or no interest in conflicts between merchants. He thought that they were a minor factor in the life of a society. Confucius was opposed to coercion, but he was not opposed to its use in order to affirm and restore the Way.[20] Reason and rational discussion—as well as the acceptance of constraining rules—are the proper technique for peaceful civil confrontation when interests conflict. This is at the heart of civil society. There is no provision for it in Confucian thought.[21]

The Public Sphere

Confucius makes no provision for a sphere where members of the public can encounter one another not as members of a family or as members of a monarch's entourage but as members of a public, meaning a collectivity constituted by relatively rational discussion and exchange of information. Such a public must have existed in Confucius' time, though in a highly restricted way. The very community of Confucius and his disciples, a fragmentary account of which comes down to us in the *Analects,* testifies to this. An interchange of views between ministers within a cabinet or a council does not constitute a civil society; neither does a secret or private discussion among the representatives of great landowning families. They certainly represent a step away from pure autocracy and toward civil society, but they are still very far from constituting it.

Nevertheless, Confucius had no more idea of a public than he had of citizenship. In his enumeration of the basic relationships—those of the living to their ancestors, of sons to fathers, of wives to husbands, of younger to older persons, and of friends toward friends—only the relationship of subjects to their ruler might be thought of as belonging to the public sphere. This is the only relation referred to by Confucius between persons who are not linked by primordial (family) ties or by common primordial conditions (generations) or by ties of friendly affection.

The relationship between a ruler and his officials is a governmental relationship. Only the relation between ruler and subjects who are not officials may therefore be said to constitute a zone in which a civil society could develop. The public is the locus of reciprocity and interchange; the relationship between ruler and subject, as conceived by Confucius, is largely unilateral. Hence, it represents only a potentiality for civil society. The relationship must become much more differentiated and multilateral if it is to undergo transformation into the public of a civil society.

Public Opinion

Confucius allowed no place for discussion in public—perhaps even in private—regarding governmental affairs. He thought that only persons occupying official positions should discuss matters of policy. It was not appropriate for the "citizens" or subjects, even those who had mastered the classics, to express views on governmental affairs unless they had an official responsibility to do so. "The Master said: 'Do not concern yourself with matters of government unless they are the responsibility of your office.' "[22] It seems that in the study of the classics, their bearing on statecraft was justified only by their relevance to the activities of an official. Study of the classics was not intended primarily to educate a class of superior citizens—scholar-gentlemen—who would create a setting of rational and informed opinion for the guidance of governmental policy. On the contrary, Confucius thought the very opposite: that the doings of government were not "the business" of the educated unless they had appointments in government as officials or counselors. If not, they were to mind their own business; and government was not their business.

Critical views about government expressed by the common people—if at all imaginable—were abhorrent to Confucius. Adherence to the Way renders critical views superfluous if not pernicious. Although there is a world of difference between the views of Confucius and those of the legalists, the legalist proposition that "a country which loves talking is dismembered"[23] is not very far from Confucius' belief. Confucius did not express himself in the harsh language used by the legalists; but with respect to their disapproval of public discussion of governmental affairs, their view was very little different from his. Confucius would, however, allow discussion within the government; the legalists would not even permit that: "At present, the prince is dazed by talk, officials are confused by words."[24]

When Confucius said, "The gentleman enters into associations . . . the small man enters into cliques,"[25] he probably did not mean what we call voluntary associations, formed for the joint pursuit of an interest or an ideal and intended to affect the state of society; he probably meant friendships in which conversations were conducted and lofty subjects discussed. He was not thinking of public and visible associations. Associations were for mutual enlightenment; cliques were presumably intended for the advancement of local and individual interests. But it is also possible that by cliques he meant conspiratorial groups that did not aim at the public good, in contrast with associations that did have such an objective. If this interpretation is closer to Confucius' meaning, then in this sense he did adumbrate the idea of civil society. But if so, it is the only such reference to a public sphere. There is no mention of discussion, nothing about contradiction and reply as a way of reaching the truth. Even in their own practice there is no dialogue between Confucius and his disciples, no give-and-take, no criticism of the views of others, such as Socrates conducted with his interlocutors, or such as Milton and Mill praised.[26] Confucian dialogues are much less sustained and of a much simpler pattern. Still, these must have been, in Confucius' time, something like philosophical debates. Surely, not long after Confucius' lifetime members of the various schools of philosophy criticized one another. Yet there is little acknowledgment of this in the *Analects* and practically no indication that it was a good thing.

There is, however, a potential place for debate in the Confucian scheme of things. Questions on problems of interpretation and application put by disciples and Confucius' answers show profound awareness that the generalizations contained in the assertions of Confucius need interpretation and application; in his conversation with his disciples he repeatedly attempts to clarify ambiguities. Yet these activities are not granted a place of prominence in the Confucian account of the proper functioning of society.

The Common People

Perhaps the organization and practice of government in China in the early centuries of Confucianism were really too far from those of a civil society for that type of society to be imaginable, even by a person of such civil disposition as Confucius. As with other political philosophers who have pondered the best or the right political order, his imagination was constrained by what he knew. The principal obstacle lay in his conception of the centers of society. He conceived of society as having one major center—

the ruler and his court—and a very large number of peripheral centers—
great families and their lineages—which were largely autonomous and relatively self-contained. All initiative and decision were concentrated in the
major center. The vast majority of the population, the common people, had
no initiative and no voice in any discussions about the society in which they
lived.

The "multitude" or the "common people" held Confucius' attention as
much as the gentleman. Confucius accepted that there was a fundamental
difference between ruler and common people. The task of the former was
to reign over the latter; the task of the latter was to support the ruler, not so
much by their acclamation as by the proper performance of their role, which
was to work hard and steadily on the land and to heed the ruler when his
desires or commands were made known to them.[27] The common people
could contribute nothing to ruling. Their virtues were hard work on the land,
submission, and devotion to the ruler.[28]

Neither Confucius nor Mencius allowed much place for the middle or
mercantile class. They regard merchants as small men because their understanding is focused on what is profitable.[29] Confucius judged them more
negatively than Mencius in this respect. There is no anticipation that the
stratum of society made up of small men would produce scholars and gentlemen. Their response to faulty government is never mentioned. Their good
conduct does not merit esteem, and their disregard for the Way does not
affect the stability, peace, or order of society—at least, this is a permissible
inference. Rulers and great landowners can affect the state of society because
they can affect the attitudes of the common people. Their failure to observe
the Way has a negative effect on the submissiveness and fidelity of the multitude. Confucius was certainly far from an egalitarian, but he was very alert
to the influence that inequality which was not properly legitimated would
have on the mass of the population. Such inequality was conducive to insta-
bility, which Confucius abominated more than poverty and "underpopula-
tion."[30]

Confucius' ideas about the common people are not wholly clear to me.
He certainly did not admire their moral qualities. Moreover, he believed that
they were worse than they had been in the past: "In antiquity, the common
people had three weaknesses, but today they cannot be counted on to have
only these. In antiquity, in their wildness men were impatient of restraint;
today, in their wildness they simply deviate from the right path. In antiquity,
in being conceited, men were uncompromising; today, in being conceited,
they are simply ill-tempered. In antiquity, in being foolish, men were straight;
today, in being foolish, men are simply crafty."[31] On top of all this, since
those who are in authority over them have lost the Way, the common people

have long been rootless.[32] One thing that is clear, however, is that he regarded the common people as of the utmost importance to the realm. Their labor, their taxes, their services, their liturgy, and their military power were obviously indispensable to the ruler. They were, therefore, to be dealt with in a manner that would ensure their maximum utility to the ruler.

Sometimes Confucius' view of the common people approximated that of the legalists, although his statements are never as harsh. The common people he regarded as instruments indispensable to the ruler, to be treated in ways that would guarantee their continuous practical value. Sometimes he appears to say that they are valuable only as a means to that end. Confucius occasionally spoke as if the common people should be objects of prudent calculations of advantage to the ruler. Actions on the part of the ruler which alienate the common people would make them less submissive and less productive, for they respond to what is done to them. The people are represented as not having any distinctive desires or aspirations to be respected by other strata of society. They are always acted upon; they never initiate. The common people are practically never regarded as having any responsibility for adherence to the Way.

The common people are, in general, viewed as entirely inert, performing routine tasks, fulfilling their duties, doing military service, performing corvée, and so on. In this sense, and only in this sense, are they integral parts of society. The common people are a passive periphery, but they are not altogether outside of society.

Confucius repeatedly said that the ruler must act benevolently toward the ordinary people. In one interpretation of this injunction, the ordinary people could never be an autonomous generator of actions required for the good of society. They form a morally inert mass incapable of initiating moral actions, capable at best of obedience and diligence in physical exertion. If not treated with benevolence, they would not be able to perform their particular indispensable function in the constitution of society. They were not to be treated simply as mechanical instruments of the ruler's desires, however, but were to be viewed simply as parts of the economic order who work and produce so that the rulers and the great families might live without exerting physical labor, perform the necessary rites, and mediate relations between Heaven and the earthly order.

In another interpretation the common people are not merely physically present and physically useful; they also have a moral standing as members of the same society as the rulers, sharing a common membership. The moral qualities of the common people tend toward inertness, but they are also capable of responding to the charismatic qualities of their superiors, the gentlemen and rulers. They themselves have no charismatic qualities.

Rulers and officials are enjoined over and over again not to act toward the common people in a manner that would overwork them. They are told not to engage thoughtlessly in wars that damage the common people. The people should be called upon for corvée only in the "right seasons." The material needs of the commoners must always be kept in mind. For example, when Confucius heard that an official—his own steward—had refused an offer of nine hundred measures of grain, he asked, "Can you not find a use for it in helping the people in your neighborhood?"[33]

The Moral Potential of the Common People

Rulers are constantly told that they must act benevolently. This benevolence might conceivably be said to acknowledge the inherent dignity of the "common people" or the "multitude." Since Confucius never spoke about rights in general, it was consistent for him to think that the common people had no rights. The people seem to lack the moral dignity which the possession of rights would confer on them. In one passage he does say that it is wisdom "to work for the things the common people have a right to." Generally, however, he does not speak of their rights, nor does he speak of their obligations to their ancestors. They have no alternatives other than submissive, productive labor on the one hand and resentment, resistance, and rebellion on the other. Their loyalty is a negative virtue; it consists in not being disloyal. The common people, left to themselves, "deviate from the right path" and are "ill-tempered" and "crafty." In the past, when neglected or not treated with benevolence, they were "impatient of restraint," "uncompromising," and "straight." They will always be submissive and diligent if their rulers adhere to the Way and practice benevolence; if not, then they will become resentful and recalcitrant. Their inertia is limited by resentment and rebelliousness. Short of that, they are at best well-behaved clods. Little or nothing emanates from them, although they are susceptible to the emanations from rulers and gentlemen.

Do the common people possess their own sort of dignity which could make them part of the larger moral order governed by the requirements of the Way? Confucius never speaks of the obligations of the common people to observe the Way. They are not responsive to the actions of others which are in accordance with the Way, but can themselves act according to the Way. Confucius says nothing of the benevolence of the common people. But what about their receptiveness to benevolence?

The lower strata can be elevated by the conduct of the gentleman, whose charismatic quality is part of the process of maintaining social order. The gentleman, like the proper ruler in relation to the multitude, calls forth and arouses in others "what is good in them; he does not help them to realize what is bad in them."[34] "The small man," like the bad ruler, "does the opposite."[35] (Confucius speaks here of others; is it permissible to think that he is referring to the common people?) Thus, the gentleman is charismatic and benevolent; he can arouse the charismatic potentiality and benevolence of others. Benevolence is enjoined by the Way. The Way is sacral law. The potential for conformity with the Way, for drawing some of it into oneself, appears in this interpretation to be widespread in society, and thus it is not entirely dependent on the study of the classics. It might be inherent in the nature of man.

The parallel between the gentleman and good government, perhaps even their identity, is evident in the proposition that to govern is to correct: "If you set an example by being correct, who would dare to remain incorrect?"[36] The same idea of the radiating charismatic power of virtue is expressed regarding criminality: if persons of prominence and power yielded to their desires, "no one would steal even if stealing carried a reward."[37]

Good desires (i.e., desires for the good, properly pursued by the rulers) will lead to goodness in the common people. "When the gentleman feels profound affection for his parents, the common people will be stirred to benevolence. When he does not forget friends of long standing, the common people will not shirk their obligations to other people."[38] A similar observation, with explicit adduction of the rites—the most particular manifestation of contact with the charismatic—is that "when those above are given to the observance of the rites, the common people will be easy to command."[39] The affinity of the charismatic qualities of the gentleman and of the good ruler is suggested by Confucius: "Just desire the good yourself and the common people will be good. The virtue of the gentleman is like wind; the virtue of the small man is like grass. Let the wind blow over the grass and it is sure to bend."[40] Also: "The common people can be made to follow a path but not to understand it."[41] Note here the implication that the common people have no power of initiation of good actions; they respond to good actions but cannot initiate them from within themselves.

Confucius insists on the need for genuineness in the goodness of rulers: "A facade of benevolence which is belied by his deeds"[42] might make a person in the service of the state or from a noble family "known," but it cannot have the same effect as genuine benevolence. The "setting of an example" has a prominent place in Confucius' counsels to rulers. "Crooked" subordinates can be made "straight" by the straightness of their superiors: "Raise the straight and set them over the crooked. This can make the crooked straight."[43] Similarly, subordinates can be induced to work hard if their superior himself works hard. In response to a question about government,

Confucius said: "Encourage the people to work hard by setting an example yourself."[44]

Yet, even though there is reason to believe that Confucius allowed for the possibility of the awakening of a moral potential or a capacity to respond to charismatic influence in the common people, it is clear that he did not conceive of a society in which there is any autonomous participation by the mass of the population. The educated outside of government were not to discuss affairs of state, and this was all the more true for the multitude. Even more than for the educated who are not officials, it is appropriate for the multitude to be silent with respect to affairs of state. Indeed, the common people are incapable of anything except manual labor and service without beneficial influences from above.

If a gentleman (i.e., a scholar and administrator) is slipshod in his "speech," meaning in the performance of his administrative duties, and is in need of correction,[45] repercussions will extend to the point at which "the common people will not know where to put hand and foot" because "punishments do not fit the crimes," and "rites and music do not flourish."[46] The common people would become irreverent, insubordinate, and insincere if those above them did not "love the rites . . . love what is right . . . love trustworthiness."[47] They are likely to be more diligent, more reverent, and more submissive if they experience beneficent influences from above. Without that benevolence, unrest and rebelliousness would be close to the surface.

The common people have a capacity for trusting their rulers, and perhaps an inclination to do so. If the common people have enough food and arms, that trust will be forthcoming. According to Confucius, trust is even more important than food or arms. Arms are the most dispensable; food, too, can be dispensed with, for "death has always been with us since the beginning of time." But "when there is no trust, the common people will have nothing to stand on."[48] Confucius' statement may be reformulated thus: by their trustfulness, the common people are firmly attached to society as a moral order within the cosmic order governed by the Way.

The common people can relapse into a turbulent state if their conditions of life are difficult. In fact, when Confucius attributes moral qualities to the common people, he is skeptical with regard to the powers of endurance of their moral disposition. Under conditions of adversity a gentleman will hold fast, but that is not so easy for the common people. Lacking constant hearts, when they find theselves "in extreme straits they would throw over all restraint."[49]

The potential moral inclination of the periphery is affected by the inclination of the center. The common people's attachment to society and their moral mood is affected for the better by the piety of their superiors toward their own ancestors.[50] They are thus affected by the charismatic quality of piety. They can perhaps be bound to their own traditions, although Confucius says nothing about traditionality among the common people. Order is maintained among the mass of the population primarily by the good example of their rulers. ("If you set an example by being correct, who would dare to remain incorrect?")[51] Confucius said that if ruled with dignity, the common people "will be reverent"; if treated with kindness, "they will do their best"; if the good among them are raised and the backward among them instructed, "they will be imbued with enthusiasm."[52]

The mass of the population will work hard if their superiors work hard.[53] This suggests that they will not work hard for their own pecuniary advantage or out of their own sense of what is right. They will do so only if their superiors set an example. If they are ruled over with dignity, they will be reverent and deferential. They will respond actively and positively to good examples embodied in the actions and attitudes of their superiors, and negatively if they are maltreated. They have no propensities toward good conduct within themselves. Confucius said that "when the gentleman feels profound affection for his parents, the common people will be stirred to benevolence. When he does not forget friends of long standing, the common people will not shirk their obligations to other people."[54] But the common people are apparently not expected to show spontaneous reverence toward their ancestors.

On another occasion Confucius said that the common people require benevolence.[55] To interpret this passage as meaning only that they are in need of the benefits provided by the benevolent acts of gentlemen might be too limited; it might also mean that they themselves will be benevolent. I think, however, that the former interpretation is the more plausible because most of Confucius' references to benevolence treat it as a virtue exercised by gentlemen and sometimes by rulers but very rarely by the common people.

Reverence, enthusiasm, and exerting oneself to do what is expected: in this way the common people certainly contribute to the harmony and tranquillity of society. It is not, however, the same as being heeded because of the legitimacy of their desires or because of their desires' origin in adherence to the Way. The common people are ordinarily outside the collective self-consciousness of the gentleman.

Confucius brings his analysis to a head when he says, "The common people can be made to follow a path but not to understand it."[56] A charismatic quality radiates from the central class; the periphery can be a recipient, but it can never be a point from which charisma emanates. Whereas the gentleman shows stability of character under conditions of adversity, the common people in contrast are severely disordered in such conditions. It is to prevent such disorder that the ruler must ensure that the common people have enough to eat even in hard times.

There is nothing in principle to prevent a person of common origin from engaging in learning and acquiring the benefits of education, any more than a barbarian is prevented from entering on a course of classical study and thereby becoming a gentleman—and, presumably, Chinese. The common people, however, "make no effort to study even after having been vexed by difficulties,"[57] and hence they are "the lowest." Still, if they were to study, they too might become gentlemen.

Confucius' view of the common people resembles in some important respects the European conception of the common people up to the eighteenth century. According to that view, the working class and the agricultural tenants and laborers, lacking property, had no stake in the country and hence were not really a part of it. This was, however, not consistently Confucius' view. To the extent that he espoused the potential of the common people to participate in the collective self-consciousness, he contributed to a rudimentary tradition of civil society.

Let me summarize the foregoing observations. The Confucian conception of the common people ranges from a conception of the charismatic incorporation of the periphery into society to the "veterinarian" conception, which sees human beings as animals who should be treated with solicitude. According to the former, the charisma of the center, discerned by study, cultivated by ritual and the reverence for ancestors, brings the peripheral common people closer to the moral order occupied at the center by the emperor and his counselors and officials. They are brought, to some extent at least, into the same moral order by benevolent action, which arouses in them the experience of the moral qualities cultivated in the centers of society. Benevolence, if it does not call forth further benevolence, at least evokes an appreciation of benevolence. Thus, the periphery comes to participate in some measure in the collective self-consciousness of the center. According to the veterinarian view, by contrast, the common people, being important for the maintenance of the ruler and his servants through the provision of food and services, must be treated in ways that will maintain their submissive diligence and suppress their inherent refractoriness and rebelliousness, which are aroused by policies that deprive them of food and physical repose and well-being. In the veterinarian conception the moral propensities of the periphery are negligible.

In both conceptions there remains a pronounced difference between the gentleman and the common people. The difference does not simply lie in the extent to which they have studied the Five Classics. Benevolence, courtesy, moderation, and inner tranquillity are very seldom attributed by Confucius to the common people. The common people cannot ordinarily exercise these virtues—and certainly not on their own initiative—but they are not inevitably insensitive to them. They can respond to them, according to Confucius, although they themselves can never generate them or possess them unsustained by external examples and without the provision of favorable conditions.[58]

By contrast, in a civil society the common people have values and beliefs of their own, and they have an intrinsic dignity which is recognized by their rulers. It is through this intrinsic dignity as residents in the territory of their society and as human beings that they are citizens. As such they possess qualities that cannot be extinguished by differences in wealth, status, power, or knowledge. Having the qualifications that make them citizens, they are entitled to share, through representative institutions, in making decisions on issues that fall within the jurisdiction of the government. They are not simply clay to be molded by the sculptor-ruler. They need to be educated and informed, but this does not diminish the validity of their rights as citizens.

Civility

Confucius omits the specifically civic category of civil society in his enumeration of the gentleman's relations with and obligations toward his ancestors, parents, wife, young people, elders, and lord. There is never any place for the citizen in relation to other citizens, although he does say at one point that "a young man . . . should love the multitude at large."[59] A similar idea is expressed when Fan Ch'ih asks about benevolence; the Master simply says: "Love your fellowmen."[60] There is no mention of service to society or to China and practically nothing of service to the empire; it is service to the emperor or to the king of which Confucius speaks. Indeed, society as such is given a secondary position.

Nevertheless, Confucius is in some important respects a great forerunner of the idea of civil society, however fragmentary and rudimentary. He does not fail to devote attention to certain elements of civility, which are the virtues of civil society. Benevolence is one such important element, although Confucius does not analyze its ramifications. When there is a possible conflict between civic virtue or civility and familial loyalty, Confucius is usually silent. When he does speak of it, he comes down on the side of familial loyalty. For instance, he prefers a son who "covers up" for his father who stole a sheep over one who gives evidence against his father regarding a similar act.[61]

This statement requires important qualifications. Many of the virtues praised by Confucius may be looked on as variant forms or components of civility. Thus, the virtues of the gentleman, although not always explicitly connected to relations with rulers, are virtues that would be highly appropriate to the workings of a civil society, even though in Confucius' time the institutions of civil society did not exist. More specifically, the first of the virtues praised by Confucius is benevolence, which, although not clearly defined, seems to mean a benign disposition toward others. Moderation, serenity, tranquillity, modesty, equanimity, courtesy, resistance to any impulse toward anger—all these are included in the idea of benevolence. They are indeed the virtues required in a civil society if the individualism, ambition, and acquisitiveness in the economic sphere are to be held in check.

It was probably not failure in commerce—Confucius did not address his discourse to merchants or craftsmen—which prompted him to say, "Is it not gentlemanly not to take offense when others fail to appreciate your abilities?"[62] He certainly could not have been thinking of a defeated candidate in an electoral contest. He is more likely to have had in mind aspirants for appointment or promotion in the civil service and in the councils of the ruler. He may also have been thinking of an adviser close to the emperor who failed to gain the emperor's ear. The meaning is the same: do not respond with anger when your objectives are not realized.

As in all other discussions of the qualities of the gentleman, the modesty of one's demands and the willingness to renounce what can be achieved only by violent action are highly appreciated by Confucius. He also counsels avoidance of actions and words that accentuate the breach between the successful and the unsuccessful or between the winners and the losers. Although Confucius did not live in a civil society, he did grasp how essential it is to maintain peace between the contenders for scarce goods in any society. Without the disposition to reconcile oneself with the failure to attain one's goals, no matter how important, a society cannot be a civil society.

Trustworthiness

It is notable that amidst the turbulence and disorder in Chinese society, only relatively rarely did those scholars who failed to obtain the classical appointments in the civil service, despite years of study and submission to rigorous examinations, join in conspiracies to displace the incumbent ruler. In this respect the scholars were also gentlemen in Confucius' sense. A gentleman must be trustworthy. Those who deal with him must be confident that he will abide by his word and will not hide malign intentions beneath an amiable exterior. The concept of trustworthiness postulates insight into aspects of other persons' dispositions. But it is not just a predictive statement that the other person will live up to his promises or to the obligations he has accepted. Trustworthiness is of course a virtue in every relationship, no less so in the civil relationship Confucius does not mention as in those he does mention, such as the relationship between father and son, husband and wife, elder and younger, lord and vassal, emperor and official. Trustworthiness, moderation, and conciliatoriness: these virtues of the gentleman are necessary virtues in civil society as well.[63]

Respect

Deference, sometimes called respect, is one of the most fundamental of Confucian virtues. It is the main feature of one's basic relations to ancestors, elders, parents, lords, and the ruler. It is the most pervasive and universal of the virtues. Except for relations between friends, all relationships in the eyes of Confucius are hierarchical, and deference or respect is the most necessary of the virtues in a Confucian hierarchical society. Since Confucius was not attempting to elaborate his view of a desirable civil society, there was no call for him to point out that mutual deference between the different social strata would strengthen that type of society. From the standpoint of an observer with an experience of civil societies, however, it is clear that deference— respect for the other person as a fellow member of society and as a fellow human being—is indeed a necessary component of civil society. It is another of the virtues—all variants of civility—of which Confucius made so much and which could contribute to the functioning of civil society.

Flexibility

Confucius said, "A gentleman who studies is unlikely to be inflexible."[64] Is flexibility a virtue of civil society? Yes. It is true that flexibility is incumbent on any realistic ruler who discovers that his ends, whether singly or in combination, are not fully realizable, or are realizable only if other ends are entirely renounced. Confucius was not doctrinaire.

Flexibility is not described in any detail by Confucius. Yet it seems to resemble Max Weber's ideal of *Verantwortungspolitik,* or political activity guided by a sense of responsibility for the concurrent attainment of a plurality of ends or satisfaction of a plurality of persons or collectivities, none of which goals is completely realizable, and each of which can be realized only to some imperfect degree and at the expense of the others. This kind of political activity calls for compromises, both among the ends sought by any particular individual and among the ends of the various contending individuals or collectivities.

Breadth

Although Confucian thought is associated with bureaucracy, Confucius' idea of the gentleman was antithetical to the narrowness of specialization often required by bureaucratic administration. He said: "The gentleman is no vessel."[65] That is, he is not an instrument for anyone to use. It is his obligation to live in accordance with the Way and to serve the emperor, not as the emperor's tool but as an agent of the Way, acting so as to bring the emperor's own actions into closer accord with the Way. This disposition can be attained only through prolonged and reflective study of the classics, not by specialized technical studies or by the accumulation of erudition. This was repeatedly emphasized by Confucius.

The quality of being a gentleman entails breadth of view. This implies a broad understanding of society and of the contending interests at work within it. Breadth of view—the opposite of the narrowness imprinted on the mind by specialization—is a necessary precondition for the concern for the common good which is the distinctive mark of the attitude of civility. There is no doubt that in this respect too, Confucius' conception of the gentleman is an adumbration of the idea of civility.

Tolerance

Another aspect of civility is tolerance. Although tolerance is one of the virtues on the Confucian list,[66] it does not extend to divergent beliefs in religious, philosophical, or ethical matters.[67] Confucius said that tolerance was required of those persons who were "in high position." What did he mean by this? Did he mean tolerance of those who depart from the Way? Did he mean tolerance toward those who neglect the rites, or those who neglect the spirits of their ancestors, or who neglect their living parents? This is not clear. Nevertheless, it seems apparent that Confucius never recommended taking drastic punitive actions against those who depart from the right standards of belief and conduct. For example, he did not recommend imprisonment or exile from society. Tolerance for Confucius was fully compatible with disapproval, a view that is very important for a civil society which admits the legitimacy of differences.

Church and State

On the relations between church and state, so important in a civil society, Confucius was silent. He was a caesaropapist in his views about religion and the state: that is the emperor being the "high priest," no issue of their separation could have occurred to him.

Nationality, Locality, and Territoriality

Nationality, where it is more or less homogeneous, contributes to civil society. It brings all the individuals residing in the territory into a single collectivity, with a single collective self-consciousness in which all participate. Confucius' ideas of Chinese nationality are obscure. He defines China only by contrast with "barbarians." The significance of China as something distinct from the Chinese states is merely touched on.

Confucius scarcely refers to territory. Nor does he refer significantly to locality. He speaks of the "village" several times, but attributes no value to it.[68] There is no expression for attachment to a territory and to the collectivity constituted by those whose ancestors were native to the territory. In view of Confucius' forceful emphasis on lineage and ancestral place, it is especially interesting that no sense of piety toward place appears in the *Analects*. He justifies emigration if the conditions of rule and life are more satisfactory in some other kingdom. Elsewhere he intimates that a gentleman should not become too attached to a particular place: "A gentleman who is attached to a settled home is not worthy of being a gentleman."[69] "Place" has practically no place in Confucius' idea of society. He did not see, probably correctly so, indications of nationality among the various kingdoms of the period of the Warring States.[70]

The empire is referred to frequently, the emperor even more often. For Confucius the empire is tantamount to Chinese society. It is a very inegalitarian society, not just in the distribution of wealth and power but, more important, in the possession of the essential quality that constitutes membership in the society. Those who are intensely in contact with the Way—the emperor as the ritual head of Chinese society as well as those who are learned in the classics from which the Way is to be apprehended and understood—constitute the center of Chinese imperial society. The rest of society is variously imagined as a material precondition or an instrument of the center or, alternatively, potential recipients of the benevolence through which the Way extends its jurisdiction. This barrier between center and periphery is the most fundamental obstacle to a civil society; bringing the center and the periphery nearer to each other in a common moral order would create the potential for the realization of civil society.

For those young Chinese to whom I originally addressed these thoughts, Confucius is available as the inspiring source of a tradition of civil society, and yet he is also *not* available as a source of such a tradition.

Let me deal first with the latter point. Confucius is entirely silent regarding the institution of civil society. He knew nothing of elections; competing political parties; representative institutions; the separation of legislature, executive, and judiciary; public discussion and public opinion; freedom of expression and the press; freedom of association, assembly, and petition or representation. He is nearly as silent on the rights of individuals. He had little interest in nationality or the constitution of society by reference to the common existence of a people living in a territory that has moral value or metaphysical meaning to them. All of those elements of civil society which are present in our modern idea of a liberal democratic national society are almost totally absent from the *Analects*.

But when we turn to the obligation of the highly educated to serve society through civil service, Confucius emerges as a point of departure for a Chinese tradition that is indispensable to civil society. That he failed to generalize his beliefs to the rest of Chinese society is less important than the fact that his interest lay preponderately in the genuinely civil virtues—the civility—of the gentleman-scholar. In this limited but crucial respect, Confucius can be regarded as an ancestor of the idea of civil society.

3

THE INTELLECTUAL HERITAGE OF
THE CONFUCIAN IDEAL
OF *CHING-SHIH*

Chang Hao

In studying the Confucian heritage of sociopolitical thought, there is no better point of entry than the idea of *ching-shih*, which, literally translated, means "setting the world in order." For one thing, it is the ideal that distinguishes Confucianism from the other major competing trends of thought in the Chinese tradition. Moreover, it is also a complex and protean notion whose multilayered meanings tap into almost all the key dimensions of Confucian sociopolitical thought. This study explores three principal layers of its meaning in the historical context of the Neo-Confucian tradition, in the hope of bringing out some characteristics of its intellectual heritage for the modern world.

CHING-SHIH AS THE CONFUCIAN
IDEAL OF VOCATION

On the most fundamental level, *ching-shih* refers to the Confucian ideal of vocation for the moral elite of society—the so-called noblemen *(chün-tzu)*. Behind this vocational ideal is a moral idealism that marks the Confucian concept of man and society. Yet, while Confucianism assumes that everyone has the innate moral potential to fulfill himself, this optimistic faith was tempered from the very beginning by a realism which acknowledged that not everyone could go through the arduous process of self-transformation required for such moral fulfillment. Out of the assumption that only a minority with the requisite moral qualities could govern, there grew the vocational ideal that it is the nobleman's privileged responsibility to set the world in order by assuming a position of leadership and rendering public service to society. In the institutional environment of traditional China, this vocational ideal of social activism was often translated into the notion of bureaucratic service or leadership in a local society. In this way the moral idealism and social activism underlying the Confucian ideal of *ching-shih* came to take on a particular political coloration. At the root of the concept of *ching-shih* was, of course, the fundamental inner-worldly orientation of Confucianism. Over the centuries the Confucian literati took pride in this orientation as the distinctive characteristic that separated Confucianism from contending traditions such as Buddhism and Taoism, whose concern with "the world beyond" or "the other shore" they scorned, regarding it as a deleterious, irresponsible outlook on life which is at odds with humanity.

Indeed, the fulfillment of humanity in this world lies at the heart of Confucian self-understanding. But Confucianism is not the secular humanism that some modern scholars take it to be, for its inner-worldly character was anchored in a transcendental belief that centered on the idea of Heaven *(t'ien)* or "the way of Heaven" *(t'ien-tao)*. The overriding concern of Confucianism may be how to realize humanity in this world, but this concern was transcendentally ordained. This transcendental anchorage of the *ching-shih* ideal often imparts to Confucian sociopolitical thought a religiously grounded tension with the realities of the existing sociopolitical order which must be kept in mind.

As the Confucian vocational ideal, *ching-shih* is characteristically predicated on the notion of self-cultivation. Simply put, Confucian self-cultivation is a process of moral transformation of the self which can be reduced to a scheme made up of three components: human nature in the raw, human nature fulfilled, and the path leading from the former to the latter. The most important component to consider in this connection is the notion of the path, which was variously conceived in the different branches of Neo-Confucianism. Focusing on the mainstream, we can identify several elements in its makeup: ethics of virtue, intellectualism, ritualism, meditative practices, and asceticism. Whatever one may say about the relative place of the other elements in the Neo-Confucian conception of this path, there is no question that the element of asceticism bulks large in it.

This asceticism was clearly reflected in the precepts for character discipline which abounded in Confucian scriptures, especially its Neo-Confucian core, the Four Books *(Ssu-shu)*. Over the centuries these precepts were refined and systematized into various recipes for self-discipline. These differed from one another in detail, but in general they comprised three interrelated elements: first, self-scrutiny, in order to launch and sustain a single-minded, unwavering pursuit of the Confucian life goal of becoming a nobleman; second, the practice of industry and hard work; third, the exercise of control over desires and emotions. This last element often had a prominent place and received special attention in many of the moral recipes. To be sure, this has been a major concern of Confucianism all along. But there was a tendency in Neo-Confucianism to intensify this concern, which often resulted in a Manichean image of the self as a battleground on which two antithetical forces of "moral reason" *(li)* and "desires" *(yü)* were locked in a ceaseless life-and-death struggle. It was on the basis of this tendency that Tseng Kuo-fan, an orthodox Confucian scholar-official of the nineteenth century, whose recipes for character discipline had a widespread influence on modern Chinese intellectuals and political leaders of all stripes, spoke of one's effort to impose control over desires and emotions as a Herculean struggle to "fight and subdue dragons and tigers" *(hsiang-lung fu-hu)*.[1] The existence of this Manichean image of self in the Neo-Confucian moral texts suggests that Confucian social activism, as symbolized by the *ching-shih* ideal, took on a strong ascetic character. Reading the Neo-Confucian literature from this perspective, one is often struck by the presence of a drive to attain total mastery over the inner world of the self. True, this does not necessarily imply the existence of a complementary drive to master the outer world of nature and society. Yet, at the same time, one must also be wary of any easy Weberian generalization about the Confucian worldview as adjustment to the world.

The presence of this threefold scheme for the moral transformation of self also points to another characteristic of *ching-shih* as the Confucian vocational ideal. In this ideal a social commitment is balanced by a self-regarding commitment to the moral fulfillment of the human individual. This latter commitment was often seen as a means to the end of achieving the former. But in the Confucian framework moral cultivation of self is also conceived as an end in itself. The orthodox Neo-Confucian commentaries on the Four Books, such as Chu Hsi's, made it clear that Confucianism envisioned twin goals: the moral perfection of the individual self as well as that of society. The relation between the two goals is one of interdependence rather than a one-way passage in either direction.[2]

At the same time, the Confucian concept of selfhood has a transcendental basis. Human nature, in the Confucian view, is never just something biologically given. It has a moral and spiritual dimension which can be fully accounted for only by reference to the sacred beyond. Because of this transcendental ground, one's selfhood can never be defined and identified exclusively in terms of one's particular social nexus, however important this is for the nurture and fulfillment of one's selfhood. Because Confucianism combined a transcendentally grounded selfhood with a sense of social rootedness and commitment, the vocational ideal of *ching-shih* crosscuts the individualism/collectivism dichotomy. In this regard, one may well compare it to Christian personalism, as both Wm. Theodore de Bary and Yü Ying-shih do.[3] In view of this characteristic of the *ching-shih* ideal, one should not just look into Confucian symbolic resources with reference to modernization; one should also ask whether there is something in the ideal that could speak to our contemporary dialogue about the relation between the individual and society in a postmodern and postindividualist era.

CHING-SHIH AS THE CONFUCIAN CONCERN WITH POLITICAL ORDER

I have drawn attention to the political orientation of *ching-shih* as the vocational ideal of the Confucian nobleman. From a cross-cultural perspective this heightened political orientation stands out, for one does not see it in the vocational ideals of other high traditions, such as the Christian concept of a calling or the Hindu concept of *karma yoga*. Underlying this political orientation was a Confucian belief articulated most clearly by Tung Chung-shu, namely, the belief that political order was not only a sort of bridge between transcendence and the human world but also something indispensable to the fulfillment of our very humanity.[4] Consequently, there was a deep-seated Confucian notion of the primacy of political order in the human world. In the Neo-Confucian tradition *ching-shih* was one of a few interchangeable concepts often used to symbolize this basic concern with the maintenance of political order.

A full understanding of the *ching-shih* ideal in this sense cannot be attempted here. But I believe an exploration of two basic categories that govern Neo-Confucian political thought—what the orthodox Neo-Confucian philosopher Ch'eng I called "doctrinal foundation of governance" *(chih-t'i)* or "the way of governance" *(chih-tao)* and the "institutional measures of governance" *(chih-fa)*—will help in a preliminary way to identify some of the characteristics of the Neo-Confucian conception of political order.[5]

For orthodox Neo-Confucian thinkers such as Ch'eng I and Chu Hsi, the "doctrinal foundation of governance" is nowhere better articulated than in the moral paradigm that lies at the core of the *Great Learning (Ta-hsüeh)*, a text often known as the "gateway to the Four Books." This moral paradigm is spelled out in its opening section:

The ancients who wished to manifest their clear character to the world would first bring order to their states. Those who wished to bring order to their states would first regulate their families. Those who wished to regulate their families would first cultivate their personal lives. Those who wished to cultivate their personal lives would first rectify their minds. Those who wished to rectify their minds would first make their wills sincere. Those who wished to make their wills sincere would first extend their knowledge. The extension of knowledge consists in the investigation of things. When things are investigated, knowledge is extended; when knowledge is extended, the will becomes sincere; when the will is sincere, the mind is rectified; when the mind is rectified, the personal life is cultivated; when the personal life is cultivated, the family will be regulated; when the family is regulated, the state will be in order; and when the state is in order, there will be peace throughout the world. From the Son of Heaven down to the common people, all must regard cultivation of the personal life as the root or foundation.[6]

This paradigm is morally idealistic in the sense that the cultivation of virtue is the root of statesmanship. Coupled with the often unstated assumption that only a few people can go through the rigorous process of moral cultivation, this moral idealism, as we have seen, has the implication of political elitism. How do such moral idealism and political elitism square with the cosmological kingship that Confucianism had so far embraced as the ideological foundation of political order?

To answer this question we must take note of two developments in the Neo-Confucian tradition that grew out of its moral idealism. One development had the promise of breaking with the institution of cosmological kingship by posing the possibility of a "dual order." This development had its roots in the classical Confucian belief in the "unity of Heaven and man" which invests the Confucian nobleman with direct access to Heaven through moral cultivation.[7] Inasmuch as privileged communication with Heaven constitutes the ultimate source of authority on earth, the Confucian nobleman has the potential to develop into a moral-spiritual center or, in Eric Voegelin's words, "the order of soul," which could bridge the gap between the transcendent and the mundane outside the existing sociopolitical order, an order focused on the cosmological kingship whose universal authority had hitherto rested on the kingship's monopoly over access to Heaven.[8]

This potential significantly increased with the rise of Neo-Confucianism, which began to move toward establishing the idea of a dual center of authority by a novel interpretation of history. According to this interpretation, after the golden age of the sage-kings, when virtue and power were blissfully unified, the unified order was woefully split into two traditions, so to speak. On the one hand, there was the tradition of moral-spiritual truth, as handed down through the transmission of *tao (tao-t'ung);* on the other, the imperial tradition of dynastic rulers, as descended through the transmission of rulership *(chih-t'ung).* With the denunciation of the later dynastic order as a "fall" from the moral-spiritual purity of the ancient era of sage-kings, a charge often made by mainstream Neo-Confucian philosophers such as Chu Hsi, the conception of the two traditions clearly pointed to a trend toward viewing the community of Neo-Confucian scholars as a rival center of meaning and authority vis-à-vis the dynastic rulers.[9]

Although the concept of the two traditions did result in some significant efforts among the Confucian literati of the Sung and Ming dynasties to elevate the authority of "teachers" *(shih)* based in Confucian academies as the custodians of *tao* to a level on a par with that of the imperial rulers *(chün),* the idea of a dual center, by and large, did not take hold in the Neo-Confucian tradition. One major reason for the abortion of this development may be located in the fact that the Confucian *tao* represented more of a truncated than a full-scale transcendence. In classical Confucianism there was already a tendency to fuse the transcendent *tao* with a moral-ritual order *(li)* centered on the institutions of cosmological kingship and extensive patrilineage. The truncated character of the Confucian *tao* became even more accentuated with the advent of Han Confucianism, when a cosmological myth emerged at the core of the Confucian worldview in the form of the much-celebrated doctrine of the "three bonds" *(san-kang).* According to this doctrine the twin institutions of cosmological kingship and extended lineage were seen not only as integrally fused with Confucian ethics but also as embedded in an all-embracing cosmic order.[10]

In Neo-Confucianism, perhaps as a result of the influences from Mahayana Buddhism and philosophical Taoism, the transcendental impulses, as embodied in the belief in the unity of Heaven and man, did become stronger. Nonetheless, these impulses never became strong enough to dislodge totally the doctrine of the three bonds. One may thus see some animated tension developing in Neo-Confucianism between its impulses toward transcendence and its entrenched cosmological myth.[11] The truncated character of transcendence, however, was at no time completely overcome. More important, the tension largely petered out after the seventeenth century, although the dichotomy of transmission of *tao* and transmission of rulership remained in the latter-day Neo-Confucian texts. In fact, as reflected in the writings of some of the orthodox Neo-Confucian philosophers of the eighteenth and nineteenth centuries, the transmission of *tao,* instead of pointing to an alternative center of meaning and authority, had degenerated into an ideological prop of the transmission of rulership.[12] In this way the Neo-Confucian development toward the idea of a dual order as a break from cosmological kingship was aborted.

Moral idealism, as exhibited in the Four Books, fed another, much more influential trend, one that, unlike the aborted development which bred tension with the cosmological kingship, took the institution for granted as its point of departure. The result was a concept of political order predicated on the formation of an elite centered on the institution of the Son of Heaven. The moral transformation of the emperor thus became the first priority of its concern with order. In the course of its development, Neo-Confucianism accumulated a wealth of literature which expressed its moral idealism in the mold of a "mirror for the Prince." Among this literature perhaps no text was more influential than a commentary from the thirteenth century, *The Developed Meaning of the Great Learning (Ta-hsüeh yen-i),* which addressed the paradigm of moral cultivation from the *Great Learning* specifically to the emperor and his family. In this interpretation of the *Great Learning,* a general moral-spiritual text was turned into a moral handbook for the ruler, thereby losing much of its original critical impulse. This text was typical of the way in which the moral idealism of Neo-Confucian political thought came to be articulated.[13]

Moral idealism not only marked the way Neo-Confucianism conceived the formation of political order but also characterized the end or goal it envisioned for that order. According to the paradigm of the *Great Learning,* a dynastic state is not the terminal community for a political order. This is why collective wealth and power are not looked on, at least by mainstream Neo-Confucianism, as a legitimate goal for the dynastic order, for ultimately a dynastic state is conceived as a stage of political order that needs to be transcended for the realization of a higher community. The text of the *Great Learning* speaks of a highest good *(chih-shan),* a kind of Confucian summum bonum that will be embodied in this ultimate higher community. Writing on this ultimate community, major Neo-Confucian philosophers such as Chang Tsai, Chu Hsi, and Wang Yang-ming often conjured up the vision of a moral gemeinschaft that would encompass all the people on earth. There is thus something of a utopianism in the way Neo-Confucianism conceives political order.[14]

This utopianism was, of course, already present in the Confucian tradition prior to the advent of Neo-Confucianism. From early on Confucianism saw an ideal order presided over by sage-kings in the distant past, during the "three ages" *(san-tai).* But this utopian vision also rested on the assumption that the ancient ideal order could be brought back in the future. Thus, Confucian utopianism was not just locked into its memory of the past; it was also accompanied by a conception of the future. But this anticipatory consciousness carried no chiliastic expectation, inasmuch as it was often infused with the pessimistic belief in a long-term deterioration inherent in the cosmic-historical process of material force *(ch'i)*. In fact, one may speak, as Thomas Metzger does, of a sense of predicament in Neo-Confucianism, considering the frustration and disappointment that must have come from a historical awareness that Confucian moral idealism cherished a forlorn hope.[15]

Nor did the presence of a utopian vision bring any radical transformative bent to Neo-Confucian political thought. As I pointed out earlier, there was a tendency for the Neo-Confucian idea of transcendence, as embodied in its notions of *tao* or heavenly principles, to become truncated by the penetration of a cosmological myth. Because, in the Neo-Confucian view, the realization of its ideal of transcendence often constituted the hallmark of the presence of a golden age, a truncated sense of transcendence means that the advent of an ideal order in the future would not involve a fundamental break from the institutional order of the present. In Neo-Confucianism, then, a future-oriented utopianism is not necessarily incompatible with political conservatism.

As we have seen, a signal characteristic of Neo-Confucianism is the priority of moral cultivation in the development of statesmanship. Correspondingly, mainstream Neo-Confucianism often spoke of the primacy of an exemplary center in the development of political order. Orthodox figures from Chu Hsi to Tseng Kuo-fan invariably upheld the vision of a good society emerging as the result of a radiation of moral-spiritual influences from the exemplary character of an elite headed by the emperor. Although this emphasis on an exemplary center by no means implied a lack of awareness with respect to the significance of an institutional order, it did mean that a premium was placed on light government. Classical Confucianism, as articulated in the *Analects,* had already envisaged a political center of "nonaction" *(wu-wei),* in the sense of forging a political order more by way of a moral-spiritual transformation from above than by institutional pressure and manipulation. This "low" posture of government was vigorously argued and defended in a debate waged by the Confucian literati of the early Han dynasty against the legalist bureaucrats' interventionist policy of imposing a government monopoly over the production and sale of salt and iron.[16] This posture of what Benjamin Schwartz calls "optimum noninterference" was emphatically reaffirmed in the early phase of the Neo-Confucian tradition by a common stand taken by many Confucian official-literati against the celebrated Wang An-shih reforms of the eleventh century, which, for the most part, boiled down to attacking major sociopolitical problems of the day by imposing heavy government. The failure of Wang An-shih's reforms more or less settled the debate, at least for the mainstream Neo-Confucianists, in favor of the principle of light government. It is by no means accidental that China would not witness another attempt at comprehensive institutional reform at the center before Western cultural influences set in during the late nineteenth century.

The Neo-Confucian notion of light government was accompanied, however, by an awareness of the significance of an institutional order. As Ch'eng I pointed out, governance involves attention both to the significance of the "way of governance" and to the "institutional measures of governance."[17] This is why two texts in the exegetical literature on the *Great Learning* came to assume central prominence in the Sung-Ming Neo-Confucian tradition. After Chen Teh-hsiu, a Neo-Confucian philosopher of the thirteenth century, wrote *The Developed Meaning of the Great Learning,* in order to spell out the moral philosophy that grounds the notion of an exemplary center as embodied in the *Great Learning,* a Neo-Confucian philosopher of the fifteenth century, Ch'iu Chun, felt the necessity to write another commentarial text, *A Supplement to the Developed Meaning of the Great Learning (Ta-hsüeh yen-i pu),* to lay out in detail the Neo-Confucian view of the institutional structures and functions of government.[18] In the Neo-Confucian tradition these two tomes came to be viewed widely as the twin Confucian texts on the way of governance and the institutional measures of government, respectively. In the Neo-Confucian view the way of governance usually takes precedence over the institutional measures of governance and occupies the foreground of attention, but this should not blind us to the fact that the significance of an institutional order is usually assumed.

Typical of a Confucian text on the institutions of political order, *A Supplement to the Developed Meaning of the Great Learning* was mostly taken up with institutional structures of a bureaucratic nature.[19] Although bureaucracy certainly was central to the Neo-Confucian view of an institutional order, it must not be assumed that its view in this regard was unproblematic. In fact, there was considerable ambivalence in Neo-Confucianism regarding the place of bureaucracy in a dynastic state. For many Confucian literati bureaucracy as a meritocracy was burdened with a civil service examination system oriented toward a careerism that undermined the moral fervor of Confucian officials. Furthermore, bureaucracy was seen as an institution staffed by many so-called subbureaucrats *(li),* whose lack of proper educational background often inclined them to be guided in their behavior by greed and other immoral impulses.[20]

More significant is a running debate in the Neo-Confucian tradition regarding the merits of a bureaucratic system *(chün-hsien)* as opposed to a "feudal" order *(feng-chien)*, reflecting a reluctance on the part of many Confucian literati to accept the former because of their preference for the latter.[21] I cannot go into all the considerations that lay behind this preference for a feudal order, but suffice it to say that it had a lot to do with the Confucian vision of the political community as a moral gemeinschaft. True, Confucianism had a practical side that allowed it to see the necessary place for coercion and management in the functioning of a government. But at the same time Confucianism was also marked by a fundamental penchant to see family as the prototype of the human community. Consequently, the hierarchy and authority that Confucianism sees as inherent in a political order must be infused by the organic solidarity characteristic of a family. From this standpoint it is no surprise that feudalism, being inseparably articulated in the Chinese memory with an ideal kinship structure known as *tsung-fa*, often had a strong appeal to the Confucian mind, whereas bureaucracy, with its legalist origin and unfeeling formalism, often proved alien if not repugnant to the Confucian longing for a moral gemeinschaft.

This longing explains why the Confucian institutional order also comprised nonbureaucratic institutions, such as schools and temples, local voluntary associations, and kinship organizations. In the Confucian view these "soft," nonbureaucratic institutions were just as important as the "hard," bureaucratic institutions in shaping a political order. Because these hard and soft institutions combined to form an institutional structure embraced in the Confucian code of *li*, a consideration of the latter will help us to further clarify the Confucian view of political order.

According to the orthodox Neo-Confucian notion of political order, an exemplary center cannot exist apart from *li* as the code of the Confucian normative order. It is *li* that puts the Son of Heaven at the center of the scheme of things. And yet *li*, as an all-encompassing normative order, as Benjamin Schwartz points out, is not self-actuating.[22] It needs the presence of a moral elite to energize and activate it. If we look only at the hard institutions of *li*, such as law and bureaucracy, a preference for heavy government comes into view. But if we also take into account the soft institutions, we see a center focused on the universal king radiating out moral-ritual influences through an all-embracing normative order that operates, presumably, not so much through compulsion as through resonance and coordination. Seen in this light, an exemplary center in the Confucian sense reflects a political order which is sui generis and defies being labeled as either "light" or "heavy," according to the modern Western conception of state.

CHING-SHIH AS THE CONFUCIAN
CONCEPT OF STATECRAFT

In considering the political thought of Confucianism, I have so far emphasized the Confucian proclivity toward moral idealism. But this proclivity
must not be allowed to obscure the realism that also resided in Confucianism
from the beginning. After all, the moral vision one finds in the Confucian
classics purports to address the lives of common people and thus recognizes
the legitimacy of the practical needs and expedient contingencies of human
life, both individual and social. Moreover, in traditional China Confucianism
was not only a moral-spiritual faith but a functioning ideology of the ruling
elite. Inevitably strains of thought would grow that addressed the practical
needs and issues a dynastic state might face. In the Neo-Confucian tradition
this practical, realistic side of Confucianism came to be increasingly associated with the idea of *ching-shih*. During the Ming and Ch'ing dynasties
writings that came out of this aspect of Confucianism were often collected
in large compilations under the name *ching-shih*. In the nineteenth century
the Confucian literati spoke of *ching-shih* as a special category for a newly
differentiated branch of Confucian scholarship *(ching-shih chih hsüeh)* that
dealt with the pragmatic problems of state and society.[23] It is as this special
category that *ching-shih* came closest to what "statecraft" means in English.
Let us now turn to a brief consideration of the ideal understood in this special
sense of statecraft.

The developments in the Neo-Confucian tradition that led up to the emergence of this persuasion in the nineteenth century must be seen against the
background of the moral idealism that dominated the orthodox conception
of political order. According to this view there was no need for a differentiated scholarship to be earmarked for statecraft because the ideas and values
regarding the goal and organization of a political order could be derived
rather straightforwardly from the moral vision of self and society laid out
in the Confucian moral philosophy of self-realization *(i-li chih hsüeh)*.[24] Almost from the start of the Neo-Confucian tradition, however, there had been
a minority of Confucian literati who balked at this view and argued for at
least a relative autonomy of statecraft thought. Dissenting from the orthodox stance, statecraft scholars conceived political order not so much in terms
of its ultimate goal—the moral perfection of self and society—as of the pragmatic order *(chih)* of a dynastic state. Its focus of attention was neither the
golden age of the "three eras" nor its possible restoration in the future, but
the vicissitudes of "order and disorder" *(chih-luan)* seen in the context of
dynastic history.

Of course, the degree of this autonomy of statecraft thought varied among

Confucian scholars who were identified with this tough-minded brand of the *ching-shih* ideal. For some the autonomy was inchoate and implicit. For others it was deliberate and prominent. Among the latter there were even some significant tendencies to justify this pragmatic order as a legitimate value for Confucianism. One sees them clearly in the thought of Li Kou and Wang An-shih of the Northern Sung, the utilitarian school of the Southern Sung, and "pragmatic thinkers" such as Yen Yüan, Li Kung, and others of the early Ch'ing, who all went so far as to champion wealth and power as morally justifiable. For them and their kindred souls there was no incompatibility between the ideal of collective achievement and growth and the Confucian vision of moral community. Indeed, the former was part and parcel of the latter.[25]

This political realism of the statecraft school was rooted in a special kind of ethics. To help define it we may refer to an ethics of absolute ends as epitomized in a celebrated maxim of the Han Confucian philosopher Tung Chung-shu: "Set straight your sense of righteousness without consideration of profit; just try to make the *tao* known without any regard for its practical consequences."[26] Such an ethic was, of course, a polar extreme influential only among the orthodox Neo-Confucians. The point to be noted, however, is that Confucianism had no place for the kind of ethics that stood at the opposite pole, namely, a raw, unvarnished utilitarianism.[27] What is found outside the orthodox circles is usually an ethics of absolute ends tempered by a tendency to come to terms with the realities of life and the world. When this accommodating tendency went far enough, what resulted was an ethics of social consequences that was marked by moral ambivalences and ambiguities in contrast to the clear-cut dichotomies and unconditional commitments of the ethics of absolute ends.

The ethics of social consequence accepted the primacy of the moral ideals upheld by the ethics of absolute ends, but this acceptance was balanced by a realization that such ideals might not be always feasible in this all-too-human world, just as the ideal order of the "three eras" might not be revived in the historical world of later ages. Thus, the ethics of social consequence involved a moral scale with a sensitivity to the pragmatic consequences and social utility of human action. It also accepted, in a relative sense, spheres of life governed by some nonmoral ends, such as wealth, heroism, and practical success.

It is this kind of ethics that underlies statecraft thought in the Neo-Confucian tradition. What was emphasized in the Neo-Confucian orthodoxy as a sharp and irreconcilable distinction between the moral and the pragmatic orientation was blurred in the eyes of the statecraft school. They might still speak the moral language of orthodoxy, dominated by dichotomies such as "rulership by moral principles" *(wang)* versus "rulership by political expediency" *(pa)*, "public mindedness" *(kung)* versus "selfishness" *(ssu)*, "righteousness" *(i)* versus "profit" *(li)*, and *tao* versus "utility" *(kung)*; but in the mind of a Sung statecraft thinker such as Ch'en Liang (1143–1194), these dichotomies no longer represented incompatible opposites. The two sides of these dichotomies, he believed, could be reconciled in a political philosophy predicated on the principle of what he called "combining *wang* and *ba*, and making use of both *i* and *li* [*wang-pa ping-yung, i-li shuang-hsing*]."[28]

This characteristic ambivalence of the ethics of social consequence was reinforced by a new trend of moral-metaphysical thought, the so-called *ch'i-monism* that began to gather momentum in the fifteenth century. This *ch'i-monism* started as a revolt against the dualistic worldview of mainstream Neo-Confucianism. In contrast to the latter, which sees the universe as made up of two basic entities, principle *(li)* and material force *(ch'i)*, *ch'i-monism* viewed it as ultimately reducible only to material force. As a result of its monistic worldview, this trend also came to reject the unmitigated dualism of conflict that often characterized the orthodox view of the relationship between moral-cosmic principles and human desires. For Neo-Confucians affected by this trend, these two sides of the dichotomy were so inseparably fused together that human desires were considered not an unmitigated evil but a qualified good. This kind of view would inevitably boost realism and blur the distinctions emphasized by the orthodox conception of the dichotomies mentioned earlier. It is thus by no means accidental that Ku Yen-wu (1613–1682), a prominent thinker whose worldview was affected by *ch'i-monism*, could uphold the moral code of *li* in an unqualified way while at the same time arguing that human selfishness is not necessarily evil and, in fact, under certain circumstances can be turned into a positive force making for the Confucian virtue of public spirit *(kung)*.[29]

Closely related to the political ethics of realism in the statecraft school's approach to political order is what can be called an institutional approach. As we have seen, the Neo-Confucian view of political order by and large broke down into two categories: the way of governance, which laid stress on the moral-spiritual force of personality, and the institutional measures of government, which focused on the institutional forces that go into making a political order. Although, in the orthodox view, both are necessary for the maintenance of political order, the way of governance clearly has priority over the institutional measures of government. It was, however, the institutional measures that dominated the attention of those who understood *ching-shih* in the sense of statecraft. Although they did not necessarily reject the way of governance, it either receded into the background or became problematic. What follows is merely an effort to see whether some general statement can be made about the institutional approach implicit in this emphasis on the institutional measures of government, which, over the centuries, had come to comprise quite a range of different views on institutional arrangements.

In developing their notion of institutional measures of governance, statecraft scholars tended to take for granted one basic institution, namely, the imperial system itself. To be sure, there was no lack of antidespotism in statecraft thought. But it rarely went beyond the behaviors and policies of individual imperial rulers or dynastic regimes to challenge the legitimacy of the underlying institution. Throughout the recurrent trends of statecraft thought in the Neo-Confucian tradition, Huang Tsung-hsi was perhaps the only exception, whose thinking regarding the institutional arrangement of the political order had broken through to the repudiation of kingship as an institution.[30]

If there was little innovation on the part of the statecraft school in this regard, it is at least significant that some of its thinkers had parted with a prevailing tendency in the Confucian tradition to justify the origin and authority of kingship in terms of cosmic order. People such as Yeh Shih (1150–1223) of the Southern Sung and Ku Yen-wu and Huang Tsung-hsi (1610–1695) of the late Ming, following the lead of Hsün Tzu (fl. 298–238 B.C.) and Liu Tsung-yüan (773–819), tended to see the rise and justification of kingship in "secular," functional terms. To them kingship arose not so much from the Mandate of Heaven as from the need of people as a group for social integration.[31] This kind of thinking at least afforded some intellectual flexibility which the conception of cosmological kingship did not allow. If some thinkers, such as Ku Yen-wu, could see the justification for kingship in terms of the need of a social group for integration, it was at least possible, as the thought of Huang Tsung-hsi suggests, for others to challenge rulership as dysfunctional on the same ground.

As for the statecrafters' thinking on institutional order based on kingship, only some preliminary observations are in order here. Bureaucracy was, of course, central to their concern. But their acceptance of the bureaucratic system was punctuated by the recurrent expression of misgivings which abated only after the seventeenth century. These misgivings need to be understood against the background of the debate over the feudal system versus the bureaucratic system mentioned earlier. It is important to note that the statecrafters' stance on this debate was never a complete preference for the bureaucratic system over that of the feudal. To be sure, they did not share the kind of moral fervor for the "feudal utopia" often found among the orthodox Neo-Confucians. But in their eyes the debate nonetheless involved a practical problem, namely, the problem of centralization versus decentralization, which still concerned them deeply.

Out of this concern grew an effort among the statecrafters to reconcile the two systems, resulting in the notion of a "mixed system" of government. Seen in the context of the time, this was a reaction against the political trend toward overcentralization in the Sung and Ming periods. According to the advocates of the mixed system, the concentration of power at the center would expose the political order to two dangers. It would entail a weakening of military power in the provinces, which would risk undermining defense against foreign invasion. Moreover, too much power at the top is apt to create despotism. The best way to prevent these two dangers is to combine a centralized bureaucracy with something of a decentralized system similar to feudalism.[32]

This idea of a mixed system was first proposed by such "utilitarian" thinkers as Ch'en Liang and Yeh Shih of the Southern Sung.[33] It found an even stronger echo in seventeenth-century political thought. Huang Tsung-hsi, for instance, suggested the establishment of the quasi-feudal (fan-chen) system, a sort of "proconsulate" along the frontier, based on the model of the late T'ang.[34] Ku Yen-wu went further in arguing for giving autonomous power and hereditary tenure to the district magistrates, making them in some way functionally analogous to feudal lords. This is what Ku meant by the principle of "imbuing the prefectural system with the spirit of the feudal system" (yü feng-chien yü chün-hsien).[35]

The concept of a mixed system also found expression in the idea of supplementing bureaucracy with large-scale kinship organizations. To see the clan system as a sort of foundation for the sociopolitical order is, of course, an ancient Chinese ideal, and certainly integral to the Chinese conception of feudalism based on the fact that during the early Chou—the classical age of Chinese feudalism—the extensive stratified patrilineage (tsung-fa chih-tu) was structurally fused with the feudal system. Thus, from very early times on the tsung-fa and the feng-chien systems had become more or less cognate ideals, symbolizing a society of hierarchical order and moral solidarity. Of course, in the statecraft tradition the ideal of the tsung-fa system did not loom as large as it did in the orthodox Neo-Confucian views of political order. But it was still alive, reflected in the political thought of some prominent figures such as Fan Chung-yen (989–1052), Ku Yen-wu, Kung Tzu-chen (1792–1841), Feng Kuei-fen (1809–1874), and Ch'en Ch'iu.[36] According to these scholars it could be used as an instrument of social control, joining the bureaucratic organizations to achieve order and stability in society. For Ku Yen-wu, however, the tsung-fa system had a further important function to perform: he saw it as a social organization for uniting the gentry-literati into a corporate body. The purpose, as Ku put it, was to "imbue the gentry-literati with the feudal spirit" *(yü feng-chien yü shih-ta-fu)*, that is, to foster their corporate consciousness as a counterbalancing social force to the centralized power of the monarch.[37]

The statecrafters' notion of a mixed system ultimately rested on the tendency they shared with the mainstream Neo-Confucians to see bureaucracy as only one instrument among others for achieving political order. Consequently, bureaucracy had to be combined with nonbureaucratic institutions. Thus, the early statecrafters' specific interest in the mixed system may have declined after the seventeenth century, but the interest in seeing bureaucratic and nonbureaucratic institutions as jointly instrumental in shaping political order persisted well into the nineteenth century, as manifested in efforts to combine bureaucracy with kinship organizations or with voluntary organizations of local society, such as the "community compact," to promote peace and stability. In this regard there was not much difference between the statecrafters and the orthodox Neo-Confucians except that the program of the former was less morally colored and more pragmatically oriented than that of the latter.

Although these views on a mixed system and nonbureaucratic institutions had a significant place in some phases of the development of the school of statecraft, their overall significance for the trend as a whole must not be overestimated, for all things considered, the institutional structure and operation of the bureaucratic system remained the principal focus of interest for the statecraft school over the long haul. This is particularly true of its final post–seventeenth-century phase. The compilation of literature on statecraft from the Ming to the Ch'ing may serve as an index of this long-term, growing concentration of interest in bureaucratic organizations. When *The Imperial Collection of Essays on Statecraft of the Ming Dynasty (Huang-Ming ching-shih wen-p'ien)* was compiled in the late sixteenth century, the essays were arranged under the names of the authors. But when *The Imperial Collection of Essays on Statecraft of the Ch'ing Dynasty (Huang-Ch'ing ching-shih wen-p'ien)* was compiled, the essays were systematically arranged under the titles of the six ministries of the central government. If this change indicates anything, it is that the statecraft school's institutional approach seems to have taken on an increasingly bureaucratic form.[38]

Over the centuries the statecraft tradition as a whole showed little inclination toward comprehensive institutional changes within the bureaucratic framework. True, Neo-Confucianism in its very early stage was marked by some strong impulses toward the wholesale remodeling of bureaucratic institutions, as reflected in the reform programs of Fan Tsung-yen and Wang

An-shih, who may be seen as precursors of the statecraft school. Such impulses, however, died away almost completely. It is significant that Pao Shih-ch'en in the early nineteenth century was probably the only figure in the Neo-Confucian tradition since its early stages who envisioned wide-ranging bureaucratic reorganization.[39] More typical was the political outlook found in *The Imperial Collection of Essays on Statecraft of the Ch'ing Dynasty*, which was oriented largely toward the fine-tuning of bureaucratic organizations. Out of this political outlook there appeared, in the course of the Ming and Ch'ing dynasties, views of piecemeal renovations such as those involved in the well-known single-whip tax reforms and the various technical reforms undertaken in connection with the management of the salt monopoly and public works.

This kind of piecemeal renovation was usually not guided by any long-range political goal such as achieving collective wealth and power or universal moral community. Rather, it displayed short-range goal-oriented thinking characterized by (1) the clear perception of a limited problem of a technical or organizational nature which a bureaucratic state might face, and (2) a cost-effective calculus of a rule-of-thumb kind based on empirical investigation of the issue involved. This kind of organizational thinking was very different from that which lay behind the idea of a mixed system. The latter was usually accompanied by varying degrees of critical consciousness, explicit or implicit, toward the existing dynastic-bureaucratic order, whereas the former, being oriented toward fine-tuning and adjustments within the bureaucratic system, usually lacked such a critical outlook. Whereas the former was characterized by a considerable impulse toward what can be called instrumental rationality, the latter featured an outlook more oriented toward considerations of dynastic security and communal solidarity. Yet both had a place in the institutional approach of the statecraft school which must be kept in view.

The foregoing is a sketchy survey of the ideas and values that flowed from the three senses in which the ideal of *ching-shih* was understood in the Neo-Confucian tradition. These ideas and values provide us with a base from which to assess the heritage of Neo-Confucian sociopolitical thought from different vantage points. Such a comprehensive assessment is beyond the scope of this essay. To conclude, I simply offer some considerations from the standpoint of modernization.

We have seen that *ching-shih*, understood as the Confucian ideal of vocation, carried a strong dose of inner-worldly asceticism. Inevitably, the Weberian question raises itself at this point: What kind of tension is generated by this vocational ideal? The answer is not an easy one. On the one hand, as I have pointed out, this asceticism was predicated on the Confucian ideal of self-realization, which channeled the tension into a relentless drive to conquer the inner world of the self. On the other hand, one does not see the same drive present in the Confucian outlook on the external world of nature and society. The tension generated in this direction was first of all tempered by the special kind of moral idealism embodied in the central Confucian ideal of *jen*. In the Neo-Confucian tradition this ideal was often identified with the worldview of "the unity of Heaven and man" *(t'ien-jen ho-i)*. The result was often an outlook that prized the value of cosmic and social harmony and thus reduced the external tension with nature and society. In other words, the relentless drive to master the inner world of the self which attended the Confucian ideal of self-realization was not transferred to the outlook on the natural and social world.

Furthermore, the ideal of *ching-shih* involved a tendency to define the Confucian life ideal and career aspirations narrowly. I have argued that the heightened political orientation of the Confucian vocational ideal meant that its inner-worldly activism was confined to the political realm of the social world. The fact that the Neo-Confucian tradition was institutionally saddled with the civil service examination system had the effect of further narrowing the political orientation of the Confucian vocational ideal to bureaucratic service in officialdom and local society. Nonbureaucratic realms of the social world and nonpolitical spheres of life were thus, more often than not, closed to the inner-worldly activism of the *ching-shih* ideal.

What we see, then, in the motivational resources that grew out of the Confucian vocational ideal was an inner-worldly asceticism held in check by other elements of the Confucian heritage, intellectual as well as institutional. What sometimes happened to this aspect of the Confucian heritage in the modern era was the weakening of the hold of these constricting elements by the influx of Western influence and the consequent release of this inner-worldly asceticism, which was then channeled into other realms of social life. The prominence of Confucian recipes for character discipline in various strains of sociopolitical activism in modern China certainly can be seen in this light.

The intellectual heritage that issued from the *ching-shih* ideal can also be evaluated in terms of institutional resources. Confucianism had long existed in symbiosis with bureaucratic institutions. But over the centuries it had evolved little intellectual impetus for a comprehensive rationalization of bureaucratic organizations. What marked Confucianism in this regard was a confined instrumental rationality, as reflected in the sporadic drives for piecemeal renovation. The underlying problem is a relative lack of vision with respect to a development state. I use the modifier "relative" deliberately. We have seen some potential in this direction in the statecraft school's vision of collective wealth and power as a legitimate goal of state. But this potential was not strong enough to overcome the Neo-Confucian mainstream's misgiving about this vision from the standpoint of its ideal of moral community. Consequently, the ideal of collective wealth and power existed largely on the periphery of Confucian political thinking under the dominance of the orthodox moral goals. In the modern era, however, when the dominance of the orthodox goals were undermined by the advent of Western influence, the marginal ideal of wealth and power was pushed to the center of attention. More important, this ideal became a principal medium through which many new institutional ideals that were to become influential in twentieth-century China, such as the nation-state and democracy, were assimilated from the West. Here we see another illustration of the important role the intellectual heritage of the *ching-shih* ideal played in the modern era: the new conceptual resources for institutional reorganization were as much a function of the shift of internal balance in the Confucian heritage as of new models introduced from the West.

I have argued before that the intellectual heritage of the *ching-shih* ideal not only involved some impetus toward organizational renovation within the framework of the bureaucratic state, but also encompassed some visions of an institutional order other than the bureaucratic state, in terms of either the mainstream's feudal utopia or the statecraft school's idea of a mixed system. Of course, one may well doubt the transformative potential of these visions of an alternative order, for they sprang in large part from the archaic institutional models of cosmological kingship and kinship-based feudalism which had little application to modern purposes. At the same time, one must not overlook the possibility of other institutional visions that lay behind these ideas of an alternative order. I am referring not only to the Neo-Confucian idea of a dual order that pitted the tradition of moral-spiritual truth against the imperial tradition of dynastic power, but also to the statecraft school's idea of a mixed system, which attempted to accommodate decentralization within the bureaucratic system. In both we see a quest on the part of the Confucian literati for an organizational autonomy vis-à-vis the authority of the imperial rulers. Of course, this line of thought had only a peripheral and often submerged significance in the Neo-Confucian vision of political order, compared to the centrality of institutional models such as cosmological kingship and kinship-based feudalism.

Nonetheless, the picture of the coexistence of these two different strains in Neo-Confucian political thought put modern intellectual transformation in a different light, as we have seen. The Chinese encounter with Western liberal modernity discredited the belief in cosmological kingship and the feudal kinship system. But at the same time it sensitized modern intellectuals to the presence of a submerged quest in the Confucian heritage for a dual order and an organizational autonomy of the gentry-literati. In turn, the modern repossession of this line of thought shaped Chinese intellectuals' receptivity to and understanding of Western liberal ideas. This is certainly true of much of the moral fervor for the ideal of democracy found among radical intellectuals such as Fei Hsiao-t'ung, as well as among cultural conservatives such as Hsiung Shih-li (1885–1968), Liang Sou-ming (1893–1988), Mou Tsung-san, (1909–1995) and Hsü Fu-kuan (1903–1982). Here we see again the subtle way in which the internal shift of balance in the Confucian heritage contributed to the modern transformation.

It should be clear by now that, seen in the light of modernization, the Neo-Confucian sociopolitical thought that was built around the *ching-shih* ideal handed down a mixed bag of functional and dysfunctional ideas and values. What has so far dominated our picture of the Confucian heritage is the way its dysfunctional elements shaped China's disastrous course of modernization. What is needed is a more complex and nuanced picture that would also allow us to see the functional elements that often, as the result of a shift in the internal balance of the Confucian heritage, played a very significant role in shaping the modern transformation. Further exploration along this line will help us attain a more balanced perspective on both the Confucian heritage and the modern transformation.

4

CONFUCIAN IDEALS
AND THE REAL WORLD

A Critical Review of Contemporary
Neo-Confucian Thought

Liu Shu-hsien

The meaning of "Confucianism" is ambiguous. Since scholars understand the term to mean different things, it is no wonder that there is a lack of communication among them. I will not discuss the extremely rich connotation of the term; suffice it to point out that it may refer to the philosophical tradition represented by Confucius and Mencius, or it may refer to the institutions and customs that emerged in the long course of Chinese history through the influence of Confucian thought. Certainly I do not deny that there is an intimate relationship between these two meanings; the interaction between them is a very complex phenomenon which needs to be carefully studied from the perspective of cultural dynamics. But when the two are not clearly distinguished from each other, confusion is almost inevitable. I approach Confucianism here in the former sense, emphasizing the transcendent character of Confucian ideals and asserting that philosophical Confucianism must be kept distinct from the politicized Confucianism which has existed since the Han dynasty. By maintaining this perspective, we find that long-accepted myths are shaken and can be subjected to a critical reexamination. After doing this, I offer a critical review of contemporary New Confucian thought in light of its relevance to modernization.

First, let us go back to the roots in order to examine the complicated relationship between ideal and practice. It is well known that the Chinese tradition has never developed a purely theoretical outlook, as in the ancient Greek tradition; it has also lacked the vision of a supernatural world, as in the Christian tradition. Accordingly, there does not seem to be as wide a gap between ideal and practice. Hence, the myth of the "perfectibility of man" arose.

On the surface Confucius does seem to suggest that there is no gap at all between ideal and practice, for he said: "Is humanity far away? As soon as I want it, there it is right by me."[1] This statement must not be taken at face value, however, for he also said: "How dare I claim to be a sage or a man of humanity? Perhaps it might be said of me that I learn without flagging and teach without growing weary."[2] Does Confucius contradict himself? Not at all. The first statement tells us that practicing the virtue of humanity is not something that is remote, and the second insists that it is also an endless process. Hence, Confucius never claimed that he was a man of humanity or a sage, for sagehood is really a transcendent ideal. Confucius was honored as a sage only by his admiring disciples. The fact that he was the last person honored as a sage in the long course of Chinese history clearly shows that the distance between ideal and fact has always been taken seriously by the Chinese. Even Mencius, the greatest ancient philosopher after Confucius, was never so honored. Human perfectibility is obviously a myth that does not apply to the real world.

In the same way, we need to look more closely at the implication of the idea of unity of man (in the gender-neutral sense of humanity) and Heaven, or *t'ien-jen ho-i*. Even though Confucius did not coin the phrase, the idea was nevertheless implicit in his thought. According to a famous story, at one time Confucius was thinking of giving up speech; when his disciple Tzu-kung became worried, Confucius' response was: "What does Heaven ever say? Yet there are the four seasons going around and there are the hundred things coming into being. What does Heaven ever say?"[3] Heaven is the transcendent creative principle that works incessantly in the universe, and Confucius was taking Heaven as his model.

This anecdote was by no means an isolated case reported in the *Analects*, for Confucius' cultural heroes, Yao and Shun, also took Heaven as their model. Confucius praised Yao in this manner: "Great indeed was Yao as a ruler! How lofty! It is Heaven that is great and it was Yao who modelled himself upon it. He was so boundless that the common people were not able to put a name to his virtues. Lofty was he in his successes and brilliant was he in his accomplishments!"[4] Specialized achievements can be praised by words, but comprehensive achievements, such as those of Yao and Shun, cannot be. Heaven engenders the natural order of things without taking any visible action. Thus Confucius praised Shun: "If there was a ruler who achieved order without taking any action, it was, perhaps, Shun. There was nothing for him to do but to hold himself in a respectful posture and to face due South."[5] Given these models, it is no wonder that Confucius said very little about the Way of Heaven; he simply preferred to follow Heaven's example and remain speechless on the subject.[6]

Nonetheless, to say that there is an intimate relationship between Heaven and man does not mean that there is not a vast distance between them. Confucius explicitly said that the profound person stands in awe of the Decree of Heaven (t'ien-ming).[7] He also said: "At fifty I knew the Decree of Heaven."[8] I have often wondered why he needed to wait until the mature age of fifty before he could claim to know anything about the Decree of Heaven. The term t'ien-ming has extremely rich connotations: it may mean one's endowment from Heaven, which constitutes the moral nature of man as set forth in the opening statement of The Doctrine of the Mean.[9] Or it may mean one's destiny, which is beyond the control of man. Although the former asserts the linkage between Heaven and man, the latter spells out the gap between them, as the Way of Heaven is necessarily beyond comprehension from a merely human perspective. Accordingly, it was not until Confucius reached the age of fifty that he fully realized the finite nature of his being and accepted the Decree of Heaven without any reservation.

My understanding of Confucius is corroborated by Mencius' claim that although Confucius was virtuous, he did not possess the empire because he did not have an emperor to recommend him to Heaven.[10] There is really nothing we can do about our destiny (ming); all that we can do is try our best and leave the rest to Heaven. This is why Confucius strove throughout his life to become a man of humanity and a sage, accepting his destiny without grudge; he had no illusions about reality but was one "who knows a thing cannot be done and still wants to do it."[11] Mencius had a similar understanding of the human situation; he too did not have any illusions about reality, which he compared to a barren mountain.[12] But even though he declared that human nature is good, it would be wrong to say that he was an optimist with a tendency to look only at the bright side of things.

The Confucian belief in human perfectibility, and specifically the Mencian theory of human nature, is often cited as the reason why the Chinese have failed to devise a "checks and balances" mechanism in their system of government. I find such reasoning one-sided. Neither Hobbes's nor Hsün Tzu's understanding of human nature as evil is organically linked to the idea of a democratic system with checks and balances. There must be additional factors to make the system of checks and balances work. Although the Chinese failed to develop democratic government in the past, I do not see any real contradiction between such a system and the transcendent ideal of humanity and creativity as espoused by Confucius and Mencius.

If there is a wide gap between ideal and practice in attaining inward sageliness, there is an even wider one in achieving outward kingliness; both Confucius and Mencius fully acknowledged that they had utterly failed in this respect. During the reign of Emperor Wu of Han, however, Confucianism was established as the state orthodoxy. Although "the Confucian state" has been used by historians in the English-speaking community to characterize the Han and subsequent dynasties,[13] the Confucian state is no more Confucian than Christendom is Christian; this is another myth in need of further scrutiny. I do not deny that some of the Confucian ideals were actualized in the Han dynasty; for example, virtues such as loyalty and filial piety have generally been accepted by Chinese society from that time to the present. When transcendent ideals are actualized, however, it is almost inevitable that they will be modified and sometimes seriously distorted, and the price to be paid is high. It was in the Han dynasty that the relations between ruler and subject, father and son, and husband and wife were transformed into a seemingly immutable pattern of domination, namely, the "three bonds," which stressed the authority of the ruler, the father, and the husband over the minister, the son, and the wife, respectively. As a result, the critical spirit of Mencius simply disappeared. The most intriguing thing is that the rulers understood this perfectly well. Emperor Hsüan of the Han dynasty told his descendants that the secret to ruling lay in the fact that "kingliness" *(wang)* and "hegemony" *(pa)* must be used together in order to achieve the best results.[14] In other words, one needs the Confucian symbols of humanity and righteousness as well as the legalist practice of law and political maneuver. In fact, the unification of China was largely due to the implementation of the legalist policies during the Ch'in dynasty, while a partial adoption of Confucian ways helped to stabilize the reign of the Han rulers. Thus, Chinese culture has been strongly influenced by the interaction between Confucian ideals and legalist practices.

Another important way in which Han Confucianism differs from pre-Ch'in Confucianism lies in its incorporation of many of the ideas of the Yin-Yang school. This represents another compromise and distortion of the Confucian moral ideal. The use of the phrase "the Confucian state" seems to imply that Confucian ideals have been largely actualized in Chinese history. This is a myth that will not bear critical examination. We must not ignore the distance between ideal and practice simply because the Chinese have adopted a "this-worldly" attitude different in character from the "other-worldly" attitude of Christianity.

My view is further corroborated by the development of Sung Neo-Confucianism. I was struck by the debate between Chu Hsi (1130–1200) and Ch'en Liang (1143–1194). Chu Hsi maintained that after the Three Dynasties, Chinese history offered nothing but a dark picture, which Ch'en Liang protested strenuously. On the surface Chu Hsi's assertion appears to be totally unreasonable, especially if we consider the fact that Chu Hsi was not a speculative philosopher but a pragmatic scholar-official who, among other administrative accomplishments, once devised a highly effective and widely emulated system for storing grain in order to deal with the famine problem. He had to have good reasons for defending such a seemingly outrageous position. Why did he feel that he had to make such a sharp distinction between the Three Dynasties and the Han and the T'ang dynasties, two of the most powerful and prosperous dynasties in Chinese history? It appears that he was trying to put down the so-called Confucian state by refusing to identify political reality with transcendent Confucian ideals. The Three Dynasties were founded on what Chu Hsi called the impartial mind, whereas the dynasties of the Han and the T'ang were founded on the mind that cared only for the profit of the emperor and the royal family. The transmission of the Way in the early period was carried out not by the rulers but by scholars, who did not occupy high positions, showing that *tao-t'ung*, the philosophical tradition, should not be absorbed into the political tradition.[15]

Chu Hsi was acutely aware of the point at issue, for he explicitly stated that Confucius, the greatest teacher of all time, was even greater than the sage-emperors, Yao and Shun. Chu Hsi's position may be understood as an attempt to set up a kind of checks and balances system against de facto rulership. Although it may not have been a very good system, it was a mechanism of checks and balances nonetheless. Chu Hsi has often been attacked by Marxist historians as an ultrareactionary who supplied the ideological ground for the establishment to defend the imperial order. This myth fails to stand up to critical examination. Ironically, Chu Hsi was a dissident of sorts in his own day. It was only after he died that his works were honored as orthodoxy and adopted as the basis for the civil service examination in the Yüan dynasty.[16] Of course, the rulers used some Confucian teachings for their own purposes; but it is essential to maintain the distinction between upholding transcendent Confucian ideals and legitimizing the political power of the rulers in the real world.

Another problem to be examined is that the Chinese seem to have failed to develop the idea of the separation of church and state, for the Confucian idea of sage-emperor seems to suggest that the two are united as one. Since the Han dynasty, however, civil servants have been recruited through the examination system; hence, even though sovereignty lay with the emperor, the scholars were entrusted to run the state. Sung Neo-Confucian philosophers such as Chu Hsi had actually attempted to separate church from state by putting *tao-t'ung*, the philosophical tradition, completely beyond the control of the rulers. Had the emperor been made into a mere figurehead, then the Chinese system would have been much closer to modern Western democracy. Unfortunately, however, the Ming dynasty went in the opposite direction and concentrated even more power in the hands of the ruler. In the early Ch'ing dynasty the situation became even worse, as Emperors K'ang-hsi and Yung-cheng wished to be seen as sage-emperors even though, in fact, they were emperors who also claimed to be sages. The publication of the famous debate between Emperor Yung-cheng and the rebel scholar Tseng Ching demonstrates that the emperor wanted to be seen as the authoritative transmitter of the *tao-t'ung*.[17]

Although the Ch'eng-Chu philosophy was firmly established as orthodoxy by Emperor K'ang-hsi, what happened after his demise was really astounding, for the philosophy simply faded away and was replaced by an evidential school that emphasized historical scholarship over philosophical speculation. Intellectual historians have been puzzled by this extraordinary phenomenon and have not been able to come up with a satisfactory explanation. Perhaps the answer is so obvious that it has been missed by most historians. Was it not the case that when the Ch'eng-Chu philosophy was honored as state orthodoxy, it lost its critical spirit and consequently its attraction for scholars as well? Perhaps because it was reduced to a mere stepping-stone for entering the civil service, it no longer vibrated with the life it used to possess. Worse still, it had turned into the hard shell that would later be denounced by intellectuals from the May Fourth Movement as a source of evil practices against humanity.

It should become clear that the attraction of Confucian philosophy to the practicing Confucians lies in its critical spirit, which is based on its ultimate commitment to transcendent Confucian ideals of humanity and creativity. Confucius and Mencius, as well as Chu Hsi, do not greatly appeal to intellectuals because they were able to solve problems at the practical level; on the contrary, while they were alive they had neither the position nor the power to do what they wanted to do, and even if they had been given the chance, there would have been no guarantee that they would be successful. In fact, the Ch'in-Han unification of China and the honoring of the Ch'eng-Chu teachings as state orthodoxy were largely unintentional consequences; they were due to other factors in interaction with Confucian ideals, which were, of course, another important factor in the shaping of Chinese culture. By the same token, contemporary Neo-Confucian philosophy is appealing not because it can solve problems at the practical level, but because of its critical stand against both traditional Chinese culture and modern Western civilization. Hence, the criticism leveled at this trend, that it fails to solve any practical problems, is as pertinent as those arguments leveled at Confucius, Mencius, and Chu Hsi in the past. We cannot predict the future influence of contemporary Neo-Confucianism, for what happens in the real world depends on the interaction of many divergent factors. The close ties between Confucian ideal and practice must not lure us into drawing any unwarranted conclusions.

I begin my critical review of the Neo-Confucian thought which has emerged since the May Fourth Movement in 1919 with a general observation. Even though Confucianism no longer occupies the central position it used to hold in the days of the dynasties, it still evidences great vitality as a philosophical movement today.[18] Moreover, what has happened in the last few decades in both industrial and socialist East Asia has forced us to reconsider the significance of the Confucian influence on economic and political development. Japan and the so-called Four Mini-Dragons—Hong Kong, Korea, Singapore, and Taiwan—have achieved phenomenal success in the business world. It is impossible not to notice that each has an unmistakable Confucian background, and so it is only natural to surmise that there must be some correlation. I fully realize that the relationship between the so-called great traditions and small traditions is a complicated one which resists generalization, but my review of contemporary Neo-Confucian thought may shed light on what has happened in real life, because philosophy is, after all, one of the factors that helps shape the character of a civilization, in either an intentional or an unintentional fashion.

Several decades ago Mou Tsung-san propounded the idea that there were three waves in the development of Confucianism, namely, pre-Ch'in Confucianism, Sung-Ming Neo-Confucianism, and contemporary Neo-Confucianism. When we study these three waves, we find that Confucianism was not simply armchair philosophy; it was often an intellectual response, informed by practical wisdom, to the burning social and political concerns of the time. In the late Chou period, when traditional ideas and practices could no longer work, Confucius instilled new spirit into traditional virtues, lifting *jen* (humanity, human-heartedness) out of the ring of virtues and making it the virtue of virtues.

Confucianism was honored as the orthodoxy from the Han dynasty, but it gradually lost its appeal to the intellectuals, who were greatly attracted by Buddhism and Neo-Taoism. Consequently, creative talents focused on these philosophies, turning the T'ang dynasty into the golden age of Chinese Buddhism. Sung-Ming Neo-Confucianism answered the challenges from Buddhism and Neo-Taoism by absorbing insights from these trends and developing sophisticated new cosmologies and philosophical anthropologies based on the spirit of Confucianism which they inherited from the past. But Sung-Ming Neo-Confucianism declined during the early Ch'ing dynasty for reasons too various to detail here.[19] Then the Chinese had to face the biggest challenge in their history—the challenge from the West. Eastern societies had little choice but to Westernize in order to survive in the modern world.

It was under such extraordinary circumstances that the contemporary Neo-Confucian trend emerged. Its aim is to conserve certain valuable ingredients inherited from the past, and in the meantime absorb new ideas and practices from the West, such as science and democracy, and make them an integral part of Chinese culture. It further aims to suggest a new path for the future of humankind, recognizing that the one-sided development of contemporary civilization dominated by Western ways has clearly shown its limitations and shortcomings. I turn now to a critical review of contemporary New Confucian thought, assessing its strengths and weaknesses in relation to modernization, and evaluating its claim as a viable alternative to Western-style modernization.

There is no consensus on who belongs in the movement, as the scope of contemporary Neo-Confucianism is not well-defined. It may include scholars with varied backgrounds, such as the thinker Liang Sou-ming (1893–1988), the historian Ch'ien Mu (1895–1990), the statesman-scholar Carsun Chang (1887–1969), and Hsü Fu-kuan (1903–1982), an expert on intellectual history. In a 1989 essay on the development of Neo-Confucian philosophy since 1945,[20] I chose to discuss four scholars—Hsiung Shih-li (1885–1968), Thomé H. Fang (1899–1977), T'ang Chün-i (1909–1978), and Mou Tsung-san—who have developed philosophical ideas of their own. I shall not repeat what I wrote there but will use it as background for further observations and reflections. In another essay on the contemporary significance of Chinese philosophy, I provide the background for understanding the emergence of contemporary Neo-Confucian thought:

If I may be allowed to borrow a dialectical scheme from Hegel in a very loose sense, I would like to suggest that the development of Chinese thought since the middle of the Ch'ing dynasty has gone through three stages which may be roughly described as follows:

(1) The Chinese were shocked to find the superiority of Western science and technology. They tried to absorb such Western achievements into their own culture, but they still believed in the basic soundness of the foundation of their own traditional culture.

(2) The Chinese were thoroughly disappointed with their own tradition; they could not find anything valuable in it. Tradition only served as the stumbling block to obstruct any move toward future

progress. Hope lay only in a quick and totalistic Westernization process.

(3) The Chinese came to realize that the West was not all positive and their own tradition was not all negative. The Western culture, as well as the modernization process, had its problems. Although many traditional "habits of the heart" had to be eradicated, some cultural insights deeply rooted in the tradition should be reconstructed in such a way that they might make significant contributions in moving toward the future. A synthesis based on the realistic understanding of the problems of humanity and its environment had to be sought.

It appears that the first wave has long been a thing of the past; the second wave has passed its peak and gone downhill; the third wave is beginning to gain momentum.[21]

Needless to say, the three waves overlap one another. It is only for the sake of convenience that they are arranged so as to appear to be successive stages. The representative of the first wave is Chang Chih-tung (1837–1909), who advocated "Chinese learning for *t'i* (substance, essence) and Western learning for *yung* (function, utility)."[22] The representative of the second wave is Hu Shih (1891–1962), who advocated "wholesale Westernization or whole-hearted modernization."[23] And the representative of the third wave may be said to be Mou Tsung-san, who advocated the revitalization and reconstruction of traditional Chinese philosophical insights. Mou was a student at Peking University when Hu Shih served as the dean of arts and was a teacher at Tunghai University in Taiwan in the early 1960s when Hsu Fu-kuan was the chairman of the department of Chinese.

The third wave coincides somewhat with the third wave of Confucianism that Mou had propounded. As opinions vary, it is not easy to sum up the ideas of the contemporary Neo-Confucian scholars. Suffice it to give an illustration that points out the direction in which these scholars have been heading. On New Year's Day 1958 T'ang Chün-i, Mou Tsung-san, Hsu Fu-kuan, and Carsun Chang issued "A Manifesto for a Reappraisal of Sinology and Reconstruction of Chinese Culture" in which they declared:

> Chinese culture arose out of the extension of primordial religious passion to ethical-moral principles and to daily living. For this reason, although its religious aspects have not been developed it is yet pervaded by such sentiments, and hence is quite different from occidental atheism. To comprehend this, it is necessary to discuss the doctrine of *"hsin-hsing"* [concentration of mind on an exhaustive study of the nature of the universe], which is a study of the basis of ethics and forms the nucleus of Chinese thought and is the source of all theories of the

"conformity of heaven and man in virtue." Yet, this is precisely what is most neglected and misunderstood by Sinologues.[24]

In section 9 titled "What the West Can Learn from Oriental Thought," they suggest that

in the first place, the West needs the spirit and capacity of sensing the presence of what *is* at every particular moment [*tang-hsia chi-shih*], and of giving up everything that can be had [*i-ch'ieh fang-hsia*]. The strength of the West's cultural spirit lies in its ability to push ahead indefinitely. However, there is no secure foundation underlying this feverish pursuit of progress. Along with this pursuit of progress there is a feeling of discontentment and of emptiness. In order to fill this emptiness, the individual and the nation constantly find new ways for progress and expansion. At the same time external obstructions and an internal exhaustion of energy cause the collapse of the individual and the nation. This is why the most powerful ancient Western nations collapsed and never did recover from their downfall. Chinese culture traces all values to "*hsin-hsing*," and in so doing achieves the capacity to "accept what is self-sufficient at the moment." Chinese thought has always regarded "retreat" as more fundamental than "advance." Complementing the characteristically Western push for progress, this will provide a solid and secure foundation for Western civilization.

The second element the West can learn from the East is all-round and all-embracing understanding or wisdom. This Chuang Tzu called "spiritual understanding" or "meeting the object with the spirit." In Western science or philosophy, principles and universals are attained by intellect and are sharply enunciated and defined. They are abstract and cannot be applied to what is concrete, because the characteristics which are peculiar to each class, and which are inexhaustible, have been eliminated. Wisdom is needed to comprehend and to deal with all the unprecedented changes of life. This wisdom does not operate by adhering to universals, but by submerging universals in order to observe the changing conditions and peculiarities.

. . . The Western world is in great need of this wisdom if she intends to understand the nature of the different cultures and to have an authentic communication with them. In addition to their knowledge, technology, ideals, and God, they must above all search deeper for the source of life, the depth of personality and the common origin of human culture in order to arrive at a true unity with mankind.

The third point that the West can learn from the East is a feeling of mildness and compassion. The Westerner's loyalty to ideals, his spirit

of social services, and his warmth and love for others are indeed precious virtues, to which oriental counterparts cannot measure up. However, the highest affection between men is not zeal or love, for with
these emotions is often mingled the will to power and its acquisitive
instinct. To forestall such an adulteration, Western civilization princi-
pally relies on its religious emphasis on personal humility and on all
merits ultimately coming from God. However, the name of God can
be borrowed as a backprop in the conviction that one's actions bear
His sanction; or else one may even selfishly wish to possess Him, such
as during a war to pray for victory. It is for this reason that Christianity
also teaches forgiveness. But extreme forgiveness tends to become complete renunciation of the world. To avoid such a fault zeal and love
must again be emphasized, thus forming a logical circle and leaving
the intermingling of love and the will to dominate or to possess still
an unresolved difficulty. The resolution lies in eradicating this will to
dominate or possess, and this is possible only if love is accompanied
by respect. In that case, if I feel that the source of my love for others
is God's infinite love, then my respect for others is likewise boundless
. . . In other words, to effect such a transformation of Western love,
God must be identified with man's heart of hearts, manifesting Himself
through our bodies as the direct communication between the life-spirits
of all authentic being, not merely as a transcendental being, the object
of man's prayers.

Fourthly, the West can obtain from the East the wisdom of how to
perpetuate its culture. Contemporary Western culture is, it is true, at
the height of brilliance, yet many observers have been concerned with
its future, whether it will perish like ancient Greece and Rome. Culture
is the expression of a people's spiritual life, and by the laws of nature
all expression drains the energy of life. If this energy is exhausted,
perishing is inevitable. To preserve his spiritual life, man needs a depth
formed by an historical awareness which reaches both into the past
and into the future and this depth connects with the life-giving source
of the cosmos . . . The West needs to develop an historical awareness
with which to tap the life-giving source. It will then come to appreciate
the value of conservation of life-energy and the meaning of filial piety,
and learn to fulfill the ancestral will in order to preserve and prolong
its culture.

The fifth point the West can learn from the East is the attitude that
"the whole world is like one family." Though there are many nations
now, mankind will eventually become one and undivided. Chinese
thought has emphasized this attitude. The Motians [Moists] advocate

all-embracing love; Taoists urge forgetting the differences; Buddhists advise commiseration and love for all things; and Confucians teach universal kindness [jen] . . . The Confucian view, however, is that all men can achieve sagehood. It has no organization, and does not require worship of Confucius since any man can potentially become like him. Consequently, Confucianism does not conflict with any religion. It has a concept of Heaven and Earth, but has no hell for those of differing views. If indeed the world is to be united, the Confucian spirit certainly deserves emulation. The same attitude can be found in Buddhism and Brahmanism, which also deserve close study.

Our list is, of course, by no means exhaustive. What we have pointed out is that the West must also learn from the East if it is to carry out its task as the world's cultural leader. These things are certainly not entirely alien to Western culture. However, we would like to see their seeds bloom into full blossom.[25]

Surely there are a number of assumptions behind this statement, and the tone appears to be apologetic. How convincing it sounds to Westerners remains an open question! But it does touch on certain serious problems of a contemporary civilization which has been dominated by the West. Therefore, it is inadequate to depict it simply as a revival of Chang Chih-tung's inclination to treat Chinese learning as substance and Western learning as function. The contemporary Neo-Confucian scholars have tried hard to see things from a global perspective, taking in valuable insights from both Asian and Western cultures. They have made a serious attempt to work out a synthesis of the East and the West, though their guiding spirit remains Confucian, for the scholars who signed the manifesto are deeply convinced that the Confucian tradition is the most open, inclusive, and creative among the various traditions of the world and may therefore serve as the best vehicle for looking toward the future of humankind.

Joseph Levenson would probably have felt that this is just another attempt to redeem the wounded Chinese ego.[26] But it appears that he failed to make the all-important distinction between the psychological stress experienced by modern Chinese scholars and the valuable insights they have come up with under such stress. What should be emphasized is not how the psychological defense mechanism of Chinese scholars works, but rather whether the ideas they expound have any merit at all. Levenson seems to have assumed that their ideas would not work simply because they emerged out of a tension-ridden psychopathological milieu. Lamentably, his premature death did not allow him to observe developments in East Asia since the 1970s, such as the marvelous performance of the Four Mini-Dragons in the business world; it is anybody's guess whether he would have revised his earlier opinions were he alive today.

The time is ripe for us to move beyond Levenson's interpretive stance and review some of the salient features of Neo-Confucian thought as articulated by the aforementioned thinkers. Several of their claims deserve our attention:

- Metaphysically, there is a creative ontological principle that works incessantly in the universe; without it there would be nothing in the world.
- Epistemologically, this metaphysical principle can be known through a realization of "the depth of reason" inherent in every human being,[27] but it cannot be reached through either logical inference or empirical generalization.
- Axiologically, there is intrinsic meaning and value in the existent beings in the world. If there were not a common source of all values, then it would inevitably follow that our values are arbitrary and relative.
- Cosmologically, the function of the creative ontological principle finds its manifestation in the formative process of the natural world, and man is a unique product of the evolutionary process of nature.
- Scientifically, since there are regular patterns in changes of nature, they may be studied by the intellect; general laws of patterns may be established by way of empirical generalization. In the process concrete details and individual differences are ignored from a methodological point of view in favor of abstract formulas and quantitative differentiation. Even though past Chinese achievements in science and technology should be preserved, Western approaches to science and technology must be thoroughly learned by the Chinese and the rest of the world.
- Psychologically, human beings are endowed with the depth of reason and the ability to realize the truth about the creative ontological principle and the intrinsic value of their own life. Therefore, the approaches of behavioral psychology and depth psychology have not exhausted the field of the psychological study of humanity. There should be room for a branch of psychology that studies the transformative process of sages and worthies from a spiritual point of view.
- Ethically, man is endowed with depth of reason, and so he is by nature a moral being, thereby answering the question: "Why should human beings be moral?" We must try our best to mold ourselves into moral and creative beings.
- Socially, as we cannot isolate ourselves from fellow human beings, the commitment to the basic family and social structures must be preserved, indeed vigorously guarded. Every human being is not only an intimate part of nature but also an intimate part of society.

- Politically, the traditional ideal that takes politics as an extension of ethics must be revised. Even though the function of government is to ensure the welfare of the people, and acknowledging that a government under the leadership of a sage-emperor may achieve a good deal more than a democratic government, the fact remains that there are not many sage-emperors and that a concentration of power may lead to terrible consequences. Hence, contemporary Neo-Confucian scholars are convinced that the Western practice of democracy through election is preferable to traditional practices. A government for the people is not enough; it must also be a government of the people and by the people. Procedural and substantive matters must be equally emphasized.
- Culturally, contemporary Neo-Confucian scholars still believe that popular tastes should not dominate people's lives. More refined cultural aspirations should be vigorously promoted and encouraged.
- Educationally, knowledge of science and technology must be emphasized in the school curriculum, but these subjects do not exhaust the whole range of education. Humanistic and moral education should also be emphasized. How to achieve a balance between the two is one of the most important concerns of modern educators.
- Finally, economically, people should be allowed to earn a good living, but infinite accumulation of wealth should not be the goal of life. There is certainly a sort of socialist tendency among Confucian scholars. But in the meantime they have also realized the importance of the right to own private property, as it has proved to be a necessary measure for the protection of the freedom of people.

This synopsis gives a very general picture of where contemporary Neo-Confucian scholars stand. I now turn to a critical reflection on and evaluation of their attempt to revive some of the traditional Chinese philosophical insights and their proposal for synthesis between the East and the West.

Contemporary Neo-Confucians have achieved a great deal at the metaphysical level. Neo-Confucian metaphysics has never denied that the world is ever changing. Changes in this world must be affirmed; the all-encompassing Way *(tao)* must be realized amidst change. Metaphysics in the Chinese sense has never developed the Greek idea of eternal Being or substance. It shows an unmistakably religious character, as it points to an ultimate concern and establishes a faith that transcends worries about life and death.[28] It finds a balance, or rather a unity, between transcendence (Heaven) and immanence (humanity).[29] Even though belief in a personal God and an organized church is absent in the Confucian tradition, it provides a spiritual path among world religions for answering some of the most deeply felt personal questions. Humans occupy a unique place in the universe, for they are seen as endowed with the ability *consciously* to appropriate the Way in their being, making them co-creators with Heaven, the symbol of the creative ontological principle which works incessantly in the universe.[30] Humans find their ultimate commitment not through logical inference or empirical generalization but through a personal realization that the finite is united with the infinite. Humans are also seen as creative agents or as a source of values. Whitehead's philosophy provides a modern approach to cosmology that draws the admiration of contemporary Neo-Confucian thinkers. The source of value is embedded in existence. The Confucian thinkers strongly believe that the proper starting point for philosophy is personal self-realization rather than cosmological speculation about the universe; even though the latter does not necessarily contradict the former, the right approach is from the near to the far, not the other way around. Eventually, however, the two approaches are found to be both complementary and supplementary, each having its proper place in a more comprehensive scheme of philosophy.

To be sure, the contemporary Neo-Confucian philosophers are no longer hostile to scientific investigation. But they can see the limitations of science and firmly reject scientism as one-sided, considering it erroneous as an ideology. The power of science lies in its quantitative measures and its claim to universality, but here we also find its limitations. Overuse of science could lead to dehumanization with disastrous consequences. Psychology as a behavioral science is worthy of study, but it does not exhaust the whole field of the human heart and mind. We need to study the psychology of the average man, but we also need to study the psychology of sages and worthies and learn more about the transformative process of human consciousness.

In terms of ethics, contemporary Neo-Confucian philosophers have inherited a great deal from the past, and have further developed the implications of Confucian ethics through a comparison with Western ethical theories such as Kant's *Critique of Practical Reason*.[31] With respect to their social, cultural, and educational perspectives, contemporary Neo-Confucian scholars hold a critical attitude toward modern development. It is in politics and economics that they seek a major departure from the past and try to incorporate valuable insights from the West.

At the ideal level the Neo-Confucian project seems appealing; but when we shift our attention to the practical level and examine how these ideals can be actualized, we might feel that there are still holes or serious problems in their conceptions of modernity. Take, for example, their attitude toward science. It is surely an improvement on the past when they affirm the value of science. But if the purpose of science is only to study the phenomenal world, while the purpose of philosophy is to uncover the truth of the Way, then science is inevitably relegated to a secondary position. Once the scientific achievements are there, contemporary Neo-Confucian philosophers are always ready to accept them. But the question is, would a person who is totally devoted to the Confucian Way pursue the career of a scientist? It is true enough that through a division of labor the scientists might concern themselves with the regularities in the natural world, while the philosophers concern themselves with ontological reality. The problem with this approach is that if a person has the ability, why would he or she go into science rather than philosophy, since science occupies a secondary position behind philosophy?

Surely this problem is not unique for the Confucian thinkers. The classical approach, Platonist or Aristotelian, would have to face similar problems. The modern world, however, seems to have rejected such an approach, and we have not seen any sign that the trend can be reversed: philosophy is slighted in our own age, while the work of scientists is much better appreciated. In theory, there is not enough justification to place the work of philosophers above the work of scientists. A nostalgic feeling toward the past which puts more emphasis on humanistic values will not help to solve our problems.

Similar problems also surface when we shift our attention to the cultural perspective. Contemporary Neo-Confucian philosophers seem to believe that a sense of direction is necessary for cultural development. But their critique of what is wrong today seems to be much more useful than their vague ideas about what is right for the future. True, a modern, liberal, permissive society faces many serious problems, including anomie, alienation, and the erosion of the social-moral fabric. There is indeed an excess of sex, drugs, and violence today, to name just a few of the apparent evils of modern civilization. But what is the solution to the problem? Are we supposed to return to the practice of censorship or to a revival of Victorian morals? The Confucian scholars know only too well that the clock can never be turned back, but they have not the slightest idea how to implement their lofty ideals in the real world.

The problem becomes even more acute when we enter into the political arena. Contemporary Neo-Confucian scholars realize that empty talk about a government for the people is not going to increase the welfare of the people or protect the human rights of the citizens. Thus, they sincerely believe that democracy is better than dictatorship for the purpose of attaining the Confucian ideal of promoting the well-being of all people. Confucian scholars, however, also insist that people must be taught about the higher values that can be realized in this life. Hence the problem remains whether it is desirable to have a "minimum" or a "maximum" government. Confucian scholars seem to waver between the two extremes. They also hold an ambivalent attitude toward the modern world of economics. On the one hand, they want people to enjoy a better life and believe that a society should produce more goods to satisfy the needs of the people; on the other hand, they see the evil of having the majority of wealth concentrated in the hands of a few capitalists and feel contempt for the life-style of a decadent society. It appears that they are not able to find a way simultaneously to protect the basic rights and freedoms of the people while helping them aspire to loftier goals. They seem to be caught in a dilemma they cannot overcome.

This partially explains the impotence of the contemporary Neo-Confucian trend as a political movement: it offers nothing concrete. Therefore the question of whether or not contemporary Neo-Confucianism will be incorporated into the mainstream depends on whether its theorists can successfully solve the problem of what they call *hsin wai-wang,* or "outward kingliness in a new form" (i.e., a viable design of a new political program to suit the needs of the time). The paradox lies in the fact that the strongest part of the tradition—well-established institutions that lasted for hundreds of years—turns out to be the weakest link in the contemporary Neo-Confucian scheme of thought.

From this analysis it becomes clear that everything boils down to one central issue: How does the traditional monistic approach square with the modern pluralistic approach? If the two cannot be brought together, then we might as well forget about the meeting of East and West. So far the contemporary Neo-Confucian attempt to synthesize the two has not been totally successful, but it is also too early to give up all hope for a possible synthesis in the future. One gleam of light comes from taking a further step in the direction pointed out by contemporary Neo-Confucian philosophers who recommend an even more radical attempt to reinterpret some of the traditional insights and a thoroughgoing reconstruction of philosophy based on a synthesis of the ancient and the modern, East and West.

One insight that may prove to be especially useful comes from the famous dictum of Ch'eng I (1033–1107): "Principle is one, but the manifestations are many."[32] A radically new interpretation of this insight helps us to overcome the dichotomy between the monistic and pluralistic approaches. Although traditional Chinese thought has tended to emphasize the monistic, this does not have to contradict the pluralistic approach. For example, Mencius discussed the so-called Four Beginnings of humanity, righteousness, propriety, and wisdom.[33] The manifestations of these four virtues are surely different from one another; otherwise there would be no need to talk about virtues at all. But Mencius also believed that what he said about humanity may apply as well to righteousness, propriety, and wisdom. This shows that

Mencius saw the four virtues as manifestations of the same principle. It is foreign to the Chinese mind to see these virtues emerging from different origins.[34]

Chu Hsi further developed this train of thought, setting forth his ideas:

> The moral qualities of the mind of Heaven and Earth are four: origination, flourishing, advantages, and firmness. And the principle of origination unites and controls them all. In their operation they constitute the course of the four seasons, and the vital force of spring permeates all. Therefore in the mind of man there are also four moral qualities—namely, *jen* [humanity], righteousness, propriety, and wisdom—and *jen* embraces them all. In their emanation and function, they constitute the feeling of love, respect, being right, and discrimination between right and wrong—and the feeling of commiseration pervades them all.[35]

Here we find no opposition between the one and the many; in fact, the one must manifest itself in the many. Chu Hsi's favorite metaphor was "the moon reflecting itself in ten thousand streams." The principle is transcendent, while the manifestations are immanent; the pluralistic tendency is not necessarily incommensurable with the Confucian version of a monistic philosophy.

In fact, there was a growing tendency to put greater emphasis on the pluralistic manifestations of the principle in the development of Neo-Confucian philosophy. For example, Wang Yang-ming (1472–1529), the great Ming philosopher, said, "The four classes of society [scholars, farmers, workers, and merchants] have different professions, but they share the same Way."[36] Scholars were traditionally considered to occupy a privileged position among the people. Wang Yang-ming's statement, however, shows that he saw things in a new light: in their relation to the Way, scholars and other classes of people are on the same footing. In conjunction with such subtle changes in philosophical ideas, the social status of merchants became much higher in the Ch'ing dynasty.[37]

Contemporary Neo-Confucian scholars went even further along this line of thinking. For example, in one of his later talks Mou Tsung-san said that the four classes are all equal and that scholars should not enjoy a more privileged position with respect to being selected as leaders of a nation, as they do not necessarily understand the operations of economics better than others; coordination should be emphasized over subordination.[38] If we can push one step further and allow manifestations of the principle to enjoy even greater autonomy, then things might appear in a completely different light.

For example, contemporary Neo-Confucian scholars should know only

too well that if detailed directives are issued from above, then creative initiatives at the grass-roots level will be effectively stifled and lofty ideas will
turn into empty talk or government propaganda without substance or meaning. It is precisely because principle is one but manifestations are many that
there is no way to determine in an a priori fashion what manifestations are
best suited to the needs of ever-changing circumstances. Therefore, freedom
of expression must be allowed to attain its greatest limit, and the search for
new visions must be positively encouraged. In short, modern democratic
practices must be adopted.

Democracy is, of course, not a panacea for all problems. Obviously math-
ematical truths cannot be decided by voting. By the same token, the value
of far-sighted intellectual vision and profound moral and religious experiences are not determined by popular taste. There is no doubt that scholars
can make important contributions to society; but for scholarly findings to
exert direct influence on the daily lives of the people takes time, and they
must go through the proper procedures. For example, when scientists can
prove that smoking is hazardous to health, the laws that govern cigarette
advertising must be revised accordingly. Even a democratic society cannot
afford to have totally relative values. Reason must still be regarded as the
final tribunal, and education is needed to raise the intellectual and moral
standards of the people. There must be a minimum consensus in a democratic society so that the system can be preserved and the basic rights and
freedoms of people protected. Early supporters of the democratic system,
such as the founding fathers of the United States of America, showed great
faith in reason. Modern man, however, seems to have lost sight of the one
principle that defies precise definition but nevertheless enables him to tell the
difference between just and unjust laws. And this principle may be identified
with the principle of *jen* (humanity) or *sheng* (creativity), the ultimate concern of the Neo-Confucian philosophers. True, the New Confucian tradition
does not have a monopoly over this principle, but it has provided some of
its most succinct expression.

If the observations made herein are not far wrong, then Neo-Confucian
philosophers should long ago have given up their dreams about the sage-
emperors or philosopher-kings. Although in modern society intellectuals
earn their living as experts in their fields, they may nonetheless as responsible
citizens offer critiques of their culture and society. Broadly speaking, such
critiques may be pursued in two different directions. On the one hand, they
can carry out a radical critique of their own tradition. As many traditions
are merely manifestations of the past, something parallel to the demythol-
ogization of Christian theology is needed when the Chinese review their own
tradition. Contemporary Neo-Confucian scholars must have the determi-

nation to dissociate themselves from the past when traditions become stumbling blocks which obstruct our progress toward the future. On the other hand, they must also carry out a radical critique of contemporary civilization. They must fight against the pollution of the natural environment, the leviathan of a military-industrial complex, and so on. Ironically, they often find that even though their expressions are modern and novel, the basic insights they rely on are not so different from many of the insights of the past, such as "the unity of Heaven and humanity." Sometimes a reinterpretation of past insights is needed; at other times a reconstruction of philosophy radically different from that of the past is required. The relation with our own past is a complicated question; there is continuity and there is breakthrough. Some people feel that Confucianism has acquired too many negative connotations to make it a viable tradition. As far as I am concerned, so long as the Confucian spirit of humanity and creativity is preserved, the name by which it is called is secondary.

Many difficulties can be overcome if we can make the necessary distinction among three possible ways of understanding the Confucian tradition: (1) Confucianism as a philosophical insight; (2) Confucianism as a political ideology; and (3) Confucianism as a storehouse of popular values. The first element is still very much alive, as has been shown by the flourishing of the contemporary Neo-Confucian movement among philosophers today. The second is at best a remnant of the past, and anyone who wants to revive it will be doomed to failure; Yüan Shih-k'ai's failed attempt to become emperor has clearly shown that it will never work again. The third element remains strong in Chinese culture. Confucianism, understood at the popular level, has an ambivalent character. Some of the success of the Four Mini-Dragons is no doubt due to the Confucian attitude of valuing diligence, integrity, education, and so on. Yet, some other Confucian characteristics may actually hinder future progress, such as the tendency to obey authority blindly and a lack of consciousness with respect to protecting human rights and exploring new frontiers. The success of Chinese communities in the future depends a great deal on whether or not the Chinese can both maximize the effects of their cultural birthright and minimize the constraints of their cultural burden.

PART II

JAPAN

Japan's unusual combination of localism and globalism makes it not only one of the most enigmatic modern postindustrial states but also a most intriguing case in comparative civilizational studies. The meaning of being Japanese is a fascinating subject for students of Japanese culture abroad and a major topic of discussion in Japanese academic circles, indeed virtually a national preoccupation on the Japanese literary scene for the last few decades. As a student of East Asian studies, I have pondered the question of Japaneseness with wonder and hope:

> Deeply rooted in her ethnic purity, attachment to the home, obsession with mother tongue, powerful creation myth, carefully constructed collective memory and elaborate ritual, Japan is embedded in the lived concreteness of being the place where the sun rises and Mount Fuji resides. Despite her responsiveness to Buddhism and Confucianism, Japan, until the Western impact, steadfastly maintained her bearings as a well protected island. The sense of crisis with which Fukuzawa Yukichi (1835–1901) urged his country-

men to "leave Asia," as dictated by a perceived Social Darwinian imperative to survive as a race, culture, and form of life, was echoed in Natsume Soseki's (1867–1816) poignant warning. Japan, by her physical and mental exertions, might indeed achieve "precipitous advance" in her competition with the West, but the danger of a "nervous collapse" was imminent. Now that the Japanese phoenix has risen from the ashes and the "economic miracle" has prompted Nakasone to proudly announce Japan is already part of the West, it is time for her to reflect critically upon her more than a century-long Faustian drive to outsmart the West at its own game. The cost is high: the sensuality of her body, the sensitivity of her heart-and-mind, the purity of her soul, and the brilliance of her spirit are all at stake. Does the vision of Heisei (bringing peace to fruition) imply a return to Asia, to home? (*Daedalus,* summer 1990)

In a deeper sense Japan may have invited the whole world to come to the Land of the Rising Sun, and yet Japan has never really left home, let alone Asia.

A most significant aspect of this apparent contradiction between localism and globalism in the Japanese experience is the inherent flexibility of Japan's rootedness. In other words, Japan's archaeological digging into its own order of things enhances the country's adaptability rather than undermines its openness to outside influence. Whether or not Japan has achieved a delicate balance between identity and adaptation, the dialectical interplay between deepening self-consciousness and broadening awareness of the other engenders a creative dynamism in the Japanese mentality rare in human history and unique in modern East Asia. There is a nervousness, as Soseki warned, in this highly energized corporate spirit, but the ability to mobilize individual and communal energy for nation building since the Meiji Restoration of 1868 is awesome. The Confucian heritage that had by then become an integral part of the Japanese "habits of the heart" was an ethic not only instrumental in the maintenance of law and order in society but also one with a great deal of transformative potential.

In " 'They Are Almost the Same as the Ancient Three Dynasties': The West as Seen through Confucian Eyes in Nineteenth-Century Japan" Watanabe Hiroshi recounts the untold story that a major contribution of the Confucian ethos for Japan's modernization was, paradoxically, its openness to Western learning. Not without a touch of irony, the Confucian glorification of the West as the concrete realization of the so-called Three Dynasties, a sort of paradise on earth, or at least the actualization of the spirit of impartiality in the human community, signaled the beginning of its own demise as the reigning ideology in modern Japan. Nevertheless, Watanabe challenges the conventional interpretation of the role of Confucianism in East Asian modernization. The assumption that Confucianism, as a conservative and even reactionary ideology, was inherently xenophobic tells only one side of the story. In fact the extraordinary receptivity of some forward-looking Japanese Confucians in embracing Western-style modernization suggests that the Confucian mind is supple enough to incorporate alien structures of thought and that Confucian symbolic resources are fluid enough to accommodate apparently conflicting value orientations. Although Watanabe is highly critical of the dogmatic "Confucian hypothesis" which sets out to establish a monocausal relationship between Confucian ethics and the rise of industrial East Asia since the end of the Second World War, his essay thoughtfully addresses the relevance of the Confucian mode of thinking to Japan's modern transformation.

Assuming that Confucian ethics was a defining characteristic of Japanese moral education designed and promoted by the state, Samuel Yamashita vividly documents in "Confucianism and the Japanese State, 1904–1945" the various editions of primary school ethics textbooks commissioned and assigned by the Ministry of Education in the first half of the twentieth century. The core values envisioned by the Japanese educational authorities as vitally important for the socialization of the young in the most impressionable period of schooling are distinctively Confucian.

The spiritual source for this thickly textured and densely ritualized form of moral education is, of course, the famous Imperial Rescript on Education (1890). Hailed as the Holy Writ of Japanese civic morality, the rescript, which consists of roughly two hundred characters, is structured around the idea of a fiduciary community rooted in the four basic Confucian virtues: benevolence, righteousness, loyalty, and filial piety. Yet, underlying the rescript is a profound religious tonality, evoking the basic motifs of imperial ancestors, empire, constitution, and the imperial throne. The benevolent and celestial voice from the exalted place of the Meiji emperor to his subjects carries a magnificently benign intonation, a request rather than a demand for a covenant from the Japanese people in order to launch a joint venture to ensure the well-being of the Way as "bequeathed by our imperial ancestors."

Yet, as Yamashita shows in his content analysis of the different editions of the ethics textbooks, issues of the sacredness of the emperor, national identity, and loyalty to the divine country loom large in modern Japanese moral education. Not surprisingly, the editions of the 1940s were unabashedly nationalistic, even frankly self-aggrandizing, proclaiming Japan "the only divine country in the world." Understandably, the Confucian values that feature prominently in the textbooks are highly selective. Conspicuously absent, from a Chinese perspective, is the cardinal virtue of humanity *(jen)* and, to a lesser degree, rightness *(i)*. Still, by stressing personal hygiene, physical fitness, loyalty, filial piety, propriety, humility, diligence, and industriousness, Confucian ethics was pivotal in shaping a new Japanese civic morality.

If the Japanese state was instrumental in developing a comprehensive Confucian moral education for the young, the social unit that was most consequential in imparting Confucian core values, notably "righteous principles and human feelings" *(jiri ninjo),* was the family. Just as Yamashita notes that Confucian moral education, intertwined with a strong commitment to the transmission of the Way of the imperial ancestors, gives a particular contour to Japanese civic morality, it is not at all clear what sort of "Confucian" institution the Japanese family is. Robert Smith, in a provocative inquiry titled "The Japanese (Confucian) Family: The Tradition from the Bottom Up," addresses the issue from the perspective of concrete praxis (orthopraxy) rather than abstract ideas (orthodoxy). Undaunted by the assertion of some of his Japanese colleagues that since 1945 the Japanese have "consigned Confucianism to the dustbin of history," Smith explores the Confucian connection in Japanese moral education, family ethics, and the civil code as they are actually practiced.

Smith's anthropological investigation, informed by a wealth of historical information, shows a remarkable continuity of the national policy to "make Confucianists of the Japanese" since the Meiji Restoration. The Japanese government made persistent calculated attempts to create a community of discourse centered on a few corporately crafted directives and exerted enormous influence in forging a common civic morality. In addition to the aforementioned Imperial Rescript on Education, the Great Principles of Education (1879), the Cardinal Principles of the National Entity (1937), and The Way of the Subject (1941) are outstanding examples. Although the initiatives from the court to instill Confucian ethics through a sort of "exegetical bonding" ended after the Second World War, the Confucian legacy is found to this day in Japanese ethical and religious consciousness and, in the case of ancestral veneration, is intertwined with Shintoist and Buddhist symbols and practices.

And yet the perception that Confucian ethics has contributed to authority, hierarchy, and status in Japanese society is still pervasive. Smith cautiously asserts that to the extent that an average Japanese still subscribes to the characteristically Confucian ring of virtues—loyalty, filial piety, sincerity, decorum, selflessness, frugality, harmony, respect, and patience—and the Confucian tradition "from the bottom up" remains vital, if often unacknowledged and even unconscious, its relevance is beyond dispute. But if

"Confucian is as Confucian does," it is quite conceivable that an anthropologist or a historian might, either by choice or by default, relegate the Confucian dimension to the background or to a residual category. To some of us this is not merely a matter of academic preference or just a question of scholarly taste. At stake is the level of intellectual sophistication and cultural competence we must emulate in order to understand, even in an exploratory stage, as complex a phenomenon as the Japanese family. Indeed, as a microcosm of the Japanese symbolic universe, the family is laden with nativistic Shinto as well as imported Buddhist and Confucian values. It is highly particularistic and yet shaped by universalizing cultural forces from India and China.

Nevertheless, the impression that Japan, by inviting the world to its motherland, thus transformed itself into a global community without experiencing the trauma of leaving home is certainly too simplistic to account for the complexity of the interplay between localism and globalism in more than a century of Japanese modernization. The collective psychology of anxiety, anguish, apprehensiveness, and disorientation so prevalent in modern Japanese literature strongly indicates that Japan's response to the challenge of the modern West since the mid-nineteenth century has been painfully difficult and ridden with crises of identity, conscience, and meaning. Its remarkable success notwithstanding, all aspects of Japan's existence—body, heart, soul, and spirit—have been profoundly affected, if not fundamentally deconstructed. Still, among the so-called Confucian societies Japan has been singularly successful in adapting to radically different worldviews, belief systems, value orientations, and institutions; indeed, its ability to assimilate Western science, technology, market economy, and democratic polity is unequaled in the world. In "Some Observations on the Transformation of Confucianism (and Buddhism) in Japan," Shmuel Eisenstadt addresses the fascinating question: What kind of historical experience and structure of consciousness has enabled Japan to be so remarkably adaptive?

Instead of providing a causal explanation, Eisenstadt invites us to consider Japan's "mode of expansion and institutionalization of Buddhism and Confucianism" in a comparative civilizational perspective as a fruitful way to approach the topic. In other words, analyzing how Japan expanded its symbolic resources by assimilating Buddhist and Confucian ideas and incorporated these two complex civilizations into its own political and social modus operandi through innovative institutional practices can help us understand Japan's distinctive pattern of modernization. Eisenstadt's thesis, simply put, is that Japan's resourcefulness lies in its astonishing power of "embedding," or transforming radically different otherness into fully indigenized and domestically efficacious "family resemblance."

In the millennium-long history of Japan's encounter with Buddhism and

Confucianism prior to the impact of the modern West, Eisenstadt observes, the obvious Buddhist and Confucian transformations of Japanese society and polity must not blind us to the amazing fact that neither the Buddhists nor the Confucians destroyed the basic institutional premises of Japanese legitimacy, authority, hierarchy, and status: the imperial system, the feudal order, and the family. On the contrary, Buddhism and Confucianism significantly empowered the hereditarily transmitted indigenous leadership to channel their universalistic tendencies in "an immanentalist, particularistic, primordial direction." Surely, Buddhist and Confucian ideas and practices have become so much a part of Japanese culture that they substantively define Japaneseness today. But the Japanese Buddhist *sangha* with its family *(ie)* trees is not Buddhist; nor are the Japanese Confucian samurai imbued with martial spirit Confucian, but they are unmistakably Japanese. Actually, Buddhism and Confucianism may have added an ethical dimension to the Japanese commitment to the center, the hierarchical order, and group solidarity; at least they have not undermined it. The Japanese social nexus—the "Confucian" family, the Buddhist liturgical community, and the imperial system—is rooted in particularistic rituals and nativist intelligence and defined in sacred primordial terms.

We draw from Eisenstadt's analysis an important lesson for understanding the Confucian contribution in modern East Asia. The variability of the tradition may enable us to see its manifestations in significantly different cultural contexts under many disguises. But as we stretch our conceptual boundaries to accommodate radically dissimilar phenomena, we are in danger of reducing the richness of the concrete historical experience to the lowest common denominator which is evidently true but flat, tasteless, and meaningless. Smith also warns us that if "Confucianism is in the eye of the beholder," its explanatory power can be easily relativized and thus diminished.

Max Weber may have been modest in confessing that, as far as religion was concerned, he was "unmusical." But by taking the religious dimension of the modern West seriously, he enriched his sociological analysis and deepened his interpretation of the rise of the spirit of capitalism. Japanese Confucianism seems more Japanese than Confucian, but the Confucian element in Japanese modernity is, beyond doubt, thought-provoking, for it addresses the intriguing issue of immanent transcendence, or in Eisenstadt's more precise formulation, "the transcendental inner-worldly orientation and experience." This attempt to define Japanese religiousness from the perspective of a comparative historical study of world religions has far-reaching implications for our understanding of Japanese modernity.

5

"THEY ARE ALMOST THE SAME AS THE ANCIENT THREE DYNASTIES"

The West as Seen through Confucian Eyes in Nineteenth-Century Japan

Watanabe Hiroshi

PROBLEMS WITH THE "CONFUCIAN CAPITALISM" HYPOTHESIS

The so-called Confucian capitalism hypothesis—namely, the theory that emphasizes the relationship between the prosperous economies of East Asia and the cultural heritage of Confucianism—seems to be slowly going out of fashion. One reason may be the remarkable economic growth in ASEAN (Association of Southeast Asian Nations) countries besides Singapore which have Buddhist or Islamic, rather than Confucian, cultural traditions. Since the Philippines has been a conspicuous exception, I wonder if a "non-Catholic East Asian capitalism" hypothesis might not come into fashion in the near future.

I do not deny the importance of exploring the Confucian dimension of the dynamics of industrial East Asia. My point is simply that it is questionable to link capitalistic prosperity with the Confucian heritage in a deterministic manner. Besides, I believe that the contribution to economic growth is not the only subject of interest in Confucian studies. Even if Confucianism has not contributed positively and directly to economic development, the Confucian aspect of the dynamics of industrial East Asia is certainly a fascinating topic.

It seems to me that many studies of this topic share three common characteristics in their method. First, they focus on the period after the 1950s, or since World War II at the earliest. Second, they pay attention to similarities among East Asian cultures rather than to their distinguishing characteristics. And third, they emphasize the differences between East Asia and the West rather than the similarities. The concept of "East Asian development"[1] itself presupposes that the East Asian economies have developed not because they are basically similar to Western economies, but because they are different from them. In other words, it assumes tacitly that some East Asian countries have been "successful" *because* of their traditions, not in spite of them.

As far as Japan is concerned, however, these three methodological features correspond to three basic problems. First, Japan's rapid industrial development, which is rather exceptional in the non-Western world, is not a post–World War II phenomenon. Japan had already become one of the imperialistic powers by the early twentieth century, having won several wars, including one with Russia (1904–5). Japan's economic development after the Second World War did not start from scratch, at least in terms of human resources and social infrastructure. The "success" of the Japanese economy in recent decades must be explained in view of its long history.

Second, although Japanese culture is a branch of the Sinic civilization in a broad sense, it is a distant branch. It is true that Chinese writing, religions, ideas, institutions, and technology were introduced to the Japanese islands not only by their native residents but also by many immigrants from the continent. But as the table I contributed to a 1990 issue of the journal *Shisō* shows,[2] Japanese society has been a poor disciple of the Confucian sages. Until the late nineteenth century it was governed by samurai warriors, not by literati. The shogun, its effective monarch, neither legitimized his position through Confucian theory nor worshipped Heaven. Instead, he worshipped the ancestor who had founded his dynasty, regarding him as a Buddhist-Shintoist god. The shogun's political institutions, laws, and rituals were barbarian, that is, non-Chinese, as deplored by Confucian scholars at the time. Professional Confucian scholars were treated just like medical doctors socially, as evidenced by the fact that they had the same hairstyle, which was very different from that of the "ordinary" people—samurai, merchants, and farmers.

Family was the most important social unit, as in China and Korea. But the family in Japan *(ie)* was something very different from that of China *(chia)* or Korea *(kajok)*. It was a kind of "corporation" (*kagyo,* literally "family business") which fulfilled some hereditary social role, rather than a lineage group. Therefore, if a man had no son, he usually adopted somebody, with or without a blood relationship, in order to continue the *ie*. This was an established custom not only among commoners but also among samurai, including high-ranking *daimyō* (local lords).[3] In some cases one adopted an unrelated man even if one had a natural son, for the successful continuation of the function of the *ie* by a competent man was more important than mere continuity of blood. A popular preacher of morals in the eighteenth century was once asked the hypothetical question: What should you do if your real father kills your adoptive father? The answer was to avenge your adoptive father's death and to dedicate the murderer's head to the tomb. In short, a man's moral duty would be to kill his real father, however heavy the emotional burden.[4] Thus, *ko,* so-called filial piety, meant simply loyalty to one's *ie* in Japan. It is no wonder, therefore, that an intellectual who had visited the West in the 1860s and 1870s wrote: "To make much of one's blood relationship is a common custom in European and American countries where morality is supported by that custom. It is not necessarily so in Asian countries. Especially in our country, people make light of blood relationship to a most terrible degree."[5] In the context of Japanese culture, Westernization thus entailed, among other things, an emphasis on natural lineage.

Because Japanese society was so peculiar, even where the same Confucian moral code seemed to be applied on the surface, and also because Japan started to industrialize much earlier than other East Asian countries, it was often argued, at least until some twenty years ago, that Japan had been "successful" precisely because the Confucian influence was much weaker in Japan than in the other East Asian countries. I am not sure whether Japan "succeeded" economically in spite of or because of Confucian influence. But it is clear that not only similarities but also differences between East Asian countries have to be investigated.

The third problem with respect to the emphasis on the differences between East Asia and the West is that it may be heartwarming for many East Asians, who have had a deep inferiority complex vis-à-vis the West, to hear that the East Asian economies are performing very well not because they are following the Westerners' path, but because they are making good use of their own traditions. Also, this theory probably sounds pleasant to the ears of conscientious Western intellectuals who are trying to overcome a Eurocentric worldview. I suspect that one reason for the popularity of the Confucian capitalism hypothesis lies in such complementary attitudes.

As far as Japan's economic growth after the Second World War is concerned, however, it is not clear whether something uniquely Japanese was an important cause or not. As is often pointed out, most so-called Japanese management techniques, which are used for enhancing efficiency and quality control as well as boosting employee morale, were inventions of the West. They are not residues of the old tradition. Even the famous lifetime employment system is to be found in the best companies in the United States and Europe. Therefore, one can argue that the Japanese "succeeded" not because they kept on being Japanese, but because they became, in a sense, 120 percent Western.

Also, the emphasis on the seniority element in promotions in Japanese organizations can be said to be related to the postwar egalitarianism promoted by the U.S. Occupation forces, rather than a residue of the old hierarchical social system. In a way the seniority system is an embodiment of this egalitarianism. It is "democratic" rather than "feudal" because in this system an employee can expect to be promoted in the future simply by becoming older every year exactly at the same rate as his or her co-workers. I think that this is one reason why in Japan, as Ronald Dore writes, "department managers do not need to hold themselves aloof to stay respected."[6] Superiors in many Japanese organizations do not need to pretend that they are in their positions because they differ from others in some quality other than years of experience in the organization. Dore asserts that "it is precisely because the principle of hierarchy is so well respected in Japan (due to the Confucian tradition?) that superiors do not *have* to behave in an authoritarian way."[7] But I am afraid his interpretation is a little too ironic. I do not think one has to say that the survival of Confucian authoritarianism is proved because people *do not* behave in an authoritarian way. I suspect that the main reason why people behave in an egalitarian way is because they are egalitarian.[8]

I do not deny that there are many differences between Japanese and Western societies. It is only natural that a society that consciously started to import industry, capitalism, and "modernity" 120 years ago should be different from the very societies that invented them. But many things that may appear to be uniquely Japanese are not necessarily traditional. In some important cases they can be regarded as the result of a kind of Westernization. I am inclined to argue that the modernization of Japan is basically nothing but Westernization.

Given the fact that the three problems I have outlined are implicit in many discussions of the Confucian capitalism hypothesis, I want to focus on a relatively neglected aspect of the Confucian dimension of industrial East Asia, namely, the roles played by Confucian beliefs in encouraging the Westernization of Japan during the nineteenth century.

WESTERN SUPERIORITY IN "HUMANITY" (IN) AND "FAIRNESS" (KO)

It has often been pointed out that until the end of the Tokugawa period (1600–1867), Confucianism provided Japanese intellectuals with philosophical reasons to confront the West. For instance, from the Confucian point of view, the West lacked cardinal morals and virtues which were supposed to be the manifestation of inner human nature, and therefore the Westerners were regarded as barbarians, close to beasts. Naturally they had to be expelled from the "holy" islands of Japan. Certainly the ideological leaders of "antiforeignism" during the last days of the Tokugawa period argued in this way.

But if that was the whole story, why did this antiforeignism evaporate so quickly after the Meiji Revolution of 1868? Why did the Japanese suddenly change their minds and start to learn from the West so eagerly? There must have been many reasons, but one of them, I think, is that Confucianism, the most influential belief system among intellectuals during the late Tokugawa period, led them to appreciate and admire the West while bolstering antiforeignism at the same time.

Relations with Other Countries

After the middle of the seventeenth century, the Tokugawa shogunate effectively and strictly controlled Japan's relations with other countries. It had diplomatic relations only with the Korean and Ryukyuan governments. As for trade, only Chinese and Dutch merchants were allowed to stay in Nagasaki, while there was semiofficial trade with Korea, Ryukyu, and the Northern Ainu people. It was illegal for a Japanese to leave the country except for a temporary stay in Ryukyu or Korea for the purpose of trade or diplomacy. In comparison with Korea at that time, which had direct contact only with China and Japan, Japan exposed itself much more to the outside world. But, in comparison with China, which had substantial trade with many Western merchants at Canton, Japan seemed to be secluded from the world in the eyes of the Westerners in the age of European expansion. For them Japan's self-imposed "seclusion" was strange and mysterious, especially in light of its active contact with the Portuguese and Spanish until the early seventeenth century.

Against this background Engelbert Kaempfer (1651–1716) wrote an essay on Japan's "seclusion." After his two-year stay in Nagasaki (1690–1692) as a doctor for the Dutch merchants, Kaempfer wrote *The History of Japan,* which was translated into many European languages and cited by many thinkers and historians (including Montesquieu, Voltaire, and Rousseau) as one of the few reliable sources of information on Japan until its "opening" to the West in the late nineteenth century. Kaempfer was the authority on Japan for more than a century, and his essay became an appendix to the 1777–1779 version of *The History of Japan,* which was later translated into Dutch.

The thrust of the essay was to justify the "seclusion" policy of Japan on the grounds that it had sufficient resources and knowledge to sustain its prosperous autarky and peace. At the beginning of the essay, however, Kaempfer explored, and ultimately rejected, an argument against the self-imposed seclusion of any people because it violated the "law of Nature" and the "law of the Creator," which mandated mutual help among the whole of mankind. Ironically, it was this argument, rejected by Kaempfer himself, that was to have the greatest impact on Japanese intellectuals. In 1801 the essay was translated into Japanese from Dutch by Shizuki Tadao (1760–1806), a scholar in Nagasaki. This was the first time that the justifiability of self-seclusion was even questioned on ethical grounds. Shizuki translated "Nature" and "the Creator" in the argument at the beginning of the essay as *ten* (Heaven or Nature), the supreme existence in the Confucian worldview. Moreover, he wrote, in summarizing the argument, that the author said that seclusion was against *ri* (principle). Sensitive intellectuals who had studied Confucianism could not easily ignore an argument based on such seemingly Confucian premises.[9]

For instance, Watanabe Kazan (1793–1841) wrote in an essay in 1838, when a British ship approached Edo (today's Tokyo) and was turned away, that an Englishman would have argued: "You deny your people any contact with foreigners permanently and strictly. Even when ships of overseas countries like ours are drifting or need water and fuel or have sick men and are asking help, you refuse it. You are doing harm to all the countries on the globe for the benefit of a single country. We are under the same Heaven [*ten*] and on the same earth. Still, you are doing harm to the same human beings . . . You should understand the 'Great Way' [*Taido*]."[10] He concluded that the Westerner would have good reason for attacking Japan by force, even if the Japanese pointed to the Westerners' past reprehensible conduct behind such a plausible argument. In Kazan's mind the mutual help and communication among nations in Europe was nearer to the "Great Way." He was punished by the shogunate for his ideas and activities in 1839 and later committed suicide.

Takano Choei (1804–1850), who could read and write Dutch, similarly wrote in 1838 that if the Japanese expelled Western ships that were bringing back Japanese sailors saved from drifting ships, the Westerners would consider Japan a country "without humanity" *(fujin)* and affection for its own people. He emphasized that Western governments cherished their people and regarded saving human life as the greatest moral achievement.[11] Choei was also jailed and killed himself in 1850 after a long secret life as a fugitive from prison.

Three years later the U.S. squadron of Commodore Matthew Perry appeared in the Bay of Edo with the firm intention of forcing the shogunate to "open" the country to the West. His formal letter to "the Emperor of Japan" (i.e., the shogun), translated from Dutch into Japanese by the shogunate's interpreters, said that Americans treated people who arrived on their shores in drifting ships with "humanity and compassion" *(ninji)* and that Japan should do the same.[12] Also, Perry sent a menacing informal letter to the shogun and condemned him for the "sin of violating the Heavenly Principle" *(Tenri)*, namely, the refusal of commerce with Western countries. In the same letter Perry also declared that he would punish the shogunate by force if it would not accept his demands.[13]

This was unconcealed intimidation consistent with the "imperialism of free trade."[14] But at the same time, it was precisely the philosophical challenge that Watanabe Kazan had anticipated fifteen years before. The hypothetical question that several intellectuals had tried to answer became a real question to the shogunate because of the use of Confucian words in the translation. Which is nearer to "the Way" or "the Heavenly Principle," Japan or the West? Can "self-seclusion" be justified by Confucian values?

According to Sakuma Shōzan (1811–1864), a Confucian interested in Dutch learning and a vassal of the *daimyo,* who was in charge of the shogunate's diplomacy, it was Japan that was nearer to "the Way." In 1858 he came up with an idea for resisting the first consul of the United States, who had been demanding Japan's much wider opening to the West. Shōzan thought that the shogunate should say to the consul at the beginning of the negotiations: "Western countries want to link all the nations in the world. Then, we would like to know whether that is because of your wish to cherish the peoples in the world indiscriminately by exchanging necessary goods, complying with the 'Fair Way and Principle of Heaven' [*Tenchi kokyo no dōri*] or because of your wicked wish to make your own profits by exploiting the world."[15] The consul was sure to answer that the former was the motive. Then the shogunate should respond:

> If so, we cannot understand what you say. In China, people have been severely suffering from the harm of opium. It is in accordance with the "Way and Principle" [*dōri*] that the Chinese government strictly prohibited the use of opium. But Britain ignored this law of the country which is in amity with it for the sake of its own profit and satisfied its wicked desire by using the formidable cannons of their ships without any consideration for people's lives. That is against the virtues of "humanity, affection, courtesy, and justice" [*nin, ji, ri, gi*] and the act of a robber. Do you call this the "fair and public way [*kokyo no dō*] for cherishing the people?"[16]

Shōzan also thought that the shogunate should take Perry's threat as a sign of the same wicked egoism.

The antiforeignists might have liked Shōzan's rebuttal to the "hypocritical" demand of the West. But some Confucian scholars responded to the challenge of the West, which was understood in a Confucian conceptual framework, in a much more serious way. Yokoi Shonan (1809–1869) was a typical example. He was a *daimyō*'s vassal who had become a Confucian and had followers among the samurai. According to Shonan, Japan was superior to other countries in the world in its respect for "humanity and justice" *(jingi)* in harmony with the "Mind of Heaven and Earth" *(Tenchi no shin)*. Therefore, Japan should always respond to missions from the West in light of the "Great Heavenly Way of Humanity and Justice" *(Tenchi ningi no taidō)*. This was his basic standpoint.[17] In 1853 he asserted that Japan should refuse the demands of the Westerners not because they were foreigners but because their behavior, as evidenced by that of Perry, did not appear to be in accordance with the Way.

But soon his perception of the West changed, and so did his opinion on the "opening" of the country.[18] In 1860 Shonan drafted "The Three Vital Policies" for the influential Fukui domain as an invited political adviser to its *daimyō*, an unusual event for a Confucian in Tokugawa Japan. Shonan wrote:

> Govern and manage things under Heaven by following "the Fair and Public Way"; then there will be nothing to worry about. Countries in the world have improved their politics and education very much. Especially in America, Washington established great principles and one of them is to abolish war in the world in accordance with the "Will of Heaven" [*Teni*]. When countries like this request us to open the country in the name of the "Fair and Public Way," Japan should renounce its policies for its own sake [*shiei no sei*] and accept the "principle" [*ri*] of commerce.[19]

It is clearly that his Confucian values and framework led Shonan to believe that Japan should join the Western state system wholeheartedly.

Politics and Society

People in Tokugawa Japan had various images of the West. For many it was simply the realm of a mysterious, devilish religion called Christianity. Since the late eighteenth century it had also been regarded as an area where scrupulous investigations of nature were popular. At the same time, some intellectuals began to suspect, based on information they got mainly from Dutch and Chinese books, that the West was a place where much was made of each human being.

For instance, Shiba Kokan (1738–1818), a painter and author, wrote in his book on Holland (printed in 1805): "All the European countries respect learning. Every king builds schools in his country and selects excellent students from among thousands to be their teachers . . . There are facilities for widowers, widows, orphans, and childless old people everywhere . . . Also, there are hospitals and poorhouses."[20] The fact that Western countries had facilities for the poor, the sick, and the orphaned was noted by many Japanese authors on the West.

As a painter, Kokan also noticed an interesting fact concerning the West: "I have never seen a palanquin carried on shoulders in paintings and illustrations of the West. They use horse-drawn carriages . . . I realized that they do not use human beings as horses and cows. They respect fellow human beings that much."[21] Moreover, Watanabe Kazan wrote in 1839: "In Western countries kings went out with few attendants because they were absorbed in nourishing people's abilities and had no custom of using people for meaningless, ornamental purposes."[22] Needless to say, Kazan was making a comparison with the Japanese shogun and local lords, who were accompanied by hundreds or even thousands of attendants whenever they went about in public.

Most intellectuals had no direct political influence, but what is important is that they were influential in forming the people's image of the West. Westerners make much of people. Westerners treat each person with respect and affection. Considering that the most important moral teaching of Confucius was *ninji* (humanity or compassion), this observation was quite meaningful. And as a matter of fact, Yokoi Shonan decisively recognized that, at that time, the West was far superior to Japan in (Confucian) morals. He wrote in 1860:

> In America the power of a president is succeeded not by his son but by an outstanding person. They [the American people] abolished the relation between lord and vassal and concentrate on the realization of "fairness and peace" [*kokyo wahei*]. They are introducing anything good and just from all over the world into their country . . . and are promoting the "life-loving sense of humanity" [*kosei no ninfu*]. In Britain, policies are always based on the sentiment of the people and every act of the government is submitted for the people's discussion. The government decides for the benefit of the people . . . Besides, many Western countries, including Russia, have not only schools . . . but also hospitals, orphanages, facilities for the deaf, and so on. Their govern-

ments are striving for the sake of the people in accordance with ethics. They are almost the same as the ancient Three Dynasties.[23]

Shonan declared publicly that Western countries were almost equal to the ancient Chinese dynasties of the sage-kings precisely because he firmly believed in Confucian values.

Shonan was not alone. Katō Hiroyuki (1836–1916), a professor at the shogunate's Institute for Barbarian Books and later the first president of the University of Tokyo, wrote in 1861 that in the West there were "fair and just" [komei seidai] regimes that aimed at the realization of "humanity and justice" [ningi]. According to Katō, they were better than the regimes of the ancient sage-kings of China. These regimes, which may be called "limited monarchies" and "democratic republics," had places for discussing national politics. Kato coined a new word for such a place: kokai (Assembly of Fairness or Public Meeting).[24]

The influence and persuasiveness of this kind of argument by intellectuals during the Meiji Revolution are manifest in the famous Five Articles, which the Meiji emperor swore before the gods in 1868 as the fundamental policies of the new government:

Article 1: Promote discussions widely and decide everything in accordance with "fair [public] opinion" (koron).
Article 2: Unify the spirits of the government and the people and advance politics.
Article 3: Make it possible for anyone . . . to realize his own wishes.
Article 4: Abolish coarse customs from olden times and stand by the "Fair Way of Heaven and Earth" [Tenchi no kodō].
Article 5: Seek knowledge in the world and promote the conditions of the emperor's reign.

Clearly, this was a plan to turn Japan into another Western country, as Confucian intellectuals understood it. This was not coincidental. The first drafter of these articles was a disciple of Yokoi Shonan. His name was Yuri Kimimasa, which means literally "Fairness and Justice of the Yuri family" (Yuri kosei).

WESTERN SUPERIORITY IN "CIVILIZATION" (BUNMEI)

Confucianism and the Concept of Civilization

Confucianists did not believe in the preposterous idea that mankind, which has limited abilities, can make unlimited progress on the earth, which has limited resources. If even the ancient Three Dynasties perished, what dynasty can hope to last forever? For them, history was the repetition of the success and failure of civilization, though the degree of both success and failure fluctuated. In this sense they were different from the optimistic believers in the idea of progress in eighteenth- and nineteenth-century Europe.[25]

But Confucianists were staunch supporters of the refinement of thought, manners, and taste. They believed that such refinement should be promoted because it is what distinguishes human beings from beasts. Moreover, they believed that the progress of life and morality would materialize only through the efforts of Confucian intellectuals, who were supposed to be model human beings. As is well known, Lao Tzu had the opposite idea. He hated intellectuals and technology. According to him, if instruments of convenience for the lives of the people increased, the country would be in disorder. He thought that only by abolishing the use of intelligence and preaching morality would people be able to live happily ever after.

During the late Tokugawa period in Japan there were a few sympathizers with Lao Tzu, such as Kamo no Mabuchi. But most Japanese intellectuals, who had some knowledge of Confucianism, including those who studied Dutch, were supporters of refinement in one sense or another. Therefore, once they acknowledged Western superiority over China and Japan in technology and science, and even in morality and politics, it was not very difficult for them to change their model from ancient China to the contemporary West. Consider the case of *bunmei,* a word from the Confucian classics which was used to translate "civilization," and which became an extremely popular catchword after the Meiji Revolution. Although the traditional term survived, the actual concept of civilization changed. For example, one of the shogun's officials who was sent to Europe in 1862 to investigate Western societies wrote down something he had heard from a Dutch intellectual living in England, using the word *jiyū*. He wrote in his report that if a country wanted to be called "civilized," it had to meet five conditions, one of which was that citizens could live "freely" *(jiyū)*, liberated from the interventions of the government. Probably he did not have the concept of a linear, limitless progress of civilization, but this early and clear example suggests the possibility that the Confucian concept of civilization worked for the acceptance of an aspect of Western civilization that would destroy the Confucian belief system in the end.[26]

Fukuzawa Yukichi and Confucianism

Fukuzawa Yukichi (1835–1901), whose portrait in a kimono with a Western hairstyle is on the ten thousand yen bill today, was the most influential intellectual leader in Meiji Japan. Among his bestsellers were *Seijo jijo* (Conditions of the West, 1866)[27] and *Gakumon no susume* (An invitation to learning, 1872).[28] He also wrote more scholastic books, such as *Bunmeiron gaiyaku* (An outline of the theory of civilization). In his writings, he advocated the introduction of "civilization" from the West and, at the same time, criticized harshly and tirelessly the old habits of mind related to feudalism and Confucianism.

According to Fukuzawa, Confucianism assisted the "refinement" of Japanese society to a certain degree, but it justified and actually helped despotic governments of the past. Also, it produced "mental slaves" of ancient sages, who were ignorant of "the universal law of progress." Confucianism was an important cause for the stagnation of Japanese society. He believed that people must engage in the practical, useful learning introduced from the West, rather than old Confucian learning. And since the mentally independent individual was the key to "civilization," people must become such individuals to promote Japan's civilization and thus to secure its independence.[29]

Certainly Fukuzawa was a severe critic of Confucianism. But it seems that he not only used many Confucian terms, but also retained several basic assumptions of Confucian thought which he had learned in his youth. I would argue that these assumptions helped him to become an advocate of "civilization." Let me introduce two of these basic assumptions.

First, he asserted in *An Invitation to Learning* that learning gives rise to difference among men who are created equal by Heaven or Nature *(ken)*. If one studies, he will be able to engage in difficult—that is, mental—work in a high position in society. If not, he will have to do manual labor in a low position.[30] This would have sounded like a cliché in China and Korea, which had Confucian state examination systems, though of course what Fukuzawa meant by "learning" was not Confucianism. But since Tokugawa Japan, which consisted of hereditary classes, had no such system for recruiting competent commoners to high positions, what Fukuzawa said was not simply the repetition of an old Confucian belief but actually a kind of declaration of liberation. Moreover, Fukuzawa thought that the principle "As one sows, so one reaps" *(jigō-jitoku)* had materialized in the West, where everyone can and must accept the consequences of his own deeds through systems of free competition.[31] For him that principle was an important aspect of the present stage of civilization. Thus, in Fukuzawa's thought, the Confucian belief that it should be learning that creates differences of social position among basically equal men combined nicely with his understanding of Western civilization.

The second example of a Confucian assumption that Fukuzawa retained was a belief in the progress of human knowledge and morality. According to C. S. Henry's footnote to his 1867 translation of Guizot's *General History of Civilization in Europe* (1828), which was one of Fukuzawa's favorite books, civilization implied "both a state of physical well being and a state of superior intellectual and moral culture . . . [and not] merely the multiplication of artificial wants and of the means and refinements of physical enjoyment."[32] This was probably a definition of civilization that any Confucianist could accept, and Fukuzawa adopted it as such. Unlike Confucianists, however, Fukuzawa did not believe in the cycle of civilization. But neither was he a cultural relativist. He still had an absolute standard for judging the state of people's morality, just like Confucianists. Therefore, he could assume a linear progress and final perfection of human morality. Also, he believed in the progress and perfection of human knowledge, which should be realized concurrently with morality. Accordingly, he often used the same word to describe the higher stage of both morality and knowledge, the word "lofty" from the *Book of Changes*. He once wrote that when mankind reaches the final stage of civilization, everybody in the whole world will be just like Confucius at seventy years of age with the knowledge of Newton.

In contrast to Fukuzawa Yukichi, Nakae Chomin (1847–1901), a representative intellectual leader of the democracy movement in the 1880s, is well known for his sympathy with Confucianism. Chomin believed in the fundamental consistency of Confucian thought, especially that of Mencius, with the principle of Western democracy. According to him, democracy and freedom are not assets peculiar to the West, but are universal principles based on human nature which Asian philosophers had also discovered. As a matter fact, he translated Rousseau's *Social Contract* into classical Chinese, which is the Latin of East Asia.

On the surface, Fukuzawa was the opposite of intellectuals such as Chomin in terms of his attitude toward Confucianism. But even in the case of Fukuzawa, some aspects of Confucianism helped him to accept modern Western ideas. Modernization theory is wrong if it presupposes a sweeping contraposition of modernity and tradition. Tradition works for modernization sometimes. But I think it is also wrong to think that the traditions of East Asia have always been working toward modernization simply by surviving. I believe that, at least in nineteenth-century Japan, Confucianism sometimes contributed to the acceptance of Westernization, which ultimately destroyed the Confucian belief system itself. Modernity is, after all, a Western invention.

6

CONFUCIANISM AND THE
JAPANESE STATE, 1904–1945

Samuel Hideo Yamashita

Few would deny the importance of Confucianism for modern Japan. It is well known that those responsible for opening the country to the West and subsequently transforming it into a Western-style industrial nation were, like the literati in China, Korea, and Vietnam, schooled in Confucianism. Confucian ideas and themes were, moreover, incorporated into the state ideology which was created in the 1880s, as the Imperial Rescript on Education so clearly reveals. Historical Confucianism was also part of the vision of East Asia that early in this century inspired many young Japanese to devote their lives to the study of Chinese civilization, to seek their fortunes on the Asian mainland, to conspire with intellectuals and political activists there, and, more tragically, to intrude in the affairs of continental and maritime Asia. All of these ideas, themes, myths, and texts that we summarily call Confucian had an impact on the broader population as well, for they found their way into the government-sponsored ethics textbooks used in the prewar educational system and were presented through that medium to two generations of Japanese schoolchildren.

This essay is a preliminary analysis of the Confucian material introduced in the ethics textbooks issued by the Ministry of Education between 1904 and 1945. It attempts to answer several questions. First, what Confucian themes, ideas, and behaviors are contained in the textbooks? Second, how is this material presented? That is, what is highlighted, and what is downplayed or excluded? Third, how did the Confucian content change, if at all, as the texts were revised and new editions issued? And what was the fate of the Confucian material in the editions of the texts issued in the 1930s and during the Second World War? In answering these questions, I look at the texts themselves and, to some extent, the stated goals and policies of those responsible for their compilation and revision. I do not, however, consider the other important facet of this issue, the reception of the Confucian content of the texts.[1] By this I mean how the Confucian material was read and "consumed" by readers.[2]

The textbooks that are the subject of this essay were issued by the Ministry of Education between 1904 and 1945. The first edition appeared in the spring of 1904, and four subsequent editions were published between 1910–1918, 1919–1933, 1934–1939, and 1941–1945. They were compiled to fill a felt need for a standard national ethics textbook. In the early 1890s there were repeated complaints about the ethics texts then being used in Japanese schools. The most serious complaint was that the texts diverged significantly from the Imperial Rescript on Education, which had been issued on October 13, 1890, to satisfy the call for some kind of national moral instruction or, more fundamentally, a national ideology.[3] The text of the rescript reads:

Know ye, Our subjects:
Our Imperial Ancestors have founded Our Empire on a basis broad and everlasting, and have deeply and firmly implanted virtue; Our subjects ever united in loyalty and filial piety have from generation to generation illustrated the beauty thereof. This is the glory of the fundamental character of Our Empire, and herein also lies the source of Our education. Ye, Our subjects, be filial to your parents, affectionate to your brothers and sisters; as husbands and wives be harmonious, as friends true; bear yourselves in modesty and moderation; extend your benevolence to all; pursue learning and cultivate arts, and thereby develop intellectual faculties and perfect moral powers; furthermore, advance public good and promote common interests; always respect the Constitution and observe the laws; should emergency arise, offer yourselves courageously to the State; and thus guard and maintain the prosperity of Our Imperial Throne coeval with heaven and earth. So shall ye not only be Our good and faithful subjects, but render illustrious the best traditions of your forefathers. The Way here set forth is indeed the teaching bequeathed by Our Imperial Ancestors, to be observed alike by Their Descendants and the subjects, infallible for all ages and true in all places. It is Our wish to lay it to heart in all reverence, in

common with you, Our subjects, that we may all attain to the same virtue.[4]

The problem, then, was that the ethics textbooks currently being used were written by private individuals and published by commercial houses and were thus, in the eyes of their critics, unreliable.[5] A standardized national ethics text seemed a likely and desirable solution, and a public call for such a text had surfaced by 1894.[6]

The first formal proposal for a standardized national ethics textbook was submitted to the upper house of the Diet in 1896. Fierce debate ensued, with a predictable split between those who favored such a text and those who opposed it. In the end those calling for such a text prevailed, and over the next two years proposals for funding the compilation of this text passed both houses of the Diet. In 1900 the Ministry of Education formed a committee—headed by the political thinker and legal scholar Katō Hiroyuki (1836–1916)—and charged it with the formidable task of compiling the first text. The committee met ten times in 1900, twenty-six times in 1901, forty times in 1902, and fifty-six times in 1903. In April 1903 the Primary School Regulations (Shogakkōrei) were revised to accommodate the introduction of the new text, and it was established that henceforth only ethics texts issued by the Ministry of Education would be used.[7] In February of the following year, the compilation committee issued its "Principles of Compilation," which read: "This text was compiled to serve as a textbook for the primary school ethics course. It was based on the principles in the imperial rescript issued on the thirteenth day of the tenth month of Meiji, it nourishes the moral character of youngsters and directs their practice of morality, and it has as its goal the teaching of the essentials of the morality necessary for a sound Japanese citizenry."[8] Two months later, in April 1904, the new ethics textbooks began to be used in schools throughout Japan. There was one for primary school students, *Jinjō shoggakō shūshinsho* (A common elementary school ethics text), and one for middle school students, *Kōtō shogakkō shūshinsho* (A higher elementary school ethics text).[9]

The content of these textbooks contains no surprises. After all, they were artifacts of a modern, Western-style educational system based on European and American models. As such, they were designed to instill in Japanese children precisely those values that would enable them to realize their own moral, intellectual, and physical potential, to lead happy and productive lives, to get along with their fellows, and to fulfill their obligations as members of families and local communities and their duties as citizens of a modern state. This is revealed in the material selected for presentation in the textbooks. Consider, for example, the tables of contents of the second edition's six volumes,[10] which were published between 1910 and 1911 and are fairly typical of the whole series:

Volume 1

1. "Studying Hard and Playing Well"
2. "Being Punctual"
3. "Let's Study"
4. "Helping Friends"
5. "Don't Fight"
6. "Be Energetic"
7. "Taking Care of Your Body"
8. "Minding Your Manners"
9. "Be Orderly"
10. "Be Gentle"
11. "The Kindness of Parents"
12. "Take Care of Your Parents"
13. "Do As Your Parents Say"
14. "Get Along with Your Siblings"
15. "The Family"
16. "The Emperor's Departure"
17. "Loyalty"
18. "Don't Conceal Mistakes"
19. "Don't Tell Lies"
20. "Your Own and Others' Things"
21. "Neighbors"
22. "Consideration"
23. "Don't Make Living Things Suffer"
24. "Don't Inconvenience Others"

Volume 2

1. "The Kindness of Parents"
2. "Filial Piety"
3. "Get Along with Your Siblings"
4. "Be Diligent in Your Work"
5. "Relatives"
6. "Learning"
7. "Diligence and Thrift"
8. "Honoring Ancestors"
9. "Compassion for Servants"
10. "Watch What You Eat"
11. "Have a Routine"
12. "Don't Be Cowardly"
13. "Help Friends"
14. "Don't Be Rude"
15. "Forgive Others' Mistakes"
16. "Don't Go Along with Bad Recommendations"
17. "Honesty"
18. "The Emperor"
19. "Kōdai Shrine"
20. "Loyalty"
21. "Keep Your Promises"
22. "Don't Forget the Kindness of Others"
23. "Perseverance"
24. "Obey the Rules"
25. "Be Kind to the Elderly"
26. "Good Children"

Volume 3

1. "The Emperor"
2. "Loyalty"
3. "Filial Piety"
4. "Siblings"
5. "Studying"
6. "Rules"
7. "Honesty"
8. "Friends"

9. "Respect for Teachers"
10. "Obey the Rules"
11. "Good Manners"
12. "Courage"
13. "Tolerance"
14. "Stay Calm"
15. "Festival Days"
16. "Valuing the Imperial House"
17. "Frugality"
18. "Charity"
19. "Don't Forget the Kindness of Others"
20. "Humility"
21. "Generosity"
22. "Good Health"
23. "My and Others' Things"
24. "Cooperation"
25. "Neighbors"
26. "Public Good"
27. "Good Japanese"

Volume 4

1. "The Emperor"
2. "Yoshihisa Shinno"
3. "Loyalty and Patriotism"
4. "Yasukuni Shrine"
5. "Resolve"
6. "Industriousness"
7. "Honoring the Imperial House"
8. "Filial Piety"
9. "Older and Younger Brothers"
10. "Servants"
11. "The Body"
12. "Independence and Initiative (I)"
13. "Independence and Initiative (II)"
14. "Determination"
15. "Broadening Your Knowledge"
16. "Dispelling Superstition"
17. "Overcoming the Self"
18. "Manners"
19. "Having Compassion for Living Things"
20. "Universal Love"
21. "The National Flag"
22. "Public Holidays and Festivals"
23. "Respect Laws and Regulations"
24. "The Public Good"
25. "Respect People's Reputations"

Volume 5

1. "Greater Imperial Japan"
2. "The Empress"
3. "Loyalty and Patriotism (I)"
4. "Loyalty and Patriotism (II)"
5. "Humanity and Courage"
6. "Valuing Trust and Justice"
7. "Sincerity"
8. "Don't Be Negligent"
9. "Be Resolute"
10. "Frugality"
11. "Starting Industries"
12. "Filial Piety"
13. "Older and Younger Brothers"
14. "An Enterprising Spirit"
15. "Perseverance"
16. "Manners"
17. "Habits"
18. "Studiousness"
19. "Friends"
20. "Masters and Servants"
21. "Virtuous Action"
22. "Generosity"

23. "Gratitude"

24. "Probity"

25. "Universal Love"

26. "The Duties of Women"

27. "Having Compassion for Living Things"

28. "Good Japanese"

Volume 6

1. "Kōdai Shrine"

2. "The Emperor (I)"

3. "The Emperor (II)"

4. "The Emperor (III)"

5. "The Emperor (IV)"

6. "Loyalty and Patriotism"

7. "Loyalty and Filial Piety"

8. "Ancestors and the Family"

9. "Sinking Courage"

10. "Cultivating Courage (I)"

11. "Cultivating Courage (II)"

12. "Independence and Initiative"

13. "Follow the Rules"

14. "The Public Good"

15. "Watching over Oneself"

16. "Starting Industries"

17. "Compassionate Goodness"

18. "Studiousness (I)"

19. "Studiousness (II)"

20. "Dispelling Superstition"

21. "Respecting Teachers"

22. "Hygiene"

23. "Citizens' Duties"

24. "The Tasks of Men and Women"

25. "Education"

26. "The Rescript on Education (I)"

27. "The Rescript on Education (II)"

28. "The Rescript on Education (III)"

The authors of these texts introduced an impressive variety of topics drawn from a wide range of sources. For instance, Buddhism contributed one broad theme, "compassion," which had many objects. Typically, one was urged to be kind to living things; accordingly, the chapter titled "Living Things" in the 1904 reader for second-year students offers this advice:

Masao found his younger sister teasing a cat, and he made her stop. One must not torment living things. [Figure 6.1][11]

One also was to have compassion for servants:

Thinking that he wanted some water, the child summoned the servant, but when she didn't come, he got very angry and went over to the well where she was busy at work and gave her a tongue-lashing. His mother heard all of this and said, "You must not treat people in this way and get angry at them. You must treat servants with compassion."[12]

This theme was clearly felt to be important, as it recurs in all five editions.

Modern secular topics were included from the outset and run through the entire series. Personal hygiene and physical fitness are the most common

Figure 6.1 "Masao found his younger sister teasing a cat, and he made her stop."

Figure 6.2 "Father goes off to a distant place."

Figure 6.3 "Otake's younger brother started to cry in the middle of the night."

ダイ三

オタケ ガ、カハイ"
サウナ コ ヲ ミ"
テキマス。コノ コ
ハ、オトウサン ガ アリマセン。
トウサン ノ ゴオン ヲ、
スレテ ハ ナリマセン。

Figure 6.4 "Otake saw a pathetic child."

Figure 6.5 "The strap on Ichirō's clog snapped."

Figure 6.6 "Bunkichi was carrying a rather heavy bundle."

ヲトコ
ハ
カウ"

Figure 6.7 "There are two people here."

topics. Youngsters were told to watch what they ate, to stay fit, and to exercise.[13] Diligence and industriousness are the next most frequently mentioned topics in this genre, followed by "independence and initiative."[14] If the sections on "enterprise" and "starting industries" are added, this complex of work-related values would rank as the most frequently occurring of the modern secular topics.[15] Other subjects include "honesty," "obeying rules," "not falling prey to superstition," "universal love," "keeping promises," "not inconveniencing others," and "being orderly."[16]

The texts make ample use of history. Roughly two thirds of the material presented features historical figures. Examples are culled from nearly all periods of Japanese history, with those from the Tokugawa period (1603–1867) being the most numerous. Interestingly, the historical figure most often cited in the entire series is Uesugi Yōzan (1757–1822), the reformist lord of Yonezawa domain who is described as the aggressive initiator of new local industries such as horse breeding, sericulture, and weaving.[17] The selfless fourteenth-century warrior Kusunoki Masashige (?–1336), famous for his loyalty to the emperor, is the second most frequently mentioned historical figure.[18] The stalwart Katō Kiyomasa (1562–1611) and the Confucians Nakae Tōju (1608–1648), Kaibara Ekken (1630–1714), Arai Hakuseki (1657–1725), and Ogyū Sorai (1666–1728), the popular eighteenth-century educator Ninomiya Sontoku (1781–1856), and the political activist Yoshida Shōin (1830–1859) each appear three or four times each.[19] Even Americans and Europeans are presented as exemplars: Florence Nightingale is remembered for her "compassion," "kindness," and "universal love"; Abraham Lincoln for his "studiousness," "honesty," and "sympathy"; and Benjamin Franklin for his "independence and initiative," "public spiritedness," "inventiveness," and "orderliness." Also mentioned are George Washington's "honesty," Christopher Columbus's "perseverance" and "confidence," William Jenner's "resolve," and Socrates' "respect for law."[20]

The texts also introduce what Carol Gluck has labeled the new "civic morality."[21] Created by the leaders of the Meiji state, this new morality was designed to instill in the general population "a sense of the nation and a civic ethos."[22] Reflecting this, the texts refer frequently to members of the imperial family, both past and present; to "Japan," "our country," "Greater Japan," and "Greater Imperial Japan"; to the "public good"; to the "duties of citizens"; to the major Shinto shrines; and to the national flag. Next to the imperial house, "patriotism" is the most frequently mentioned element of the new national morality. It is almost never presented abstractly but, rather, is mentioned as a quality embodied by selfless patriots, chiefly modern military men.[23] The favorite is a certain "Comrade Kiguchi," who appears in the first four editions of the texts: "As he approached the enemy, he didn't flinch one bit and blew his bugle three times," enabling Japanese troops "to advance and wipe out the enemy." But Kiguchi "was hit by a bullet, dying with his bugle pressed to his lips."[24] Comrade Kiguchi is representative of a platoon of selfless individuals cited in the texts who risk life and limb and, in some cases, give their lives for their monarch and country.

It is the Confucian material, however, that dominates the first four editions of these textbooks. "Learning" and "study" are the most frequently mentioned Confucian topics and are generally presented in one of two ways. They may be described as inherently valuable. Ninomiya Sontoku, for example, is depicted as someone who managed to pursue his studies despite adversities of every kind,[25] and the Confucian scholar Arai Hakuseki, who is said to have doused himself with buckets of water to remain alert while memorizing Chinese characters, appears as a model of "studiousness."[26] But learning and study are also considered essential to the nation. "In order for our country to prosper," says the first edition, "each and every citizen must become a good person. What is important here is that everyone receive an education, cultivate his virtue, and polish his knowledge."[27]

"Filial piety" is the second most common Confucian topic, and its importance is established early on. The first volume of the first edition opens with three sections on this theme:

1

Father goes off to a distant place. Otake, together with her mother, sees him off. [Figure 6.2]

2

Otake's younger brother started to cry in the middle of the night. Mother picked him up and held and comforted him.
One must not forget one's mother's kindness. [Figure 6.3]

3

Otake saw a pathetic child. She had lost her father.
One must not forget one's father's kindness. [Figure 6.4][28]

Filial piety occurs in some form in every volume of the first four editions. It is always represented by Japanese figures, including Ninomiya Sontoku, Kusunoki Masashige and his son, a pathetic girl named Ofusa who seems to spend all of her waking hours helping her father in his straw sandal business, and many others.

After learning and filial piety, "loyalty" and "courage" are the next most frequently mentioned Confucian topics. Their appeal is understandable, given Japan's long history of warrior rule, the survival of warrior values in certain quarters, and their demonstrated value to the state. Exemplars range from famous historical figures such as Kusunoki Masashige, whose names were practically synonymous with these qualities, to lesser-known person-alities.[29] Even emperors and courtiers were pressed into service.[30] But the favored subjects of this genre were military men, especially heroes of the last two wars that Japan had fought—the Sino-Japanese (1894–95) and the Russo-Japanese (1904–5) wars.[31] The authors of the texts generally distin-guish between courage and loyalty but usually join patriotism with loyalty, as in the phrase "loyalty and patriotism" *(chūkun aikoku).*[32]

In addition, the five cardinal Confucian social relationships are intro-duced. As the preceding discussion suggests, the relationship between par-ents and children receives the most attention. This theme is treated explicitly in descriptions of filial piety and the family and is implicit in much else that the texts cover, as in the chapters "Keeping Promises," "Being Orderly," and "Manners." Also predictable is the attention given to the relationship be-tween rulers and subjects, which appears in discussions of loyalty, patriot-ism, and courage. The relationship between siblings, especially between older and younger brothers and sisters, is emphasized as well. Youngsters are repeatedly urged "to help" their siblings and "to get along with one another." A helpful older sister, for instance, is featured in the 1903–4 text for second-year students:

> The strap on Ichirō's clog snapped, and Oume is rejoining the two parts.
> Siblings must get along well with one another. [Figure 6.5][33]

In another parable Ninomiya Sontoku is said "to have worked nonstop from morning until night to provide for his two younger brothers."[34] Typi-cally, the texts also stress the benefits of cooperation between siblings, as though additional incentives were thought necessary.[35]

Friendship was encouraged, and readers were urged to help their friends whenever possible. This theme is introduced in the story of a youngster who helps a friend carry a large and unwieldly bundle. The 1910–11 version reads:

> Bunkichi was carrying a rather heavy bundle. Along the way Kotarō, seeing this and feeling sorry for him, changed places with him and carried the bundle. [Figure 6.6][36]

The story of Bunkichi and Kotarō proved durable, appearing in the first four editions. The benefits of friendship were also highlighted. In the fourth edition, for example, the friendship of two warriors from the feudal domain of Mito leads to the discovery of a way to produce the high-quality steel needed in the furnaces that made heavy artillery.[37]

The last of the five relationships, that between husband and wife, is presented under the headings "Men and Women" and "Fathers and Mothers," but it does not occur as often as do the other four kinds, although it is implicit in much else that is discussed.[38]

The presence of Confucian material in the textbooks should not be surprising. First, Confucianism was central to the thinking of those who oversaw the design and compilation of the first textbooks. Most of them had been born before the Meiji Restoration and thus had the rudiments of a Confucian education; that is, they had some knowledge of the Chinese classics and some facility in classical Chinese.[39] Their "Principles of Compilation," which is filled with Confucian ethical language, is revealing: the new ethics texts were "to cultivate the moral nature" *(tokusei o kan'yō suru)* of youngsters and "to direct their practice of morality" *(dōtoku jissen o shidō suru).*[40] Similar phrases occur in the first edition as well: "What is important is that all . . . cultivate their virtue and polish their knowledge."[41] Second, the text was, by design, "based on the principles of the rescript [on education]," which, as we have seen, included Confucian material.[42] Finally, Confucianism was of value to the state. This may explain why "learning" and "study" are shown to be valuable not only in themselves but also for the prosperity of the state. The instrumental value of "learning" is even more explicit in later editions. A passage in the last edition reads: "The advances in a country's civilization and the increases in its wealth and power are dictated largely by the educational level of its citizens."[43] What was true of "learning" and "study" was also true of other Confucian concepts and, indeed, everything introduced in the texts. This suggests, then, that Confucianism supplied one of several different conceptual vocabularies introduced in the texts, perhaps the dominant one, and this was done partly by historical accident and partly by conscious design.

Confucianism informs the ethics texts in another, more subtle way. Material of Confucian origin appears simply as part of the prevailing Japanese discourse on morality; that is, the prevailing discourse on ethics was highly Confucian. Consider the language used by the compilers of the first text, who spoke of "nourishing the moral character" (literally, the virtuous nature) of the students and "directing their practice of morality." Both phrases implicate what might be called archaic Confucian narratives: "Nourishing the virtuous nature" echoes Mencius' use of "nourishing," his notion of "extending and developing the four beginnings" to achieve virtue, and his arguments for the existence of innate moral tendencies—as presented, for example, in the parables of Ox Mountain and the child about to fall into a well. Similarly, "directing their practice of morality" voices the same practical concerns that were a staple of Confucian ethical thinking from Confucius' time. These themes also owe much to latter-day readings of venerable Confucian tropes; that is, the authors of the texts were using a language that alluded to the Confucian classics and thus can be called Confucian, and this was the kind of language that the educators and Ministry of Education officials used when they discussed moral education.

The use of moral exemplars is another Confucian device that appears to have been a staple of contemporary moral discourse. Its importance in the texts is obvious. The textbooks rely so heavily on instruction by emulation that at times they seem little more than catalogues of either exemplary or inadvisable behavior. Although this feature of the texts is sometimes ascribed to the influence of Western educators—chiefly Johann Friedrich Herbart (1776–1841)—it calls to mind the extensive use of moral biography in China, Korea, Japan, and Vietnam.[44] Indeed, this was featured in the distinctive historiography that was developed in China early on and formalized both in the biographical sections (Chinese: *lieh-chuan*) of the Standard Histories that confirmed dynastic succession and in private historical writing, and was widely imitated in the rest of the Sinitic world, including Japan.[45] In the fourth and fifth editions of the ethics texts, students are instructed not only to model their behavior on that of exemplars, but also "to become models" *(tehon ni naru)* for others.[46] The ubiquity of this device in all the texts suggests that it was deeply embedded in contemporary moral discourse, or at least that of the governing elite.

There seems little question, however, that the use of moral exemplars, like so much else in the textbooks, was made with certain ends in mind. The predictability of the Confucian material is revealing in this regard. First, the characters face adversity of some kind (e.g., poverty, unsympathetic employers, illness), which they overcome through self-discipline and effort and then achieve, in the end, some admirable moral quality (e.g., courage, studiousness, loyalty). The writers of the texts were eager to encourage these particular moral qualities in their readers, and they attempted to do so by telling the same story over and over, using different subjects in each instance. The underlying narrative structure made the same point, while the different subjects brought relief.

The hope was clearly that the texts would produce "good Japanese" *(yoi Nihonjin)*—citizens who would study hard, be compassionate and filial, respect their elders, be helpful to their friends, and generally abide by the five Confucian relationships. "Good Japanese" were also those who paid their taxes, obeyed the laws and regulations created by the state, contributed to its standing in the world, and, if necessary, died for their country. Those who did not embrace these values or failed to perform these actions were not, by definition, "good Japanese." Distinctions such as this between "good" and "bad" Japanese are typical of the kinds of "dividing practices," as Michel Foucault puts it, that modern states have used to objectify, categorize, and thus control their subjects.[47] The process of subjectification would be complete when Japanese not only acted in accordance with the new ideology but also saw themselves as "good Japanese."[48] In this respect, the Japanese ethics texts were typical artifacts of a modern educational system designed by government authorities to construct willing, obedient, and informed subjects. As such, they were not so different from the textbooks then in use in the United States and Europe during the same period.

The ethics textbooks changed over the life of the series in both obvious and subtle ways. Chapter titles were continually revised; illustrations were redrawn; emphases were altered; and sections were moved about, with both deletions and additions. Even the style of the texts changed, gradually at first and then dramatically in the 1940s. All of this affected the texts' Confucian content.

The revisions found in the second and third editions, which were published in 1910–1918 and 1919–1933, respectively, are quite obvious. The entries are fuller or more focused than those of the first edition. Consider this excerpt from the section titled "Learning" in the 1903–4 edition:

> When he lived in his uncle's house, [Ninomiya] Kinjirō gathered rapeseed and exchanged it for rapeseed oil, and he studied every night. When his uncle said, "Instead of studying, how about doing your chores?" Kinjirō thereupon studied after he finished the things he was ordered to do.[49]

The version in the second edition reads:

> [Ninomiya Kinjirō's] uncle said, "It would be better for you to do your chores instead of reading." Accordingly, Kinjirō worked well into the evening and then studied.[50]

The third edition substitutes two young and obviously modern men for Ninomiya Kinjirō:

> There are two people here. Both were once in the same school. One never heeded his teachers' admonitions and instead loafed and, as a result, became a pathetic person. The other listened to his teachers' instructions and studied, and he became a fine person. [Figure 6.7][51]

The appended comment observes: "Seeds that are not sown do not sprout." The contrast represented in the text and the accompanying illustration leaves little doubt as to the course readers were to follow and what would happen if they did not.

The entries in the second and third editions are more realistic; characters are more lifelike and "rounder," as E. M. Forster puts it, with personal histories and even personalities. This is true even of august personages. For example, the empress is barely a presence in this entry from the second edition: "The empress went to a hospital to visit wounded and sick soldiers. Every single person there shed tears and felt the deepest gratitude."[52] She is, however, a fuller, rounder entity in the third edition: "From her childhood onward, the empress was modest and felt compassion for lesser beings. When she became crown princess, she attended the openings of schools and in wartime made bandages and offered them to the soldiers. After she became empress, she turned her attention to education and industry and showed compassion for the poor. Many are the things for which one should be grateful."[53] In attempting to explain the empress's modesty and compassion, the biographical narrative of the second passage even gives us a glimpse of what might be called her personality.

Direct discourse is used more often in the second and third editions than in the first. Characters who speak directly seem more lifelike and credible. Compare the lesson "Not Inconveniencing Others." The first edition reads: "This child's father has spotted her throwing some trash away at the side of the road and stops her. One must not inconvenience others."[54] In the third edition the same passage reads: "Ochiyo was about to throw out some trash at the side of the road. Her father stops her, saying, 'If you throw trash out there, you'll inconvenience people.'"[55]

Direct discourse is used even more extensively in the fourth and fifth editions, with the exemplars making longer and longer statements. Hortatory in nature, these lessons were obviously written to be remembered, recited, and perhaps even used, or at least mimicked. In the fourth edition, when Kusunoki Masashige is commanded by Emperor Go-daigo "to attack [Hōjō] Takatoki and bring peace to the realm," he responds: "No matter how strong the rebel army is, I believe that by using clever strategies when attacking it, victory is certain. When our forces engage each other, though there is one in ten thousand chances that we will be defeated, if you hear that Masashige alone has survived, you may be assured that the way will be opened for [your] sacred forces."[56] And of course, the entry continues, Masashige's forces wipe out those of Takatoki.

These changes—fuller biographical narratives, greater realism, more extensive use of direct discourse—enhanced the explicitly Confucian content of the texts. They made the exemplars and behaviors presented in the texts more believable and thus more persuasive, heightening the impact of the lessons. To the extent that the use of exemplars is Confucian, all of these changes can be interpreted as strengthening the impact of the texts' Confucian content. This emphasis was further encouraged by the addition of chapters on the Rescript on Education, which was reprinted in its entirety and explained in the more advanced texts.[57]

One other change also added to the number of Confucian topics: the introduction of more historical figures from the Tokugawa period, including famous Confucian scholars and others who exemplified Confucian values.[58] This was a response to a Ministry of Education recommendation to increase the quantity of "early modern material."[59] The revisions made in the second and third editions were designed to encourage readers to adopt the norms presented in the texts and to work at becoming "good Japanese." It is no coincidence that the second and subsequent editions appended a summary section at the end of each text that contained a composite picture of a "good Japanese." There was no ambiguity about what qualities one should possess. The expectation was that the readers would transform themselves into approximations of the ideal, that they would become "good Japanese" and see themselves and others in these terms. Foucault calls this process of self-transformation "subjectification" and describes it as "the way a human being turns him or herself into a subject."[60]

The most dramatic revisions appear in the fourth and fifth editions. Beginning in the fourth edition, for example, even the thoughts of the exemplars are cited, something that had not been done in earlier editions. Readers are told, for instance, what two students, Tarō and Takeko, thought about a rousing speech by the principal of their school: "After hearing the speech, Tarō and Takeko thought, 'We ourselves have become third-year students, and thus we should unite our hearts, obey our teachers' instructions, and try to make our school even better.' "[61] In the same edition, the political conscience of the pro-imperial activist Yoshida Shōin is revealed:

[I] believe that our country is ruled by an emperor who represents a ten-thousand-year lineage. We have been the subjects of emperors from the time of our ancestors. The emperor loves his subjects with the magnanimity of his imperial forbears and sect, and his subjects, inheriting their predecessors' spirit, are completely loyal and just to the emperor. The emperor and his subjects form a single body, and loyalty and filial piety converge—this is what makes our country superior to all others. And it is important that all Japanese understand how precious is our national polity.[62]

This innovation opened up a whole new dimension of state-sponsored moral instruction. Surely, it is no coincidence that all references to what Confucians called the "good mind" *(ryōshin)* are eliminated in the fourth edition. In preceding editions this "good mind" was described as what enabled one "to distinguish between right and wrong" and what kept one from "doing the wrong thing."[63] The good mind also had been, from the seventeenth century onward, the moral basis for direct antigovernmental action, the basis for resistance. Nor is it coincidental that the government had been cracking down on those seen as posing a threat to the "national polity"— chiefly socialists and communists—since the spring of 1928. By the time the fourth edition was released, the government had arrested over two thousand leftists.[64] Maruyama Masao's observation is relevant here, namely, that an independent moral conscience was not legally protected in Japan before 1945, as it was in the West, and that the Japanese state from the Meiji Restoration to the end of the Second World War intruded freely into the private, "interior, subjective sphere" of its citizens' lives.[65]

Models were more important in the fourth edition. As before, paragons of a particular virtue are paraded in the textbooks, but if their value as exemplars was once tacit, it is now explicit. The word "model" *(tehon)* appears for the first time, and readers are even advised "to become models" for others.[66] The reader for second-year students, for example, features Tarō and Takeko:

> When the whole class was assembled, Tarō and Takeko became second-year students. They are completely familiar with everything; school is like home. The cute first-year students have entered the school, and Tarō and Takeko, feeling like older brothers and sisters, look after them. When they get to school in the morning, they call them over and play with them. The new second-year students, Tarō and Takeko, study well and play hard and have become even better children and *believe that they will probably be models* for the first-year students.[67]

In the opening section of the text for third-year pupils, the principal of a school speaks of students who, after graduating, have become models.[68] Here, too, the message is clear: one should not only imitate the behavior of the models but also be models for others.

At first glance this renewed interest in modeling may seem to point to a further deepening of the texts' Confucian content, but in fact it does not. Rather, the chief concern here is not the moral cultivation of the individual but the state. This was in keeping with the guidelines for revision issued by the Ministry of Education; the new text was "to transmit the essentials of a morality appropriate to loyal and good Japanese subjects" and "to clarify further the concept of a national polity."[69] The state was now everything, and Tarō and Takeko counted for very little except as its subjects. When one considers the combined impact of this change and the introduction of passages representing the thoughts of the fictional and historical characters presented in the texts, Maruyama's analysis seems apt, and both the significance of these changes in the Confucian material in the texts and the direction in which they point are evident.

As many commentators have pointed out, the most dramatic revisions are in the last edition of the texts, which first began to appear in 1941.[70] In sum, the content of this edition is highly nationalistic, which is hardly surprising, given that the Japanese had been waging an aggressive war on the Asian mainland for several years, were on the verge of war with the United States and its allies when the first volume was issued, and were fully at war with the Allied forces when the other volumes were published. Yet this was not a sudden or dramatic change, for the texts had gradually become more and more nationalistic over the years, beginning with the second edition. One of the criticisms of the first edition was that most of the lessons impart only what is necessary to be of use in society and to succeed in business, and the introduction of many more entries that centered on the state and the imperial house was a response to this criticism. This trend continued and was apparent even in the third edition, which appeared in an era of democracy and internationalism, and was intensified in the fourth edition, which, as we have just seen, was revised with an eye to creating "loyal and good Japanese subjects" and to "clarifying the national polity." But this trend assumed its most extreme form in the fifth edition.

These revisions are ubiquitous, with repeated references to "Japan," "the country," and "our country."[71] Various representations of Japan appear often: the rising sun; the flag; the emperor, empress, imperial house, and divine ancestors; the national anthem; and the Ise, Izumo, and Yasukuni shrines.[72] The descriptions of Japan, its people, and its culture are telling: the Japanese are described as the politest people in the world.[73] Indeed, they are said to take such special care when they speak that they are able to express the deepest and most profound sentiments.[74] Even the change of seasons in Japan is described with such enthusiasm that naive readers could easily have been led to believe that spring and fall in Japan were unlike spring and fall anywhere else in the world. "The Country of Japan," a chapter in the second-year reader, is typical:

A bright and pleasant spring has arrived. Japan is a country with beautiful spring, summer, fall, and winter scenery. It is a country with beau-

tiful mountains and rivers and seas. And it is in this fine country that
we were born. Both father and mother were born in this country as
well, and uncle and aunt were born here, too.

> Japan is a fine country,
>   a pure country.
> The only divine country
>   in the world.
>
> Japan is a fine country,
>   a strong country.
> A glittering and great
>   world country.[75]

As in this passage, Japan is frequently described in the fifth edition as superior to all other countries because it is divine.[76]

One of the most important, though subtle, changes was the addition of
references to war. The imagery, symbols, and language of war are introduced
at regular intervals, as is the paraphernalia of war—helmets, canteens, fire
drills, tanks, aircraft, and other things that suggest combat.[77] Servicemen
often appear as conquerors and occupiers, as ordinary citizens fulfilling their
national duty, and as selfless heroes willing to die for their monarch and
country.[78] All of these allusions and references to war constitute what one
critic has called "a structure of attitude and reference" within which children
reading the texts could locate themselves.[79]

The wartime edition brought a second change that had profound implications for the Confucian material. The first-person pronouns "I" and "we"
generally replace named figures as the main subjects of the texts. The exceptions are historical figures who could not be elided very easily with the reader
and whose temporal distance actually made them ideal models. This change
is especially conspicuous in the readers for first- and second-year students.
"I" (watakushi) and "we" (watakushitachi) replace Tarō, Takeko, Masao,
and others who had appeared in earlier editions. The "I" here "does not
make his or her parents worry"; "sweeps the garden"; takes care of the house
while another runs an errand; "politely bows to a visiting aunt, helps her
mother, and carries out the tea"; "gets her own schoolbag together"; "tries
on a lord's helmet"; "goes fishing for minnows"; "plays hard"; brings water
to the house; and writes a letter to a soldier.[80] The "we" of these texts is
described as looking after younger students; "truly feeling gratitude" for the
kindness of the emperor and empress; trudging to school in a blizzard; "joining together to collect all sorts of things to sell so planes and tanks can be
made"; watching a portable shrine pass by; and going on a school excur-

sion.[81] And, of course, it is "we, all together" *(watakushitachi . . . mina so-rotte)* who advance to the next grade,[82] and the "collective we" whose "ancestors have been loyal to emperors for generations" and who perform the "supreme obeisance" on the emperor's birthday.[83] As these examples suggest, the individual reader was encouraged, even expected, to make the leap from self to family, then to school, and finally to the nation. Apparently this was so by design, for the structure of this progression echoes the commentary in the teacher's manual accompanying the text: "The new national morality encompasses the so-called social morality and individual morality."[84]

Finally, the last edition was distinctive in one other way: it attempted to engage its readers on an affective rather than a conceptual level by introducing highly poetic language designed to elicit emotional responses. Consider the opening section of the second-year text:

> The classrooms have changed.
> The desks have changed.
> How wonderful!
>
> The first-year students have started school.
> [We] have lots of younger brothers and sisters.
> How wonderful!
>
> The books are new.
> The notebooks are new.
> [We] have become second-year students and are happy![85]

This is a far cry from the descriptive narratives that opened the chapters in earlier editions. "The Rising Sun Flag," a chapter in the third-year text, is typical:

> A blue, clear sky.
> Flying just at the eaves,
>   the rising sun flag
> is truly dignified.
>
> Snowbound houses.
> Flying just at the eaves,
>   the rising sun flag
> somehow seems warm.[86]

This attempt to engage the readers on an affective level was actually mandated and had been the stated aim of the compilers of the fourth edition, who wrote that "emphasis will be placed on developing the affective and volitional aspects of the youngsters' moral character . . . and special care will be taken to affect their feelings."[87] Their design was realized in the fifth edition.

These changes, however, adversely affected the Confucian content of the ethics texts. The submersion of the individual in ever-larger collectives that culminated in the state, as well as the appeal to emotion, countered the idea of moral self-cultivation. The intense nationalism that informs the texts, with its insistence on loyalty to the emperor and sacrifice for the nation, left little room for other, potentially competing norms. One could argue that the activities of the "I" in the first- and second-year readers suggest that Confucian virtue survived; after all, the needs and concerns of parents were satisfied, and parental commands were faithfully fulfilled. Nonetheless, this may simply reflect a greater interest in the family as a subset of the state than in filial children.

The careful conflation of loyalty and filial piety is revealing in this regard. From the mid-thirties, Ministry of Education writers insisted that being loyal to the emperor and filial to one's parents were one and the same thing. In *Kokutai no Hongi* (Cardinal Principles of the National Polity of Japan), which was released in 1937, one reads: "For us to show loyalty to the Emperor is in effect a manifestation of the manners and customs of our ancestors, and this is why we show filial piety to our forefathers."[88] The writers of *Kokutai no Hongi* took some care in defining the relationship of loyalty and filial piety. "Filial piety directly has for its object one's parents," they write, "but in the relationship toward the emperor finds a place within loyalty."[89] And when they add, "There is no filial piety apart from loyalty and filial piety has loyalty for its basis," the priority of the state over the family is clear.[90]

In my opinion, the fate of Confucianism in the last edition can be described in two ways. There certainly were, to be sure, residues of a Confucian ethical language that stressed the importance of spiritual growth and development. These residues, however, were now nothing more than a language of action; in those places where Confucian terminology survived, it was carefully misread to serve the needs of the state. "The national ethics course," reads a passage in section 3 of the Rules for the Implementation of the National School Law, "is based on the principles of the Rescript on Education, directs the practice of national morality, nourishes the moral character of youngsters, and makes them aware of the righteous moral mission of the imperial nation."[91] The phrases "directs the practice" and "nourishes the moral character of youngsters" come from the original "Principles of Compilation" but have been dramatically miscast: the morality of the individual has become the "practice of national morality," while "nourishing the moral character of youngsters" is placed between "national morality" and the "righteous mission of the imperial nation." What now matters most is "citizens' morality" *(kokumin dōtoku)* and loyalty to the "imperial nation," not "nourishing the moral character of youngsters" or "directing their practice of morality." The teacher's manual accompanying the fifth edition is absolutely clear on this point: "Citizens' morality encompasses what is called social morality and individual morality,"[92] and "the well-spring of filial piety, friendship, harmony, trust, modesty and respect, and universal love is loyalty."[93]

That the ethics textbooks used in Japanese schools between 1904 and 1945 contain Confucian material is indisputable. The texts introduce major Confucian concepts such as learning, filial piety, loyalty, and courage. They stress the importance of the five cardinal social relationships—those between rulers and subjects, husbands and wives, parents and children, siblings, and friends. They also rely almost exclusively on biography as a medium of moral instruction and assume the efficacy of biographical narratives. Moreover, the exemplars presented in the texts include Japanese Confucians from the early modern period such as Arai Hakuseki, Itō Jinsai, Ogyū Sorai, and many others.

There are two explanations for the presence of Confucian material in the texts. First, those who compiled the early texts had had a Confucian education, and so their conceptions of morality were still unmistakably Confucian. This was true even of those who were well versed in Western philosophy, such as Katō Hiroyuki, and may point, as Matsumoto Sannosuke once suggested, to the determinative impact of a Confucian education on the first generation of modern Japanese intellectuals.[94] Revealing in this regard are the recurrence of words such as "cultivation," "nourishment," and "moral practice" in the policy statements of those who designed the first texts.

The second explanation is that government authorities found Confucian ethical discourse eminently usable. Confucian moral traits and behaviors were still familiar to the Japanese, even in the early years of this century, and supplied a means for the state to cultivate willing subjects. After all, the Confucian material presented in the texts constituted a language of service and subordination that configured social relations along vertical lines, recognizing as given the authority of parents, teachers, and the imperial family, accepting larger collectives such as the family, schools, military, and the nation, and encouraging youngsters to serve, even to sacrifice themselves for these collectives and their betters.

Telling in this regard is the selectivity with which the Confucian material was used, especially with respect to what was excluded. "Humanity" *(jin;*

Chinese: *jen*), a central Confucian concept, is not featured, and "righteousness" (*gi*; Chinese: *yi*), sometimes translated as "justice," is mentioned only infrequently, perhaps because neither was regarded as particularly useful. Even more significant is the deletion of the notion of the "good mind" (*ryōshin*; Chinese: *liang-hsin*) from the fourth and fifth editions for the reasons given earlier. The deletion of "good mind" was, however, only one of many revisions made in the 1930s and early 1940s that transformed the meaning of the Confucian material in the texts. Equally important was the intensification of the texts' nationalistic content, the introduction of war, the displacement of named characters by first-person pronouns, and the calculated appeal to the readers' emotions. In the end, what survived was barely recognizable as Confucian.

What must be noted, however, is that from the outset the ethics texts were being revised continually. One need only compare the first, second, and third editions to see this. Those responsible for the texts took the task of revision seriously, and assiduously worked at improving the texts and keeping them up-to-date. Beyond the varying format, layout, and illustrations, the most important changes were the texts' increasing realism, the use of direct discourse, fuller biographical narratives, the addition of historical material, and the gradual exclusion of non-Japanese exemplars. Ultimately, these changes increased the efficacy of the texts as instruments of state control and thus ensured that scores of Japanese youngsters would be imbued with values, behaviors, and a broad outlook that, though identifiably Confucian, had been appropriated by a modern Japanese state and reshaped to serve its needs.

7

THE JAPANESE (CONFUCIAN) FAMILY

The Tradition from the Bottom Up

Robert J. Smith

Roderick MacFarquhar has noted that "most contemporary East Asians do not share the elite's concern about identity as Chinese or Japanese but do care about what it means to be an individual in a Confucian family. Confucius was right to emphasize the family's role as the root of stability, and it is incumbent on those who wish to understand Confucianism to examine the traditions from the bottom up, not from the top down."[1] Although I doubt that many contemporary Japanese think of themselves as members of a *Confucian* family, they certainly are preoccupied with the benefits and costs of what it means to be a member of a *family*. Nonetheless, it is an injunction calculated to delight the heart of any anthropologist, for it suggests the need for some intensive field research. Because I have been unable to conduct such research for this essay, it is in the main a review of the programs and policies that were calculated to make Confucianists of the Japanese.

There is little doubt that the family in contemporary Japan remains the source of moral order. The central question, then, is easily posed: To what extent has the Japanese family ever been Confucian, and to what extent is it today? Would that the question could be so easily answered.[2] Even the most casual survey of the vicissitudes of Confucianism in Japan suggests the need for caution. Indeed, I was tempted to indicate just how cautious one must be by titling this essay either "Confucianism Is in the Eye of the Be-holder" or "Confucian Is as Confucian Does." That is to say, how Confucianism is described, the praises sung of it, the importance assigned to it, and the terms in which it is denounced all are very strongly colored by the historical period in which the assessments are made, the position in the social hierarchy of the person expressing the opinion, and—not least in recent times—the age and gender of those whose views they are.

I hasten to add that in these respects Confucianism seems to me rather like all other philosophical, ethical, and/or religious systems of whatever time or place. An example, drawn from personal experience with one such system, involves one of the myriad subcategories of the southern United States brand of Protestantism. Fifty years ago its construction of Christianity was a finely crafted one that had no place for Catholics, who were thought of as idolaters, or for Quakers, of whom few had ever heard. Depending on the particular church and the position of its minister on the issue, it was not always entirely clear that Methodists and Presbyterians were Christian either.

Be that as it may, did my relatives and neighbors think that they themselves led Christian lives? Of course they did, or tried to. Were it to be pointed out that someone had committed some "unchristian" act, the usual explanations were that all are conceived and born in sin, that everyone backslides from time to time, that no one is perfect, that it had all happened before the miscreant had found God—or perhaps it was that Christ had found *him*. It is all now too far in the past for me to recall the full inventory of shifting grounds on which our neighbors and relatives took their unshakable Christian stands. Would they have agreed—and do they still—that the United States is a "Christian country"? Of course. They have never doubted it, for among other things, our uninterrupted string of victories in war[3] is taken as a sure sign either that we are on God's side or that he is on ours. Yet I wager that in the course of conducting interviews on the subject, you could collect scores of definitions—some of them flatly contradictory—of just what the term "a Christian country" might mean. There is bound to be some overlap, to be sure, but no consensus. Are we then to conclude that the United States is *not* a Christian country? I think not.[4] But I submit that consensus on the religious and ethical dimensions of Christianity is not much more likely to be achieved than agreement as to precisely what Confucianism might be and whether the Japanese family is a Confucian institution.

It is possible, of course, that I am looking in the wrong place for an authoritative definition, and would be better advised to seek it among the philosophers, the theologians, the ethicists, or the intellectual historians. My reading of the relevant sources, however, strongly suggests that consensus at the top is even more difficult to achieve than at the bottom. In any event, my anthropological training predisposes me to start at ground level. Setting aside for the moment questions of authenticity and authority ("What is Confucianism?" and "Who says so?"), I have asked a hopelessly unrepresentative sample of Japanese colleagues, acquaintances, and friends whether contemporary Japanese think of themselves or their families as Confucian. The spontaneous answer is a resounding no, often supplemented by a dismissive reference to the conservative, reactionary, or feudal (a favorite term of opprobrium in Japan) character of its teachings. The implication is that one's grandfather or great-grandfather may have been taught Confucian ethics and might even have internalized them, but in 1945 the Japanese consigned Confucianism to the dustbin of history.

Because I am generally suspicious of the claim that any society has made a complete break with the past,[5] the results of further inquiry suggest that contemporary Japanese are likely to attribute very limited aspects of the institution of the family to what they regard as residual Confucian influence—the emphasis on respect for parents, which is associated with the duty to perform the ancestral rites, and the assignment of low status to women. Note, however, that the ancestral rites are viewed in a generally positive light, the status assigned women in a highly negative one. In the popular view, then, Confucian teachings are credited with the former and charged with the latter.[6] Have the centuries of promotion by the authorities of what they regarded as (or represented as) Confucian teachings left the Japanese only this?

Because it is impossible to review the entire history of their efforts, I take up only the period since the Meiji Restoration of 1868, and that in barest outline. I emphasize family law and the educational system, for if the authorities ever intended to make Confucianists of the Japanese, it was through the schools that they proposed to achieve their aim. My purpose is to try to show how very difficult it is to untangle the many elements that went into the formulation of educational policy.[7] Only some of them are traceable directly to Confucian teaching, and of these many are represented by their promoters as having other (often Western) origins.

I hope to show that it is impossible to advance a plausible argument that the Japanese family today is Confucian in the strict sense. It is equally impossible to argue that it has been completely purged of the effects of attempts by the authorities to structure it in terms of selected Confucian principles.

WHAT IS (JAPANESE) CONFUCIANISM?

The question is answerable in at least as many, and probably in far more, ways as it is for (Chinese) Confucianism. Julia Ching tells us that it may refer to the ethical teachings of the historical Confucius; it may refer to the centuries-long development called the Confucian tradition, which ranges from the profoundly practical to the metaphysical: "And it may frequently refer, to the uncritical mind—even among the educated—to the twentieth century Confucian 'vestiges': to the ethical teachings concerning political loyalty, filial piety, female chastity, and justice or righteousness, or to the 'Confucian' social structure, in which these teachings have become embedded."[8] She goes on to say that the term "Neo-Confucian" is even more ambiguous, which hardly augurs well for any attempt to illuminate the Japanese situation. Before turning to that issue, however, note her use of the words "uncritical mind," which suggests to me that she is referring to people very like my southern friends and relatives, who, without thinking a lot about the matter or consulting higher authorities, are quite able to list the distinctive characteristics of what they believe to be "Christian teachings."

There is one obvious difference between the role of Confucianism in China and Japan, where it has always been only one of many competing ideologies, philosophies, and ethical systems, and never, as in China, "a way of life encompassing the ultimate standards for Chinese social and political order."[9] Given the centuries of Japanese heterodoxy, it follows that from time to time, purists of various persuasions have accused both Japanese Buddhists and Japanese Confucianists of promoting alien religions and philosophies. Not surprisingly, then, both Buddhists and Confucianists often have chosen to forge alliances with adherents of Shinto and, on occasion, with one another. The course of these developments has been characterized by one observer in this way:

> Japanese Confucianism started as a cultural ideology serving the political needs of the Tokugawa Bakufu, and its flexibility made it useful for other social purposes as well. To these initially different conditions was added the internal intellectual dynamism retained by the Japanese Confucianists, whose attitude toward Confucianism was dictated by a sense of social utilitarianism. As time went on, Japanese Confucianism diverged further and further from its origin as a politicized cultural ideology and became a collection of social and ethical codes in support of certain kinds of social actions.[10]

This position is perhaps the most widely shared of all those taken with respect to the role of Confucian teachings in Japan. As John Haley writes:

> Legal rules could and did reflect ethical concerns. Indeed, law was an attempt by government to enforce the proscriptions of Confucian or Neo-Confucian ideology . . . Confucian thought encompassed what

may be called a natural law or moral order. It was not, however, of deistic origin. Confucian ideology was more of a sociology in which social harmony and a consequent political stability were the principal aims of public policy and were to be achieved by adherence to behavioral norms rooted in familial and status relationships. Those below owed filial piety and loyalty to those in authority who, in turn, owed benevolence as a reciprocal but not conditional social duty.[11]

Although for a time Confucianism had been discredited along with everything else associated with the shogunate, it gained currency again with the consolidation of conservative power in the late 1920s and 1930s. And it was in the 1930s, as Ronald Dore writes,

that pilgrimages to the Mito school became popular, that educational historians began writing fulsome books of praise about their Tokugawa forerunners, that the Shingaku movement was revived, that Tokugawa-style swordsmanship was brought back into the schools and that the selected writings of certain Tokugawa Confucianists became most popular in high school curricula. The decade when Japanese society was being reduced at the hands of fanatics to its most stifling condition of oppressive irrationalism was the decade in which the ideals of the Japanese educational world were closer to those of its Tokugawa past than at any time since 1870.[12]

Is it any wonder that today's Japanese, if they have thought about it at all, are likely to view Confucianism in a negative light? Not so long ago, after all, it suffused the world of Bushido and provided the language, if not the content, of Japanese authoritarianism at its most repressive stage.

Yet there is much to recommend the position that identifies humanism, rationalism, historical-mindedness, and ethnocentrism as characteristics of Neo-Confucian thought, each of them in varying degrees and contexts conspicuous in Tokugawa discourse.[13] As for humanism, while some have pointed to Confucianism's emphasis on the spiritual equality of human beings, others remind us that it was quite possible for the Japanese to: "reach this egalitarian point of view from any one of the three religions familiar to most Japanese: Confucianism teaches the universality of Heaven's Way— Tendō—in which the potential for moral action is granted without favor; Buddhism believes in spiritual salvation for all human beings; and Shinto nourishes the view that a divine spirit or *kokoro* joins all beings and things without differentiation."[14]

Indeed, we may enlist the aid of no less exalted a personage than Tokugawa Ieyasu himself in illustrating how elusive the historical sources are for the most central values of the Japanese. This little tale, whether apocryphal or not, is worth volumes of formal exegesis:

> At Suruga Castle one evening after the Osaka campaign, Ieyasu summoned his attendants before him and spoke thus: "As you know, I was born in the very midst of the period of turbulent warfare. Every day, from dawn to dusk and since my boyhood, my body and soul have been given to the councils of war. I have had little time to pursue learning. However, there is a line from a text I have studied which I have always retained in my mind. I have always acted according to the principle expressed in that one line in attempting to establish by deeds the fortunes of my family. What do you think that line is, and where does it come from: the Confucian canon or the biographies of the sages, or the words of Buddha? I should like you to think about it," he ordered.
>
> Among those in attendance on that occasion were some who possessed great learning. They ventured one answer after another, only to be told they were incorrect. Soon all admitted that they did not know the answer. Then Ieyasu spoke thus: "From the statements you have just made suggesting the presence of the line in the Four Books and the Five Classics, or in the sayings of the sages and the scholars, this line must indeed be an important text in literary studies. However, as you know, I am unlettered, and therefore I am not certain of its source. At any rate, the line which I learned in my boyhood and which I have always retained in my mind runs, 'Requite malice with kindness.' It has been useful to me on many occasions, great and small. That is the secret formula I wish to confide to you today," said Ieyasu smiling.[15]

Were the Japanese ever Confucianists in, say, the same sense as the Koreans? No one claims that they were. Nevertheless, there are many ways in which the Confucianist concern with hierarchical relationships and its emphasis on harmonious families as the basis for harmonious states seems to have influenced Japanese society. Be that as it may, it is just as likely that the Japanese selectively utilized Confucian teachings to reaffirm and strengthen characteristics of their society, which was deeply rooted in the pre-Confucian past.[16]

Presumably one of the domains in which Confucianism did not simply reinforce and justify older social practices is the treatment of women, for it is widely argued that they enjoyed a far more favorable position in Japanese society before the introduction of Confucianism. It may well be, however, that the decline of women's status in Japan actually began with the popularization of Buddhism. Setting aside questions of historical priority, Peter Nosco is more concerned with examining those aspects of Tokugawa Confucianism that were alien to long-established Japanese orientations:

> Confucian philosophy tends to appear in Tokugawa literature as appealing more to the intellect than to the heart, and being more rational than emotional. In fact, Confucianism seems to emerge in Tokugawa literature as a highly charged metaphor for a complex set of identifications that would include Chineseness as opposed to Japaneseness, *giri,* or a preoccupation with moral behavior, as opposed to *ninjō,* or a resignation to the demands of the heart, craftiness as opposed to wit, and even stuffiness or aloofness as opposed to a more casual demeanor.[17]

THE EDUCATIONAL SYSTEM

The *Analects* had been widely disseminated among warrior and commoner classes alike well before the Meiji period.[18] By the late Tokugawa the Four Books and Five Classics had become the core curriculum in almost all domain schools; National Learning *(kokugaku)* had been introduced into about one third of them, "Western learning" in about one quarter.[19] The Confucian ethic clearly had ramified widely throughout Japanese society and was an important source for moral concepts not only in the warrior class but among the commoners as well.[20] Indeed, it is often observed that despite the intensive efforts of the ideologues to shore it up, Confucian influence in Japanese society at large actually began to ebb sharply with the introduction of Western educational goals after 1868.[21]

The Great Principles of Education *(kyōgaku taishi),* issued by the court in 1879, established Confucian teachings as the basis for public education. This document represents the victory of Motoda Nagazane (Eifu), Confucian tutor to the Meiji emperor, over the supporters of an education founded primarily on Western learning. In Motoda's view the goal of education was the development of moral men,[22] and therefore it was incumbent on the designers of the educational system to devise a national orthodoxy. To counter the liberalism and Western-inspired scientific learning that had come to dominate the educational enterprise, the Imperial Rescript on Education *(kyōiku chokugo)* was issued in 1890. In it was reaffirmed the traditional stance, combining elements of Confucian ethical teaching, National Learning, and Shinto statism with a Western orientation to learning.[23]

So goes the story as it is often told, but in fact the tale is a good deal more complicated. The "traditional stance" referred to is said to have developed

throughout the Tokugawa period. How was it constituted? As Martin Collcutt writes:

> Early in the period Hayashi Razan, Yamazaki Anzai, Nakae Tōju, and
> Kumazawa Banzan, in their efforts to liberate Confucian teachings
> from Buddhist influence [the Five Virtues had become an integral part
> of popular Buddhism], advocated an alliance of Confucian ethics and
> Shinto devotion . . . At the same time, from the Shinto side, Watari
> Nobuyuki was urging a Shinto-Confucian synthesis as a way of freeing
> Ise Shinto from Buddhist contamination. In Edo, Yoshikawa Koretaru
> and his successors, as hereditary Shinto ritualists . . . were advocates
> of pure *(yuitsu)* Shinto . . . During the eighteenth and nineteenth cen-
> turies, scholars advocating "national learning" *(kokugaku)* mounted
> an increasingly determined attack on both Confucianism and Bud-
> dhism.[24]

From this mix, it would appear, the framers of the Imperial Rescript on
Education included a little something for everyone—except, perhaps, the
Buddhists. In light of the amount of credit or blame later given the rescript
for its role in promoting the dissemination of the Confucian ethic, it comes
as some surprise to discover that from its promulgation conservatives had
objected strongly to its alien Confucian flavor. In 1912 its real author, Yoshikawa Akimasa, rejected the charge:

> As people know, the Imperial Rescript on Education was based on the
> four virtues: benevolence, righteousness, loyalty, and filial piety. The
> making of these four virtues the foundation of the national education
> was, however, strongly criticized at the time, and some scholars even
> declared that these virtues were imported from China and ought never
> to be established as the standard of the nation's morality. Others have
> said that, should such old-fashioned virtues be encouraged among peo-
> ple, it would mean the revival of the old form of virtue typified by
> private revenge, etc. But I strongly upheld the teaching of those four
> principal virtues, saying that *the essence of man's morality is one and
> the same irrespective of place or time,* although it might take different
> forms according to different circumstances, and that therefore the
> aforesaid four virtues could well be made the moral standard of the
> Japanese people.[25]

Here Yoshikawa takes the universalistic view that because "the essence
of man's morality is one and the same irrespective of place or time," it does
not much matter where we find the texts with which to teach it.[26] One may
doubt that any such universalism motivated those who later produced two

documents that had enormous influence on the preparation of school text-books in the immediate prewar years, "The Cardinal Principles of the National Entity" *(kokutai no hongi)* and "The Way of the Subject" *(shinmin no michi)* in 1937 and 1941, respectively.[27]

Did the textbooks used in the secondary schools of the Meiji period faithfully reflect the injunctions of the rescript? E. Patricia Tsurumi has carried out a survey of the language *(kokugo)* and morality/ethics *(shūshin)* texts of the first thirty years of the Meiji period (1870–1900),[28] with intriguing results:

> During the Meiji period, primary schooling was carefully designed to impart values as well as to provide elementary scientific knowledge and to teach the rudiments of reading, writing and arithmetic. Some of these values were obviously new and foreign . . . But many of the ideals taught to Meiji schoolchildren would have been very familiar to young samurai pupils or even to commoners who went to school before the Meiji Restoration . . . Such traditional values included frugality, obedience, patience, endurance, courage, selflessness, modesty, decorum, harmony and honesty, with prime importance placed upon loyalty and filial piety. Indeed, the other values were usually treated as part of one or both of these two essential qualities.[29]

Although much Western material was introduced,

> even in the 1870s the content of Japanese language and ethics courses was by no means solely Western. The Primary School Regulations issued in September 1873 stipulated that ethics lessons in the first and second grades should not use textbooks but instead should be given orally by the teacher. Since the majority of the teachers came from the Confucian-oriented samurai class, it is highly likely that many of their talks on morality concerned loyalty, filial piety, respect for status and authority in a hierarchical social order, and all the virtues which were to be cultivated along with these qualities.[30]

Tsurumi also notes: "Certainly ethics texts published after the 1890 rescript contained heavy doses of loyalty and filial piety. But although both the ideal Confucian society and the new Japan were hierarchically ordered worlds, there was always room in primary school ethics textbooks for individuals who rose suddenly from very humble beginnings."[31] She finds, further, that

> the Meiji child was presented with a rich if sometimes confusing array of ideals. Assuming that formation of the mature adult's system of

values begins in childhood, the citizens of Meiji Japan had rare opportunities to choose among different systems of morality, or at least to become acquainted with different systems. One might have gained the beginnings of an ideology or individual self-reliance and achievement in a Meiji classroom. Or one might have made one's start towards becoming a Confucian gentleman. Or, as the Meiji oligarchs hoped, one might have acquired a staunch allegiance to the country's official moral code.[32]

The situation had changed rather dramatically by the early 1930s, as Dore has suggested. Un Sun Song has examined the ethics and language readers used in elementary schools during a later period, between 1933–1941.[33] Although the former took up only about 7 percent of instructional time and the latter almost 40 percent, unlike Tsurumi, Song believes that the ethics texts are the more important for their ideological content. The three mileposts in the development of the textbooks in question are the Imperial Rescript on Education (kyōiku chokugo, 1890), the Cardinal Principles of the National Entity of Japan (kokutai no hongi, 1937), and the Way of the Subject (shinmin no michi, 1941). The elementary school ethics text (jinjō shōgaku shūshin-sho), which was in use at the outbreak of the Second World War, contains two heavily Confucian sections. One, "The Ethical Drive: The Confucian Relationships," is accompanied by a teacher's manual note: "The purpose of this chapter is to teach the pupils to work constantly at cultivating their morals, to make themselves men of ability, and to become national figures."[34] The name of Confucius figures prominently, and the relationships discussed include those between brothers, sisters, relatives, friends, and neighbors. The second of the two sections, "Filial Piety," also is accompanied by a teacher's manual note: "The purpose of this chapter is to clarify the true nature of the family in our country [and to teach the children] to respect our ancestors and family, and to fulfill the way of dutifulness."[35]

Following the end of the war, it was the concern of the Occupation forces to restructure the educational system along American lines, which they did with a vengeance. In late 1952, in the waning days of the Occupation, Amano Teiyū, Minister of Education, apparently perceiving a need to replace the outlawed Imperial Rescript on Education, drafted a document titled "An Outline of Ethical Practice for the Japanese People." Leaked to the press, it raised such a storm of criticism that Amano withdrew it, canceled plans to have it published, and instead distributed it to the schools as his personal views on the subject of education. The document uses certain key words that have a long history in Japanese thought, some of them specifically Confucian. These include three terms for "morality" or "morals": (dōgi), which has traditional Confucian associations; *dōtoku,* a more common Confucian term that now is more familiar as the translation of "morality" in Western philosophy; and *rinri,* the standard translation of "ethics." The word *wa,* which is generally used in Confucian contexts, occurs in expressions such as *fūfu no wa,* the Confucian ideal of marital harmony. By far the most clearly Confucian terminology used is *jinrin no kankei,* the five basic moral relationships, which is almost never encountered in any other context.[36] For all the survivals of Confucian vocabulary, what those who viewed Amano's document with such alarm failed to realize was that the Ministry of Education would never have issued such a document in prewar Japan, for Amano concluded that, "albeit in the vaguest terms, the individual is given his place in society and his duties are no longer summarised in terms of loyalty and filial piety or of correct behavior in the traditional five human relationships of Confucianism."[37] Nevertheless, Amano's statement makes it clear that the family remains the link between the individual and the state; society is a collection of families, not of individuals.[38]

In 1958 the Ministry of Education introduced into the curriculum an entirely new course, to be taught one hour a week. Called *dōtoku,* it was made compulsory in 1962, but schools were not required to use the Ministry-approved ethics texts designed for the course. Betty Lanham, who has compared the prewar *shūshin* texts with these postwar *dōtoku* ones, reports that the similarities are fewer than the differences.[39] Not surprisingly, she finds that the prewar lessons on ancestor worship, loyalty, etiquette, and respect for teachers are gone. The *shūshin* texts' sections on sibling relationships and filial piety, among their most "Confucian," have been deleted, but in the postwar books there still are stories emphasizing gratitude to one's parents and to national figures of historical importance.

How is Confucianism represented in the middle and high school textbooks on ethics and society today? The topic is discussed only in the section titled "Chinese Thought":

> Confucian Chinese thought, as discussed in the textbooks, has nothing to do with religion. Confucianism is presented as a moral system which guides human conduct in the family, in society, and in politics. It is a philosophy dealing with present-day reality and with man's moral conduct in its human relations within the familial, social and political spheres of Chinese society. Confucianism, which is not founded on any religious belief, is closer to the philosophy of Socrates than are Buddhism and Christianity.[40]

The textbooks stress the five virtues and the concept of *jin,* and point out that the notions of benevolence, loyalty, filial piety, respect, and sincerity exerted great influence on the thinking and conduct of the Japanese people. Confucianism is characterized as a moral code designed for both ruler and subject, with its goal of "the attainment of a perfect society."[41]

FAMILY LAW

It is not in moral and ethical education alone that we must look for Confucian influence, of course. At the end of the Tokugawa era, the new Meiji government faced the staggering task of creating viable new values for an old society. They realized that they had to achieve unity within the country while at the same time changing many indigenous customs in order to gain recognition by the Western powers as an equal. Robert Epp writes:

> Motivation for the discovery of Western civil codes was external and internal. The external motive was of course the pressure of the Powers and their forced treaties; the internal motive was the Confucian tradition in which all samurai had been schooled. This was a tradition which stressed the need for properly ordered interpersonal relationships if the state was to be strong, an end obtained by perfecting the individual. The individual in turn was perfected by study . . . [After the 1860s] both ethical and national sanctions supported the need to study and to regulate interpersonal relationships. Therefore it was natural for the Japanese to inquire into and investigate the Western means of achieving this end: a civil code.[42]

An early attempt to adapt the Code Napoléon to Japanese usages dragged on for almost a decade. The eventual collapse of that effort and the long delay between 1878 and 1898 gave the traditionalists time to regroup, and in the end they were successful in reasserting the values they cherished. When the Meiji Civil Code *(minpō)* was finally promulgated thirty years after the Restoration, it turned out that its drafters had filled their new wineskins with old wine.[43] On the face of it, it seems a doomed course of action, but the new wineskins remained intact for two generations. It may well be, as Eric Hobsbawm suggests, that in this endeavor at least, Japan is unique: "A 'modernization' which maintained the old ordering of social subordination (possibly with some well-judged inventions of tradition) was not theoretically inconceivable, but apart from Japan it is difficult to think of an example of practical success."[44]

The Civil Code provided all Japanese with a "traditional" family form, specified the rules of inheritance and succession, and assigned to the institution of the family the familiar Confucian role of foundation of the state. Yet, as a foreign observer correctly noted at the time, the adoption of the

Civil Code of 1898 nonetheless marked the transition of Japanese civil law from its long-standing Chinese basis to the Roman, adding only that "of all the social relations with which the new code deals, the family remains the least affected by occidental influences."[45] Munroe Smith's assessment, coming as it does within a few years of the promulgation of the code, seems to me defensible still. Smith does not say that the Japanese family "remains Confucian," but it would be difficult to sustain any other interpretation of his remark.

Hiroshi Wagatsuma writes:

> It was . . . an axiom of Chinese political philosophy generally that stable families ensured a stable society and that filial piety was a civic duty . . . The Japanese family, as a system of legal and political organization, was based upon these Confucian political principles . . . The family system was often regarded as synonymous with the ethical system, or at least as a conceptualized set of behavior patterns that had normative implications. These patterns strongly reflected Confucian ethical notions. Emphasis was placed on the individual's respect, obedience, and "piety" toward his parents, especially toward his father, and upon the observance of rank order within the family. Respect was required from a person of lower rank to a person of higher rank, that is, from children to parents, from younger siblings to older ones, from wife to husband, and generally from younger members to older members. The picture of a family governed by Confucian ethics often took on a "patriarchal" quality, although the benevolence of parents and a harmonious solidarity among family were equally emphasized.[46]

But there is a curious anomaly here. John Pelzel notes that although Japanese borrowing of Chinese terms and concepts was extensive,

> in few other areas of kinship were Chinese influences so direct and so obtrusive as in the propagation of marriage ideals and the dyadic concept of kin ties: and in few others was this influence so at variance with what seem to have been the basic Japanese ways.
>
> In early times filial piety was taken over as the main conscious principle governing the relations between parents and children, as were Chinese ideas about the subordinate status of women as daughters, sisters, and wives, and about the arranged marriage. Significantly, however, the other kin dyads stressed in the Chinese ideal—e.g., the tie between brother and brother—were hardly noted in Japan, then or thereafter, and the borrowed ideas about even the arranged marriage, the filial relations, or the subordination of women had little practical

significance until the Tokugawa period gave cachet to philosophical Confucianism. It is true that if one reads only the didactic, philosophical, and historicizing literature of the years from mid-Tokugawa through early Meiji, one is impressed by the prominence given these Chinese conceptions. Yet the *Twenty-Four Examples of Filial Piety* and similar homilies, as well as the *School for Women,* a book of precepts for the demure female, were widely disseminated for the first time only in the late seventeenth century.[47]

Recently widely disseminated or not, by the late nineteenth century these "Chinese Confucian" concepts were sufficiently well established among the warrior class to define for them the parameters of propriety. That the members of the Confucianized elite who were charged with framing the Civil Code of 1898 held very firm notions on the subject of proper familial relations is suggested by their reaction to what they were to discover about the typical Japanese family. The committee undertook to educate itself about prevailing customs by means of a nationwide survey. They were shocked to find that 90 percent of commoners practiced anomalous (e.g., not conforming to "Confucian rules" as they understood them) forms of marriage, kin reckoning, and household formation. So unorthodox did most of these practices seem to the members of the committee that they were moved to take corrective measures. Pelzel writes:

> The code they wrote reflected their own ideals, rather than the "anomalies" their survey revealed, and so put the Chinese model forward. In subsequent generations, the development of a national culture, and of mass education, literacy, and communications transmitting its standards, as well as widespread social climbing in terms of its symbols, gave greater currency and realization to that model than it had ever had before, even as in most other ways the Japanese were sprinting ever faster away from traditional Chinese prototypes. Of course, the same post-Meiji generations saw other cultural developments that diluted the Confucian orientation . . . Nevertheless, it is ironic that the clearest kinship influences from China gained status at only that time when Western ideas were also beginning to enter Japan.[48]

The Civil Code of 1898 was to remain in effect for less than fifty years—a circumstance not often mentioned by those who attribute to it such formative power in the construction of the prewar Japanese household. The code that replaced it went into effect in 1947,[49] and among the many results of the reforms it embodied, it is commonly observed, is that the Confucian definition of the role of father and husband has disappeared, and an egalitarian, more democratic definition of the new father and husband predominates.[50]

The problem is that this point of view greatly oversimplifies the issue by ignoring the considerable variations in Japanese family structure found historically. Toshio Fueto, for example, argues that those who see a need to revise the postwar Civil Code must examine inconsistencies between that code and what he calls the realities of family life in Japan. And so he poses an intriguing question: To what extent does the family structure visualized in the postwar Civil Code differ from social reality as compared to the extent to which that visualized in the Meiji Civil Code differed from the social reality of the time? He goes on:

> There are two types of family structure in Japan: the Confucian type and the popular type. The Confucian type was characteristic of the nobility, the great landowners, the great merchants, and the military class of feudal Japan; and the more indigenous popular type was characteristic of the farmer, fisherman, and the city commoner of feudal Japan. Neither type was democratic in the modern sense: the characteristic absolute authority of the family head—usually the husband or father—was more manifest in the Confucian type; but equally suppressive of individualistic thinking was the role of tradition and custom underlying the apparent co-operative spirit of the popular family type. In the intervening centuries, there has been considerable fusion of elements of each type, and their present-day distinction has become more one between rural and urban populations.[51]

This distinction between the elements of the population who were Confucianized and those who were not is routinely drawn. I once asked a Japanese anthropologist about what I thought to be a surprisingly high rate of extramarital sexual activity by men and women alike reported for a village in Kumamoto prefecture in the mid-1930s.[52] The answer, delivered without hesitation, was that the older people in these places behaved with such impropriety because they knew nothing of Shushigaku, the teachings of Chu Hsi!

THE ANCESTORS, RELIGION, AND THE QUESTION OF ORIGINS

One widely held view has it that the clearest answer to the question of whether or not Confucian elements survive in the Japanese family lies in an examination of the ancestral rites. At one extreme is Nobuyuki Kaji, who argues that Confucianism is far more than a secular moral and ethical code,

and that the essential religiosity of Japanese Confucianism is evidenced by
the rites of ancestor worship. Although his position is extreme, it is worth
setting out for the construction he puts on Confucian teaching: "The ideal
of filial piety has long been interpreted in Japan simply as respect for parental
authority, but that is a mere part of what Confucius taught. The Confucian
ideal consists of continuing the ancestral cult by worshiping dead ancestors,
by paying respect to living parents, and by giving birth to progeny. To Confucianists, filial piety embraces obligations toward one's ancestors and descendants equally as strong as the obligation to honor one's parents."[53] Furthermore, the religious aspects of Confucianism are deeply rooted in the
Japanese consciousness: "The Japanese family is an excellent example. Even
during and after the great upheavals Japan experienced in the wake of World
War II, the custom of venerating ancestors remained unaltered. And today,
erecting graves and holding memorial services for dead ancestors is more
popular in Japan than ever before. *However, people have the misconception
that these rituals are of Buddhist origin.*"[54]

I think he is wrong. Few Japanese today have any considered opinion
about the *origin* of the ancestral rites, but they are in no doubt whatsoever
that the *idiom* in which they are conducted is Buddhist. Are these rites still
assigned importance? Although a 1988 survey strongly suggests that they
are, Michio Ozaki advises caution:

> It is obvious that our attitude towards systems or institutions from the
> past, not only concerning the family, does not suddenly change at one
> point in time. In the survey, one out of three respondents answered
> positively to the proposition that it is the eldest son's duty to look after
> his parents and one out of four respondents to the proposition that the
> name of the family must be continued, even by adopting a child. Fur-
> thermore, to the proposition that the family tomb should be treasured
> and passed on to posterity, the overwhelming majority (over 80%) of
> respondents gave an affirmative reply.[55]

But note that it is in Tōhoku and Hokuriku—and rural areas elsewhere—
where support for the obligation of the eldest son to care for his parents and
importance of continuity of the family name is strongest. Concerning the
family grave, however, Ozaki notes:

> there is very little difference by age-group, occupation or by region . . .
> Many specialists consider this high rate of support for treasuring the
> family tomb is not in the same nature as the ideology of ancestor wor-
> ship which was one of the bases of the old family system . . . With the
> shift from extended to nuclear family, people were cut off from their

ancestral tombs, particularly during the years of high economic growth when many people from rural areas became concentrated in the urban areas. As a result, the significance of the tombs changed, and they were no longer the chains that bound you to distant ancestors, but monuments to the memory of your mother or father, or at the most, your grandparents.[56]

Both Kaji's comments and Ozaki's survey results serve to open up an important area of inquiry. The question is not whether Confucianism is a religion. It is rather: Does Confucianism, broadly defined (or, perhaps better, undefined) have anything at all to do with religion in Japan? Not many students of either subject have had a great deal to say on the issue in just those terms. Robert Ellwood and Richard Pilgrim are exceptions, and they open their discussion of the several ways Confucianism has figured in Japanese history with a bow to Edward Gibbon's *Decline and Fall of the Roman Empire,* in which he wrote: "To the common people all creeds were equally true, and to the magistrates all were equally useful." The insight seems to me to fit the Japanese situation almost perfectly. Ellwood and Pilgrim write:

> The "rules" by which religions are tacitly expected to operate in Japan are, more than anything else, Confucian. As so often in Japan, Confucianism plays the role of a moral and ethical substratum that, its preconditions being met, allows a harmless surface diversity. Indeed, one could argue, as many have, that these principles go back beyond Confucian influences on early Japan to the values inherent in ancient clan structures and an agricultural society with their demands for loyalty and cooperative effort; Confucianism did not so much create as articulate the values by which Japanese society works.
>
> Fundamental to Confucian principles is the family. Thus, one "rule" or expectation of religion in Japan is that it inculcate the value of loyalty to family. Families in turn see themselves as part of extended families and as rooted in a village or district. Religious practices that express solidarity with those units are well regarded. The basic Confucian model is the patriarchal family. Religions that express that in their own structure, as in the concept of hereditary succession of leadership, would on that score be regarded as conforming to expectation.
>
> Virtually all religions that have endured in Japan have adapted external forms agreeable to the patriarchal family model and have made their peace with the state.[57]

It is difficult to conceive more persuasive testimony to the power of Confucian ethics in the domain of Japanese religions, but there is a caveat that commands our attention. It is that the "rules" in question may actually antedate the introduction of Confucian teachings into Japan, a claim advanced by partisans of many persuasions, who appear to share only their determination to find indigenous origins for what they obviously regard as a singular institution—the Japanese household. Although the intensity of the debate has waxed and waned over the centuries, I think it fair to say that there is scarcely a shred of evidence to support either view of the origins of ancestor veneration in Japan. The question of origins aside, it is apparent that the practices are an amalgam of indigenous (Shinto), Confucian, and Buddhist elements. Should we wish to claim them as evidence of Confucian influence (although purists will argue that ancestor veneration is not supported by Confucian teaching), there is little danger of responsible contradiction.

CONFUCIAN IS AS CONFUCIAN DOES

I offer three illustrations of testimony to the assertion made in the heading of this section.[58] The first is straightforward enough, and reminds one of the story of the students who, introduced to poetry for the first time, discover unwittingly that they have been writing prose all their lives. It is an excerpt from a letter written in 1991 by a Japanese woman in her early forties:

> You asked me if I thought my family was in any way influenced by Confucianism. I know very little about Confucianism [*jukyō*], so I borrowed a library book called *Rongo to Kōshi*. After reading it, I realized something for the first time. The thoughts and ideas of Kōshi, who is the father of Confucianism, have entered into the fundamental ways of thinking in our daily life. This came as quite a surprise to me.
>
> In Japan today, Confucianism has nothing to do with religion, but rather is cultural and a part of our basic education. For example, one of the famous sayings of Kōshi is: "What you do not want done to yourself, do not do to others." We are conscious of this advice not only in our daily life, but in our family life as well. The saying reminds us of the opposite sentiment expressed in the Christian Bible: "Do unto others as you would have them do unto you." The difference between the two highlights the difference in our assumptions about the proper way to live, even if our life-styles today seem very similar.
>
> Another of Kōshi's sayings, "Look at the complexion [*kao iro*] of a man," has also influenced our family life, for we often say, "You can understand what I want to say, even if I don't say it." Anyway, I find that it is true that we have been influenced by *jukyō*, even though we don't realize it. It can be said that *jukyō* has entered our ethical system.

The second letter is rather different. The writer is in her late twenties:

I am not familiar with Confucianism, so I am not sure how to answer your question. Like other children, I was taught to respect older people and superiors [*meue no hito*], at home and at school. Piety toward grandparents, parents, teachers, and anyone elder was officially taught in the classes of morals [*dōtoku*] in elementary school. We read stories, watched TV dramas made especially for those classes, and had to recite such things as: "We must respect older people, must help weaker people, must not be selfish, must be nice to everyone," and so forth. Nevertheless, I was a very rebellious kid.

And, as if to confirm what has been said about the ancestral rites, this rebellious kid, who admits to having grown up to be a rebellious woman, continues:

My mother was always serious and strict about visiting the graves [*o-haka-mairi*] of both her family and my father's. From the time I was about twelve until I turned twenty, I thought it wasn't important to go to the graves. But my mother always insisted, saying that we owe our existence to the ancestors. I started going on my own only after I returned to Japan from studying abroad, and ever since then I have visited my ancestors occasionally. I go to the graves before I go abroad to ask for their protection and help, and the first thing I do when I get back to Japan is go to thank them and tell them that things went all right. I think I visit my ancestors more often than most people my age, and I do believe that they always help me and lead me to the better way.

The third set of comments is taken from a letter written to me by a former student, a Hawaii-born sansei who has lived in Japan and on the U.S. mainland. He now teaches at a high school in Honolulu. His letter was unsolicited:

I find that I must use my Japanese language abilities quite a bit, as a number of my students are from Japan, many of them here for the ESL program. Most are diligent, but some are really "out to lunch." It might have something to do with the current culture in Japan. I am most impressed by the kids from Korea. They arrived speaking hardly any English, but now they can carry on a decent conversation. They work hard, are humble, and carry around a lot of Confucian virtues that are absent in the new breed [*shinjinrui*] of Japanese. The Korean students are a joy to work with.

THE CONFUCIAN VIRTUES

I conclude with a list of what are generally agreed to be Confucian values, characteristics, and imperatives. The terms are gleaned from the sources cited herein and many others. All are, of course, translations from the Chinese and the Japanese, and are therefore suspect for the simple reason that true equivalence of terms of such weight and power can never be achieved.[59] At the head of the list, of course, are loyalty and filial piety, followed in alphabetical order by benevolence, courage, decorum, endurance, frugality, harmony, honesty, modesty, obedience, patience, respect, selflessness, and sincerity.

What moral code, what ethical teaching, what set of principles (dare we ask, what religion) fails to extol these virtues? If, on the one hand, we assert that they are specifically, if not exclusively, Confucian, then there can be no doubt that the Japanese family in particular and Japanese society in general are Confucian as well. If, on the other hand, we mean only to say that insofar as the family that looms large in the lives of most Japanese is conceived to be the sine qua non for a stable society, then I think it equally the case that the Japanese family and Japanese society are Confucian still.

8

SOME OBSERVATIONS ON THE
TRANSFORMATION OF CONFUCIANISM
(AND BUDDHISM) IN JAPAN

S. N. Eisenstadt

In this essay I explore some aspects of the specific mode of expansion and institutionalization of Confucianism and Buddhism in Japan in contrast to the modes of their expansion and institutionalization in mainland Asia. This exploration is based on the assumption that there is, indeed, a sharp difference between the impact of the expansion of Confucianism on the respective institutional and ideological formats of Korea and Vietnam on the one hand and Japan on the other. The institutionalization of Confucianism, first of all in China itself, and then in Korea and Vietnam, transformed the basic premises of the social and political order in these societies, and in the structure of their centers and their ruling strata, in comparison with those of preceding regimes.[1]

In both Korea and North Vietnam there have developed as a result of the expansion or adoption of Confucianism new regimes—more imperial than the older patrimonial or feudal-patrimonial regimes—and of centers, even if there were not as fully articulated as in China, the like of which persisted in South Vietnam, as well as new structures of the ruling elites and systems of stratification.[2] This change was effected by the transformation of feudal, or rather feudal-patrimonial, ruling groups into something similar to the class of Chinese literati, that is, to an autonomous bureaucratic-cultural elite, recruited according to distinct, independent criteria and organized in relatively autonomous frameworks.

In Korea, by partial contrast, Confucian elites have never achieved the kind of autonomy and independence that characterized the Chinese empire. Aristocratic and patrimonial tendencies remained very strong. The Confucians encountered strong Buddhist opposition, in alliance with large sectors of the older aristocracy and some of the rulers.[3] Once the Confucian institutions and elites became predominant, however, even the aristocracy was "Confucianized." True enough, aristocratic families and lineages continued to be much more important in Korea than in post-T'ang China. But their importance was manifest in their success in monopolizing, at least in part, the Confucian bureaucratic literati positions—but not in abolishing these positions—and in reverting to a distinct "semifeudal" aristocratic type of polity. In other words, they were already at play on the Confucian playing fields, according to Confucian rules, even if they manipulated those rules to their advantage. In North Vietnam the Confucian state was even more coercive than in Korea and in some ways more truly "imperial" in its permeation of the periphery than it was in China.[4]

The story of Confucianism—as well as of Buddhism—in Japan is radically different. True, both Confucianism and Buddhism have greatly influenced the entire cultural and social ambience of Japanese society. Their influence was indeed far-reaching, and it is, as is well known, impossible to understand the history of Japanese society and culture without taking this influence into account. Confucianism and Buddhism were also instrumental in generating many areas of cultural creativity, as well as in establishing the realm of private meaning in many sectors of Japanese society. They have contributed greatly to religious-cultic life in Japan and have deeply influenced the pattern of creativity in these areas, and they were also of considerable importance in transforming the general cultural ambience and climate.[5]

Under the impact of Confucianism and Buddhism, and contrary to many non-Axial civilizations (e.g., ancient Egypt, Assyria, and Mesoamerica)—which, unlike Japan, were also pre-Axial civilizations—there developed in Japan sophisticated intellectual, philosophical, ideological, and religious discourses, as manifest, for instance, in the development of the intensive debates between various Neo-Confucian schools and schools expounding the so-called nativistic learning of the Tokugawa period.[6] But the nature of the influence and impact of Confucianism and Buddhism in Japan was different from that of Confucianism in China, Korea, and Vietnam or of Buddhism in, above all, the countries of Southeast Asia.

Institutionally, in Japan neither Confucianism nor Buddhism has changed the structure of the center or of the ruling elites. The "importation" of Confucianism did not develop in Japan those central institutional forces that shaped the Confucian regimes in China, Korea, and Vietnam—namely, the examination system and its crystallization of the stratum of the literati and the imperial bureaucracy. Thus, whereas the famous Confucian saying that one should have educated rulers implied in China (and to a lesser degree in Korea and North Vietnam) the crystallization of entirely new types of autonomous ruling classes, in Japan it led to attempts to educate those that already existed—mostly various types of aristocratic rulers. This fact also had, as we shall see, a far-reaching impact on the political behavior of Confucian groups in these different settings.

Buddhism in Japan developed some distinct characteristics that distinguished it from Buddhist communities in India, China, and Southeast Asia. The most important of these characteristics was the development of very strong worldly orientations and of a highly sectarian familistic organizational structure among Buddhist groups or sects. On the organizational level, Buddhist sects developed in extremely personalized and familistic directions. Buddhist sectarianism in Japan was rooted not in strong transcendental orientations but in its having become embedded in the emphasis on personal "enlightenment" on the one hand, and on concrete social nexus or "groupism," with tendencies toward hereditary transmission of leadership roles, on the other.[7] As Shigeru Matsumoto puts it:

> This particularistic tendency also dominated various aspects of culture having their root in more ancient times. Hereditary families and school artists with their secret traditions appear on a large scale during the Heian period, and many of them continued to thrive in the following period. The same pattern came to affect even the Pure Land Shin sect of Buddhism soon after the time of its great founder, Shinran. Shinran represented a radical break from the particularistic, continuous, hereditary tradition by emphasizing the absolute trust of each individual person in the universal-saving power of Amida Buddha. The penetration of Pure Land Shin Buddhism into the villages certainly helped to break their closed traditional structure and brought the possibility of a more universalistic religious organization extending beyond the villages. Yet, from the very beginning, the headship of the sect has been inherited in the line of its founder, Shinran, generation after generation. The priesthood in each temple has also been largely hereditary. Moreover, the relationship between main temples and branch temples, and between a temple and its member-followers [danka], came to be conceived in terms of family relationship or the oya-ko symbolism.[8]

All in all, from these observations one may argue that Norinaga, through his stress on lineage or hereditary continuity, points to an important aspect of the traditional Japanese value system.

In close relation to such far-reaching institutional changes, some of the major premises or concepts of Confucianism and Buddhism were also transformed in Japan. We have seen how Buddhist orientations become transformed in a this-worldly direction. The ontological conceptions that stressed (as in all Axial civilizations) the chasm between the transcendental and mundane orders, between "nature" and "culture," were shifted in a more "immanentist" direction.[9] This led to a much stronger emphasis on the mutual embeddedness of the cultural and natural orders and a very heavy emphasis on nature as given rather than as constructed according to transcendental principles.

It is, however, probably with respect to the conception of the national collectivity and its relation to the broader Confucian and Buddhist civilizations, as well as with respect to conceptions of authority, especially imperial authority, that the ideological transformation of Buddhism and Confucianism was most fully manifest. The crux of this transformation was the redirection of the universalistic orientations of Buddhism and Confucianism in a more particularistic, primordial direction. Buddhism, as well as Confucianism, had a powerful impact indeed on the definition of the overall "national" Japanese community and on the basic concept or premises of authority in Japan—the heavy emphasis on commitment to center, on hierarchy, and on group solidarity. Confucianism and Buddhism imbued these definitions with a very strong moral or metaphysical dimension.

But the impact of Buddhism and Confucianism did not change the basic institutional premises of these definitions. Above all, they did not change the sacral, particularistic components of Japanese collective self-definition and of the system of legitimation of authority within it—unlike in Vietnam and Korea, not to mention China itself. If anything, it has strengthened these definitions and the legitimation of the social and political order in such sacral-primordial ties by combining them with a strong ethical dimension.[10] True enough, the encounter with Confucianism and Buddhism did give rise to continuous reformulations and reconstructions of the definitions and symbols of the Japanese collectivity. But such reformulations have never basically changed the ontological and social import of these symbols. Japan's first encounter with Buddhism had transformed the concept of sacred kingship into a sacred liturgical particularistic community, rooted in the older Shinto concept, and all the subsequent formulations of the nature of this community have only strengthened this conception. As M. Wahida writes:

This liturgical community was believed to have its exemplary model in the mythical sacred history as it was to be delineated in Japanese mythology. Moreover, it was believed that the state, as a liturgical community, could be renewed whenever the Enthronement Festival was celebrated. The Enthronement Festival was indeed the supremely important occasion, when the ideal national community on the level of mythical sacred history could be translated into reality and represented on the dimension of profane history. Among the families taking part in the celebration of the festival were those who had long served the ruler's personal household in the performance of their magico-religious, economic, and military functions. When the structure of the *ritsu-ryo* state was completed in the eighth century, the families charged with the magico-religious functions were integrated into the *Shingi-kan,* while those with economic functions were mostly systematized into the Ministry of the Imperial Household of the *Dajō-kan.* In addition, the military families and groupings who had served as Imperial guards were incorporated into a special system of bodyguards and palace guards. In short, the state at the beginning of the eighth century constituted a perfect cosmos as a liturgical community.[11]

At the same time, the strong universalistic orientations inherent in Buddhism and more latent in Confucianism were subdued and "nativized" in Japan.[12] When Japan was defined as a divine nation, this meant a nation protected by the gods, a chosen people in a sense, but not a nation carrying out God's universal mission.[13] Parallel developments took place with respect to the basic conception of political authority and of accountability of rulers. These concepts were also greatly transformed from the original Chinese-Confucian concepts prevalent in China, Korea, and Vietnam. Unlike in China (as well as Korea and Vietnam),[14] where, in principle, the emperor, even if a sacral figure, was "under" the Mandate of Heaven, in Japan he was sacred and seen as the embodiment of the gods, and could not be held accountable to anybody. Only the shoguns and other officials could be held accountable, and even then in ways not clearly specified, and only in periods of crisis, as for instance at the end of the Tokugawa regime.

The differences between the modes of expansion of Confucianism and the impact of such expansion on the institutional structure in China, Korea, and Vietnam and of Buddhism in the various countries of mainland Asia, on the one hand, and of both Confucianism and Buddhism in Japan, on the other, are closely related to differences in the structure and composition of their respective elites, as well as of the orientations and activities of their respective sects. These differences are very close to those that can be identified in the case of Islam, that is, differences in the structure of the cultural elites (especially their relative autonomy), their relation to the ruling elites, and their place in the ruling coalition.

In mainland Asia the Confucian and Buddhist elites were highly autonomous. The Confucian elites constituted a new, distinct, autonomous political-cultural stratum recruited in principle—if not always in practice— through the examination system, the basic contents of which were set up and promulgated by them.[15] The Buddhists, at least in the area of religion, were also highly autonomous—and not totally embedded in the existing structures of power and family.

In Japan, by contrast, both the Confucian scholars and the Buddhist sects were deeply embedded in the existing power, kinship, and family settings. Although the Confucian academies in Japan were often relatively independent institutions, they were highly dependent on the rulers for public offices.[16] The Confucian scholars served in Japan at the courts of the rulers according to the criteria set up by the rulers, and they served at the rulers' pleasure. The Buddhist sects thus became strongly embedded in the familistic settings that predominated in most sectors of Japanese society.

The different modes of expansion of Confucianism had some very important repercussions on the nature of the sectarian activities that developed within them. From the very beginning, the development of sectarianism in Confucianism and Buddhism differed greatly from that in the major monotheistic civilizations. Given the strong other-worldly orientation, Buddhist sects were not oriented—as was the case in the monotheistic civilizations—toward reconstructing the political centers of their respective societies.[17]

The various Hindu sects, as well as Buddhism itself, did indeed have a far-reaching impact on the structure of the secular spheres of their respective civilizations.[18] First, they extended the scope of the different national and political communities and imbued them with new symbolic dimensions.[19] Second, they could also change some of the bases and criteria for participation in the cultural communities—as was the case in Jainism, in the Bhakti movement, and, of course, above all, in Buddhism, where an entirely new civilizational framework was constructed.[20]

Buddhism also introduced new elements onto the political scene—above all that special way in which the Sangha, usually politically a very compliant group, were able, in some instances, as Paul Mus has shown, to become a sort of moral conscience of the community, calling the rulers to a degree of accountability.[21] This impact was of a different nature from that of the struggles between the reigning orthodoxies and the numerous heterodoxies that developed within the monotheistic civilizations—Judaism, Christianity, and Islam. Although the reconstruction of political centers was not the major orientation of Buddhist sects, even in these societies there did develop a mode of involvement in the political arena that posed potentially subversive challenges to the authorities.

The mode of involvement of the Confucian elites in the political centers in China, Korea, and Vietnam developed in a rather different direction from that of the Buddhist Sangha, and was in many ways closer to the sectarian activities in the monotheistic civilizations. Confucianism was indeed very strongly oriented toward the political centers. But, given the strong (in contrast to the monotheistic traditions), almost exclusively this-worldly orientation of Confucianism, the potentially heterodox groups of literati rarely challenged the political center and order. They were, however, very active politically, and often engaged in intensive discourse about and moral criticism of the rulers.[22]

As in all other Axial age civilizations, there developed in China numerous secondary religions, such as Buddhism and Taoism, as well as numerous schools within the central Confucian fold with strong other-worldly orientations. As the official Confucian "orthodoxy" was not greatly concerned with this other-worldly orientation or with pure speculation, these sects never developed into heterodoxy in the doctrinal sense; and so long as they did not impinge on the basic institutional implications of the imperial order, with the political-cultural predominance of the literati and bureaucracy, they were more or less left alone. But once some of these sects did attempt—as was the case with the Buddhists under the T'ang—to impinge on the basic institutional framework of the Confucian order, to construct the world according to their own premises, the Confucian literati and bureaucracy behaved like any other "monotheistic" orthodoxy, engaging in fierce political struggle and wide-ranging persecutions.[23] Moreover, throughout the various periods of Chinese history there have been continuous attempts by the ruling literati to define the limits of Confucian orthodoxy.[24]

At the same time, there were many noteworthy attempts at reform in China grounded in the Confucian and Neo-Confucian visions, especially from the Sung period onward. Neo-Confucian groups were much concerned with the reconstruction of the imperial order in accordance with the metaphysical and moral visions they articulated, and these had a far-reaching impact on certain aspects of policy, such as land allotment and taxation, and to some extent the details of the examination system itself.[25] They were continually politically active, and often critically engaged in the political discourse. Unlike the sects and heterodoxies of monotheistic civilizations, however, the Confucians have but rarely challenged the basic political premises of the regimes, the very foundation of the imperial order. This was probably to no small extent due to the fact that they conceived the political or political-cultural arena as the main, possibly the only, institutional ground (as distinct from the more private contemplative one) for implementing the Confucian transcendental vision.

Thus, both Buddhist sects and groups of Confucian (especially Neo-Confucian) literati in mainland Asia participated in the political arena, thus constituting, at least potentially, a challenge to the existing political regimes—even if in ways that differed greatly from those prevalent in the monotheistic civilizations.

It was, indeed, this strong, relatively autonomous, and often critical political involvement, posing political challenges to the regime, which almost entirely disappeared in Japan. Here most Buddhist sects and Confucian schools became either supporters of the existing political order—performing religious or cultural functions for the existing powers, imbuing the political process with proper Buddhist (or Confucian) ethical values and orientations—or politically passive.

The major new sectarian orientations that developed in Japanese Buddhism, most clearly manifest in the Pure Land sect, were in principle inclined toward the perfection of the individual, seemingly without any direct political charge—certainly without any effort to change the premises on which the political realm was based. They were also very strongly inclined toward strengthening the national community; but this could, contrary to Confucian teaching, lead to a certain political passivity or withdrawal.[26] It was only in Nichiren's case that some more active political overtures—beyond the "simple" struggle for power—could be identified with Japanese Buddhism, but even these were basically entirely embedded within the framework of premises prevalent within the Japanese political order. There did not develop among these groups in Japan—unlike in at least some of the Neo-Confucian groups in China and, in a different way, in Theravada countries—a specifically sectarian political dynamic.

Of course, the various Buddhist sects and monasteries in Japan, especially in late medieval times, developed into very powerful political and economic forces, and many of them enjoyed great autonomy and power vis-à-vis the shoguns. They engaged in intensive struggles among themselves and with the feudal lords or the shogun. But most of these battles were fought over economic resources and political power. The religious dimension was quite weak.

Some Neo-Confucian scholars, such as Hayashi Razan, attempted to present themselves as the bearers of the official ideology, hoping to have their schools certified by the authorities and declared orthodoxies. Sometimes their attempts succeeded, but only to a limited extent, especially in periods of turmoil during the late eighteenth and early nineteenth centuries, when the status of orthodoxy was in fact bestowed on them. Yet, given the basic premises of the Japanese political order and its legitimation in some combination of sacred primordial terms, the rulers were not as interested in the promulgation and imposition of uniform orthodoxies as was the case in China, at least to some degree. Accordingly, they tended to supervise the intellectual or religious activities of these academies—and of the Buddhist monasteries—to a much lesser extent than in China. On the whole, these academies and religious institutions did perform useful functions for the regimes, but the entire dynamics differed from those prevalent in China, Korea, and Vietnam. It is also because of the basic characteristics of Japanese Buddhism, especially its "groupism" or group loyalties, which were continuously reinforced over individual autonomy, that, contrary to some assertions, Kamakura Buddhism understandably did not develop in the direction of a "reformation."[27]

A rather similar picture developed with respect to the Confucian groups in Japan. Some of the Neo-Confucian scholars hoped to initiate fully established orthodoxies, but they were not on the whole successful, for the rulers did not generally encourage this tendency. The mode of participation of the Buddhist and Confucian groups in the political process in Japan was very much influenced by the fact that neither Japanese Buddhism nor Confucianism ever became a fully autonomous orthodoxy—and hence never gave rise to far-reaching heterodoxies. The shoguns were mostly concerned with what may be called the civilizing features of their cultural activities.[28] But, given the basic non-Axial premises of the Japanese political system, the shoguns were not interested in establishing orthodoxies in the full sense of the word.

One of the paradoxical results of the fact that Confucianism did not become in Japan—in contrast to China, Korea, and Vietnam—the main channel for recruitment of the ruling group was that it had a wide-ranging impact, pointed out by the Confucian scholars, on the development of a well-educated public in Tokugawa Japan. This relative weakness in Japan of the direct impact of sectarianism on political transformation culminated in some of the most important characteristics of the Meiji Restoration, which distinguish it from other great modern revolutions—namely that, despite the broad structural changes it effected in all spheres of society, it was characterized by the weakness, even the lack, of utopian, universalistic, and missionary revolutionary ideologies and by the concomitant reconstruction of the legitimation of the new modern regime in "restorationist" terms.[29]

• • •

Thus, to sum up briefly, the transformation of Buddhism and Confucianism in Japan in its symbolic dimension was manifest in the weakening of their transcendental and universalistic orientation, and in their being channeled in an immanentist, particularistic, primordial direction. These transformations took two paths. One emphasized the more transcendental, other-worldly orientation and experience; the other hemmed in these orientations in this-worldly, immanentist directions and frameworks. Such hemming in did not entail the obliteration of the transcendental and other-worldly orientations but rather bracketed them in special segregated arenas. Such bracketing gave rise to the development of sophisticated philosophical, religious, and aesthetic discourse, and created a continuous tension between such discourse and the prevalent intellectual hegemony. But at the same time, this bracketing did not undermine the core of the basic ontological and social premises, even if it did give rise to their continuous reformation.

These transformations could already be identified in the first encounter with Confucianism and Buddhism and then again, in a much more complex and sophisticated way, with the development of New Confucian schools in the Tokugawa period. Throughout these periods Confucianism and Buddhism imbued the basic premises of Japanese order, such as the strong emphasis on commitment to the center—defined in strong primordial-sacral (or natural) terms—on hierarchy, and on group solidarity, with very strong new moral and metaphysical dimensions. They were also important in giving rise to manifold forms of cultural discourse, and in the reconstruction of the realm of private meanings and of public discourse of many sectors of Japanese society.

This gave rise to a widening of the range of discourse and to the reconstruction of more sophisticated and influential discursive modes. It also gave rise to a continuous broadening of the scope of participation of various sectors of Japanese society and cultural creativity, and in the political and ideological discourse that developed within it. And yet, as we have seen, the definition of the religious or "cultural" community that developed within Japanese Buddhism or Confucianism was distinctively national and did not strongly emphasize those transnational, civilizational dimensions that could be found in most other Buddhist communities or those universalistic orientations typical of most Confucian and especially Neo-Confucian schools.

On the whole, both Confucianism and Buddhism in Japan have continually reinforced some of the basic prevalent political orientations, premises, and symbols of legitimation of authority in Japan—the emphasis on the national community, defined in primordial terms, minimizing most references to universalistic orientations—thus greatly transforming certain basic tenets of "original" Chinese Confucianism. Moreover, however much of their discourse was couched in Neo-Confucian terms, it was set within a strongly restorative and nativistic framework and premises—even if the framework and premises were continuously reformulated in ever more sophisticated ways. On the institutional or organizational level this transformation entailed relatively little autonomy for the major Confucian schools and scholars and the Buddhist sect leaders and seers, embedding them into the prevailing social settings and networks, be they familial, regional, or political.

Accordingly, however great the impact of the spread of Confucian education and learning on the dynamics of Tokugawa society, neither Confucian (nor Buddhist) groups were active participants in the toppling of the Tokugawa regime. They did not perform those sectarian political roles that, for instance, the Puritans did in the English Revolution. It was, as is well known, different groups of disenchanted and rebellious samurai that toppled the Bakufu. Of course, they were greatly influenced by the development of new modes of public discourse. But the more intellectual groups were not active, autonomous participants in this process of rebellion, even if they provided part of the background for the disintegration of the Tokugawa regime.

The foregoing analysis points out that the essential characteristics of sectarian movements and their impact on political dynamics are not necessarily derived from their beliefs or their ritual practices, but rather stem from the way in which, and the extent to which, these beliefs become transformed into components of the basic premises of their respective civilizations. It is, indeed, the transformation of such beliefs into the components of the premises of civilization that generates, first of all, in all Axial civilizations the very tendency toward sectarianism, toward heterodoxy, and toward the confrontation between orthodoxy and heterodoxy. Yet, while some tendencies toward sectarian organization and activities are to be found in all these civilizations, the specific characteristics and impact of such sects vary greatly according to their respective premises and institutional features. Most important from the point of view of this analysis is the fact that, within the "same" religion, the impact of such sects varies widely in different settings and societies. Also, such variations are greatly, although certainly not exclusively, dependent on whether in any particular setting in any civilization the given religion constitutes only a distinct pattern of belief, ritual, and worship, or whether it has become a component of the basic ontology and beliefs of the civilization and of the concomitant characteristics of the religious elite and its relations with other elites. It is, indeed, these differences that explain the basic relations of such sects to the existing powers and the important variations in their organization and ideologies, as well as—even if not necessarily to the same degree—their more purely theological doctrines.

PART III

SOUTH KOREA AND TAIWAN

The Confucian phenomenon in South Korea brings to mind Ernest Cassirer's famous saying in his essay on Giovanni Pico della Mirandola: "The center was everywhere; the periphery nowhere." The case of Confucianism in South Korea, the paradigmatic "Confucian" society in East Asia, seems to suggest that the Confucian center is nowhere and yet its periphery is everywhere. Not without a touch of irony, as Koh Byong-ik notes that according to the *Manuals for Religions in Korea,* self-styled Confucians constitute no more than 2 percent of the total population. Yet the seemingly exaggerated claim "All men are Confucians!" makes sense in the Korean context. Koh's pithy essay, "Confucianism in Contemporary Korea," helps us to understand the complex problem of Confucian self-identification, as well as Confucianism's legacy, relevance to modernization, and future transformation in present-day South Korea.

Paradoxically, the apparent waning of Confucianism as an official ideology, as an educational institution, and as an articulation of personal faith does not undermine its presence as a code of ethics in government, school, and family. Indeed, an overwhelming majority of Korean Buddhists and Christians continue to identify their convictions and practices as characteristically Confucian. Since Confucianism is not a religion with an organized membership, it is compatible with and complementary to religions that are not strictly exclusionistic. Often the adjectival "Confucian" can be attached to "Buddhist" or "Christian" to designate a particular style of being religious. For example, those who take ancestral veneration seriously may consider themselves Confucian Christians or Confucian Buddhists. If we broaden the scope to include daily ethical behavior, we could even describe Confucianism as the civil religion of Korean society.

Kim Kwang-ok's ethnographic description in "The Reproduction of Confucian Culture in Contemporary Korea: An Anthropological Study" offers several fascinating cases to substantiate the claim that the Confucian tradition still provides the core values for this multireligious society. The inherent moral elitism in the "Confucian forest" may appear to be confined to a distinct class *(yangban)* and a particular area (Andong), and the typical Confucian institutions, notably the village schools and the famous academies, are somewhat idiosyncratic in the larger social context. Yet, what they signify is moral force with political power and social influence rather than the utopian vision of an imagined community. Of course, the deliberately constructed symbolic communities which reenact well-established Confucian rituals to honor famous ancestors, national heroes, or renowned scholars may lack the infrastructure to ensure institutional continuity, but they are often vitally important in sustaining the Confucian discourse in the public sphere.

The Korean moral fabric woven by family, school, and government has such a thick structure of Confucian ethics that, even though South Korea is the most Christianized of all East Asian societies, its social network (both the vertical order and the horizontal relationships) is remarkably Confucian in character. The style of Confucian culture in action, as depicted by Kim, is reminiscent of Durkheim's *conscience collective*. Korean society, so conceived, is not an adversarial system but a fiduciary community. Surely, in political culture or economic ethics, a fiduciary community may be even more tension-ridden than an adversarial system; but its pattern of legitimacy, its basis for authority, its justification for hierarchy, and its status consciousness are grounded in shared values, common sense, accepted ritual, and the rhetoric of assent. Undeniably, the Confucian heritage in Korean society is a double-edged sword: it has contributed to family cohesiveness, educational excellence, social harmony, and political stability. Yet, it has also perpetuated authoritarian, factional, gerontocratic, and male-oriented ideas and practices.

Whereas, as Kim notes, President Park Chung-hee of South Korea learned the benefit of promoting Confucian teachings of loyalty and filial piety after he had crossed swords with the Confucian literati of Kyoungbuk province, the Nationalist government in Taiwan under the leadership of Chiang Kai-shek and later his son Chiang Ching-kuo has been a staunch supporter of Confucian ideology from the beginning. Ambrose King, in "State Confucianism and Its Transformation: The Restructuring of the State-Society Relation in Taiwan," narrates how the Confucian conception of the role of the maximum state (to provide for, to enrich, and to educate the people) has actually led the government to assume full responsibility for economic development in Taiwan. He further notes that the Confucian moral and political persuasion supported the "people's-interest orientation of the authoritarian party-state," a pivotal influence in the transformation of Taiwan into a newly industrialized country.

The main thrust of King's essay, however, is to show the unintended consequences of "the state-led development of an ever-expanding market economy": the emergence of an autonomous middle class, the creation of a public sphere, and the advent of civil society. While assuming that state Confucianism has contributed to the Taiwanese "economic miracle," King believes that democratization in Taiwan has had different political and social dynamics. As the power of the state is overshadowed in many critical economic areas by newly released social forces, institutional Confucianism, he believes, will inevitably decline. In its place a new Confucian humanism predicated on the communal critical self-consciousness of the intelligentsia may become the de facto civil religion. Having endured and flourished in a market economy, the Confucian persuasion will face the real test of its survivability in the democratic polity. King seems cautiously optimistic that the transformation of state Confucianism, as an integral part of China's quest for political modernity, will eventually give birth to full-fledged civil society. This is reminiscent of Edward Shils's assertion that civil society "entails the participation of individuals in the civil collective self-consciousness of society as a whole." Since a vibrant civil society is a precondition for a sustainable and flourishing democracy, King believes that the prospects for Taiwan's democratization are encouraging.

Thomas Gold, by contrast, concludes that "as Taiwan becomes increasingly pluralistic, a new moral order and institutions will draw on the Confucian repertoire, but the dominant influences will come from elsewhere." "Civil Society in Taiwan: The Confucian Dimension," Gold acknowledges the positive role that the Confucian "habits of the heart" have played in shaping the moral responsibility of the intellectual, the spirit of protest, family enterprise, personal networks, pragmatism, and social conscience. He also cites the example of the 1990 National Affairs Conference, which included "some political prisoners released just to attend," as an indication of the improved relationship between the party-state and society and a symbol of "the dramatic emergence of civil society." We are reminded of Shils's observation that the extension of a barrier "which would bring the center and the periphery nearer to each other in a common moral order also has potential for the realization of civil society."

Nevertheless, both King and Gold are in agreement with Lucian Pye that the crisis of authoritarianism will inevitably lead to a fundamental break with the Confucian tradition in Taiwan. They would perhaps also accept Samuel Huntington's judgment that Confucian political culture is in principle incompatible with democratization. As Huntington insists, however, "Confucian democracy may be a contradiction in terms, but democracy in a Confucian society need not be." For him the central question is: What elements in Taiwan today are favorable to democracy, and how and under what circumstances can these supersede the undemocratic thoughts and practices in the cultural tradition? Still, is it really inconceivable that the New Confucianism, as Liu Shu-hsien envisions, can facilitate the transformation of state Confucianism into intellectual Confucianism, which in turn will encourage the development of a Confucian style of democracy in Taiwan? Given the prominence of authority, hierarchy, and status in the Confucian tradition, we may have to accept the possibility that a spirit of equality and bureaucratic elitism, openness of political access and concentration of power, and the rhetoric of human rights and duty-consciousness may coexist.

9

CONFUCIANISM IN
CONTEMPORARY KOREA

Koh Byong-ik

This essay begins with two recent surveys of the religious affiliation of Koreans today and then briefly examines the complex
problems of Confucianism, including Confucian self-identification, the legacy of Confucianism, and its relevance to modernization and to possible future transformation.

A SHRINKING MINORITY

It is generally believed that at present Korea is the most Confucian country in all of East Asia, more so even than Taiwan or
mainland China, not to mention Hong Kong or Japan. Missionaries and travelers to Korea in the nineteenth century expressed
surprise to find that the most rigid Confucian systems and values
permeated almost all facets of Korean life. Many modern sociologists and economists also believe that Koreans today still retain unmistakably Confucian behavioral traits and ways of thinking.

Statistics, however, reveal a bewildering picture. According to
the *Manual for Religions in Korea,* published in 1984 by the
Republic of Korea's Religious Affairs Office of the Ministry of
Culture and Information, the number of Confucians was only
slightly under 800,000, while Buddhists numbered 7.5 million
and Christians (Protestants and Catholics together) totaled about

7 million. Confucians amounted to only about 2 percent of the total population, Buddhists about 19 percent, and Christians 17.5 percent (Table 9.1).

Statistics are very often deceptive, however, and in the case of Confucianism this is obviously so. Since Confucianism is not an organized religion and hence has no registration procedures, it is always difficult, in fact almost impossible, to define any person as Confucian or non-Confucian. The statistics in Table 9.1 are derived from a government census taken in October 1983 and are based on self-identification (i.e., the respondents were asked to fill in their religion on the census sheet). Those who answered "Confucian" amounted to only 2 percent of the total population. But the fact that about 800,000 people declared themselves followers of Confucianism is, in itself, amazing, since Confucianism has no organized body, such as a church or temple, with which people can affiliate themselves, as does Christianity or Buddhism. Those people very probably identified themselves solely on the basis of predilection and inner convictions, and thus the number should not be considered small. Also to be weighed is the fact that over 60 percent of the total population responded "no religion." A substantial majority of this supposedly nonreligious population is, as we shall see, actually Confucian; they observe the basic Confucian rituals, such as ancestral services and burial rites, and subscribe to Confucian values. When judged by the statistics alone, however, Confucians make up only a very small minority of Korean society today, and if a similar census were to be taken ten years from now, this minority would almost certainly be even smaller.

Confucian values and practices are transmitted not through schools, worship services, or the mass media, but only through spontaneous family indoctrination. As the family becomes nuclearized and family unity wanes, the transmission of Confucian values also inevitably wanes.

Table 9.1 Religions in Korea

Religion	Population	Percentage
Buddhists	7,507,059	18.92
Won Buddhists	96,333	0.24
Protestants	5,337,308	13.45
Catholics	1,590,625	4.00
Confucians	786,955	1.98
Heavenly Way	52,530	0.13
Others	216,809	0.54
Subtotal	15,587,619	39.26
No religion	24,082,240	60.73
Total population	39,669,859	100.00

Note: From census of October 1, 1983.

LOW VISIBILITY

Confucianism as the dominant ideology has been fading in Korea, as is also the case elsewhere in East Asia. It lost its most important function as the orthodox state ideology after the fall of the monarchy in the early twentieth century, and in subsequent years it could no longer claim any leading role in the modernizing and Westernizing republican polity. Not a single word in the nation's constitution refers to Confucianism, and within the entire school system no part of the curriculum is designed to foster Confucian values and practices. The closest thing to Confucian ethics in the curriculum is elementary school civics, but it essentially teaches general good citizenship.

Even the heavily didactic proclamation by the president of the republic in 1968, the "Charter of National Education," which since then has been recited at every educational and cultural ceremony, emphasizes diligence, thrift, cooperation, creativity, and loyalty in general terms, not as specifically Confucian values or in Confucian phraseology. Saemaul Undong (the New Community Movement), which since the 1970s has contributed much to rural development through an emphasis on the moral values of diligence, self-reliance, and cooperation, makes no reference to traditional Confucian values.

On the social level, the landowning *yangban* class, which was the major bearer of the Confucian tradition for over four centuries, underwent gradual disintegration and dissolution during the first half of this century owing to modern education, land reform, armed forces conscription, civil war, and the ensuing displacement and migration, not to mention rapid urbanization and industrialization. The rural villages, which had been inhabited mostly by the members of one clan and were the main seat of grass-roots Confucianism, became desolate and were often abandoned when most of the better-off families moved to the urban areas in search of opportunities for themselves and better education for their children. The agrarian population decreased rapidly from more than 60 percent in 1960 to a mere 27 percent in 1980.

Confucianism as a scholarly pursuit has disappeared since the introduction of modern education. The elaborate and painstaking pursuit of Neo-Confucian epistemology and an understanding of human nature, which attained an unparalleled status and scope through the elite scholars and thinkers of the Chosŏn kingdom (1392–1910), as exemplified in the expositions of Yi T'oegye (1505–1570) and others, has ceased to be a concern of even the most ardent Confucians.[1] The termination of the civil service examination system in 1895 brought about a general discarding of the use of written classical Chinese, which had been the unquestioned vehicle of education and literary activities. Thus, modern intellectuals, who know Chinese characters but have no knowledge of classical Chinese composition, are virtually cut off from the traditional literary treasures of Confucian learning and scholarship.

The *hyanggyo*, traditional Confucian schools in the capital and the provinces, and the *sŏwon*, private academies (Chinese: *shu-yüan*), survive only in their decaying edifices, having lost the functions of education and public opinion formation. Also, with no prayers and no worship of any deity, Confucianism had no direct influence on arts such as sculpture, painting, architecture, music, and folk dance. In all, Confucianism today is hardly visible on the surface and rarely manifests itself in any organization or institution. It survives only at the most basic level of the popular consciousness and in the routines of daily life.

SURVIVING PRACTICES

Although most of the Confucian facade has been torn down and has vanished, there are still some organizations that have the expressed aim of enhancing and disseminating Confucianism. The centuries-old Songgyungwan, the center of Confucian studies in the capital and the national Confucian shrine, has continued to exist, with only brief interruptions, to this day. It still performs the rites for Confucius with ancient music and dance twice a year and theoretically still controls the operation of the local Confucian schools, or *hyanggyo*. Its former function as the center of advanced Confucian education has been partially maintained insofar as it has developed into a modern university with a college that is devoted exclusively to the study of Confucianism.

There are still traditional local *hyanggyo* buildings scattered all over the country, totaling as many as 231 at present, some of which continue to perform the regular ceremonies for Confucius but which have mostly discontinued their other functions. There is a similar situation with the private academies, or *sŏwon*. They suffered a severe blow in the middle of the nineteenth century, when the powerful ruling regent, Taewon-gun (1820–1898), took the unprecedented measure of closing most of the academies for their alleged role in fostering antigovernment public opinion. Except for a few very important and prestigious academies, most of them, totaling as many as 375, merely survived as the custodians of the relics and writings of the founder-scholars and other books and woodblocks. As the nation's economy has developed in recent years, a new trend has begun among the descendants of the founders of the academies to restore and maintain them, but not to enhance Confucian culture so much as to glorify their ancestry.

Whatever the significance of the surviving Confucian edifices, Confucianism as a moral teaching and a way of life has by no means been discarded altogether. Since it permeated the minds and behavior of the people for so long, through intensive and constant inculcation and broad institutional binding, it still can be perceived in today's daily life. Strong family consciousness has been the core of Confucianism, and this survives. Although the family structure has changed considerably during the last decades, from extended families to nuclear families, and the divorce rate has risen from 0.28 percent in 1965 to 1.16 percent in 1980, the family is still stronger than nearly anywhere else in the world. As for property inheritance, the eldest son gets the lion's share, but the remaining sons and daughters receive graduated shares, unlike in Japan, where primogeniture prevails, and in China, where the equal division of property among the sons is the rule. Although the revised civil code of 1977 recognizes the separate property rights of conjugal partners, in reality the concept of communal family property still prevails. It is customary for unmarried female workers to send their meager wages back to their family in the rural areas to support their parents or to help their male siblings receive an advanced education.

Ancestral memorial rites and funeral ceremonies constitute the backbone of the Confucian heritage, and probably nowhere else are these ceremonies more intensively and extensively observed than in Korea. As for the significance of the ancestral memorial rites, according to the Korea Gallup survey mentioned earlier, even 57.1 percent of Christians favor them. Since memorial ceremonies are observed for five generations of ancestors on their death dates, this means each individual observes at least ten rites a year. Added to this are the ceremonies on holidays such as New Year's Day and Chusok, the harvest moon festival. The cost, labor, and time involved in these ceremonies are by no means small, and often they are a major source of family debt. Participation in these ceremonies by close descendants is considered an important duty, often requiring distant travel. Of course, these occasions contribute to the solidarity of the family and clan.

Funeral and mourning ceremonies for parents were thought to be a direct reflection of filial piety, so they tended to be rather elaborate, costly, and drawn-out affairs. These Confucian ceremonies were strictly modeled after the formula laid down in the *Chu-tzu chia-li* by Chu Hsi in the twelfth century.[2] In today's modern industrial society they have become burdensome and wasteful in terms of cost, labor, and time for both the immediate family and the participating descendants. The government has stepped up efforts to trim these ceremonies drastically. In 1973 it laid down the "Guideline for Family Rituals" as a presidential decree, and in 1980 promulgated it as law. According to the law, ancestral ceremonies may be held only for parents and grandparents instead of for the full five generations of ancestors. Funeral ceremonies have been simplified, and the mourning period for parents has been reduced to one hundred days instead of twenty-seven months. The law is, however, proclamatory in nature and has not been strictly enforced. No charge has yet been made for any violation. Since such violations generally do not arouse a sense of guilt, they are almost ubiquitous. Graveside ceremonies on Chusok, for instance, are becoming even more prevalent because transportation is more convenient, and because this outdoor gathering of scattered relatives provides an opportunity for families to reinforce a sense of solidarity. The ancestral memorial services and funeral ceremonies will certainly undergo adjustment and transformation, much in line with the directions set out in the "Guideline," but they should survive in Korea for a long time to come.

The continuation of the male family line is also one of the most important duties of any descendant. Thus, the preference for boys, in spite of government efforts to dispel it, is still strong and affects family planning projects. Adoption is almost solely for the purpose of continuing the family line, so a male heir is always adopted from among close relatives. Since a consciousness of ancestry was very strong in premodern Korea, the publication of clan genealogies (*chokpo;* Chinese: *tsu-p'u*) was a flourishing enterprise during the Chosŏn kingdom. In Korea the compilation, augmentation, and publication of clan genealogies is still prevalent today to an extent probably unparalleled in East Asia.

The most striking example of how staunch the traditional family concept can be and the degree of adherence to traditional values is the opposition to marriage between people whose family origins can be traced back, at least over four centuries, to the same ancestral place of origin. Since there are close to 1 million people with family names such as Kim, Lee, and Pak, and since even the branch lines of these clans usually have hundreds of thousands of members, it is not surprising that couples from the same branch line form conjugal partnerships, possibly without even being aware of their clan origins. According to present law such marriages are illegal. The revision of this outdated prohibition has long been the subject of heated debate, and demonstrations by fundamentalist Confucians still do not ebb. So far no revision has been passed by the National Assembly.

"ALL MEN ARE CONFUCIANS"

Since the census shows only a very superficial and incomplete picture of the religious tendencies of Korea today, efforts have been made to get a clearer picture. Korea Gallup attempted a small but significant survey to analyze the religious characteristics of Koreans, based on a survey method designed by Yoon Yi-hum, professor of religious sciences at Seoul National University. The survey was conducted on a sample of four hundred persons picked through quota allocations. Along with the conventional self-identification method, it attempted an in-depth investigation through one-on-one interviews. The conventional self-identification method yielded the results shown in Table 9.2. The results roughly correspond to the general trend seen in the government census cited earlier. Christians constituted over 30 percent and Buddhists around 20 percent of the population, whereas Confucians numbered less than 1 percent. Also, nearly half the respondents checked "no religion," which is comparable to the response in the government census of over 60 percent.

But the in-depth interview revealed quite a different picture of the religious climate in Korea. It was designed to measure the respondents' degree of adherence to specific values and rituals of the religions to which they subscribe. Since the design of the survey itself reflects how Confucian theory and practice are conceived in Korea today, it would not be out of place to introduce the design here in some detail.

The interview questionnaire was divided into two basic categories: "conviction" and "practice." The "conviction" category covered the Confucian values and was divided into three subcategories, each of which was in turn divided into three to five items, making twelve items altogether. The major items were:

Filial piety and loyalty
Three Cardinal Virtues and Five Ethics *(san-kang wu-lun)*
Benevolence, Righteousness, Courtesy, and Wisdom *(jen-i li-chih)*
Self-cultivation and family ordering *(hsiu-shen ch'i-chia)*
Veneration of the ancient sages and wise men
Inviolability of tradition

Table 9.2 Korea Gallup survey of religions in Korea

Religion	Number	Percentage
Buddhists	77	19.25
Protestants	106	26.50
Catholics	20	5.00
Confucians	2	0.50
Others	6	1.50
No religion	189	47.25
Total	400	100.00

Belief in the inherent goodness of human nature
Sacredness of the Four Books and Five Classics *(ssu-shu wu-ching)*

These "conviction" items were mostly so ambiguous that no respondent could give a straightforward "yes" or "no" answer with any certainty about his own inclinations. Measurement of these items could yield at best only vague tendencies. The second category of "practice," however, which covered actual behavior and daily practices, elicited more tangible and measurable responses. This category was also divided into subcategories and further into thirteen items:

  a. Basic exclusive practices
      Ancestral memorial ceremonies
      Filial piety
      Seniority deference
  b. General practices
      Primogeniture and patrimonial rights
      Regular ancestral graveside rites
      Three years' mourning for parents
      Bridal homage to parents-in-law at weddings
      Endogamy prohibition
  c. Participation in community activities
      Clan ancestral memorial ceremonies
      Clan meetings and compilation of clan genealogies
      Confucian organizations
      Local Confucian school *(hyanggyo)* activities
      Propagation of Confucianism

The respondents were classified into one of four "grades" of Confucianism—active (core), normal, marginal, and outside—depending on their degree of commitment to the items in both categories.

This survey, conducted with a provisional design and on a small scale, nonetheless revealed some very interesting phenomena. First, the discrepancy between the number of people who identified themselves as Christians and the number of those assigned through the interview was negligible, while in the case of Buddhists, the self-identified number was less than half that established by the interview.

Second, those who checked "no religion," when measured against the "conviction" and "practice" items, turned out to be predominantly Confucians. Out of the 189 who checked "no religion," an absolute majority of 183 (96.8 percent) could be counted as Confucians (see Table 9.3).

Third, an unusually strong tendency was found for Confucian values and

Table 9.3   Results of interview

Religion	Self-identified members	Found to be "Confucianized"	Percentage
Buddhists	77	77	100.0
Protestants	106	81	76.4
Catholics	20	18	90.0
Confucians	2	2	100.0
Others	6	5	83.3
No religion	189	183	96.8
Total	400	366	91.7

practices to permeate other religions. Even those who identified themselves as Christians and adhered to Christian values and practices were very much inclined to Confucian values and practices as well, and when measured against the itemized scale, a substantial majority of Korean Christians were found in fact to be at least "marginal" members of Confucianism. Statistically, 90 percent of Catholics and 76.4 percent of Protestants in Korea could be regarded as Confucians according to their convictions and practices. This confirms the statement of a well-known Christian theologian, who said, "Our Christians are Confucians dressed in Christian robes."[3] In the case of Buddhists, the figure was as high as 100 percent.

Fourth, the end result was that among the four hundred interviewees, 91.7 percent (366) were all at least "marginal" adherents of Confucianism.

BASIS OF BELIEFS AND PRACTICES

The survey indeed leaves much to be desired and should be used only with great care, but the results are nonetheless indicative of general trends in the religious characteristics of Koreans.

If we assume the general validity of the survey results, how should we interpret the phenomenal growth of Christianity in Korea in recent decades? Today almost one quarter of the total South Korean population is Christian, the largest proportion of any "Confucian" nation, and yet over 90 percent are Confucians for all practical purposes. How do we reconcile the two obviously contradictory figures?

Three factors seem to be operating in producing this unusual phenomenon. First, Confucianism as an integrated ideology is fading, but not to the extent that the deeply imbued values and daily practices are being eradicated. These legacies still continue their hold on the minds and behavior of the population in general, though it has been considerably weakened, and that explains why most young Koreans may be depicted as Confucians for all practical purposes.

Second, Confucianism can be said to have been relatively tolerant toward other religions. The primary reason for this may be the fact that Confucianism had neither an organized constituent membership nor the missionary zeal to propagate itself. But another important reason seems to be that its humanistic moral teachings can be applied universally, and its rituals and practices are devoid of direct allegiance to any specific founder or savior. Confucianism tolerates and is tolerated by other religions, and thus it can permeate into and be accepted by other religions.

Third, Confucianism is not concerned with salvation. Since those who are in distress and despair can hardly expect to find consolation and spiritual support in Confucianism, they tend to turn to other salvational religions. In this respect Confucianism on the one hand and Christianity and Buddhism on the other are not contradictory but rather complementary.

Confucianism is declining with respect to the number of those who identify themselves as followers, but it is surviving as the basis of the beliefs and practices of the majority of the Korean population, in spite of the fact that they often turn to other religions for salvation.

HERITAGE AND MODERNIZATION

The survival and continuation of Confucian values and practices in an unfavorable atmosphere is due primarily to the older generation. With the passing of this generation, the Confucian heritage will certainly continue to wane. There are, however, new influences at work which, while not in direct support of the Confucian tradition, militate against its further decline, such as a nationalism that searches for its identity in tradition and heritage and an apprehension of the extravagances and moral disintegration caused by industrialization. No attempt is being made to revive Confucianism, but its legacy will, with much adaptation and transformation, remain for a long time to come.

Both the hitherto widely accepted perception that Confucianism was a major hindrance to modernization and development and the recent growing claim that the Confucian heritage is the major driving force behind the spectacular economic development of the Four Mini-Dragons of Asia may be equally one-sided and farfetched. As for the case of Korea, rapid economic development has been achieved primarily by drastically departing from tradition, not by adhering to it. Successful development is due, first, to structural or organizational innovations that permitted the mobilization of human and material resources; second, to the external and internal situations that forced the successful drive; and third, to the inherent cultures that supported and sustained it. Many of the characteristics of Confucianism can be interpreted as either supporting or hindering modernization. It depends on how they are structured and organized in given situations.

FUTURE TRANSFORMATION

The very fact that Confucianism has never been an organized religion and has never really been exclusionistic could now be seen as an advantage by which to expand and propagate itself throughout the wider world. Confucianism is not likely to become an independent, integrated world religion in the future, but instead it can endeavor to become the basic moral teaching of human relations by permeating and being accepted into all religions and ideologies without arousing conflict with their essential beliefs. Confucianism might thereby lose its identity as an integrated ideology, and ultimately even its name, but as the Taoist sage said, "The Tao [Way] that can be told is not the eternal Tao."[4] Confucianism could gain new life and a broader horizon by diffusing itself throughout the ever-changing world.

10

THE REPRODUCTION OF CONFUCIAN CULTURE IN CONTEMPORARY KOREA

An Anthropological Study

Kim Kwang-ok

It was a rainy afternoon in late October 1991 when a funeral procession attempted to enter Seongkyunkwan University, a private university of the Confucian Foundation, carrying the coffin of a student who had committed suicide during an antigovernment demonstration. The bereaved family and fellow students wanted to hold a farewell ceremony at the university where he had studied.

The procession was halted by a group of Confucians who came from all over the country in order to keep the coffin from passing by the *munmyo* where Confucius and his disciples are enshrined. Since Confucius is the supreme saint, they felt that the sacred place should be protected from any kind of pollution.

Confucians, dressed in ritual robes, and students, wearing T-shirts with political slogans, were both sitting in confrontation on the street in front of the main gate of the university. Actually, it would not have been difficult for the students to break the line formed by the few old gentlemen. Neither were they daunted by the well-prepared and experienced riot police. But they dared not cross the line.

Female student representatives knelt down before the old men and, in tears, begged for their special permission but the stubborn Confucians refused to accept their petition. They told the students that, although they were personally sympathetic toward them, they would not allow them to violate the thousand-year-old tradition. There was no possibility of compromise. Both groups sat in silence for hours in the cold autumn rain. Spectators became afraid that the old men might catch cold. Already some of them had fainted. Still, they insisted on maintaining their stand. They felt that contemporary society was on the brink of collapse because the traditional ethical system and principles of human beings were deteriorating. Therefore, they argued, they could not step aside. They asked the students to understand them and not to contravene their last desire to preserve the "national" tradition and ethics.

In a discussion behind the curtains, a young Confucian suggested that the students might break through the side wall of the university, and thus enter the campus without violating the traditional Confucian regulation whereby a corpse that meets its end under abnormal circumstances may not enter his or her house through the main gate. Instead, it must be transported into the house through a hole made in the side wall. Accordingly, some of the students were prepared to demolish the wall, but others objected since doing so would involve damaging public property and would thus give the police an excuse to arrest them. In the end, therefore, with the implicit consent of the Confucians at the front gate, the corpse was carried through the rear gate.

Later, in November, as a reaction to this incident, Confucians from all over the country gathered at the meeting hall of the national head office of the Confucian Association to discuss how to modernize the organization and how to popularize Confucian teachings among the younger generation in contemporary sociocultural settings.

The case just mentioned raises two important points: Confucian culture is still at work in the everyday lives of the Korean people, and it is now being renovated or reproduced. This essay attempts an understanding of Confucian culture as practiced in contemporary Korea—its political, social, and cultural meaning and functions. This is not a philosophical argument or an ethical analysis, but an ethnographic approach by an anthropologist. I focus my observations on the area of Andong, which is generally regarded as one of the exemplary places in Korea for the preservation of traditional cultural elements. It produced a great number of famous Confucian scholars and politicians during the Chosŏn dynasty, and it still maintains aspects of traditional culture. It is in this region where many well-organized lineages compete with one another for social prestige and influence in local politics.[1]

Those engaged in Confucianism may be classified into four categories. First, there are the leaders who are active in institutional organizations, such as Seongkyunkwan University in Seoul, local Confucian temples, and Confucian associations. Second, there are local Confucian elites who, as members of *yurim* (Confucian Forest), study and practice the Confucian learning and traditions in their local societies. Third, there are common people who do not belong to any particular religion but who practice Confucian culture in their daily lives. And last, there are the academicians who specialize in the study of Confucian philosophy, regardless of their own religious affiliation.[2] Andong is an ideal place to understand Confucianism as it is practiced today because its society contains all four of these groups.

Contemporary Korea is characterized as a "multireligious society"[3] in that Buddhist, Protestant, Roman Catholic, shamanic, and Confucian communities are found together, with none of them being prominent in terms of population and degree of sociopolitical influence. The 1984 census reports that more than 91.7 percent of those surveyed can be considered Confucians in that they practice Confucian rituals and ceremonies, regardless of their actual religious affiliation. Also, about 49.7 percent of the respondents identified themselves as Buddhists and 36.3 percent as Christians.[4]

It is typical that members of a Korean family have different religions and that most of them are not completely devoted to one particular religion. A woman who identifies herself as a Christian might visit a shaman in search of fortune (for her husband's new enterprise, her daughter's success in the college entrance examination, and so on). Therefore, it is difficult and even misleading to characterize Korean society with reference to a particular religious sect. Nevertheless, one may say that the Confucian cultural heritage is deeply rooted in people's everyday lives. A Christian might refuse to perform ancestral ceremonies in a Confucian way but still be concerned with his ancestor and kinship relationships. Although highly educated intellectuals criticize the familism and patriarchal ideology, they are still bound to their own kind of familism and male preference. There have also been age-old arguments, ever since Christianity was first introduced into Korea in the eighteenth century, about the ways to incorporate the deeply rooted Confucian tradition into Christianity. All these indicate that Confucianism still works as one of the basic elements of the Korean social structure and its cultural system.

What is even more interesting is that we are now faced with a resurgence of Confucian culture, despite the fact that Korea has undergone the modernization process, with successful economic development and industrialization. It is true that many intellectuals of the younger generation are skeptical about this resurgence, and Christian leaders severely criticize the movement. Nevertheless, the revival of Confucian culture can be observed in contemporary Korea as a careful design and program by those adhering to the ideology, just as it has been politically manipulated by successive regimes since the liberation from Japanese colonialism in 1945.

This essay presents a sociological explanation for this phenomenon by observing Confucian cultural elements that have been revived and popularized in the modern Korean political and cultural contexts and by analyzing people's interpretations of these elements.

THE CONFUCIAN TRADITION AS A CULTURE OF DISTINCTION

In order to have a vivid picture of Confucian culture in practice, it is useful to focus on the members of the local Confucian association, called *yurim*, since they are the most persistent as well as the most conspicuous adherents of the tradition. The superiority of Confucian culture is intentionally dramatized by its members. The *yurim* is a voluntary association, and membership is said to be open to anyone. In reality, however, most of the members are descendants of those of the *yangban* class of the last Chosŏn dynasty, who possessed a strong sense of cultural and moral superiority over others and who were devoted advocates of the Confucian tradition. One may enumerate a number of different ways in which Confucians assert and reinforce this distinction.

First, they have detailed knowledge about their ancestors and family histories. Genealogical awareness is one of the most important resources by which they relate themselves to prominent ancestors. When they introduce themselves, they are expected to produce some information about their clan, lineage, and family background. Therefore, members of the Confucian elite usually keep writings and other related materials about their ancestors, by which they may provide evidence of a superior family background. Marriages are also contracted according to the relative prominence of the clan reputation.

Second, self-cultivation is the core concept of the Confucian way. With the phrase *su-ki ch'i-in* (first cultivate yourself and then you can rule others), Confucians always emphasize the importance of examining moral and philosophical knowledge and practicing what one has learned. For them, knowledge is not important in itself; it must be practiced. Cultivation means to determine one's proper position in the network of social relationships and to behave properly according to one's position. That position is located in the hierarchical order on the one hand, and in the horizontal network on the other. Harmony is achieved only when people practice their proper roles. Harmony refers to the harmonious relationship between Heaven and man, between nature and man, and between man and man. The ideal of the noble man, *kunja*, is realized when one does his best to effect harmony in everyday life in terms of sincerity and respect for others. To keep one's relationships in the proper way means to adopt a proper manner and decorum.

Third, Confucians experience the distinctiveness and superiority of the Confucian culture through complicated rituals and rites, *le-i,* both on religious occasions and in everyday life. Rituals provide the opportunity to reveal the degree of one's cultivation, while at the same time they are occasions for educating people about Confucian culture. Through refined manners it is believed that one can develop sufficient reason to be able to control emotion and desire. Confucians look down on those who do not suppress desire. For instance, some of them regard emotionally expressive Westerners as failing to make the distinction between human reason and animal nature. People in Andong proudly call their hometown "the home of etiquette" *(le-hyang),* in contrast to the southwestern part of Korea, which is called "the home of art" *(ye-hyang).*

Elite qualities are thought to be gained through continuous participation in the enculturation process. Gestures, accent, and special speech behavior, including vocabulary, tone and speed of talking, politeness, self-possession, self-respect and pride, decency and discipline, delicacy of thought, taste and propriety, generosity and forbearance, candor and consideration, special knowledge and loyalty toward tradition, and a firm attitude in the face of external challenges—all these are qualities that constitute the distinctive repertoire of the elite.

Fourth, this elitism is reflected in one's views on job classifications. As self-cultivation through learning and practice is the essence of the Confucian way of becoming a noble man, being a scholar is regarded as the highest ideal. Commercial activities and menial work are looked down on. In the past anybody engaged in commercial activity was ostracized from his lineage and his name erased from the genealogical record. Nowadays a businessman is distinguished from a merchant in that a businessman is regarded as having a white-collar job while a merchant is regarded as carrying out menial work in pursuit of profit. The director or owner of a manufacturing company is qualified to become a member of the Confucian elite because he does not engage in menial labor but rather creates employment opportunities in the public interest.

Since education is the most important mechanism by which people become proper human beings, jobs related to education, such as being a teacher or professor, are highly respected. The job of university professor is one of the most prestigious in Korea, as this represents the model of the noble man. The next highest professions are court judge and high-ranking civil servant because these are related to the administration and governing of people. In their dealings with administration, ordinary people still maintain the traditional idea of the parent-official. The examinations for becoming a government official or a judge are regarded as the equivalent of the national examination during the traditional period.

A noble man refrains from desires for material comfort and selfishness. In particular, he is not supposed to calculate his own interests in terms of money, nor directly involve himself in money dealing. Gaudy fashion and material possessions run counter to Confucian ethics; simple living and a decent life-style are important. A Confucian gentleman's house should not be too colorfully decorated. He should refrain from dancing or singing. Since one's writing is the mirror of one's personality and reflects the quality of one's self-cultivation, people begin studying calligraphy at an early age. In this regard the Confucianists prefer to call calligraphy *seodo,* "the way to cultivate through writing," rather than *seoye,* "the art of writing." The motto of the Confucian elite urges them to live a frugal life, with a love for learning: *ch'eongbin hohak.*

CONFUCIAN INSTITUTIONS

A man should be a member of a *yurim* in order to earn social recognition as a proper Confucianist. With Seongkyunkwan in Seoul as the model, local Confucian temples, or *hyangkyo,* are the basic formal institutions. These temples are sacred places, as Confucius and his disciples are enshrined there for annual commemoration rituals. There are 231 local Confucian temples and 261 Confucian associations, called *yudohoe* (Association for the Confucian Way) or *yurim* (Confucian Forest), throughout the country. Moreover, numerous Confucian academies and clan organizations are closely related to these Confucian institutions.

In principle, each county has one Confucian temple and one Confucian association. If some counties have two organizations, it is because during the Chosŏn dynasty they belonged to different administrative units or cultural areas. Andong county has two temples, called Andong Hyangkyo and Yean Hyangkyo, and, accordingly, two Confucian associations. Yean was originally a part of the Greater Andong Administrative Region. Since it was the seat of T'oegye, the greatest scholar of the Chosŏn dynasty, a separate association and temple were established there. Andong Hyangkyo is said to have been second only to Seongkyunkwan in terms of its size, grandeur of construction, number of members, extent of its properties, and the authority it enjoyed during the Chosŏn dynasty. The buildings were completely destroyed by bombs during the Korean War, however, and the area later became the site of Andong Teachers' College.

In February 1988 a new temple was opened near the newly established

Andong National University. National assemblymen of the region, the mayor of Andong city, and the chief administrator of Andong county, the president of Andong University, heads of educational institutions at various levels in the Andong area, the governor of Kyoungbuk province, and nationally known university professors participated in the special ritual to install tablets of Confucius and of his eighteen Chinese disciples and eighteen Korean Confucian scholars. More than a thousand Confucians came from all parts of the nation. Numerous nationally known Confucian academies and temples sent their blessings, and many political figures, including the president, sent congratulations.

The chief instructor of Seongkyunkwan was given the title of chief supervisor of the entire ceremony, and representatives of various temples from other regions were appointed supervisors of the ceremony out of courtesy. With the pride that Andong Hyangkyo was the most authoritative Confucian institution in Korea, leading figures of the temple performed the main body of ritual. The mayor of Andong made the first libation, the eldest member (eighty-nine years of age) of the Andong *yurim* made the second, and the head of the provincial association made the third, according to tradition. Then thirty-six Confucian leaders made libations to each of the thirty-six Confucian saints besides Confucius.

Each Confucian academy, or *seowon,* is under the supervision of a local Confucian temple and is usually established in commemoration of a prominent scholar. A *seowon* consists of two parts, the shrine and the educational area, including a lecture hall, studies, a library, and a dormitory. In the past, therefore, a *seowon* was a sacred religious place and at the same time functioned as an institution of higher education. There were two ways to establish a Confucian academy. The official national academy was called *saaek seowon,* "the academy which received the board from the king," because the king gave the name of the academy in his own writing on a board. Since it was an institution with royal approval, the academy enjoyed superior authority and prestige. Another type is the local or private academy, which is built by local Confucians to commemorate a prominent scholar. This kind of academy is formally installed with unanimous recognition by members of the local Confucian society. Once established, these private academies perform commemoration rites under the supervision of the local Confucian temple.

In cases of both national and local academies, the enshrined scholar is labeled *bulch'eonwi* "tablet not to be removed." In the case of an ordinary man, his tablet is removed from the ancestral hall after four generations, and thereafter the domestic ritual for him ceases to be observed. Tablets of the spirit of a great scholar, however, are made objects of ritual commemoration for generations. This title is further divided into two categories. There are national *bulch'eonwi,* whose titles were granted by the king in recognition of the quality of the individual's life in relation to the state, such as those who sacrificed themselves in times of national crisis (for example, Admiral Yi Soonshin and General Kim Shimin during the Japanese invasion), or those who lived exemplary lives of great scholarship (for example, Yi T'oegye and Yi Yulgok). The second category includes the *bulch'eonwi* created at the local level by the unanimous consent of local Confucians after evaluating the quality of life and scholarship of the person concerned.

Because *seowon* were built only for those who were *bulch'eonwi,* whether national or local, descendants of the figure enshrined have been regarded as proper *yangban,* and the lineage segmentation was constructed with the honored person as its apical ancestor. Since lineages of this status have maintained an exclusive marriage network among themselves, political power and social influence have also tended to be concentrated in these clans. For this reason it was extremely important for a clan to have such an ancestor if they hoped to pursue social status and political opportunities. If an ancestor was disqualified in a legal case, descendants would continuously petition the king for a reinstatement of his title. This was not only an act of filial piety but also, or perhaps more important, a political struggle for the sake of the descendants themselves.

In 1895, by the special order of the prince regent, Confucian academies all over the nation were demolished except those designated by the king. In the Andong area all the local academies were disbanded, with only two exceptions. One is Tosan Seowon, which was designated by the king to enshrine T'oegye. The other was Byoungsan Seowon, for Ryoo Seong-ryong, which was saved by the wisdom of one of his descendants, who was the magistrate of Andong at that time. He postponed the destruction of the academy until the retirement of the prince regent. After that, however, people rebuilt their academies, and at present there are fifteen local academies under the supervision of Andong Hyangkyo. There are also some lineage shrines *(sawoo)* for their prominent scholars. These local academies and private shrines are also under the supervision of Andong Hyangkyo in that rituals are performed by its members. In addition, members of Andong *yurim* take part in rituals held in Yean region, including at Tosan Seowon.

Rituals at *seowon* are observed only by Confucians. In most cases Confucians from other areas and provinces are also invited to participate. The wider the region from which ritual participants come, the greater the authority and fame of the *seowon* concerned. Therefore, academies compete to show off their fame by inviting well-known figures to attend their ritual occasions. University professors and nationally known Confucian leaders are favored. Tosan Seowon once invited the seventy-seventh-generation descendant of Confucius from Taiwan to be the honorary director for two years, and nominated an ex-president of Seoul National University to succeed him.

RITUAL AT BYOUNGSAN SEOWON

Byoungsan Seowon was established to commemorate Ryoo Seong-ryong, who was one of the prominent disciples of T'oegye and served as prime minister under King Seonjo (1568–1608), especially during the period of national crisis caused by the Japanese invasion (1592–1598). As an ancestor with the *bulch'eonwi* title, he is also commemorated at his family shrine by his descendants on the dates of his birth and death. Commemoration in the academy, however, is performed by Confucians beyond the kinship category. It is held on fixed dates in the third and ninth months of the lunar calendar.

Traditionally, the ceremony has taken place at midnight. Recently, however, the time was changed to 9 o'clock in the morning in order to facilitate participation by local high school students. In principle, the ritual is observed only by Confucians, but it was opened to high school students in order to give them an opportunity to be exposed to their tradition and history.

At the autumn rite of commemoration in 1991, a nationally prominent Confucian, a descendant of Yi Eonjeok, who was highly evaluated by T'oegye, was invited from Kyoungju, in the southern part of Kyoungbuk province, to serve as chief supervisor of the ceremony. An old man, one of the leading figures of the Confucian Society of Jeonbuk province, was given the role of the first sacrificer, and a Confucian of the Kwon clan from Bonghwa, a county located in the north of Kyoungbuk province, was given the role of the second sacrificer. A Confucian of the Andong Kim clan made the third libation. The entire ceremony was supervised by a man from Andong Hyangkyo, and other assistant roles and positions were filled by local Confucian academy members. Representatives of the high school students were allowed a special opportunity to make additional sacrifices. After the ceremony all the participants performed another ritual for sharing food and wine with the spirit, *hyang-eum-le*. It was conducted according to traditional protocol. The participants then changed into street clothes and chatted.

A special network of relationships is established among Confucian academies beyond local boundaries. Primogenital descendants of famous lineages and local Confucians are kept busy traveling all over the country to participate in rituals and ceremonies of other lineages and Confucian institutions.

In 1988 a voluntary association was organized in Andong. Under the initiative of some professors specializing in T'oegye's philosophy, three hundred people of various ages gathered in a middle school located in the vicinity of Tosan Seowon. These included educators, primogenital descendants of local lineages, descendants of T'oegye's disciples, and members of *yurim* from various places in Korea. They named the association *Bak-yak-hoe* after the name of the west wing of Tosan Seowon, and proclaimed that they would try to learn the Confucian teachings by practicing them in their daily lives. According to the leaders of the association, it is necessary to realize Confucian ethics and teachings in a concrete way, especially when social justice and human rights have so seriously deteriorated and morality is threatened with destruction at the national level. They maintain that since T'oegye is the model of a noble man who emphasized the importance of practicing Confucianism in everyday life, people should reevaluate him from a new perspective and try to realize his teachings. The association has held various public lectures and academic conferences on Confucianism in the modern context. Within three years, membership increased to two thousand, mostly from the area of Kyoungbuk and Kyoungnam provinces. In addition to T'oegye, they included four other nationally famous Confucian scholars of the Chosŏn dynasty as their ideological mentors, and expanded their area of influence by holding meetings in various places in Korea.

Another voluntary association is *Dam-soo-hoe* (society of clean and still water), which was established mainly by primogenital descendants of prominent lineages in Korea. Membership is rather selective because of the elitism shared by the founding members. The name of the society symbolizes the notion that pure-mindedness is the greatest need in the "chaotic" social and cultural atmosphere of contemporary Korea, which is described as being dominated by "rotten morality." Friendship should be as clean and constant as water, without artificial taste, flavor, or color. Members hold meetings for friendship and for mutual help during various ritual and social occasions. They visit places related to their respective ancestors and to the ideal scholars of the traditional period.

CONFUCIAN CULTURE IN LOCAL PERFORMANCE

Various activities of the Confucian tradition are observed both at the official and at the private level. In addition to the domestic ancestral worship ceremony, ceremonies at the lineage level are organized in a more elaborate fashion. As a result of economic development, people can afford expensive ceremonies for ancestors. Recently it has become fashionable to reconstruct the grave and memorial stone of an ancestor. Formal ceremonies are conducted by the Confucian society for the occasion, especially in the case of the erection of a memorial stone. All the expenses are covered by the lineage concerned, and Confucians are invited from the farthest possible areas. If the local *yurim* does not perform the ritual, the stone is not recognized as proper. The ritual for the erection of a memorial stone is, in this regard, not only a practice of filial piety, but also an occasion to establish social relationships by sharing the historical community created by the activity.

The Construction of a Symbolic Community

Kim Kyehaeng, the second son of the primogenital descendant of the ninth generation of a localized lineage of the Andong Kim clan, was the first Confucian scholar from the area to hold a high government position during the early Chosŏn period. He was honored by local Confucian scholars because he paved the way for scholars of the so-called Youngnam faction to take up government positions. Despite the power he held as the king's supervisor, he lived a very frugal life. Upon his death he was honored by the king as a model pure-minded official, *ch'eong-baek-ni,* and was given the title *bul-ch'eonwi.* Land was bestowed by the king, and a local Confucian academy was established at his place of worship. A lineage segmentation took place with Kyehaeng as the focal ancestor.

At a special meeting in 1988, the Andong Kim clan decided to erect a memorial stone for him. His descendants were not able to do so at the time of his death since he had made a specific request in his will to avoid all unnecessary extravagance. More recently, however, his descendants began to consider it their moral duty to glorify their honorable ancestor. They argued that it was a matter of face for the entire Andong Kim clan, in view of the fact that other clans with ancestors junior to Kyehaeng had memorial stones for their ancestors. Also, they emphasized that the plan would popularize the virtue of his life in a modern world where morality has been destroyed.

After two years of preparation, they consecrated a memorial stone in May 1990. More than nine hundred Confucians came from all over Korea, representing the various associations they belonged to, and five nationally famous traditional Confucian academies sent long scrolls listing the names of their members who had particular ritual roles to play at the ceremony. In order to honor him, the ceremony was held by the Confucian association of Kyoungbuk province rather than by that of Andong county.

At 9 o'clock in the evening, the nine hundred participants gathered at the open ground wearing ritual dress. The ritual roles were distributed and announced. It took an entire night for the organizing committee to select 120 persons out of the nine hundred registered and to allocate roles and positions for the actual ceremony. The primogenital descendant of T'oegye became the chief supervisor of the ceremony, *do-jip-le;* the primogenital descendant of Kyehaeng took the role of the first sacrificer of ritual food; and the primogenital descendant of Ryoo Seong-ryong was selected to be the second sacrificer. The mayor of Andong made the third libation.

It was a spectacular scene, with nine hundred men of various ages, wearing ritual robes and hats, lining up in front of the newly erected memorial stone in the fresh air of a spring morning. All the participants were provided with rooms and meals for three days and were given their traveling expenses. After the ceremony the participants paid homage at the *seowon* to Kim Kyehaeng, where they were given a collection of his essays and written documents about him.

Various suborganizations of *hyangkyo* organize public lectures on traditional culture and Confucian ethics in collaboration with official institutions. Special training programs for local teachers include lectures on Confucian philosophy and studies of local Confucian scholars. These are designed to give teachers a sense of pride in their local culture and history based on the Confucian tradition. Also, classes on the Confucian classics are open to general readers. For children simplified versions and comic books of the Confucian classics are produced.

The city council awards special prizes to filial sons and virtuous women on the recommendation of the local Confucian society. Although the women's liberation movement criticizes the awards as contributing to the perpetuation of sexual inequality, it is done in all counties of the nation, as it is widely regarded as a positive national tradition. In the same regard, the traditional initiation ceremony, *kwan-le,* is reproduced by the city council for teenagers, through which Andong has gained a reputation as the seat of the tradition.

Ancestor worship is a cultural mechanism through which people learn about their history and cultural distinctiveness. In line with the recent tendency toward "cultural nationalism," the material cultures of the past are being reevaluated. Confucians have a special interest in the preservation of the writings and possessions of their ancestors, and reproduce genealogical records and written materials concerning them. Such activities enable them to discover the hidden or forgotten history of their own lineage in a new light as well as their social and political relationships to other lineages and clans.

Opening private museums for local scholars is also in fashion. This is financed by the lineage or clan concerned in order to preserve collections of all kinds of objects related to their prominent ancestors, such as clothes, shoes, fans, hats, personal belongings, stationery, letters from the king and from friends, diaries, certificates, books they read and wrote, and so on.

Private History in the Public Context

In the spring of 1985 the lineage of Kim Seong-il organized the opening ceremony of a lineage museum which contained valuable relics and written materials related to their ancestors of over eight hundred years. About five hundred Confucians came from all over the country. Professors of history, philosophy, and cultural studies were also selectively invited. The whole ceremony was conducted in a traditional Confucian way under the supervision of the local Confucian society. The event was announced in the mass media, and details of the ceremony were broadcast on a local television channel, thus allowing ordinary people to participate indirectly.

On the eve of the ceremony, after all the ritual roles were distributed among those attending, the Confucians enjoyed chatting about philosophical discourses and debates. Some of them read aloud poems or phrases of Confucian teaching written by their ancestors in order to demonstrate their scholarship. Others engaged in a discussion of the "authenticity" of a ritual. The debates were enlivened when their ritual pattern was compared with that of other lineages and academies in other parts of Korea. The participants argued about differences in the physical arrangement of their own *seowon* and the format of rituals and those of the so-called Kiho school, represented by Yulgok. They expressed their sense of superiority over the Yulgok school and the Noron faction in terms of ritual authenticity and quality of scholarship.

During the mid-Chosŏn dynasty government officials and scholars were divided into two factions called Dong-in, man of the east (camp), and Seo-in, man of the west (camp). The east camp was later divided into Nam-in, man of the south (camp), and Buk-in, man of the north (camp), while the west camp was divided into Noron, theory of the senior (group), and Soron, theory of the junior (group). Politics during the latter half of the Chosŏn dynasty consisted of bloody struggles between the Nam-in and Noron factions.

Kim Seong-il belonged to the east camp Nam-in, and later the majority of Confucian scholars in the Andong area joined this faction, with T'oegye's philosophy as their ideological basis. T'oegye and Yulgok differed in their interpretations of Confucian thought, and each had his own theories. Followers of T'oegye became the main force of the Nam-in faction, while those of Yulgok became members of Noron. Differences in the theory and practice of rituals and rites between the two factions resulted in recurrent bloody political attacks and counterattacks. Therefore, even today there is a deep-rooted antagonism between descendants of scholars of these two factions.

Through participating in various activities organized at the public and private level, people learn the proper way of self-introduction, manners and etiquette, patterns of verbal and nonverbal behavior, the use of refined vocabulary, and so on. Those who are ignorant about their ancestors are regarded as non-*yangban* and are looked down on. Since people of the younger generation today are not well aware of the importance of these traditions, the local *yurim* organizes classes in traditional culture, where young people can learn about genealogy, reading Confucius' and other scholars' teachings in simplified and modernized interpretations, and etiquette. Clan and lineage councils organize cultural movements to help the young feel connected with their roots *(ppurich'atki woondong)*, in which descendants are taught histories relating to their ancestors and make pilgrimages to places related to their family history.

Historical buildings and written materials of earlier scholars are registered as national or local cultural treasures and preserved by the state. This enhances the social prestige of the families concerned and reinforces the cultural superiority of the Confucian tradition.

It has also become fashionable for people to seek out locations connected with their ancestors. Places where a famous ancestor was born, once lived, or spent some years in exile for political reasons are of special significance. Also important are places where the ancestor died in battle against foreign invaders, or any location cited in the ancestor's essays or poems. Descendants make lists of local Confucian academies where their ancestors once studied or are now worshipped. They organize tour groups to visit these places, publish essays on their visit, and reprint documents concerning the places. They try to identify the descendants of friends of the ancestor or of people who served the ancestor, to express gratitude to them. If they are wealthy enough, they make donations to the academies related to the ancestor, participate in ceremonies there, and even purchase land or buildings related to the ancestor.

By taking part in the pilgrimages, people enter into the imaginary world of their ancestors, create their own past, and through the process of sacred ritual come to identify with their ancestors. Moreover, pilgrimages provide an experience for constructing a conceptual map of their own world beyond the limits of time and space. By visiting these sacred places, people renew their historical consciousness and expand their historical community beyond local boundaries.[5] Through these activities they reconstruct or solidify the social network of communication. Interregional relations among local Confucian societies are established which cover the whole country.

CONFUCIAN CULTURE IN A PRACTICAL CONTEXT

Confucianism in Korea, as a civic culture rather than a religion, should be understood in the context of cultural and political history. It has been noted that the Confucian tradition in relation to politics emphasizes the notion of hierarchy and the ideal of *ch'ung-hyo* (loyalty to the state and filial piety to parents). These two sets of ideals and value systems of Confucianism have been manipulated both by the state and the counterforce of the society in national and local politics throughout Korean history.

During the Japanese colonial occupation (1910–1945), the cultural nationalism and literati elitism of the Confucians struggled against the Japanese military suppression and cultural colonialization programs. The colonial government deliberately attempted to Japanize Korean culture by forcing Koreans to accept Shintoism as the state religion and to change their personal names to the Japanese style with new Japanese surnames. At the same time, speaking the Korean language and writing in the Korean alphabet were strictly forbidden. As an essential part of this "cultural" policy, Korean history was distorted and rewritten from a negative perspective by the colonial scholars.

Because of their strong sense of nationalism and cultural superiority, many Confucian leaders committed suicide or organized violent resistance against Japanese colonial rule. The majority of the Confucian elite in the Andong area sacrificed their property and went into exile as a result of their anti-Japanese activities. Some established private schools based on nationalistic teaching in their belief that education was the only way to retake the nation. Others lived in China, where they led the Korean government-in-exile and organized military operations against the Japanese army. Of course, the Japanese government propagated the ideal of *ch'ung-hyo* in their colonial education program for the Koreans. The Confucians, however, emphasized Korean nationalism over the notion of the state on the one hand, and on the other maintained their sense of the cultural superiority of the literati tradition over Japanese military dominance.

In the political struggles after the liberation, Lee Syngman's party, backed by the United States and those who had cooperated with the Japanese colonial government, defeated the Nationalist party, led by those who were active in the anti-Japanese movement. The First Republic proclaimed its fervent anticommunism, supported by Christians and those who had cooperated with the Japanese. During the height of McCarthyism, the families of anti-Japanese fighters were suspect because their nationalism at times conflicted with the government's anticommunist policies. This widened the gap between the state ideology and the people's perception of their nationalism, which followed the Confucian tradition. Although they were supportive of the new government in their enthusiasm for the reconstruction of their nation, the Confucian elites in general maintained an attitude of reserve toward the Christian-oriented Syngman Lee.

Under the influence of the Confucian elite, the majority of voters in Andong supported the opposition party in the general elections. At the first general election Kim Sihyun was elected the national assemblyman from Andong. As the primogenital descendant of a locally prominent lineage of the Andong Kim clan, he joined the independence movement of the government-in-exile in China after he graduated from a university in Tokyo. He had been sentenced to life in prison for his abortive attempt to assassinate Syngman Lee. After the First Republic was toppled by the student revolution in April 1960, he was released from prison. By the time he ran for a seat in the National Assembly in the 1960 general election, he was too old to move about freely, and his physical condition had deteriorated as a result of his long imprisonment. He also had no money to organize his election campaign. But he was nevertheless elected by an absolute majority and was given unanimous support by the local Confucian society.

With the Third Republic, born out of a military coup d'état in 1961, the tension between state authority and Confucian culture heightened. At first people were critical of the legitimacy of the new government. The government denounced the cultural tradition in its pursuit of modernization, and it promoted the regulation of family ritual in order to simplify the traditional marriage and funeral rites. This regulation dealt a heavy blow to the Confucians, to whom rituals are so important for establishing their cultural distinction. At the same time, the new government initiated diplomatic relations with Japan. The mutual antagonism between the newly emerged military power elite and the civilian tradition was inevitable, and the Confucian tradition of literati elitism supported the latter.

The tension between the military regime and the Confucians heightened when Park Chung-hee criticized the literati tradition in his election campaign. Before gatherings of elderly Confucians in Taegu, the capital city of Kyoungbuk province, he openly criticized Kim Seong-il[6] as an example of a narrow-minded Confucian scholar who lacked a sense of responsibility toward the nation and who wasted national energy on empty theory and futile debate (kong-li-kong-ron).

This provoked serious counterattacks by the Confucians throughout Kyoungbuk province, the very base of political support for Park. As a compromise, Park visited Tosan Seowon to pay a special homage to T'oegye, and he designated the academy as the property of the national culture. In order to solidify his political resources under the strong influence of Confucian tradition, Park renovated Confucian relics, including the Tosan Seowon, and printed the likeness of T'oegye and Yulgok on paper currency. Scholars who had sacrificed themselves in the resistance against the invading Japanese forces were recognized, and their shrines were reconstructed. The government also provided financial support for local lineages to open private museums honoring their scholar ancestors.

Local Confucians understood this series of actions by Park as an expression of nationalism and respect for the national culture and history molded by the Confucian tradition. Gradually they came to favor Park, emphasizing that he had been educated at the normal school and had served as a teacher before he entered the army. They were content with Park's emphasis on morality and his simple life-style. Although intellectuals and college students criticized Park's favorable attitude toward Japan, the old Confucian elite acknowledged that Park had an understanding of the literati tradition because of his educational background.

Park manipulated the people's memory of their historical experiences based on Japanese colonial exploitation and the total destruction and poverty caused by the Korean War. He emphasized that the existence of a strong government was necessary in order to achieve economic prosperity and national security against the threat of communist invasion. Hence, the ideal of loyalty to the state, *ch'ung*, was emphasized. People were indoctrinated to perceive the nation as a family, with the president as the patriarchal head. While some liberal Christian leaders criticized the deterioration of human rights and democracy, Confucian leaders collaborated with the government in their belief that the authority of the government was necessary to achieve national security and prosperity. It is quite interesting to note in this connection that the government used the idea of the Confucian authority system while it denounced Confucians as being responsible for the nepotism and conservatism that delayed economic and scientific development.

Confucianism emphasizes the importance of orderliness, which is to be realized through the proper exercise of both the vertical order and horizontal relationships among members of the society. Harmony is achieved only when all members of society identify their respective positions in the social order and behave accordingly. This is the way to self-cultivation, and the road to achieving this cultivation is to know oneself. Confucianism is therefore not a religion but a "way," and the essence of the Confucian way is to practice respect *(kyoung)* and sincerity *(seong)*. John F. Kennedy's speech in which he emphasized that people should ask not what the country can do for them but what they can do for the country was frequently quoted approvingly by the Korean government, and the Confucian ideal of citizenship was understood as being similar to this.

During the past several decades the most serious question the Korean people have raised in the political sphere is that of the legitimacy of the regime rather than that of democracy. Many would argue that, if a regime is legitimate, it does not matter whether or not it is democratic. The tradition of patrilineal rule led people to be relatively uncritical about the nepotism around the president. They were gradually persuaded to accept the government's idea that a change of power from the present majority party to the opposition party was not desirable as long as the regime was successful in creating economic development and ensuring national security. Antigovernment activities were regarded by the regime as procommunist, and Confucians regarded them as unfilial acts against the great family of the nation.

In this regard one may say that Confucianism has contributed to, or at least cooperated in, the establishment of the absolute authority of the state during the past several decades by providing an ideological base for loyalty to authority and to the establishment. Andong became the loyal supporter of state authority, and the Confucians' challenge to the legitimacy of regimes that had emerged by military coup d'état was not as strong as that of the intellectuals and the college students. Only candidates from the government party have been successful there in the various elections from the Third Republic to the present. In reality, however, the Confucian community in Andong is not homogeneous, in that disputes have arisen every time an election has been held. There have been heated debates over whether to support or attack the regime, which lacks the legitimacy of power. On the one hand, the Confucian community has encouraged people to exercise loyalty to the state by applying familism to the concept of the state, but on the other hand, they were critical of the military origins of the government.

Confucianism and Business

Korea's "miraculous" economic development since the 1970s has been achieved through the leadership of the government, which has exercised patriarchal authority. Confucian culture has thus been adopted into the area of economic activity. Regardless of their membership in a particular religious sect, heads of economic institutions and organizations have exercised Confucian patriarchal authority and privilege in their actual business management.

New employees are indoctrinated to regard their workplace as a family, with the company director or president as a family head who enjoys patriarchal authority. In the case of a large company, the head uses his own office, toilet, and dining room, as the head of a family has his own space separate from that for the other members of the family. An elevator is reserved for his exclusive use. Employees arrive at work before he arrives, and are expected to remain until he leaves his office. They are taught to identify themselves as members of a big family which is named for the company, such as the Hyundai family, the Samsung family, or the Daewoo family. Juniors behave vis-à-vis their seniors according to Confucian codes of etiquette.

Business culture, which is based on the idea of a vertical relationship, is said to have originated in the mix of a military system and the Japanese style. But it is also deeply rooted in the Confucian way of doing things. Because the head always emphasizes the importance of harmonious relations among the members, the Confucian behavioral codes, which depend on attributes such as differences in age, kinship status, sex, and sociopolitical status, are expected to be observed.

Poongsan Metal Company

Poongsan Metal Company was founded by a descendant of Ryu Seong-ryong from Poongsan township of Andong. Because of government support for the development of a national security industry in the 1970s, the company grew rapidly to become one of the major industrial firms in Korea. With headquarters in Seoul, it has several factories all over the country. Its headquarters employ more than a thousand white-collar workers. Over 80 percent of the management positions are filled with people from Andong. The majority of the executive board are either descendants of the founder's lineage or people who have some marriage relationship to his clan.

Because of these relationships through ancestors, workers of the company easily adopt pseudo-kinship terminology for use among themselves. They call one another by kin terms such as elder and younger brother or uncle and nephew, according to their age difference and kinship or marriage relationship. As they share the local dialect and accent as well as other cultural codes of behavior, they appear to be part of an imagined family. On account of this one might suppose that it would be difficult for junior employees to function in a businesslike way. An undemocratic atmosphere may prevail as they identify one another in terms of kinship or pseudo-kin relationships. In order to minimize the negative consequences of this internal structure of the company, seniors always emphasize Confucian ethics with regard to the relations between senior and junior, between father and son, and between brothers.

By employing people of the same cultural background, the company saves time and energy in training newcomers in its moral and cultural codes. They are already well enough educated in Confucian ethics to adapt to the hierarchical order of the workplace, and their sense of loyalty is already guaranteed by the social relationships based on kinship and affinal ties. This works well in most situations. The seniors, however, are not well trained to deal with abnormal occurrences, such as labor disputes, which are confrontations between people of different cultural codes.

The Poongsan Metal Company uses Byoungsan Seowon as an educational facility for the newly employed. The president of the company asks newcomers to think of themselves and their company in relation to Ryu Seong-ryong, who, as a great scholar-official during the Chosŏn dynasty, sacrificed himself for the nation. He emphasizes that the company is not private but public in the sense that the industry contributes to national security. He tries to rationalize his business in the context of history by referring to national heroes such as Prime Minister Ryu Seong-ryong, and attempts to indoctrinate his workers with the idea of loyalty to the state. Members of the executive board emphasize the importance of morality and etiquette among all members of the company. At an employment interview the president considers an applicant's quality of self-cultivation and manners rather than actual knowledge because a proper family background guarantees harmonious relations in the company.

TriGem Computer Company

TriGem is one of the leading computer companies in Korea. It was founded by collaboration between Lee Yong-t'ae and Kim Chong-kil. Kim is the primogenital descendant of Kim Seong-il, and Lee is related to him through marriage (his grandmother is the daughter of a primogenital descendant of Kim Seong-il). Later on another Lee, the youngest brother of the primogenital descendant of T'oegye, joined the company. Lee's elder sister is Kim's wife. In this regard the company represents cooperation among three major clans and is solidified by marriage relationships. The principals refer to one another with kinship terms such as elder brother, younger brother, uncle, and so on. Dr. Lee was elected the president of the International Society for T'oegye Studies, and the company provides a great deal of financial help for the institute, including holding worldwide conferences and other activities for their respective lineages.

Since companies are perceived by many Koreans as extended families, it seems only natural that business should operate on the basis of Confucian ethics and familism. For instance, it is not strange to find nepotistic management in business. The principle of primogenital inheritance according to the patrilineal descent rule is also practiced in filling the chairmanship of a company. Samsung and Hyundai, two gigantic business complexes that filled the presidencies of their member companies with the sons and nephews of their respective founders, are not criticized as much in Korea as one might expect.

Since the Western concepts of free market and contract are not well established in Korea, the pattern of business management based on familism and patriarchal authority is in conflict with the general tendencies of civil society. In the turmoil of labor disputes in the 1980s, the most serious problem turned out to be that business administrators and managers were not ready to accept demands for democracy in business management. For them it meant the deterioration of the harmonious relations which had been maintained by their Confucian ethics.

THE REGENERATION OF CONFUCIAN CULTURE

Why has the Confucian tradition reemerged, and how has this been accommodated in the current situation in Korea? It is to be understood in the context of sociocultural change at the national level. The past forty or so years have witnessed the process of a deconstruction of the traditional class system by a new social system and a new worldview. At the same time, the Confucian tradition as an elite culture is no longer the exclusive asset of any particular privileged class. Access to the tradition is much easier for everyone. As a consequence, the Confucian tradition in Korea today no longer functions as a system by which one class distinguishes itself from others. Descendants of the traditional upper class try to "generate" and "invent" more refined aspects of the Confucian culture in order to set themselves apart.

Another explanation may be drawn from the fact that Confucianism is a multifaceted ideological set and has been treated differently by people of different political orientations. During the 1930s the illegitimate military regime tried to utilize the idea of loyalty to the state as a means of blind emotional indoctrination. Although liberals of the Christian and Buddhist communities were active in antigovernment movements during the period, most Confucian leaders kept silent on the issue of human rights and social justice, and at times cooperated with the authoritarian government by supporting the idea of social order based on patriarchal government authority.

Confucianism began to be interpreted from different perspectives by university professors and students in their criticism of the military-based regime. "Politics by educated people and civilians" *(munmin jeongch'i)* was the leading slogan of opposition leaders and antigovernment movement activists during the 1980s. *Mun* means literature or the literati tradition, and *min* designates civilians as opposed to the military. The major implication of *munmin* is that the educated literati or educated civilians should lead the country rather than an "ignorant" or "meanly educated" military junta. This elitism of the literati tradition is backed up by Confucian discourse. As Tu Wei-ming puts it, "Theoretically, and occasionally in practice, Korean intellectuals have exercised their right to criticize the state and the symbolic resources used by the state to legitimize both its *modus operandi* and its very existence."[7]

Studies on Jeong Yak-yong of the late Chosŏn dynasty, a prominent Confucian scholar with revolutionary ideals and critical attitudes toward the exploitation of the peasants by the power elite, became fashionable among academics. His works were reproduced and translated into Korean, and his democratic ideals were reanalyzed. This trend was perceived as a message for intellectuals to engage actively in sociopolitical problems with a sense of responsibility, on the one hand, and as an indicator of the superiority of the literati tradition, symbolized by the advanced ideology advocated by past Confucian scholars, on the other.

Also, during the 1980s intellectuals and college students began to perceive the negative impact of economic development and an authoritative political process—unequal distribution of economic opportunities, political alienation, social marginalization—as the inevitable results of a coalition of the military elite, technocrats, and capitalists. As the movement of the intellectuals developed, some began to criticize the elitism inherent in the Confucian tradition and sought to understand the dynamics of the historical process from the viewpoints of nonelite people through *minjung munhwa woondong*. Instead of *yangban* culture, which had been monopolized and symbolized by the Confucian elite, activists in the popular cultural movements emphasized the significance of popular culture. Peasant music and dance, shamanism, and peasant rebellions were the main topics both in academic discourse and in actual performances. To them, to be an elite in Korea meant to be a puppet of (neo)colonial power, a collaborator with the dictatorship, an egoist maximizing one's own interests by exploiting the majority of poor peasants. Therefore, Confucianism gradually became their major target.

Yet in their ritual of rebellion students used the Confucian pattern of ceremony in their announcement of the purpose and legitimacy of their intention before calling on the spirits of their protector through a shamanistic performance. Confucianism and shamanism are thoroughly mixed in antigovernment movements: the former was used in the effort to establish the legitimacy of the rebellion in the context of national history and the literati tradition against the abnormal succession of power by an illegal military junta, and the latter was used to symbolize the dynamic of people's power in the fight against the immoral power elite.

Although the radical intellectuals criticize the Confucian tradition in their effort to popularize the folk tradition, the criticism is based on their antagonism toward the traditional estate system, which was epitomized by the privilege of the *yangban* class. It is interesting to note that they posit their antigovernment movement and concern for the popular culture in the intellectual history of Korea, which is itself based on the Confucian tradition. Whether or not they share the same Confucian elitism that teaches intellectuals to have a distinctive sense of responsibility and criticism, their pragmatic idealism seems deeply rooted in Confucian political culture.

RESPONSE TO THE SOCIOCULTURAL CURRENTS

The revival of the Confucian tradition may also be interpreted as a new moral movement in the sense that it appeared as a reaction to the rapid economic development and modernization process which resulted in the destruction of the traditional moral and ethical system. During the past several decades the major driving force of antiestablishment movements in Korea has been criticism of the government for the lack of democracy, the suppression of human rights, and the perpetuation of social injustices. Contemporary Confucian scholars criticized the moral status of the political elite. In the past only the moral duties of the governed were emphasized, but now people began to question the morality of political leaders. They argued that the elite should lead exemplary lives before the people, as the Confucians of the traditional period would try to exemplify the way of a noble man.

Another explanation can be sought in connection with the recent development of cultural nationalism. As the influx of foreign cultural elements increased under the political slogans of "Korea in the World" and "The Creation of Korea as an Advanced Nation" by the government during the 1980s, intellectuals became seriously concerned with the issue of national identity. Especially during the latter half of the 1980s, in preparation for the Seoul Olympiad, cultural nationalism became fashionable among the people.

Confucian leaders were in conflict with students on the issue of violent reactions against the government. The Confucian circle was of the opinion that criticism should be refined in the manner of gentlemen, while the students emphasized the violent dynamics of the nonelite people. More recently the popular cultural movement has been attacked as representing only one level of society, neglecting the refined aspect of upper-class culture in the search for national identity. It is in this context that Confucianism is discussed as one of the possible solutions. Ancestor worship, rituals, and ceremonies in the Confucian way, cultural tradition based on Korean Confucianism, together with Confucian ritual robes and foods are all regarded as important aspects of the cultural heritage. The way of drinking and table manners as well as other traditional behavior based on the Confucian tradition are recognized as national trends toward a refined culture.

The revival of Confucianism is also a reaction against the process of modernization based on American-style pragmatism and economic wealth and modeled on Western standards. Through the New Village Movement, first launched in the late 1960s, the government denounced the Confucian tradition as a hindrance to modernization. Muted by the public discourse, the Confucian tradition became the private culture of localized elite groups. Now, people have begun to realize the importance of cultural nationalism and have tried to restore Confucian culture in their search for cultural identity.

The capitalist value system replaced the Confucian concept of quality of life. Personal income became one of the most important indicators of status. The traditional value system which emphasized the refinement of emotion and control of physical and material desires gave way to the uncontrollable and competitive pursuit of material and physical comfort and satisfaction. People of the older generation began to stress the need to restore the esprit of the Confucian gentleman *(seon-bi-jeong-shin)* and return to an education in ethics.

Consumption patterns raise serious social and economic problems. Confucians feel uneasy about recent trends in which economic morality is destroyed and simple living is not respected. They also point out that people have become more egoistic and have lost their concern for public and communal life. All of these changes can be expressed in one phrase: the destruction of order. In this context a rehabilitation of the superiority of spiritual life over material life is necessary, and the Confucian value system is needed to meet this goal.

As we have seen, Confucian culture saturates the Korean people's lives and is the core of Korean culture. Confucianism itself is a multifaceted value system, and therefore it is interpreted differently according to the political or social situation. As I mentioned earlier, Confucian culture has been made, reshaped, and regenerated by different groups with different purposes. It is interesting to see that the Confucian tradition is thought to be able to bridge the gap between state authority and the people's experience of community.

Confucian culture in Korea is represented by familism, intellectualism or literati elitism, and the importance of ritual or the moral life. Familism developed a communal ethic and a strong sense of history among the people. They could manipulate the ideal of familism in their construction of society and in their dealing with the state. The tradition of intellectualism provided a basis for distinctive aspirations for education in Korea on the one hand, and the sense of noble responsibility of the intellectuals toward their society on the other. The social application of familism and the intellectualist tradition have been the driving forces behind economic development and the pursuit of civilian politics. Also, man cultivates himself and expresses the quality of his personal cultivation through rituals. Etiquette, manners, decorum, refinement of verbal and nonverbal behavior, which are necessary for social order and harmony, are required by the ritualization of life. Despite criticism of the negative aspects of Confucianism in the modern context, these reasons for positive appreciation are emphasized by the Confucians as they try to construct a community based on cultural superiority in the face of foreign influences and the immorality of economic pursuits.

The problem of Confucianism in contemporary Korea is that it lacks organizational refinement. In contrast to other religious communities, the Confucian circle is not well organized. Seongkyunkwan is not the headquarters, and local *hyangkyo* do not constitute a concrete system, since there is no formal relationship between the academies. It is therefore quite common for Confucian cultural traditions to be monopolized by prominent local clans or lineages. Sharing the ritual of the same tradition means constructing the symbolic boundaries of community. Here the image of community for the Confucians is different from that of the power group and that of the antigovernment movement leaders. Although the Confucian tradition is recognized as an aspect of national cultural tradition, so long as it remains the elite culture, it will be continuously challenged by those in other social sectors.

It is also interesting to note that Confucianism in Korea is now engaged in a real conflict not with other religious sects but within its own community, between the liberal younger generation and the conservative older generation. And this is a reflection of the larger national cultural turmoil. In a word, people in Andong have a strong sense of their cultural superiority, which is based on a local history that produced numerous prominent scholars, civil servants, and statesmen, including many active leaders of the independence movement during the colonial period. Although Andong is now backward with respect to industrialization and economic prosperity, local residents are proud of having maintained the Confucian tradition as their cultural identity throughout the political-cultural hardships at the national level. In this regard, the recent revitalization movement of Confucianism is understood in the context of the people's search for a new culture to construct their own community for civilian politics by which they can cope with state authority on the one hand and the ever-increasing influx of Western culture on the other.

11

STATE CONFUCIANISM AND ITS TRANSFORMATION

The Restructuring of the State-Society Relation in Taiwan

Ambrose Y. C. King

The rise of the East Asia region, manifested first in Japan as a supereconomic power and subsequently in the so-called Four Mini-Dragons as newly industrialized countries (NICs), has captured the interest and imagination of scholars of different persuasions. Among the explanations accounting for this phenomenal success in economic modernization, a post-Confucian thesis emphasizing the role of Confucian cultural values has been articulated in various forms. What I address here is the challenge of democracy confronting those countries that can be broadly conceived as post-Confucian states.

No student of politics today can afford to be unaware of what Lucian Pye calls "the crisis of authoritarianism."[1] The crisis of authoritarianism, in most cases, is concomitant with the challenge of democracy. Speaking on democracy, Ernest Gellner has provided a vivid description:

> Looking at the contemporary world, two things are obvious: democracy is doing rather badly, and democracy is doing very well . . . Democracy is doing very badly in that democratic institutions have fallen by the wayside in very many of the newly independent "transitional" societies, and they are precarious elsewhere. Democracy, on the other hand, is doing extremely well in as far as it is almost (though not quite) universally accepted as a valid form.[2]

John Dunn perceptively points out that "democratic theory is the moral Esperanto of the present nation-state system, the language by which all nations are truly united, the public cant of the modern world, a dubious currency indeed."[3] He further suggests that "all states today profess to be democracies because a democracy is what it is virtuous for a state to be."[4] Indeed, the Four Mini-Dragons (South Korea, Taiwan, Hong Kong, and Singapore) have demonstrated remarkable success in economic development, but are they able to take up the challenge of political democracy? In a broad sense, the nature of the political systems of the Mini-Dragons can be characterized as authoritarian. How can these authoritarian systems be transformed into democratic ones? I intend to analyze the transformation of Taiwan's state system, which showed a marked discontinuity with the state Confucianism of imperial China. The theoretical focus of the analysis is on the state-society relationship and changes in it. The existence and viability of a civil society are believed to be necessary conditions for the development of a political system that is democratic in nature.

STATE-SOCIETY RELATIONSHIPS IN IMPERIAL CHINA

The single most important factor that shaped and molded the social-political structure of traditional China was the establishment of a centralized bureaucratic state in the hands of its first emperor, Shih Huang Ti of Ch'in. Under the Ch'in empire, which grew from the collapse of the feudal substates through war, political unity was achieved for the first time in Chinese history. In the Han dynasty, which was the immediate successor of the short-lived Ch'in, while the basic state structure of the Ch'in remained relatively unchanged, Confucianism was elevated to the status of state ideology. The Confucian cultural system was then integrated with the political structure, which had a strong legalistic character. Thereafter the interpenetration of culture and politics was in a significant way the fundamental social-political reality of imperial China. What should be noted is that the state ideology of the Han was an amalgam of Confucianism and legalism which provided the legitimation for the imperial rulership of successive dynasties. From the Han onward, Confucianism became what can be called *institutional Confucianism* as the result of the mutual penetration of the cultural system and the political structure.

Institutional Confucianism refers to an institutional-cultural complex.[5] It refers to political institutions, including imperial authority, as the keystone of the state system, the imposing bureaucracy as an instrument of the imperial state, and the literati and gentry as a status group linking the state

with society. All these institutional structures were intermingled with Confucian cultural values. As the keystone of the state system, imperial authority
was embodied in the concept of a cosmically based universal kingship. Benjamin Schwartz argues that "the centrality and weight of the political order"
was one of the most striking characteristics of Chinese civilization.[6] He
writes, "The kingship or locus of the authority which he occupies *(wei)* is
an institution which comes to constitute the major link between human society and the ruling forces of the cosmos."[7]

The universal king embodies within his person the supreme authority over
both the sacred and the secular realms of sociopolitical life. Max Weber
showed unusual insight in noting that "secular and spiritual authority were
combined in one hand, the spiritual strongly predominating."[8] The legitimacy of the universal king was based on the well-known theory of *t'ien-
ming,* or the "Mandate of Heaven." The universal king was conceived as the
Son of Heaven. Under the vast heaven, the universal king had, to use
Schwartz's expression, "all-encompassing jurisdictional claims over the social-political life of the people."[9] Since, according to the theory of the Mandate of Heaven, imperial power was a religiously consecrated structure, it
precluded the possibility of the development of a powerful priesthood or
independent religious force, as Weber pointed out. The nonexistence of independent religious forces in China made the Chinese monarch a "pontifex"
who ruled the sociopolitical world "in the old genuine sense of charismatic
authority."[10] Furthermore, according to the Confucian ideal of the sage-king,
the ultimate form of politics must be a form of "ethocracy," that is, ethical
politics. In Confucianism there was no recognized autonomous realm of
politics, separate from or independent of morality. Confucian thinkers never
intended to develop, and indeed never could envisage, institutional constraints on imperial authority. As Leon Vandermeersch points out, there was
nothing in China comparable to Montesquieu's three powers.[11] And in the
same vein, political pluralism was hardly conceived as a desirable state of
political affairs.[12]

Bureaucracy was an indispensable institution of the imperial state. In fact,
"bureaucratic power is usually thought to be the essence of state activity . . .
[and] it is sometimes considered to be identical with it."[13] The Mandarins
(i.e., scholar-officials) of the bureaucracy were the governing class of the
Chinese state par excellence. Their status and prestige were defined in cultural terms, and qualifications for office were decided by a competitive examination based on the Confucian classics. Under institutional Confucianism the state, exemplified by the kingship institution, was entitled to make
all-encompassing jurisdictional claims on the sociopolitical affairs of the empire. Hsü Fu-kuan posits a strong thesis for the state by saying that the pivot

of the Chinese autocratic system, the foundation for which was laid down in the Ch'in and Han dynasties, was that "outside of the imperial domination, no independent or resisting forces were allowed to exist."[14] Jacques Gernet advances a similar argument. He writes: "The only problem for the Chinese state in the course of its long history, was to prevent the development of powers other than its own, such as that of the merchants, the armies, the religious communities, and to prevent dangerous splits at the top."[15]

What should be reiterated here is that the state institutions (kingship and bureaucracy) were permeated by Confucian ethical values. The problem of the power of state Confucianism must be considered at the same time as the problem of duty. The Confucian ideal of ethocracy was based on the concept of duty or obligation instead of right or power.[16] To say that the state has an all-encompassing jurisdictional claim on the sociopolitical life of the people is tantamount to saying that the state has a comprehensive responsibility "to provide [for], to enrich, and to educate" the people.[17] Seen from this perspective, it is not difficult to agree with Karl Bunger that "the Chinese emperor had no 'right' to rule, but a 'Heavenly Mandate' (t'ien-ming), i.e., a duty to fulfill. It was his duty to keep the human society in good order (zhi). The guidelines for this order had to correspond to a cosmic order which was believed to include moral principles."[18]

Whether from the viewpoint of power or duty, the state had a "positive" interventionist or transformative stance toward society. In China's long imperial history, as Chang Hao argues well, imperial power could take either a "heavy" form, in which the throne "used the machinery of state to dominate and transform society," or a "light" form, in which the political-bureaucratic center "relied mainly upon its moral and ritual influence to achieve order in society."[19] Michael Loewe's characterization of the basic attitude toward the role and duty of the government in the Western Han dynasty is also suggestive. He thinks that a more precise way to identify the government's role in economic affairs is to use the terms "modernist" and "reformist" instead of "legalist" or "Confucian."[20] Not all thinkers or scholar-officials in all dynasties would have agreed that the role or responsibility of the state (i.e., government) lies in the greatest exploitation of natural resources for the benefit of the people.[21] The crucial fact is that in the notion of universal kingship, ideologically the political system of imperial China had the right and the duty to intervene in the socioeconomic activities of society. But empirically the level of "generalized power" of the state, as S. N. Eisenstadt argues, was rather limited,[22] and the state's penetration into society reached only to the door of the subcounty level, where "informal government," represented by traditional elite groups such as the gentry and by a variety of nongovernmental social institutions, tended to dominate the scene.[23]

True enough, "the rationalism of the bureaucracy was confronted with a resolute and traditionalistic power . . . This tremendous power of the strictly patriarchical sib was, in truth, the carrier of the much discussed 'democracy' of China, which had nothing whatsoever in common with 'modern democracy.' "[24] All these factors indicated that the power of state Confucianism in actuality was circumscribed; yet this should not lead us to think that the state was weak vis-à-vis society.

The bureaucratic domination of the state over society was most clearly manifested in the nature of Chinese cities. The Chinese city, which was "an imperial fortress, actually had fewer formal guarantees of self-government than the village . . . [Furthermore, it] was predominantly a product of rational administration."[25] The cities in China lacked political autonomy, had no "city law," no concept of a citizenry.[26] As a result, the Chinese city was an administrative entity but not a political society or civil society. The Confucian bureaucratic state had in effect prevented the emergence of civil society in China. Therefore, in large measure the state-society relationship in imperial China was rather unbalanced and lopsided. Admittedly, in the long imperial history there were some periods in which the omnipotence of state power was more imaginary than real.[27]

THE ROLE OF THE STATE
IN TAIWAN'S ECONOMIC DEVELOPMENT

For a very long time, at least up to the early 1970s, despite the fact that Taiwan had achieved considerable success in economic development, its political system was seen as an ossified one.[28] Structural features of the political system had experienced little basic change since the Kuomintang (National People's party or Nationalist party, hereafter KMT) moved to the island in 1949. But it would be a mistake to think that the party-state was inactive or passive while the economy was making aggressive advancement. The party-state had in fact made successful functional adaptations in coping with the problem of political modernization, that is participation, legitimation, and integration.[29] A fundamental fact, often not fully recognized until recently by students of Taiwan's modernization, is that the party-state played a vital role of guidance in Taiwan's rapid and successful economic development.[30] Roy Hofheinz, Jr., and Kent Calder argue that "Eastasia has an advantage over us in the way it is organized and motivated—that its political system, broadly conceived, gives it an 'edge' in crucial areas of economic competition."[31] Talcott Parsons, in an analysis of the institutional pattern of economic development of the West and the Third World, writes: "In the case of the original development of industrialism, I have argued that it could not have occurred without the freeing of private enterprise from certain types of political control. But in the present case, I shall argue that political authority is usually a necessary agency and that under certain conditions, far from obstructing, it is likely strongly to facilitate the process."[32]

Speaking on the case of Taiwan, Alice Amsden makes the claim that to understand Taiwan's economic growth it is necessary to understand its potent state. She convincingly demonstrates that "Taiwan is simply a particularly striking example of the positive association between state interventions and the acceleration of economic growth that is now generally accepted to prevail in cases of Third World capitalist development."[33]

At this juncture it is worth examining the nature of the state of the Republic of China. Taiwan has been under the hegemonic rule of the KMT since 1949. Until the early 1980s party and state were interwoven, with no clear boundaries between them. It is not inappropriate to characterize the political system as that of one-party authoritarianism, under which no independent organized political force was allowed to exist. Indeed, the party-state of Taiwan saw itself as the custodian of Chinese culture, but the relationship between Confucianism and the party-state was fundamentally different from that which existed between Confucianism and the imperial state in China. Although Confucianism is not an insignificant living force in the political life of Taiwan, institutional Confucianism was completely deconstructed. Taiwan made a marked departure from institutional Confucianism in both political institutions and political culture. It is clear that Confucianism no longer serves as a state ideology intermeshed with political authority.

The ideology of Taiwan's party-state is the *san-min-chu-i* (Three Principles of the People) of Sun Yat-sen, which is a creative and adaptive amalgam consisting of both Chinese and Western values and concepts.[34] Though the KMT is somewhat Leninist in structure, its ideology is categorically different from Leninism. Sun's three-stage development theory of nation building (i.e., military rule, democratic tutelage, and constitutional democracy), shows unmistakably that he was firm in his commitment to political democracy. Government in Sun's proposed system would be powerful, but sovereignty would remain with the people. Indeed, Sun's concept of the political system was unequivocally democratic.[35]

What should be emphatically pointed out is that although a new constitution was promulgated in 1946, it did not bring China to the stage of constitutional democracy, as Sun's theory prescribed. Instead, the civil war between the KMT government and the Chinese communists accelerated to an unprecedented level. In an atmosphere of war, the first session of the National Assembly convened in Nanking in 1949. The Assembly elected

Chiang Kai-shek as the president of the Republic of China, and also adopted the "Temporary Provisions for the Duration of Mobilization to Suppress the Rebellion."[36]

Upon establishing its rule over Taiwan, the KMT government declared martial law in 1949. In the early years of its rule the government was pre-occupied with issues of national security, as military invasion by the Chinese communists seemed possible and imminent. Throughout the 1950s, 1960s, and the early 1970s, the KMT government, despite its vigorous develop-ment-oriented economic policies, made no serious efforts to establish con-stitutional democracy. Under martial law strict control of political and other rights—including the right to organize new political parties—was imposed. The hegemonic domination of the party-state over society was never seri-ously challenged until the late 1970s.

The government, while making the recovery of the mainland its national policy and spending a disproportionate amount of the budget on the military, shifted its strategy decisively to precipitate economic development in the early 1950s. The KMT started first with land reform, which was ideologi-cally sanctioned by Sun's doctrine and was considered by party-state elites a political necessity for ensuring the stability of the island. The process of land reform was peaceful and bloodless, and the results were far-reaching, economically and politically, with the creation of the most equitable rural scene in all of Asia.

Immediately after the completion of land reform, the party-state succes-sively launched two four-year economic plans (1953–1956 and 1957–1960) with import substitution industrialization as a development strategy. Under this strategy the indigenous industrial sector was nourished and assisted by the state through a protectionist trade policy. In the early 1960s the govern-ment shifted its strategy from import substitution industrialization to export-oriented industrialization, under which three successive four-year plans (1961–1964, 1965–1968, and 1969–1972) were successfully pursued, resulting in the tremendous growth of manufacturing industries in the pri-vate sector. Chu-yüan Cheng writes:

> At almost every critical turning point, the guidance from the govern-ment has proven to be vital. In the transformation of Taiwan from an inward-oriented economy to an outward-oriented economy in the 1960s, the government used tax and credit as leverage to induce pri-vate-sector activity. In recent decades, the government took initiatives to upgrade Taiwan's industrial structure. In July 1979, a 2,210-hectare industrial park was created in Hsin-Chu to be the Silicon Valley of Taiwan . . . More recently, the government has offered new tax incen-

tives to attract venture capital to new enterprises in high-tech industries.[37]

The story of Taiwan's economic development has been fully analyzed elsewhere.[38] What needs to be said here is that in Taiwan's miraculous development, the party-state has, from the very beginning, played the role of guidance and control. It has not only enjoyed a highly autonomous status but has also used its power to transform the society.

What were the factors making the party-state so overwhelmingly an agency for developing and transforming society in Taiwan? It has been argued that the interventionist stance of the party-state toward society may resonate directly with traditional practice in imperial days.[39] Indeed, students of Taiwan's development believe that the party-state's role in a regulated capitalist economy has much to do with the traditional Chinese cultural structure.[40] It is important to note that no less a policymaker than K. T. Li, who was one of the major architects of Taiwan's economy, attributes the state's development-oriented policy to Sun's Doctrine of the People's Welfare. He writes: "All economic activities were aimed ultimately at improving the people's living standard. This is the essential meaning of the Doctrine of People's Welfare which conceives 'to provide and to enrich the people' as the basic fundamentals."[41]

As I mentioned earlier, the Confucian idea of the state is that it has comprehensive responsibilities to provide for, to enrich, and to educate the people, and this concept is well incorporated into Sun's Doctrine of the People's Welfare. In this connection it should be noted that as early as 1949, President Chiang Kai-shek told KMT members: "We must frankly admit that our party has done more for the political phases of our National Revolution than for the economic and social phases. Many of our members speak for social reform in theory, while in practice they rarely go into the heart of society and work for social improvement. Thus they incurred the criticism of being 'leftists in thought but rightists in action.' "[42] This shows that the leadership of the KMT government, in the aftermath of its defeat on the mainland, had critically reflected on the inadequacy of its rule-oriented policies in the past and had consciously shifted to development-oriented policies in land reform and economic growth in Taiwan. The leaders of the KMT deliberately gave greater scope over Taiwan's economy to Western-trained technocrats. Indeed, K. Y. Yin, the first major architect of Taiwan's economy, who was an American-trained electrical engineer, was given a free hand to design and implement Taiwan's economic strategies. Moreover, the party-state even established, outside the conventional bureaucratic structure, new institutions to guide and implement development-oriented economic plans.

The unflagging support of the top leaders of the party-state made it possible for the modernizing technocrats single-mindedly to pursue economic goals.[43] As a result of economic development, a free market economy was being developed.[44] Such a free market economy was hardly embraced out of the convictions of the KMT government. What Sun Yat-sen advocated was a sort of mixed economic system under which state enterprises and private enterprise coexist. He wrote: "All matters that can be and are better carried out by private enterprises should be left to private hands, which would be encouraged and fully protected by liberal laws. All matters that cannot be taken up by private concerns and those that possess monopolistic character should be taken up as national undertakings. The property thus created would be state owned and managed for the benefit of the whole nation."[45]

Under Sun's system the state or public sector definitely has a more prominent role than in the free market system. The shift from state-regulated capitalism to a free market system in Taiwan was believed to be due to the influence which the United States exerted on the KMT government.[46] American aid agencies were of the belief that "a shift from state to private ownership would contribute to the operating efficiency of . . . enterprises, hasten overall economic development and decrease the [government's] financial burden in subsidizing [public] activities."[47] Neil A. Jacoby, analyzing the impact of U.S. aid, wrote, "By far the most important consequence of U.S. influence was the creation in Taiwan of a booming private enterprise system."[48] The shift of weight of the public sector vis-à-vis the private sector was unmistakably clear. According to Chu-yüan Cheng: "In the 1960s, about 48 percent of the industrial output value originated from publicly owned and managed enterprises. The share has been continuously declining. By 1986, only 14.8 percent of all production originated from the public sector, indicating that the pace of growth in the private sector has far exceeded that in the public sector."[49]

Since the 1950s Taiwan has successfully developed into a newly industrializing country. In the process of development the state has always played a vital role in guiding and shaping the nature of the economy. Indeed, the nature of the state is a form of authoritarianism. In Taiwan the authoritarian form of the state seemed to contribute to economic growth as in other NICs of the East Asia region.[50] John Lee, in his study of political change in Taiwan from 1949 to 1974, observed that "people in Taiwan do not have a firm belief in democracy as to act democratically on all occasions. They believe that policies should be in the interest of the people but they seem to prefer authoritarian and informed ways of decision-making to rules of law called for by open processes of political competition."[51]

These findings show that the political attitudes and values influenced by the Confucian persuasion were more congenial to, and supportive of, the people's-interest orientation of the authoritarian party-state, at least until the early 1970s. But, intended or not, the ever-expanding market economy which was sanctioned and indeed pushed by the state was becoming more and more autonomous throughout the 1970s and 1980s, and along with it a viable civil society was coming into existence.

THE EMERGENCE OF CIVIL SOCIETY: RECIPROCAL RELATIONS BETWEEN STATE AND ECONOMY

I have argued that the party-state enjoyed a hegemonic rule over society. It is, of course, nonsensical to regard state autonomy as the total absence of constraint. Up to the mid-1970s the state did have a significant impact on the economy and society. Yet, along with the growing force of the economy, particularly in the private sector, the market-based society gradually asserted its status as a less dependent entity. Alice Amsden argues that Taiwan's case "demonstrate[s] the reciprocal interaction between the structure of the state apparatus and the process of economic growth."[52] Furthermore, "the Taiwan state, which appeared on its arrival from the Mainland to be an unlikely instrument for the promotion of development, proved to be a most effective one. At the same time, changes in the nature of the state itself appear to have been an important by-product of economic development. The state, in short, can be said both to have transformed Taiwan's economic structure and to have been transformed by it."[53]

The reciprocal dynamic between the power of the state and the power of society is the key to understanding the changing state-society relationship since the 1960s. Owing to the state's development strategies, the socioeconomic structures of Taiwan have undergone a fundamental change. A basically agrarian society was transformed into an industrial society. The urban working class and the urban middle class emerged as a result of industrialization and urbanization. By 1980 only 18 percent of the working population was engaged in farming, but the work force in industry had increased from less than 15 percent of the population in the 1960s to more than 35 percent in 1980. What is striking is that the middle class has risen to more than 31 percent. The number of people belonging to this class is now around 6 million. Whereas the old middle class, which was a product of the state's development, tended to be politically conservative, the new middle class has become more reform-minded. Surprisingly or not, studies show consistently that more than 50 percent of the electorate identify themselves as middle class. Moreover, this is the class that showed the strongest identification with the KMT in elections.[54] At this juncture it should be mentioned that Taiwan's development has produced a distinguishing characteristic, namely, to use Thomas Gold's expression, "the bifurcation of the economy from the polity."[55]

Not only has this phenomenon of bifurcation produced extraordinary results in the political system in terms of power distribution between the so-called mainlanders and the Taiwanese, but also it has had an important impact on the state-society relationship. For a long time the primary source of tension between the mainlanders and the Taiwanese was the dominant position of the former over the latter. At the national level all the high positions in the government and the army were initially occupied by mainlanders. Of the three elective bodies of the central government—the National Assembly, the Legislative Yüan, and the Control Yüan—the mainlanders constituted the great majority since they were elected in 1946 on the mainland to represent all provinces of China. Because the government of the Republic of China claimed to be the sole legitimate representative government for all of China, it justified its perpetuation of a national government by having all central government units staffed by mainlanders, not Taiwanese. Despite being virtually denied a road to national political power, the Taiwanese were deliberately encouraged by the KMT's policies to engage in economic ventures and activities. By the 1970s it had become evident that a division of power had emerged between the mainlanders and the Taiwanese, with the former controlling the political sector and the latter dominating the economic sector.

Nevertheless, the more basic structural change was not the division between economic and political power along ethnic lines but the emergence of an increasingly potent civil society vis-à-vis the powerful state. In the 1970s a growing demand for liberalization and political participation became obvious. A vigorous democratic political movement entered the political arena. One-party authoritarian rule began to be questioned. In particular, the ossified political structure of the three national representative bodies was challenged by independent politicians, who were sometimes called *tang-wai* (outside the party) figures. The KMT government was not totally insensitive to these demands. Consequently, a series of supplementary elections were held in 1969, 1972, 1973, 1976, 1980, 1983, and 1985. Although the KMT was consistently able to win about 70 percent of the vote, the independent politicians took the other 30 percent. The KMT's one-party authority was being seriously challenged.

What is significant to note is that in the 1980s, apart from elections, through which anti-KMT political views were widely voiced, another totally new movement took place in Taiwan's civil society. This movement was social in nature but different from the democratic political movement. In fact, a total of seventeen social movements have been recorded and analyzed, including a consumers' movement, a nature conservation movement, a women's movement, an aborigines' human rights movement, a New Testament church protest, a teachers' rights movement, and a veterans' welfare protest. Hsiao Hsin-huang argues that the various movements, though with different specific objectives, "all demand a change in the existing state-society relations. The most commonly shared goal is to search for more autonomy for civil society across class boundaries. The state, rather than an adversary class, was taken as a critical target to which the participants have made strong and direct appeals."[56]

How could the democratic movements and social movements have developed so vigorously in the 1970s and 1980s? Fundamentally, as I have pointed out, they were the direct result, intended or not, of state-guided economic development. What Alfred Stepan has written about the political evolution of Latin America seems to be equally applicable to Taiwan. He writes, "The state played a central role in setting the conditions that allowed crucial developments in civil society to take place at all."[57]

Thus, one should avoid taking a sociological stance of structural determinism, treating politics as a mere epiphenomenon of the economy. The state system in Taiwan has always been an autonomous force. The political development of electoral competition in the 1970s and 1980s was, in fact, engineered from the very center of the political system in which President Chiang Ching-kuo played a decisive role. In order to understand fully Taiwan's movement toward democracy and its restructuring of the state-society relationship, the politics of growth must be autonomously assessed parallel to and together with the economics of development.

In a substantive way the KMT government, far from being stagnant, as was often believed, was sensitive and responsive to the changing political reality. Long before the Chung-li incident of 1977, which is believed to be a watershed event in Taiwan's postwar political development,[58] the KMT government was prepared to take an accommodating approach toward the sociopolitical forces. Yet it was determined to ensure that change would take place within the existing constitutional framework, as Ramon Myers writes, "offering more pluralism but determined to control the parameters of political competition."[59] The burgeoning social movements of the 1980s are probably better interpreted as the result of the democratic transformation of the authoritarian state than that of a weakened party-state.[60]

Chiang Ching-kuo, like his father, enjoyed supreme authority and made himself popular among the people after becoming the premier in 1972. While vigorously pushing the modernization program in the economic realm, he actively engaged in political reform by initiating a process of "Taiwanization," thus bridging the gap between the state and society. Chiang was fully cognizant of the changing spirit of the society. He said in November 1986: "The times are changing and so are the environment and the trends. To fit in with these changes, the KMT must adopt new concepts and new forms according with the basic spirit of the democratic and constitutional system. Only by doing so can the KMT be in line with current trends and forever be together with the public."[61] It should be remembered that in May 1986 the party-state, obviously with Chiang's blessing, agreed to enter a dialogue with *tang-wai* members. This symbolized nothing short of the KMT's de facto recognition of the *tang-wai* as a legitimate competitor in the newly developing political order.

In this regard it is worth mentioning that what changed was not only the socioeconomic structure but also people's political attitudes and values. A citywide survey on motives of the Taipei electorate by Hu Fu and You Yinglong in February 1981 revealed that 47.3 percent and 43.9 percent of the voters, respectively, answered that "to exercise civic rights" and "to perform civic duties" were the "most important reason(s) for their taking part in the election."[62] According to another islandwide survey conducted in 1985, as much as 85 percent of the population (twenty to seventy years of age) said that they had the right to appeal to the government about its officials; that they would expect officials to be more responsive to the needs of the people; and that they would express dissenting views on government policies.[63]

Judging from these findings, we can see that Taiwan was evolving into a political culture that showed a marked break with Confucianism, although the influence of the latter was far from dead. The intellectual climate in Taiwan, though complicated in content and confused in expression, had long ceased to accept the idea that the state, as the guardian of the people's well-being, has an all-encompassing power over social-political life, as was conceived in Confucian political-ethical philosophy. Intellectuals of different persuasions share a loose consensus on "the idea of individual moral autonomy, some kind of 'democracy' and—albeit with reservations—capitalism."[64] Thomas Metzger, after examining the ideological mode of Taiwan's experience, writes: "In the R.O.C., however, there was an 'elective affinity' between the ideological mix that was realized and the other aspects of a political center that indeed came to focus increasingly on instrumental rationality, using this standard to revise the inherited culture and so to promote an effective program of modernization leading today even to full political pluralism."[65]

Lucian Pye makes the strong claim that:

Taiwan, in spite of all its lingering Confucian rhetoric, has made a greater break with Confucian attitudes toward authority than has China, Korea, or Vietnam . . . Taiwan has probably gone further than the other three states in abandoning Confucian ways—but ironically, it has been the most vigorous in its support of the Confucian tradition. The erosion of Confucianism has taken place because the politics of status and prestige have had to give way to utilitarian values of a materialistic nature. Taiwan has become a society so energized by economics that politics has yielded up its pretensions of importance. Moreover, to the degree that the status of officialdom has been redefined, Taiwan has tended toward a pluralistic polity and away from a dutiful, disciplined Confucian society which defers to government authority.[66]

Taiwan's modernization is too dynamic for us to know where it is leading, but one thing is certain: structurally and culturally Taiwan has made a marked departure from institutional Confucianism, and a new, more balanced state-society relation has emerged in the process of modernization.

CONFUCIANISM, CIVIL SOCIETY, AND POLITICAL MODERNITY

Daniel Bell, speaking on "American exceptionalism," writes:

What is the distinguishing feature, then, of the United States, one that has been its strength throughout its history? It is simply that the United States has been the complete civil society (to use the Hegelian term), perhaps the only one in political history . . . In Hegel's sense, there was no "State" in the United States, no unified, rational will expressed in a political order, but only individual self-interest and a passion for liberty. In every European nation (with the partial exception of Britain), the State ruled over society, exercising a unitary or quasi-unitary power enforced by an army and a bureaucracy.[67]

In the case of China the state ruled over society throughout its imperial history. In fact, no concept of civil society was ever articulated; in the strict sense no counterpart of the word *society* existed in the Chinese language. Jacques Gernet is not wide of the mark when he asserts: "One could say that in China, the state is all . . . In China, the state was an established reality from the beginning, or in any case from the time when the formula was worked out in the state of Qin [Ch'in], before it was extended to the whole of the Chinese realm. It was the great organizer of society and of territory."[68]

Indeed, people in Europe did not begin to apply the term *state* to their political entities until as late as the seventeenth century, whereas in China the concept of the state already existed in the Spring and Autumn and Warring States periods (eighth to third centuries B.C.).[69] In terms of world comparisons, what made China fundamentally different from Europe was that China, since the Ch'in and Han dynasties, had become a centralized unitary state with a single politico-religious order of state Confucianism, while Europe remained a multistate system with a higher degree of pluralism.[70]

As we have seen, in the imperial system politics and culture were mutually penetrating and closely interwoven. Nevertheless, the Confucian normative (ethical) paradigm of state or politics was never fully realized. What was actualized was an institutional Confucianism, under which the state was legitimized by a Confucian cultural-political ideology, and in which the state, personified by the emperor or Son of Heaven, had all-encompassing claims over the social-political order. The leadership of the state, according to the Confucian ideology of universal kingship, had comprehensive responsibilities toward the population. Imperial China, which could legitimately be called a state Confucianism, took an interventionist and transformative stance toward society. The imperial domination effectively prevented the emergence of civil society. This is a structural problem that is fundamental to the development of the modern state in China.[71]

The modernization that has taken place in Taiwan since the 1950s has resulted in the fundamental transformation of state Confucianism. A civil society has emerged owing to the development of a market economy and political pluralism. A new state-society relation has come into existence. In the process of transformation the party-state played a dominating and guiding role in developing strategies for the economy. Probably nothing is more strikingly dialectical than the fact that the vibrant market economy, which was the very creation of the state, has in turn transformed the state. But, as I hope I have made clear, politics was never a mere epiphenomenon. The state has always enjoyed an autonomous status. No economic, deterministic argument could explain fully the transformation of the state. In point of fact, to explain Taiwan's case the self-transformation of the state is as important as, if not more important than, the impact of the market economy. The state's people-oriented developmental and transformative strategies toward the economy and society were reminiscent of the Confucian tradition, but Confucianism was no longer the state ideology.

Institutional Confucianism has been fundamentally restructured. Institutional Confucianism has become what may be called intellectual Confucianism, by which I mean Confucianism in Taiwan today is nothing more than a philosophical-cultural system, like Hegelism, liberalism, and so on.

Although the KMT has been organized as a Leninist-style party, the KMT government neither intended in theory *(san-min-chu-i)* nor tried in practice to have total control over society. The political center of the party-state in Taiwan is, to use the concept of Thomas Metzger and Ramon Myers, an "inhibited and accommodative one,"[72] which provides ample room for the development and growth of the economy and society. The story of state Confucianism and its transformation is still an unfolding process. It is part of the great drama of China's search for political modernity.

12

CIVIL SOCIETY IN TAIWAN
The Confucian Dimension

Thomas B. Gold

Rapid economic development in the Confucian societies of East Asia has revived the once moribund debate over the relation between development patterns and traditional cultures. For these particular societies, at least, mounting evidence indicates that certain arrangements between elements of traditional Confucian culture and modern institutions can facilitate economic growth, even though the same culture interrelated with different institutions can and does obstruct it.

Now that the authoritarian political systems which seemed to be an inherent part of the economic development pattern are giving way before broad-based societal pressures for democratization, we need to inquire whether there is some Confucian dimension to this political process as well, or whether in fact the emergence and strengthening of civil society—which scholars agree is necessary if not sufficient for democracy—requires expunging the Confucian elements. Can Confucianism contain an elective affinity for both authoritarianism and the type of pluralist democracy that arises along with civil society? As with the economy, are they mutually exclusive, or is the matter more one of institutional arrangements?

This essay addresses these questions. First I explore the concept of civil society; then, after describing the nature of civil society in Taiwan up to 1994, I evaluate the relation between that and what Tu Wei-ming has called "Confucian habits of the heart."[1]

CIVIL SOCIETY

The dramatic progress toward democracy in authoritarian regimes of the right and Marxist-Leninist regimes of the left has focused renewed attention on the concept of civil society as a necessary component of democracy. Unfortunately, the term itself has undergone numerous permutations.

Civil society was originally synonymous with the state. Hegel then separated the two terms, seeing civil society as the sphere between the family and the state, in which individuals pursue their self-interest. This necessarily brings them into association with others. Shlomo Avineri writes: "Self-interest and self-assertion are the motives of activity in civil society; but these can be realized by the individual only through inter-action with others and recognition by them. The mutual dependence of all on all is inherent in every individual's self-oriented action."[2] Marx and Engels utilized the economic aspect of Hegel's definition of civil society, defining it as "embrac[ing] the whole material intercourse of individuals within a definite stage of the development of productive forces. It embraces the whole commercial and industrial life of a given stage."[3]

Antonio Gramsci provided a major elaboration of the concept in his *Prison Notebooks* of the 1930s, and this has had the greatest impact on the current discourse. In Gramsci's view, civil society refers to the superstructural realm of social relations and organizations, including economic, political, and cultural behavior,[4] "that is, the ensemble of organisms commonly called 'private.' "[5] The leading social group, which would be the bourgeoisie in capitalist society, exercises hegemony through its leadership of the interrelated spheres of economic, political, and cultural life in civil society. Through the state, in Gramsci's view, this same ruling group exercises political dominance. Within civil society (which is "intertwined in practice" with the state),[6] organizations representing various interests form alliances and consolidate strength ("war of position") and struggle for power, launching frontal assaults ("war of manoeuvre") at the crucial moment.[7] This contestation can bring about a revolutionary transformation. Gramsci also emphasized the role that intellectuals play in the revolution.[8]

Related to, but not dependent on, civil society is the emergence and expansion of a public sphere. Jürgen Habermas has analyzed in detail what he specifies as the "bourgeois public sphere," which "may be conceived above all as the sphere of private people coming together as a public; they soon claimed the public sphere regulated from above against the public authorities themselves, to engage them in a debate over the general rules governing relations in the basically privatized but publicly relevant sphere of commodity exchange and social labor."[9] In other words, the bourgeoisie delineated a specific realm apart from the expanding state, limiting the state's authority.

This struggle over the public sphere has particular relevance to the present-day transitions from authoritarianism to democratization. In *Tentative Conclusions about Uncertain Democracies,* the final volume of their tetralogy, *Transitions from Authoritarian Rule,* Guillermo O'Donnell and Philippe Schmitter include a chapter titled "Resurrecting Civil Society (and Restructuring Public Space)," which traces the manner in which a "generalized mobilization" occurs once so-called soft-liners in a regime have prevailed over hard-liners and extend certain rights and guarantees to the citizenry.[10] This stage of liberalization precedes the democratization stage.

According to their analysis, authoritarian regimes destroy the autonomous realm of civil society and monopolize the public sphere as a central feature of their control over real and potential opponents. As the transition gets under way, "exemplary individuals" test "the boundaries of behavior initially imposed by the incumbent regime," a challenge that revives "collective identifications and actions" and then "repoliticizes society."[11] Citizens from all walks of life begin to participate in political activity, holding the state accountable for its actions. That is to say, there is a dialectical relationship between a mobilized citizenry and a crumbling authoritarian state.

To sum up, the concept of civil society, as I use it, refers to a realm of autonomous organizations outside the state (or, in a Leninist system, the party-state), whose members organize themselves, define their group boundaries, administer their own affairs, and engage in relations of many types with other similarly constituted groups and with the state. These organizations vary in their degree of formal institutionalization. Many of their activities, in particular contestation with the state, take place in the newly constituted public sphere through the media, publications, popular culture, debates, demonstrations, and explicitly political activity such as elections. I do not see a civil society or state dichotomy. Rather, an important stage in the emergence and consolidation of civil society is the legitimation by the state of a sphere of autonomous citizen activity. The state helps to set and administer the ground rules for civil society.

Introducing an important 1988 collection, John Keane distinguishes three ways in which the state–civil society schema may be understood: (1) as an analytic approach, identifying the complex patterns of interaction among institutions and actors; (2) as an aid to strategic political calculation, providing tactics and goals for social movements or for states in the process of consolidating power; and (3) in a normative sense as a fundamental way of maintaining democracy by limiting the state and preserving pluralism.[12]

I use the concept in the first and third senses, although, as I make clear in the end, unlimited civil society risks deteriorating into anarchy. Political entrepreneurs in Taiwan have used civil society in Keane's second sense, having a conscious project of establishing autonomous organizations and compelling the state to legitimize both these associations and the idea of an autonomous sphere.

CIVIL SOCIETY IN TAIWAN PRIOR TO 1945

Civil society resembling that in the West has emerged in Taiwan over the course of the island's spectacular economic development, in particular since the mid-1980s. Nonetheless, it has grown out of a very different tradition and structure from that of the West.

Under the Chinese

To what extent did civil society or a public sphere exist in Taiwan prior to industrialization and social change under the Kuomintang (KMT) capitalist development state? Answering this question involves a brief foray into the issue of the relevance of applying the concept of civil society to traditional China. Recent research has addressed this.[13] Although traditional China did not conceive of society as an autonomous realm separate from the state, there were numerous self-regulating corporate groups and voluntary associations such as "guilds, native place associations, clans and lineages, surname associations, neighborhood associations and religious groupings such as temple societies, deity cults, monasteries, and secret societies."[14]

As an indication of distinctive Confucian habits of the heart, these groups handled many of the tasks normally thought in the West to be the responsibility of the state: maintaining social order, building public works, dispensing welfare, handling dispute mediation, and so on. The scholar-gentry elite in particular, as an exemplary elite, had an obligation to the state to do this. These activities also helped in the elite's continuous self-cultivation to become Confucian "superior men." As other chapters in this volume argue, individuals in a Confucian system had obligations but no rights. On occasion, however, these groups did mediate between the state and their members.[15] One example of this is the community compact model utilized by Zhu Xi, "a mechanism for the promotion of community spirit and a sense of shared responsibility for the community welfare."[16]

One aspect of the Confucian tradition potentially conducive to the emergence of civil society in our sense was remonstrance.[17] Loyal officials were duty bound to point out critical shortcomings to the emperor, although such whistle blowing might bring harm to the remonstrator. This intraelite duty was tied to the concept of the Mandate of Heaven, I would argue, as it offered the emperor a chance to get his house in order before mass social movements—a type of proto–civil society—arose which could end the dynasty altogether.

Citing research by Mary Rankin and William Rowe, Elizabeth Perry and Ellen Fuller argue that in the late nineteenth century "something resembling European civil society emerge[d] in China."[18] It was in the form of intellectual-led cross-class movements, not of organized institutions, however. The warlord and Republican period saw the "high point of movement politics in China."[19] The iconoclastic May Fourth Movement, during the 1910s, explicitly called for the overthrow of the Confucian value system and its institutions ("the Confucian shop"), which activists accused of being the major obstacle to the development of democracy and science.

The situation in Taiwan was somewhat different owing to its status as China's frontier, separated from the mainland by a dangerous body of water. The reach of the Qing state into Taiwanese society was weaker than on the mainland, creating an even larger vacuum for social groups to fill.[20] Mainlanders commonly immigrated as individuals. On the island they created or sought out organizations to substitute for families and lineages, such as "sworn brotherhoods, secret societies, and religious associations."[21] Migrants set up voluntary associations to facilitate adaptation to the new environment.[22] Conflict over land and water and between regional groupings in a weakly governed frontier territory fostered communal strife. The voluntary associations played an active role in this violence, even fueling it as people created ever more organizations for protection.[23]

Some major lineages did form on the island, and they fulfilled many of the same quasi-governmental functions as their counterparts on the mainland.[24]

Under the Japanese

The Japanese Occupation (1895–1945) introduced an unprecedented level of control and social penetration by the state.[25] The Japanese coopted local elites, such as the five major Taiwanese capitalist families, who, in Confucian fashion, continued to help the state in some welfare and social order capacities.[26] There were several popular social movements, but most pressed for integration and equal treatment with the Japanese, local autonomy, and elections, not independence.[27] China's anti-Confucian campaign of the May

Fourth era, and the anti-imperialist movements of much of the first half of the twentieth century, passed Taiwan by with very little impact.

CIVIL SOCIETY SINCE RETROCESSION

The Retrocession of Taiwan to Chinese control in 1945, and, especially, the retreat of the KMT Nationalist regime to the island in 1949, had a major impact on the nature of civil society and its subsequent evolution.

Preemption and Cooptation

For most of the first four decades after Retrocession, the KMT attempted to preempt or coopt the emergence of civil society. But a number of contradictions in the KMT and the system it erected actually created a fertile soil for the sprouting and then the full-blown flowering of civil society.

At its height, the KMT functioned as a Leninist-style vanguard party with an explicit mission of social transformation and national salvation. In Leninist fashion (it was reorganized by agents of the Comintern in the early 1920s along the lines of the Soviet Communist party), the KMT established a corporatist system, establishing its hegemony over political society, the military, civil society, and the public sphere.

Political Society. The national Republic of China and Taiwan province governments (controlling virtually identical territory) were little more than executive arms of the party; there was scant separation between party and state. Based on the 1948 Temporary Provisions for the Period of Mobilization of the Suppression of Communist Rebellion (lifted in 1991), the KMT granted extensive emergency powers to the president, enforced martial law (1949–1987), and created numerous organizations to maintain internal security, which acted as a shadow government. The members of the national legislature were frozen in place (until 1991), new political parties were forbidden (until 1989), social movements and strikes were banned, and the media were tightly controlled.[28]

The Military. In Maoist terms, the party controlled the gun, with a system of political commissars monitoring loyalty and indoctrinating troops in the party's ideology.[29]

Civil Society. In Taiwan's very weak civil society, the party-state exercised hegemony over the economy and market through its ownership of numerous enterprises in all fields, especially upstream and heavy industry, and the banking system, as well as monetary and fiscal policy. In the superstructure the KMT employed corporatist tactics, selecting one group to represent particular social interests. It penetrated those groups and prevented the emergence of competitors. Although some groups could represent the interests of their members to the leadership, they functioned primarily as instruments of control of farmers, workers, businessmen, students, residential communities, and so on.[30] One could put a Confucian spin on this, arguing that, as in traditional China, social organizations worked to help the state, not challenge it. For instance, the Association for the Promotion of Industry and Commerce was founded to coordinate business activities with national policy and to strengthen unity within the industrial and commercial world.[31] But citizens did not have the freedom to establish competing organizations if they so desired, or to gain access to the public sphere to make a case for a particular point of view. Religious and service organizations likewise assisted the party-state.

The educational system was highly ideologized (Confucianism as well as Sun Yat-sen's Three Principles of the People were required studies). It was controlled by the party and monitored by the internal security apparatus.

Public Sphere. The party also closely restricted the public sphere. It either owned or indirectly controlled the media (for instance, the publishers of the two largest daily newspapers were members of the Central Executive Committee).[32] Mandarin Chinese was made the official language, and media use of other dialects, such as Taiwanese (spoken by the majority of the island's residents) and Hakka (another widespread dialect), was tightly regulated. Martial law did away with, for example, the freedom to assemble or strike. Through hegemony over the educational system and the media, the KMT monopolized the definition of reality, asserting that Taiwan was only one province of the Republic of China, and that calls for Taiwan's independence, constitutional revision, multiparty elections, and so on were tantamount to treason. The KMT constructed and enforced a "collective national-popular will," in Gramsci's terms, which theoretically articulated the national mission of anticommunism, mainland recovery, and the Three Principles of the People.[33] Questioning that mission, in particular by advocating Taiwan's independence, could draw a charge of sedition.

Unassailable Hegemony

The unity of the mainlander elite, strengthened by a party purge in 1950[34] and reassertion of control over the armed forces, facilitated implementation of this corporatist system. The subethnic division of labor, whereby mainlanders (themselves by no means homogeneous on the mainland) dominated virtually everything, leaving only small-scale business to the Taiwanese, put the elite in an almost unassailable position.

Until the mid-1970s there were very few challenges even attempted against this hegemony. When a small group of mainlanders led by Lei Chen attempted with a few Taiwanese to establish a new political party around 1960, the regime dealt with them quite harshly.[35] A decade later a group of intellectuals involved with the magazine *The Intellectual* called for political reforms. Many of its members were young KMT rising stars, and the movement had something of the feel of traditional remonstrance. It was tied into a patriotic movement, complete with street demonstrations, to urge the government to resist the perceived Japanese encroachment on Diaoyutai; again, this was a case of urging the government to action. The *Intellectual* ferment was shut down in 1973 with the arrests and firing of university professors.

Throughout the middle years of the 1970s, an emerging core of dissident intellectuals, many of whom were former KMT members, attempted to break into the public sphere, primarily through publishing magazines such as *China Tide* and *Taiwan Political Review*. They became the core of the non-KMT opposition movement, the *dangwai*. At the same time several Taiwanese writers began to publish serious fiction about the island, featuring farmers, workers, prostitutes, fishermen, and small businessmen. This corpus was dubbed *xiangtu wenxue* (nativist literature) and attracted a sizable following, not least because it gave prominence to the unglamorous common people of the island, a subject never broached before.[36]

Inherent Contradictions

Although this system was virtually unbreachable for more than three decades, it contained a number of contradictions that opened the way for the emergence and strengthening of civil society in the 1980s, and then a transition to democratization.

First, although the KMT is Leninist in structure, it is not Marxist. It does not see the world in class terms, it does not claim infallibility, it does not present itself as the instrument of the laws of history, and it does not aim to eliminate private capital. Its ideology calls for the "restriction" of private capital, and for state capital to dominate the commanding heights of the economy, with an important role for foreign capital as well. "Restriction" is a moving target, and the KMT recognized early on that it could not run the entire economy, so it yielded to, and then cultivated, a private capitalist class. So long as businessmen did not attempt to translate economic wealth into oppositional political activities, they enjoyed great scope for entrepreneurship. There was thus the potential for creating the material basis for civil society through a market economy. In Marxist terms, as I noted earlier, this expansion of commercial and industrial life did in fact constitute civil society.

Second, the KMT claimed to be embarked on a three-stage course of democratization.[37] There was a military stage, completed on the mainland, a long tutelary stage, and then a final stage of constitutional democracy. Unfortunately, the exigencies of civil war had resulted in the suspension of the 1946 constitution, but a Western-style democracy remained the official goal. The regime referred to itself as "Free China," in contrast to Communist China on the mainland. It was only fair to raise questions about constitutionalism and freedom, especially given the dramatic improvement in the standard of living along with widespread literacy, education, and knowledge of constitutional democracy elsewhere in the world.

Third, as part of democratization the state had implemented local self-rule in Taiwan in 1949, inaugurating elections for county magistrates and city mayors in 1950. Elections have been held on a regular basis since that time. An elected Taiwan Provincial Assembly was established in 1959. Although the state prohibited new political parties, non-KMT members could and did contest some seats, even winning on occasion and assuming office. There were real issues at stake in many elections. Beginning in 1969, and continuing through 1989, elections were held for supplementary seats added to the national bodies—the National Assembly, Legislative Yüan, and Control Yüan. Although the members elected in 1947 held on to their seats until elections held in 1991 and 1992, popular political participation had been extended from the local to the national level, and the contests grew increasingly heated from the late 1970s on. At the local level the KMT organization was little more than a gloss on powerful patron-client networks which could go off on their own, given suitable conditions.[38]

These decades of electoral experience proved significant when the authoritarian facade began to crumble. As new members took their seats in the legislative bodies, they began to exercise their rights of interpellation, holding government officials accountable for their policies, something most cadres were unaccustomed to.

Fourth, the émigré KMT regime set up something of a division of labor, where mainlanders controlled the national political, military, and economic bodies, while Taiwanese had great scope over business activity. Education was free and compulsory. Sooner or later, if the KMT could not recover the mainland, and given the high emigration rate by the children of mainlanders, it would have to recruit Taiwanese into important positions in the party and state.

Fifth, foreign interests were extremely influential in Taiwan's development. The United States government has had long-standing influence over the KMT government since mainland days. Through its control of vital civilian and military aid, it compelled the initially bankrupt and vulnerable regime to cultivate private business activity and to soften some aspects of its authoritarian control in order to present a more convincing freedom-loving image to the American Congress. On the private side, U.S. economic, missionary, educational, and service organizations also contributed to cracking the monolith. As Taiwan's economy became increasingly export-oriented, beginning in the 1960s the number of resident foreigners increased, as did the number of ROC passport holders traveling abroad and seeing the world. American popular culture was everywhere—television, translated publications, radio, films, rock and roll. Integration into global economic, social, and information networks raised the Taiwan populace's awareness of alternatives to their current system.

A sixth factor contributing to civil society was the safety valve: it was relatively easy to leave Taiwan for study abroad, and only about 5 percent of those who did so returned. Some who went were potential dissidents. Overseas Taiwanese maintained an interest in the island's affairs. Many joined organizations such as the World United Formosans for Independence (WUFI), the Formosan Association for Public Affairs, and others, which closely monitored the situation on the island and lobbied American politicians to withhold aid pending improvements in the political environment.[39] Long residence abroad trained many Chinese from Taiwan in the formal and informal aspects of democratic politics.

In sum, then, a number of factors provided fertile soil for the potential emergence of civil society, given conducive conditions. The rapid economic growth and social structural changes of the island during the phenomenal growth years of the 1960s and 1970s helped.[40] Taiwan's diplomatic setbacks during the 1970s and 1980s, as well as the generational transition in the regime, also created the need to recruit new people into leadership positions, and to reintegrate an increasingly complex society in a more imaginative, and less coercive way.[41] By the mid-1980s the situation on the island had changed dramatically, with the full emergence of civil society in all its manifestations.

Civil Society in the 1990s

I cannot review the democratization process or the current situation in great detail here.[42] But I will draw attention to some of the significant elements of civil society in Taiwan by the early 1990s.

First, to use the Marxist definition, the place of private capital and the market had risen to dominance on the island.[43] With 1952 as the base year, private industrial production had risen 162 times by 1990, while state-owned production had increased 25 times. Private industrial production accounted for more than 80 percent of value added at 1981 prices since 1983.[44] The state was still a major player in upstream and heavy industries, but it was gradually permitting private ownership there as well, and was also liberalizing and privatizing the banking and finance system. Taiwan's bourgeois class had expanded dramatically. Although business was dominated by small and medium-sized family enterprises, there were several large and powerful conglomerates, as well as complex networks among entrepreneurs. Capitalists had begun to flex their political muscle, although not always successfully.[45] Foreign capital was also a major player in the economy.

Second has been the rise in autonomous organizations. On January 27, 1989, the president promulgated a new Civic Organizations Law laying out the regulations for the establishment of professional, social, and political organizations. The last type was the most significant, as, at long last, the state permitted the formation of new political parties. The Democratic Progressive party (DPP), established in September 1986 by the former *dangwai,* could finally register as a legal party and end the charade of not existing. By the November 1993 elections for county magistrates and city mayors, there were more than seventy parties, although "more than 90 percent exist as hollow registered groups."[46] The only other opposition party of consequence was the New party, established in the summer of 1993 by disgruntled KMT mainlanders upset at what they saw as the direction in which KMT Chairman Lee Teng-hui was taking the party: toward Taiwan independence and a too cozy relationship with big business. Elections in Taiwan had become increasingly intense, and the KMT had begun to reposition itself as an electoral rather than a hegemonic commandist party, although none of the other parties could match it for organization or finances.[47] Among professional organizations there has been the notable emergence of think tanks, some connected with political figures, some with wealthy businessmen, some with scholars. They have aggressively put policy suggestions into the public sphere.[48]

Third has been the emergence of a social movement sector. From a base of virtually zero during martial law, Taiwan now has dozens of movements of varying degrees of institutionalization and permanence, representing single- or multiple-issue causes. A listing of the more prominent ones would include consumer protection, environmental protection (and antipollution), labor, women, students for campus democracy, aborigine rights, mainlander veterans' rights to visit the mainland, anti–nuclear power, farmers opposed to liberalized imports, the charismatic New Testament church's movement against government harassment, members of the middle class unable to afford housing, stock market investors opposed to transaction taxes and a declining market, teachers, the handicapped, victims of political oppression, and Hakkas.[49] The Association for a Plebiscite on Taiwan organized a mammoth rally in Kaohsiung in October 1991 calling for Taiwan's readmission to the United Nations and a plebiscite on the suitable name to use.

Fourth has been the expanded participation in the public sphere. Of significance was the lifting, in January 1988, of the restrictions on publishing new newspapers. New papers started up, morning papers established evening editions and vice versa, and all of them added pages. In an intensely competitive environment Taiwan's press corps now rivals those of Britain and the United States for irresponsible reporting and smothering a story with aggressive overkill. The party-state maintains a monopoly over television ownership but, under protest, has granted increased coverage to opposition politics. Early in 1993 the government also lifted its ban on new radio stations. Opposition politicians as well as opportunistic businessmen have operated private cable television stations which broadcast shows from the mainland, among other offerings. There are frequent street marches, and public space once monopolized by the regime is now shared by civilians. The Chiang Kai-shek Memorial complex has been the site of several mass sit-ins, for example. First Chia-yi then other locations have erected monuments memorializing the victims of the February 28, 1947, massacre, an event formerly not even acknowledged.[50] Archives have been opened, and scholars have begun to conduct research on this once totally taboo topic. The government has issued its own white paper as well as a formal apology and reparations. The subject of Taiwan independence, although still seditious, has become an issue of public debate. In the elections of 1989, 1991, and 1992 DPP and various political figures included a call of independence in their platforms. When the issue of rejoining the UN was first raised in 1991, the KMT forcefully opposed it, although it allowed a public airing of the matter in a televised debate between Vice Foreign Minister John Chang and DPP legislator Frank Hsieh. By the middle of 1993 the Ministry of Foreign Affairs had coopted the cause, saying that rejoining the UN had top priority on its agenda. In 1993 and 1994 it induced several nations to attempt to raise the issue (stifled by the mainland delegation) and sent a high-powered group of its own to New York for support.

If one event could symbolize the dramatic emergence of civil society and the restructured relation between the party-state and society it would be the 1990 National Affairs Conference (literally, "a meeting to decide the country's destiny").[51] President Lee Teng-hui called this meeting to defuse increased political tensions surrounding a number of sensitive issues: direct election of the president and vice president (rather than by the National Assembly, which was dominated by delegates elected on the mainland); election of the governor of Taiwan and mayors of Taipei and Kaohsiung, all of whom were appointed; constitutional revision to reflect the real territory controlled by the ROC; relations with the mainland (and thus Taiwan's international status); and structural reform of the National Assembly, Legislative Yüan, and Control Yüan. The 130 delegates included some political prisoners released just to attend. The calling of this conference clearly indicated that Taiwan's once invincible political center was now severely "inhibited" and had to engage in discourse with powerful social forces.[52] It also showed efforts by the state and citizens to establish new modes of civil(ized) discourse.[53] Soon after the summer conference, the state began to explore concrete measures to implement ideas arising from it, including direct election of the president and governor and the mayors of Taipei and Kaohsiung. Stalwart anti-KMT political figures long in exile, such as Peng Ming-min, George Chang, and Shi Ming, returned from the United States and Japan in 1992 and 1993, and immediately plunged into political activity. This again is highly symbolic of the trends toward reconciliation and a public effort to build a new fiduciary community.

A CONFUCIAN DIMENSION?

It seems clear that civil society, in the sense discussed at the beginning of this essay, has definitely emerged and taken root in Taiwan in spite of a weak traditional base for it. Groups are interacting with one another and with the state in a very complex fashion. A new set of rules of the game is in the process of being formulated; in the meantime Taiwan often appears to be gripped by anarchy as the inhibited state faces great challenges in establishing and administering new rules to deal with a fast-growing social-political situation.

Can we discern a Confucian dimension to the situation of civil society in today's Taiwan? An essay by the sociologist Ann Swidler provides a useful way to approach this question.[54] Swidler suggests conceiving of culture as a "tool kit" of skills and habits, a repertoire to construct what she calls "strategies of action." Culture provides not only valued ends to actions but also means. In an unsettled period, in particular, culture helps to construct new strategies. What has gone into the tool kit of the constituent elements of Taiwan's civil society?

It is clearly a mixed assortment. Civil society is far from homogeneous. Many of the activities have a strong flavor of traditional remonstrance. Intellectuals and other citizens have felt impelled to organize and inform the leadership about severe problems such as environmental degradation and unaffordable housing. Drawing on Confucian habits of the heart, they look to the authorities to solve problems, and they expect results. The intellectuals also appear to want to be treated as "insiders," another Confucian legacy. Much of the protest is couched in moralistic terms, and the authorities have to demonstrate their moral qualities as well as their efficacy by determinedly and sincerely addressing these issues.

Much of business life at the core of civil society also draws on Confucian habits: family-based enterprises, the importance of personalistic networks, the acceptance of a major presence of the state in the economy, pragmatism, diligence, paternalistic management, and so on. What is driving civil society and helping to redesign Taiwan's political and social institutions, however, are the more radical actors. Their emergence is an outgrowth of changes in the economy, social structure, personnel in the party-state and society, ties to the outside world, and purely situational factors. Many of the ideas they draw on to construct strategies of action are decidedly non-Confucian, as are the language and the symbols they use. These come directly from a range of foreign, mostly Western, thinkers and activists.

For instance, they have pressed for the legal protection of autonomous groups which, in many cases now, advocate ideologies quite at variance with that of the state. Rather than trying to become insiders or helping the authorities do their job, these groups want to replace the authoritarian, hierarchical elite and create a new set of "democratic" institutions. There is no guarantee that they would not become as elitist—a solid Confucian trait—as those they would replace, but the important thing is that they represent a distinct challenge to the state's monopoly of orthodoxy. They disagree profoundly with the Confucian idea of a single locus of power and legitimacy. They also challenge the state's legitimate right to interfere in the life of individuals, who are to be empowered to make decisions and accept responsibility for them.

With the public advocacy of Taiwan's independence, they are also directly challenging the officially constructed "national popular will," and thereby the KMT's legitimacy. Eschewing Confucian-style compromise and harmony, many radical elements in civil society savor confrontation, adopting a Western market image of political and social as well as economic life. The state-initiated National Affairs Conference may be read as a very Confucian effort to harmonize divergent interests, and some participants temporarily suppressed their hostility to the regime and attended. Since then, however, the level of rhetoric has become even more shrill than before. The public sphere has become the locus of debate over fundamental issues once rarely discussed even behind closed doors. Groups in civil society are establishing horizontal alliances among themselves rather than seeking patrons in the elite.

Taiwan is very much in an unsettled transitional stage. The KMT-led fiduciary community, employing values and symbols from Confucius and Sun Yat-sen, among others, is being torn asunder. Confucian ethics were conducive to economic growth but appear to be a fetter to further, inevitable political evolution. Although many elements in civil society can be accommodated into the old community, other aggressive actors are waging a "war of manoeuvre," sensing that the time is right to tear down the old set of institutions and build a new set. There appears to be a mass base in society for this "war." As Taiwan becomes increasingly pluralistic, a new moral order and new institutions will draw on the Confucian repertoire, some elements of which are also found in the West, but the dominant influences will come from elsewhere.

PART IV

HONG KONG, SINGAPORE, AND OVERSEAS CHINESE COMMUNITIES

Since the founding of the People's Republic of China in 1949, the official ideology of the new regime has been Marxism, Leninism, and Mao Tse-tung Thought. While scholars abroad, notably Stuart Schram and Benjamin Schwartz, and more recently Chinese intellectuals such as Li Zhehou and Jin Guantao have noted a firm Confucian sedimentation in the ideologically constructed Sinicized Marxism, Beijing's official position has been harshly critical of China's feudal past and strongly anti-Confucian. Surely the radical iconoclastic attack on Confucius in the early 1970s during the Cultural Revolution was motivated by a blatantly political conspiracy and was thus an aberration, but the overall ideological thrust of the Chinese Communist party has been hostile to the Confucian tradition. Of course, this by no means implies that the habits of the heart in mainland China have ceased to be Confucian. On the contrary, recent anthropological, sociological, and political surveys all point to the pervasive presence of Confucian ethics in belief, attitude, and behavior across all social strata throughout China. The deliberate attempt by the Chinese communist leadership to promote Confucian studies for nationalist reasons after the T'ien-an-men tragedy of 1989 is a new development, and the implications have yet to be assessed. In short, the fate of Confucianism in Communist China, to put it mildly, is infelicitous.

Not surprisingly, Hong Kong, specifically New Asia College at Chinese University, has been the center for contemporary New Confucianism. It seems ironic that the commercial capital of South China, noted for its vibrant merchant culture, has provided a hospitable environment for the revitalization of the preeminent scholar-official tradition of the literatus. Or perhaps, as Ambrose King suggests in his brief discussion of intellectual Confucianism in Taiwan, "The Transformation of Confucianism in the Post-Confucian Era: The Emergence of Rationalistic Traditionalism in Hong Kong," what has been revived in Hong Kong is neither the scholar-official nor the literary tradition, but a mode of Confucian spirituality separable from and critical of institutional or state Confucianism. The issue is further complicated by the fact that although New Confucianism, as Liu Shu-hsien defines it, has found a tentative home in Hong Kong since the 1950s, it was basically incongruent with the ethos of the Cantonese-speaking metropolis. Indeed, none of the leading New Confucians managed to become acclimated to Hong Kong, even though they have resided there for decades. Their refugee status and exile mentality have been so strong that their writings, especially those in a personal and autobiographical vein, convey a profound existential sense of alienation and homelessness. To be sure, several generations of New Confucians have been trained in Hong Kong; but it would be farfetched to characterize New Confucianism as an indigenous Hong Kong intellectual movement.

Understandably, King, in addressing the Confucian influence in Hong Kong, takes Weber's spirit of capitalism as its point of departure. In light of S. N. Eisenstadt's critical insight, King reformulates the Weberian thesis in order to examine the "internal transformative capacities" of Confucianism and their impact on the modernization of Hong Kong. Basing his analysis on a series of empirical studies, King discusses the emergence of "rationalistic traditionalism" as the mentality of Hong Kong's business community as it has engaged in an impressive march toward modernity since 1949. He acknowledges that "the impact of Confucianism on the direction of modernity in Chinese societies was not quite the same as that of Protestantism in Europe," but maintains that "Confucianism does contain the seeds of transformation, and in the right institutional settings these seeds could bear fruit to influence positively the course of economic development."

King constructs his argument for rationalistic traditionalism by examining the role of family values—filial piety, frugality, and respect for elders—in the economic culture. Having established the relevance and even the centrality of the familistic ethos in Hong Kong's economic sphere, he makes the critical observation that a distinctive feature of rationalistic traditionalism is that the Confucian values are not necessarily cherished affectively for their intrinsic goodness. Rather, they are being "selectively preserved" mainly for their "extrinsic usefulness in pursuing economic goals." This "cognitive selectivity" enables the Chinese business community in Hong Kong to translate "utilitarianistic familism" into a dominant cultural code. Obviously it is not institutional or state Confucianism but social and popular Confucianism that provides an ethic for the man in the street. If we follow Robert Smith's clue in perceiving the tradition from the bottom up, rationalistic traditionalism may very well, as King claims, be a general cultural phenomenon in Confucian East Asia.

John Wong, in "Promoting Confucianism for Socioeconomic Development: The Singapore Experience," frankly warns against the "perils of simplistic cultural explanations." After recounting several arguments in favor of the Confucian thesis, Wong insists that for the hypothesis to be taken seriously by his fellow economists, it must be argued in "a testable hypothesis." Specifically, he notes that it is not enough to show that the Confucian ethos is conducive to increased personal savings. One must also demonstrate that such savings have been productively invested in business or industry rather than squandered on noneconomic spending. Similarly, analysts fall short of establishing the link between the Confucian ethic and economic development if they cannot be more specific than simply noting that Confucianism holds education and learning in high social esteem. Unless it can be shown that Confucian values have "operational implications" for significant economic activities such as upgrading skills and manpower training, observers are not in a position to defend the Confucian thesis.

The economic dynamism of East Asia, Wong asserts, is due primarily to the adoption of the basic development strategy employed in Singapore as well as in South Korea and Taiwan, namely, the successful "transition from import substitution to export orientation" in a favorable international economic climate. Having identified both domestic and international factors that are particularly congenial to Singapore's economic vitality, Wong singles out the government's "correct choice of development policies and strategies" as the critical factor in providing the basic framework for mobilizing capital and labor, "the real resources" for economic growth. Thus, Wong concludes that "Singapore's past industrialization progress can be captured and analyzed using conventional neoclassical economic theory."

While Wong does not see any need to resort to cultural explanations such as the role played by Confucianism for Singapore's economic development, he chronicles the government's campaign to promote Confucian ethics in schools in the 1980s and offers an interpretation of the underlying reasons for such a course of action. He also gives an informed account of Singapore's decision to address the thorny issue of "national ideology" in 1989. Intent on constructing the national creed rooted in shared values, the government, acutely aware of the sensitivity of ethnic minorities, formulated four cardinal principles: (1) community over self; (2) upholding the family as the basic building block of society; (3) resolving major issues through consensus instead of contention; and (4) stressing racial and religious tolerance and harmony. With telling effectiveness, Wong states that the current Singapore political leadership identifies and emphasizes the positive aspects of Confucianism "in order to strengthen their cultural identity and use it as a social bulwark against negative Western cultural inroads."

Eddie Kuo's focused investigation of Singapore's government-sponsored movement to revitalize Confucian ethics, "Confucianism as Political Discourse in Singapore: The Case of an Incomplete Revitalization Movement," details an elaborate process involving quite a few top leaders, including the prime minister and the minister of education. Not since the Meiji Imperial Rescript on Education have we witnessed such a national effort to deal with ethics on so grandiose a scale. Kuo interprets the movement as a conscious response to a moral crisis occasioned by economic prosperity. It seems that the political and intellectual leaders of Singapore perceive neither urgency nor necessity in exploring the genetic reasons for the economic dynamism of industrial East Asia. To them the burning concern is to devise a future-oriented strategy. If by fostering and encouraging Confucian values Singaporeans may keep their bearings in a complex and fluid multicultural society, the question of the Confucian contribution to economic vibrancy in the past is of only secondary importance, if not of purely academic interest.

The movement to promote Confucian ethics involving curriculum development for secondary schools and a national campaign to promote civic morality in Singapore was, therefore, a well-coordinated government attempt to formulate a common creed for the country with a view toward the future. Whether it was designed as an integral part of social engineering or simply occurred as an unintended consequence of mass mobilization, the continuous national debate precipitated the emergence of a public sphere. The Chinese community, especially those not well versed in English, vocally expressed their views on the matter. Anti-Confucian rhetoric, reminiscent of the iconoclasm of the May Fourth generation, clashed with sentiments of ethnic pride and the desire for cultural identity. Liberal-minded intellectuals trained in England and the United States criticized Confucian ethics as authoritarianism, gerontocracy, and male orientation in disguise, whereas high school teachers of Chinese background embraced it as Singapore's main cultural heritage. Kuo enumerates the favorable conditions that prompted the Confucian discourse to attract such attention in government, the mass media, school, and business, and he analyzes the dilemmas and paradoxes surrounding the movement.

Although the movement is at best incomplete, the original intention of sensitizing the Singaporean Chinese to the positive values of their Confucian heritage has been realized. Even the specific aim of incorporating Confucian ethics into the moral educational component of the primary and secondary school curriculum has been partly achieved. The Confucian experiment in Singapore, however, makes it glaringly clear that the cultivation of civic morality works essentially from the bottom up; the leadership may and should set high standards of conduct, but it can provide a source of inspiration only through exemplary conduct. It is unlikely that "a sense of shame," as Confucius would have it, can be imposed from above. It is worth noting that Kuo also refers to the "White Paper for Shared Values," announced in January 1990 and adopted by the Parliament a year later. According to him, the White Paper (apparently the final text resulted from an elaborate process of consensus formation) asserts five principles, not the four John Wong ascertains. The additional principle in Kuo's version is "community support and respect for the individual." If Wong's four original principles are rooted in the Confucian tradition, the fifth suggests the need to revitalize Confucianism in the modern liberal democratic spirit.

Still, in light of the Confucian traditions in Hong Kong and Singapore, it is highly problematic to define modernity purely in terms of the European and American experience, that is, in terms of market economy, democratic polity, and individualism. The modernizing process may compel Hong Kong and Singapore to follow institutional imperatives dictated by these Western ideas and practices, but what constitutes a functioning modern enterprise in Hong Kong or Singapore may not depend on its degree of Westernization. S. Gordon Redding argues in "Societal Transformation and the Contribution of Authority Relations and Cooperation Norms in Overseas Chinese Business" that these relationships and norms can be brought to bear on the general managerial issue: "the function of a legitimate moral base for stabilizing vertical order." He begins from an assumption based on earlier research that Confucian ethics helped establish authority relations in modern enterprises in Hong Kong, Singapore, and overseas Chinese communities. A more challenging question concerns the applicability of this seemingly idiosyncratic description of Chinese practice to the business world at large.

Implicit in Redding's empirical work on the managerial style of overseas Chinese family business is a heuristic question: In what sense can the Chinese modus operandi be generalized into a nomothetic principle? Availing himself of Eisenstadt's idea of "transformative capacities," Redding examines the role of Confucian ethics in fostering stability and adaptiveness, maintaining legitimacy of cooperation, and providing the ethical base for Chinese family business, and thus bringing about societal transformations in overseas Chinese communities. He further contends that so long as Confucian ethics help to establish "a moral base for the legitimization of authority at the level of the firm" and for the "facilitation of reliable transactions," ensuring "a state infrastructure that allows stable decentralization," they comprise universal and necessary conditions for sustainable economic growth.

Without addressing the Confucian dimension in East Asian modernization directly, Gary Hamilton straightforwardly examines a phenomenon transcending temporal and geographic boundaries. In "Overseas Chinese Capitalism" he challenges virtually all interpretive literature based on country-specific or comparative studies, asserting that Chinese capitalism, past and present, is neither elite-based nor dependent on an explicit political system. Rather, it is a form of capitalism carried out by heads of peasant, merchant, artisan, and scholar households, featuring family enterprises which use "consanguineous relationships as the organizational medium for the economy."

Hamilton further observes that this kind of capitalism, rooted in kinship ties (relatives) and primordial territorial affiliations (fellow regionals), mainly consists of "household-based firms linked together into investment, production, and distribution networks." These networks, highly demand-responsive, seem to have dominated the economies of "Hong Kong, Singapore, Taiwan, Thailand, Malaysia, and to a lesser extent Indonesia and the Philippines." They are flexible, innovative, and expansive; with a preference for small and medium-sized enterprises, they also possess the know-how to span political boundaries, bypass bureaucratic restrictions, and transcend sovereign states. Hamilton's provocative thesis raises doubts about state and institutional Confucianism but lends support to social and popular Confucianism. Indeed, this historically situated and sociologically constructed Chinese "network capitalism" may not have benefited from the political arena, but it is definitely embedded in and nurtured by the rich symbolic resources of and dense interpersonal communication among overseas Chinese societies seasoned in Confucian ethics.

13

THE TRANSFORMATION OF CONFUCIANISM
IN THE POST-CONFUCIAN ERA

The Emergence of Rationalistic
Traditionalism in Hong Kong

Ambrose Y. C. King

The striking empirical phenomenon of success in economic de-velopment in particular, and modernization in general, of East Asian societies, namely, Japan and the Four Mini-Dragons—Tai-wan, South Korea, Singapore, and Hong Kong—has captured the attention of students of modernization from various disciplines. Peter Berger believes that there is a distinctively East Asian form of modernity in the making.[1] Edward Tiryakian argues that the epicenter of modernity has begun to shift from North America to East Asia.[2] The success of East Asia, which constitutes such a sharp contrast to the ineffective struggle of most of the econom-ically backward Third World countries, calls for an explanation.

Broadly speaking, there are two theoretical tendencies in the current literature on East Asia. One, the "institutionalist" inter-pretation, emphasizes specific economic, legal, and political in-stitutional arrangements within the societies at issue.[3] The other, or "culturalist" interpretation, emphasizes specific cultural fac-tors.[4] The culturalists attribute the success of Eastern societies to their common cultural heritage, that is, Confucianism. Herman Kahn and others have put forward what may be called a post-Confucian thesis, which holds that the set of values with which the people grew up, conventionally labeled Confucian, provides them with the mentality and work ethic believed to be conducive to economic development.[5] This post-Confucian thesis, though still in a rudimentary form, can be seen as both Weberian and anti-Weberian at the same time. It is Weberian because, like Weber's Protestant thesis, it argues for the critical role of cultural factors in economic development; it is anti-Weberian because it contradicts Weber's view that the failure of capitalism to develop in traditional China was largely due to the effects of the Confucian ethos. Thomas Metzger writes: "We consequently are led to ask: why in this kind of world are some societies more effective than others in coping with their problems and rising to the challenges of modernization? While Weber had to explain China's failure, we have to explain its success, but paradoxically our answer, like Weber's, emphasizes the role of the indigenous ethos."[6]

This essay is not intended to join the great controversy over Weber's Protestant thesis, which has often resulted in sterile debate. One point, however, should be made clear: the post-Confucian thesis, though interestingly provocative, probably cannot fundamentally challenge Weber's original thesis. The Weberian thesis asks why the indigenous development of the West in the seventeenth and eighteenth centuries led to capitalism and the indigenous development of China did not. To Weber the adoption of capitalism is theoretically a separate issue. As Talcott Parsons has commented: "Weber's concern was with the conditions which made it possible for 'capitalism' to develop in the West, and why this did not occur in other societies. Now it can perhaps be said that attention must be centered on the conditions of its spread from the West to other societies all over the world."[7]

The spread of capitalism from the West to other non-Western societies has been extremely uneven. And the success of non-Western societies in assimilating capitalism very much depends on their "conditions," which involve both institutional and cultural factors.[8] If we speak only of the cultural conditions involved in assimilating capitalism, we are resorting to the post-Confucian thesis, which in effect hypothesizes that Confucian values are providing the motivational drive for economic development in East Asian societies.

Ironically, from the beginning of this century, especially since the New Culture Movement of May Fourth in 1919, most intellectuals have held the view that the root of China's backwardness lay in its cultural traditions, especially its Confucian values. Not surprisingly, they vigorously attacked all aspects of Confucianism, particularly the Confucian family system. Their antitraditionalism was total and uncompromising. What some of the leading intellectuals advocated was nothing short of wholesale Westernization. The May Fourth cultural revolution was aimed at a total rejection of China's past.[9]

Indeed, this view which holds that Confucianism is inimical to China's development is not totally dissimilar to that of Weber and is in opposition to the post-Confucian thesis. Students of China's development may ask, then, which view is theoretically and empirically more defensible, in light of the striking economic success of some East Asian societies. I am of the view that no definitive verdict can be given on this issue. A fundamental cultural fact must be recognized, namely, that East Asian societies no longer exist in a Confucian sociopolitical order. The May Fourth leaders' Confucianism has long since been deconstructed, if it has not totally died. We are now living in a post-Confucian sociopolitical society, and the cultural systems of the post-Confucian societies are a mixture of indigenous values and Western influences. In this essay I argue that insofar as Hong Kong is concerned, a kind of Confucianism which I call *rationalistic traditionalism* has come into existence. This, I believe, is an important contributing factor in making Hong Kong one of the most successful newly industrialized societies.

I am not arguing that rationalistic traditionalism (a transformed value orientation of Confucianism) is the only factor responsible for the success of Hong Kong's modernization. No student of development of any sophistication would think that a Confucian heritage is enough to explain the successful modernization of East Asian societies.[10] There is no gainsaying that Weber was not a monocausalist. His thought is not determined by any single factor; he was as much concerned with institutional factors as with cultural ones.[11]

The suggestion by S. N. Eisenstadt that what is required for a reexamination of the Weberian thesis is "a shift of attention from the allegedly direct, causal relationship between Protestantism and capitalism (or other aspects of the modern world) to the internal transformative capacities of Protestantism and to their impact on the transformation of the modern world"[12] seems to me most appealing. He writes: "The crucial impact of Protestantism in the direction of modernity came after it could not fully realize its initial totalistic socio-religious aims. Thus the special importance of Protestantism, from a broad comparative point of view, was that . . . it contained within itself the seeds of such a transformation and that in certain settings these seeds could bear fruit generously to influence the course of European civilization."[13]

Although the impact of Confucianism on the direction of modernity in Chinese societies was not quite the same as that of Protestantism in Europe, I am of the view that Confucianism does contain the seeds of transformation, and in the right institutional settings these seeds could bear fruit to influence positively the course of economic development. In the pages that follow I discuss how the seeds of Confucianism have grown into a rationalistic traditionalism.

Hong Kong has been rapidly industrialized and modernized since the 1950s. By 1985 Hong Kong's per capita income was U.S. $6,282. In terms of employment, 35.6 percent of the labor force was engaged in manufacturing, 54.4 percent in commerce and other service industries, and only 1.8 percent in agriculture. According to the United Nations' classification, in 1971 Hong Kong had the second highest per capita consumption of extrasomatic energy in Asia, next only to Japan. From the standpoint of energetics, Hong Kong belongs among the "ecological phase 4 societies," in which "the total use of energy by human communities, unlike in phase 1, 2, and 3 societies, is no longer running more or less parallel with population size."[14]

Hong Kong is an international city of the first order, but 98 percent of its population is ethnic Chinese, with only 2 percent non-Chinese in origin. Although Hong Kong is considerably Westernized, the Chinese population is very conscious of its ethnic and cultural identity. According to a 1982 survey of a wide cross-section of the Chinese population, with two-thirds of the sample under thirty-five years of age, the majority of the respondents (76 percent) claimed to be Chinese in terms of internal characteristics, be they values or traits. Fifty-seven percent maintained they were Chinese because they preserved values such as filial piety, frugality, and respect for teachers. Furthermore, a survey of a representative sample of students from two universities in Hong Kong showed that they perceived four main areas where differences between modern Chinese and Westerners continue to exist. The first is in family life, where the Chinese endorse filial piety and have reservations about voicing opinions different from those of their parents.[15] That the Hong Kong Chinese identify their "Chineseness" most saliently with the familistic values, particularly with filial piety, is a good indication that they have maintained the core value of Confucianism.[16]

The importance the Hong Kong Chinese have attached to the familistic ethos is also manifested behaviorally, in spite of the fact that as many as 73 percent of the households surveyed in 1974 consisted only of nuclear families. In a survey of 3,753 married men and women in 1967, R. E. Mitchell found that 32 percent of the husbands and 54 percent of the wives claimed to be ancestor worshippers. Furthermore, 65 percent of the married sons and 44 percent of the married daughters gave money to their parents, and many of these younger adults were themselves sacrificing financially in order to help their parents in this way.[17] S. K. Lau, in his 1976–77 survey of a sample of 550 on sociopolitical behavior of Chinese residents in Hong Kong, found that at both normative and behavioral levels the Chinese manifested their primary concern with the family. Lau writes: "The significance of the family is clearly evident as 85.6 percent of the respondents rated either 'the family more important' or 'both family and society equally important' as against 13.5 percent of them who considered 'society more important' . . . The significance of the family is further indicated by the fact that 86.6 percent of the respondents stated that they spent most of their spare time with their families."[18]

The importance of the familistic ethos also extends to the economic sphere of life. The "traditional" Chinese family was a highly particularistic structure,[19] and its particularism was nowhere more evident than in economic organization where people with familial ties or kinship relationships were given preferential employment. Such a practice of preferential employment based on familistic particularism is called nepotism. How prevalent is nepotism in the Hong Kong economy? The economic structure of Hong Kong is disproportionately dominated by small industry. Among 26,149 factories surveyed in 1971, there were 23,765 small factories (90.9 percent) employing no more than fifty workers.[20] In these small factories, according to a 1978 survey, about half (47 percent) of the 415 factory owners employed relatives in their work force.[21] In another survey of 346 factories in Kwun Tong, an important industrial section of Hong Kong, Victor Mok concludes: "It is rather customary for a Chinese proprietor to put a trusted man in each department as some kind of supervisor to safeguard his own interests. Beyond direct kinsfolk and clansmen, a person who comes from the same place of origin, speaking the same dialect and probably being a remote relative would be next in line of reliability."[22] Employing relatives is not confined to small factories. A 1969 study of twenty-seven large Chinese industrial firms showed that among the twenty-three from which information was obtained, fourteen (61 percent) employed family members.[23]

All these findings suggest unequivocally that the familistic ethos is a significant force in influencing Chinese social and economic behavior in the rapidly industrialized and modernized Hong Kong.

In Weber's diagnosis one of the essential elements of Confucianism which constitutes a great barrier to the rise of capitalism is precisely the Chinese kinship system, or the Confucian family ethos. He writes: "Family piety, resting on the belief in spirits, was by far the strongest influence on man's conduct. Ultimately family piety facilitated and controlled . . . the strong cohesion of the sib associations . . . Chinese ethic developed its strongest motives in the circle of naturally grown, personalist associations or associations affiliated with or modelled after them."[24] Students of Chinese culture today would hardly disagree with Weber's views on the traditional Chinese family ethos. He continues: "For the economic mentality, the personalist principle was undoubtedly as great a barrier to impersonal rationalization as it was generally to impersonal matter of factness. It tended to tie the individual ever anew to his sib members and to bind him to the manner of the sib, in any case to 'persons' instead of functional tasks ('enterprises'). This barrier was intimately connected with the nature of Chinese religion."[25]

Weber's analysis of the familistic aspect of Chinese society is indeed penetrating and insightful, and has won more confirmation than refutation in the literature by contemporary social scientists. C. K. Yang writes: "Recent findings do not, in general principle, contradict Weber's interpretation of the implications of the Chinese kinship system as an inhibiting influence against capitalist development."[26]

I agree that Weber's assessment of the traditional Chinese family ethos as an impediment to economic development is basically sound, although there is an error in Weber's interpretation of Chinese civilization, namely, his denial of the existence within Confucian China of any transcendental tension.[27] What I argue is that the Chinese in Hong Kong no longer live uncritically under the traditional Confucian familistic persuasion, though they remain "modern Chinese" in the sense that they still, ideologically and behaviorally, attach importance to some Confucian familistic values. But they do not necessarily deem such values intrinsically good in the economic sphere of life. They have adopted a rationalistic, instrumental attitude toward familistic values, thus turning them into a cultural resource to achieve other purposes. Through a continuous process of cognitive selection, the Hong Kong Chinese have, whether consciously or subconsciously, transformed Confucianism into a kind of rationalistic traditionalism. By this I mean that traditions are not necessarily always treasured affectively for their intrinsic goodness but are selectively preserved mainly, though not exclusively, for their extrinsic usefulness in pursuing economic goals.

Hong Kong is often called the meeting place of East and West. Indeed, a sensitive casual visitor to the city will notice the influence of both Western and Chinese cultures. But the great Confucian tradition had never been truly developed in Hong Kong when it was ceded to the British in the late nineteenth century. Rich in Chinese folk traditions such as *fengshui, shen,* and *gui,* as well as in the elements of Confucian familism which I have just discussed, Hong Kong has developed a full set of institutional arrangements which are Western in nature. As Stephen Boyden and his associates point out: "The way of life of the Chinese people in Hong Kong is profoundly affected by modern Western culture. For example, their livelihood depends upon striving for material wealth and status defined by the West, and the education system is a British one."[28] Striving for material wealth, however, is nothing new or alien to traditional Chinese. Weber was in fact fully aware of the much-bewailed "crass 'materialism' of the Chinese."[29] In Hong Kong, says the anthropologist James Hayes: "The pursuit of wealth has long been a common goal . . . It has drawn generations of businessmen from the West and from China alike. The Colony has always afforded an outlet for talent for which Kwangtung is famous. For centuries its immigrants have been described by other Chinese as lovers of money, subordinating all else in its pursuit."[30]

Hayes's observation on the Chinese quest for wealth is not atypical among Chinese outside mainland China. Maurice Freedman writes: "Shrewdness in handling money was an important part of the equipment which ordinary Chinese took with them when they went overseas in search of a livelihood . . . The Chinese were economically successful in Southeast Asia not simply because they were energetic immigrants, but more fundamentally because in their quest for riches they knew how to handle money, and organize men in relation to money."[31] E. J. Ryan, in a study of a Chinese trading community in Indonesia, discusses the "focal value of wealth," writing: "In the day-to-day course of events, it is around this value that energies are mobilized, interest centred, the very life and household organized, and in the service of which social relations are patterned."[32]

In China's great tradition, wrote Weber, "Confucius might not disdain the acquisition of riches but wealth seemed insecure and could upset the equilibrium of the genteel soul."[33] Nevertheless, the folk religions of China fully sanctioned the act of "getting rich." The god of wealth is probably the most widely worshipped god in Chinese folk religion. In present-day Hong Kong wealth no longer upsets the equilibrium of the genteel soul. Indeed, "most people in Hong Kong are imbued with a relatively strong sense of purpose. This sense of purpose usually centres on the desire to promote the prosperity of the family."[34] For a long time business and industrial activities in matters relating to material wealth have been regarded as socially acceptable pursuits. The impulse to pursue material wealth is evident not only among entrepreneurs and managers but also among workers. Attitude surveys of Chinese workers regularly find that monetary rewards are high on their list of priorities.[35]

In traditional China government officials constituted the ruling stratum. Literary education was the yardstick for measuring social prestige and the basic qualification for office. The Chinese literati were a status group with a particular mentality, the Chinese ethos, which has been characterized as the status ethic.[36] The Chinese masses believed that literary education bestowed an extraordinary power on officials. Weber observed: "High mandarins were considered magically qualified. They could always become objects of a cult, after their death as well as during their lifetime, provided that their charisma was 'proved.' "[37]

In Hong Kong, by contrast, literati never came into existence as a status group, despite the fact that the Chinese have a high level of achievement motivation.[38] In a study of child-rearing attitudes and practices in Hong Kong, David Ho finds that "the most frequently mentioned personal characteristics expected of the child when grown up were those concerned with competence and achievement, followed by those concerned with moral character, sociability, and controlled temperament."[39] The most outstanding feature of the learning environment in Hong Kong is the pressure put on the student, both by parents and by teachers, to study for examinations. Education is seen by most people as a prerequisite for material wealth.[40] In Hong Kong the cult object is not the literatus or even the high mandarin but the successful industrialist and businessman. Shipping magnates and commercial managers rank highest in the occupational status hierarchy.[41] This preference is manifested throughout the Chinese communities of Southeast Asia.[42]

In the sociopolitical context of Hong Kong, there seems not to have occurred the phenomenon that Everett Hagen calls "withdrawal of status respect,"[43] which, I suspect, has happened in other East Asian societies. The overwhelming status value accorded to industrial and business elites can be explained only by the fact that, unlike in imperial China, the most promising route to social eminence for the Chinese in Hong Kong is not by becoming officials and scholars but through gaining wealth in the business world. A career in politics was denied to the Chinese in the colony, so that "wealth was, in fact, the only means by which a Chinese individual in Hong Kong could come to have any influence at all on community affairs, and the only means by which he could stand out in society as an important person."[44] Industrial-business elites are status groups par excellence in Hong Kong. As a consequence, the pursuit of wealth has become a powerful motivation for Hong Kong Chinese and has led them to channel their energy into economic activities.

The intense motivational drive of the Chinese for material wealth and social status has created in them a pragmatic and instrumental or rationalistic attitude toward traditional values in dealing with men and economics. As I mentioned earlier, Confucian familistic values are still alive in Hong Kong. If we look more closely, however, we find that these values have been transformed. It may well be argued that a new kind of rationalistic traditionalism has appeared in the social-cultural sphere of Hong Kong. I turn now to a discussion of this transformation.

In our study of small factories in Hong Kong in 1971, my colleague and I found that Confucian familial values still played an important role among Chinese factory owners. More often than not, however, the practice of recruiting relatives was justified on rational grounds and was not simply the result of the cultural legacy of Confucian familism. We concluded:

> It is true that the owners/managers of the small factories are in large measure traditionalistic, paternalistic and conservative, but it is far from being true that they are persons with an inevitable and almost built-in disposition for nepotistic inclination which is often the mental characteristic of the so-called "patrimonial manager." On the contrary, what strikes us most is that the Chinese owners/managers are pragmatic, practical and serious. The above-mentioned fact of hiring relatives should not be interpreted as an indication that kinship relationship is cherished as a goal value in itself; instead it is more or less used as an instrumental mechanism to secure one whom they feel they can trust. It is indeed our contention that the Chinese traditional familistic system has been modified by Western business ideology and practical necessity, or by the functional prerequisites, if you so wish to call it, of the industrial system. As such, it may have enhanced rather than undermined the economic performance of the small factories.[45]

In a survey of 255 Hong Kong employers in 1976, S. K. Lau found that most of them (85.1 percent) considered that "aggressiveness" was either an important or a very important trait for an employee to possess. And in the eyes of employers the "ability to do the job" was also rated very high as a characteristic of the employee; 57.3 percent considered it important, and 32.9 percent considered it very important. With regard, however, to the characteristic "related to me through kinship or other ties," more than two thirds of the sampled employers deemed it not important (32.5 percent) or extremely unimportant (34.5 percent). Lau concluded: "Though there are still traditionalistic elements of various sorts embedded in the managerial attitudes, they can in many cases be justified on rational and pragmatic grounds, in view of the specific economic and labor conditions in Hong Kong."[46] It may be that nepotism is still widely practiced in Hong Kong mainly because it has been utilized as a cultural resource for positive economic reasons. Wong Siu-lun's distinction between passive and active nepotism with regard to Chinese businessmen and industrialists is very useful. He writes, "We can expect them to shake off passive nepotism whenever circumstances permit, while they may keep active nepotism because it can serve them positively."[47]

In view of the Chinese economic mentality and behavior discussed earlier, I can fully echo what Maurice Freedman has said: "The people of the Sinoinfluenced cultures are to an unusual extent pragmatic-empirical problem-solving, rather than submissive and fatalistic in a problematic situation."[48] Since Hong Kong is a place where both Western and Chinese traditions coexist, the Chinese can theoretically become what Robert Park calls "marginal men." The theory of social marginality has not produced convincing evidence that marginal individuals tend to make creative adjustments in situations of change, and there are some who argue that such individuals are more prone than others to anomie and thus to becoming carriers of trends leading toward social disorganization.[49] Hong Kong's modern Chinese, however, seem to have no "identity" problem. They identify themselves as Chinese and, "at the grass roots level, there is no evidence for a sense of loss or cultural disintegration among the Hong Kong Chinese."[50] On the contrary, the Chinese have shown a remarkable ability to move in and out of the two traditions. Marjorie Topley, an anthropologist who has resided in Hong Kong for many years, observes that "people do not usually turn to Western ideas because they come to believe them more 'true' than the traditional ones. Rather, they follow some Western practices because they find them effective in some circumstances and some Chinese practices for similar reasons. People may move in and out of Chinese and Western traditions, at least at the present time. The effect is the proof—if it works, it is true."[51]

The ease with which Hong Kong Chinese move in and out of different cultural traditions is due to pragmatic-empirical considerations and, more often than not, is based on cost-benefit calculations. The process is one of cognitive selectivity in which the individuals exercise rational judgments. S. K. Lau has argued that "utilitarianistic familism" has become the dominant cultural code in Hong Kong. He writes:

> Briefly, utilitarianistic familism can be defined as a normative and behavioural tendency of an individual to place his family interest above the interest of society or any of its component individuals and groups, and to structure his relationships with other individuals and groups in such a fashion that the furtherance of his familial interests is the primary consideration. Moreover, among the familial interests, materialistic interest takes priority over all other interests.[52]

It should be pointed out that utilitarianistic familism, unlike traditional Confucian familism, is characterized by a marked element of rationality. "As a faction-oriented entity," writes Lau, "the familial group exercises rationality in both family organization and member recruitment so as to maximize the efficiency of resource mobilization and utilization. The vagueness or fluidity of the boundary of the familial group is both the result and cause of rational consideration."[53]

Given these findings, it could be said that, though Confucianism never existed in Hong Kong as a systemic, intellectualized cultural system, the Chinese tradition of which the Confucian familial ethos constitutes the core is still operative in Hong Kong. In a large measure, modern Hong Kong Chinese ideologically identify more with Chinese traditions than with Western traditions. They are not, however, sentimentally bound by traditions in their economic behavior. Hong Kong Chinese have an active self-awareness in the sense that they are capable cognitively of assessing the practical utility of the various elements of Chinese tradition for achieving their social and economic goals. Chinese traditions are not always cherished as something intrinsically sacred or good; instead, they are more often than not treated as cultural resources to be tapped and utilized according to instrumental considerations. This does not mean that the Chinese familistic values in Hong Kong have been thoroughly changed. What I argue here is that modern Hong Kong Chinese have been able to use the "personalist principle," which, according to Weber, was intimately concocted with Confucian ethics in a rational and selective fashion aimed at achieving personal economic goals.[54]

People follow traditions, but they are not traditionalistic; Confucian traditions are preserved and practiced mainly because they serve current rationalistic ends. I venture to argue that it is not the Confucianism Weber came to know but rationalistic traditionalism, or rationalistic Confucianism, which seems to be an important contributing factor to the economic success of Hong Kong. If there is a "post-Confucian" culture, then it is, for Hong Kong, the culture of rationalistic traditionalism.

As the foregoing discussion should have revealed, the assimilation of capitalism in Hong Kong has been facilitated by the cultural "conditions," to use Parsons's expression, provided by a transformed type of Confucianism, or by what I call rationalistic traditionalism. It is clear that the Confucianism discussed by Weber is now dead and never took root in Hong Kong at all. Weber's Confucianism can probably be identified as imperial Confucianism or institutional Confucianism, which was a complex and sophisticated combination of state ideology combined with a set of strategic institutions, including the literati, the examination system, and above all universal kingship and the imperial bureaucracy. In Hong Kong there is only social Confucianism or the Confucianism of everyday life, which refers to a set of Confucian beliefs and values accepted widely by the man in the street.

What I wish to stress is that this social Confucianism is not a rigid belief system. It consists of a group of guiding social principles for the conduct of familial and extrafamilial relationships. In the post-Confucian era the strategic imperial Confucian institutions are all dead or deconstructed in the

Chinese societies of East Asia. But Confucian social-cultural beliefs and values have found new and more dynamic expressions in non-Confucian institutional settings. Moreover, these beliefs and values, as I have suggested, can be effectively utilized as resources for modernizing purposes. That Confucianism contains the seeds of a transformative capacity is amply manifested in the newly emerging rationalistic traditionalism of the post-Confucian era. Rationalistic traditionalism is not necessarily unique to Hong Kong. It is rather, I suspect, a general cultural phenomenon of secularization in other East Asian societies also pursuing economic development. I have not attempted or intended to confirm or refute the Weberian thesis. I have, however, tried here to give substantive meaning to the "post-Confucian" thesis.

14

PROMOTING CONFUCIANISM FOR
SOCIOECONOMIC DEVELOPMENT
The Singapore Experience

John Wong

The dynamic economic growth of postwar Japan, and more recently of the four Asian newly industrialized economies (NIEs) of South Korea, Taiwan, Hong Kong, and Singapore, has been regarded as a rare economic phenomenon of modern times. All five economies are scarce in land and poor in natural resources, but they have managed to overcome these constraints by intensifying the development of their human resources through education and the upgrading of skills, thrift, hard work, and industrial discipline—traits that are commonly identified as Confucian values and that constitute the mainstream cultural traditions of these societies.

Japan's economic performance in its totality is actually more impressive than anything that has been achieved by any Western economy. Apart from its spectacular postwar economic recovery and expansion, Japan has been able to sustain high economic growth long after the growth momentum of high-performance postwar economies such as that of West Germany have tapered off. Consequently, Japan today has developed into a truly world-class economic superpower, second only to the United States. In fact, Japan's current per capita income in nominal terms has already surpassed that of the United States. Japan has achieved its present level of economic development in just half the time it took Britain.

In a similar context the economic performance of the NIEs has been an even greater miracle. For about three decades these NIEs have consistently chalked up nearly double-digit rates of growth, based primarily on the expansion of manufactured exports. With their combined population of only 1.4 percent of the world total, they succeeded in 1989 in capturing a staggering 8.4 percent share of the world market for their manufactured exports. The average per capita income of these four NIEs in 1992 was around U.S. $12,000, which was about the level in Japan in the mid-1980s. The NIEs should be fully developed economies by the turn of the century. In fact, the World Bank has already "graduated" Singapore and Hong Kong to the "developed economy" status. (See Table 14.1 for main performance indicators.)

Such spectacular economic achievements have inevitably generated a great deal of interest among scholars as well as journalists who want to explain this success. To be sure, standard neoclassical economic theory is rich enough to provide a reasonably adequate explanation for the economic growth of these East Asian economies. For instance, their high economic growth was generally attributed to their high levels of domestic investments, which were matched by their equally high levels of domestic savings. Their export competitiveness was clearly linked to their high labor productivity or low unit labor cost. Above all, their adoption of export-oriented development strategies was the single most important policy variable in bringing about the dynamic transformation of these economies toward the global level of competition and efficiency.

Economic theory, however, often fails to provide a satisfactory explanation for the root causes of many economic phenomena, especially with regard to the fundamental institutional and social forces that have brought about those economic changes. Both West Germany and Japan were dynamic economies in the postwar period; but why did only Japan successfully sustain its growth-inducing forces for so long? How do we explain the export-oriented development strategies which were so successfully carried out in the NIEs but not in other LDCs (less developed countries)? Why do many East Asians generally show such a strong preference for education and schooling regardless of the actual rates of return on education? What has allowed entrepreneurship to thrive in these societies? Beyond such "hard" inputs as capital, labor, and technology (which are amenable to quantification) lie many "soft" components, such as people's attitudes and motivation, belief systems, patterns of social relations, religious practices, and so on— all of which are capable of exerting a strong influence on the workings of the "hard" economic inputs. Hence the search for more fundamental explanations among the more broad-minded social scientists.

Table 14.1 China and other Asia-Pacific economies

Country	Area (thousand sq. km)	Population 1991 (in millions)	Total GNP 1992 (US$, in millions)	Nominal GNP per capita 1992 (US$)	Real GDP growth (%)							Annual export growth (%)		Manufacturing exports as % of total exports, 1992	Foreign exchange resources, 1992 (US$, in billions)
					1960–70	1970–80	1980–90	1991	1992	1993		1970–80	1980–92		
China	9,561	1,162.2	506,075	470	5.2	5.8	9.5	7.0	13.0	13.4		8.7	11.9	89 (1993)	47
Japan	378	124.5	3,670,975	28,190	10.9	5.0	4.1	3.4	0.9	−0.6		9.0	4.6	98	73
NIE															
S. Korea	99	43.7	296,136	6,790	8.6	9.5	9.7	8.3	4.8	5.7		23.5	11.9	93	17
Taiwan	36	20.8	212,400	10,215	9.2	9.7	7.1	7.2	6.6	6.2		28.5	16.0	93	82
Hong Kong	1	5.8	77,828	15,380	10.0	9.3	7.1	4.0	5.0	5.5		9.7	5.0	95	35
Singapore	1	2.8	46,025	15,750	8.8	8.5	6.4	6.9	5.8	9.8		4.2	9.9	78	40

Sources: World Development Report, 1994 and earlier years; for Taiwan, see *The Statistical Yearbook of the Republic of China, 1993*; and ADB, *Asian Development Outlook, The Straits Times*, (Singapore), April 13, 1994.

To the extent that all of these East Asian societies share the mainstream cultural heritage of China as embodied in Confucianism, such Confucian ethics as are manifested in the emphasis on thrift and hard work, respect for education, and reverence for authority were seen, prima facie, as having direct bearing on these societies' economic success. In this way Confucianism was conveniently singled out as the most important exogenous explanation for the industrial takeoff of East Asia, much like the Protestant ethic for the rise of modern capitalism in the West.

PERILS OF SIMPLISTIC CULTURAL EXPLANATIONS

Development economists have long ago learned that, historically, any society or culture is just as capable of initiating industrialization, provided its positive forces are identified and activated to spark off the dynamic economic growth process.[1] At the same time, economists are also aware that there are clear differences in the economic performance of different ethnic groups within a country which can be explained in a satisfactory manner only by cultural or social rather than economic factors.[2]

Back in 1979, before the NIEs had risen to their present worldwide prominence, Herman Kahn, in his characteristically provocative way, was among the first to link emphatically the economic success of East Asia to the dominant cultural traits operating in these Neo-Confucian societies.[3] In a similar vein two eminent overseas Japanese economists, Michio Morishima and Harry Oshima, also traced the economic success of East Asia directly to Confucian values. While Morishima attributed Japan's success to the working of the Japanese variant of Confucianism, Oshima argued that the more rational, pragmatic, and utilitarian nature of Confucian culture was more conducive to modern economic growth than the social values of either Hinduism or Mahayana Buddhism; hence the differences in economic performance between East Asia and South Asia.[4] Roderick MacFarquhar has gone even further in arguing that post-Confucian "collectivism is better suited to the age of mass industrialization."[5]

Suffice it to say that any explicit argument attributing the industrial success of East Asia to Confucian values, or even any strong statement to this effect, is bound to stir up heated controversy, and often runs dangerously close to cultural determinism. To begin with, there is a serious methodological problem in pinpointing Confucianism or a similar cultural explanation as a fundamental cause of the successful economic development of East Asia. Such arguments, as rightly pointed out by Lawrence Lau, are often tautological in the sense that they merely repeat the same observed facts in a different way, with little or no explanatory power.[6] The same is of course also true of the opposite view: early in this century, when China was poor and backward, many scholars from Max Weber to the young Chinese intellectuals involved in the May Fourth Movement blamed Confucianism for having caused China's backwardness, and their arguments were equally tautological in nature.

Not surprisingly, most scholars are ambivalent toward the actual role of Confucianism in economic development, and they prefer to take the more cautious "necessary but not sufficient" position. Instead of treating Confucian values as the structural factor or the primary force for the industrial takeoff in East Asia, they have generally followed a more acceptable approach by arguing that Confucian values have merely reinforced or facilitated the growth-supporting forces once the economic modernization process in these societies was under way.[7] Similarly, there are others who have wisely chosen the eclectic approach, focusing on how certain positive aspects of Confucianism, such as its emphasis on education and manpower development, effectively contributed to the successful economic growth of East Asia.[8] It is clear that not all aspects of Confucianism but only the part referred to by Peter Berger as "vulgar Confucianism" (rather than intellectual Confucianism, as traditionally embraced by the gentry class of old China) is likely to be directly relevant for modern industrialism.[9]

Thus, for economists to take it more seriously, the argument must be expressed in a testable hypothesis. It is not enough just to argue in general terms that the Confucian ethos is conducive to increased personal savings and hence higher capital formation. It must also be demonstrated forcefully and specifically whether such savings have been productively invested in business or industry or have been squandered on noneconomic spending, such as in the fulfillment of social obligations, which is after all also a part of the Confucian social system. It is not enough just to generalize that Confucianism holds education and learning in high social esteem. It must also be shown how Confucian values have actually resulted in effective manpower development in terms of promoting the upgrading of skills and not in encouraging merely intellectual self-cultivation or self-serving literary pursuits. A typical Confucian gentleman in the past would have shown open disdain for menial labor and would have looked down on the blue-collar factory employment of today. In short, more rigorous research using modern social science techniques is needed to test the "operational implications" of the whole Confucian thesis; otherwise the argument will remain a futile intellectual debate, always bordering on the tautological.

ECONOMIC DEVELOPMENT IN
MULTIRACIAL SINGAPORE

From the outset Singapore's contribution to the debate about Confucianism and economic development has sharply differed from that of the other NIEs. Historically and geographically Singapore is an integral part of Southeast Asia, which is highly heterogeneous in terms of culture, language, religion, and ethnicity. In contrast to the other East Asian NIEs, with their cultural homogeneity, Singapore has never been a "pure" Confucian society. To add to the complications, the government of Singapore, alone among the NIEs, mounted a public campaign in the 1980s to promote Confucian values among its Chinese population. Furthermore, it is quite difficult to establish a direct causal relationship between Confucian values and Singapore's economic development. In fact, neither any Singapore leader nor any serious Singapore scholar has ever openly claimed a specific role played by Confucianism in Singapore's successful economic development.

Singapore's economic development since the 1960s is broadly summarized in Table 14.2. Per capita GNP in 1960 was only S$1,330 (U.S. $760). By 1990 it was S$21,658 (U.S. $12,376), surpassing the level of several OECD countries, including New Zealand, Ireland, and Spain.[10] This sixteenfold increase in per capita GNP over a period of thirty years is by any account a remarkable record of successful economic development.

The Singapore economy started off in 1960 with entrepôt trade as its lifeblood, which amounted to 43 percent of the total trade, or 94 percent of total exports. After the current People's Action party (PAP) government took office in 1959, every effort was made to transform the stagnating entrepôt economy into a thriving economy based on manufactured exports and tradeable services. In 1990 entrepôt trade accounted for 16 percent of the total trade, or 34 percent of total exports. The decline in the economic importance of the traditional entrepôt activities was precipitated by the growth of the manufacturing sector. In 1960 manufacturing accounted for a mere 11 percent of Singapore's total GDP at current market prices; but it rose to 20 percent in 1970 and further to 29 percent in 1990.[11]

Singapore has thus emerged as the most industrialized economy in Southeast Asia. By 1990 its manufacturing sector was made up of 3,728 industrial establishments, employing 352,676 workers and producing S$70.9 billion worth of output, 67 percent of which was for direct export.[12] The industrial structure has matured and become broad-based over the years, having shifted from dependence on traditional industries such as food and beverages or textiles and garments to more capital- and skill-intensive activities such as electronics, chemicals, machinery, and transport equipment. Furthermore, the economy in recent years has also diversified from manufacturing into services, with tradeable services such as finance and banking, and with communications and tourism making increasingly important contributions to economic growth.

There is no single-factor explanation for any economic success. Singapore's success story, much like those of other nations, was due to a multitude of economic factors interacting with the "right" government policies.[13] The policy variable seems to have been more crucial, as appropriate policies were needed to initiate and sustain the development momentum by creating the necessary institutional environment for the working of the economic forces. In retrospect the string of policies adopted by Singapore in the 1960s was actually not very different from those introduced in other LDCs, particularly South Korea and Taiwan, which essentially boils down to a basic development strategy that led to the transition from import substitution to export orientation.[14]

It may be added that the timing also happened to be right for the working of these policies. The international economic environment during Singapore's crucial period of industrial takeoff, around the late 1960s, was exceptionally conducive to export-oriented developing economies. This was a period of free flow of capital and technology from developed economies, which, blessed with unprecedented prosperity and full employment, allowed easy market access to the labor-intensive manufactured exports of developing countries in accordance with the liberal Kennedy Round of multilateral trade negotiations. Hence, not just Singapore but all the other dynamic NIEs were also able to harness the forces of international capitalism to produce a high rate of economic growth.[15]

The correct choice of development policies and strategies thus provided the basic framework for the real resources, such as capital and labor, to be mobilized for dynamic economic growth. All the NIEs started off as capital-poor economies, but Singapore's initial conditions were even more disadvantageous than those of the other three NIEs. In the initial phase of industrialization, Hong Kong had benefited from an influx of capital, skills, and entrepreneurship from China, while Taiwan and South Korea had been recipients of substantial U.S. economic aid. Singapore was all along on its own.

Under the circumstances, the Singapore government had made a conscious policy choice from the outset by pragmatically incorporating foreign investment as one of its main sources of economic growth, with the provision of liberal incentives to attract foreign capital. Subsequently the government introduced the compulsory Central Provident Fund (CPF) scheme to increase forced savings as well as to mobilize housing and infrastructural development. At one stage 50 percent of a worker's pay was locked up in the CPF.

Table 14.2 Singapore: Basic economic indicators

Indicator	1960	1970	1980	1988	1989	1990p
Gross domestic product						
At current market prices (S$m)	2,149.6	5,804.9	25,090.7	49,694.2	56,235.1	62,711.3
Annual change (%)	9.9	15.1	22.3	16.5	13.2	11.5
At 1985 market prices						
Annual change (%)	8.7	9.4	9.7	11.1	9.2	8.3
Per capita GNP (S$)	1,329.6	2,825.3	9,940.6	17,700.3	19,412.9	21,657.6
Gross fixed capital formation (GFCF)						
At current market prices (S$m)	204.9	1,888.5	10,203.1	17,344.1	20,683.2	23,840.7
GFCF as % of GNP	9.4	32.2	42.2	34.7	36.7	37.3
Annual change (%)	21.7	11.8	20.2	8.2	17.7	14.7
Gross national saving (S$m)	−52.3	1,129.7	8,282.0	20,659.8	24,379.7	28,504.3
As % of GNP	na	19.3	34.2	41.4	43.3	44.6
As % of GFCF	na	59.8	81.2	119.1	117.9	119.6
Unemployment rate (%)	4.9	6.0	3.0	3.3	2.2	1.7

Index of industrial production (1989 = 100)	na	18.7	56.2	90.8	100.0	109.5
Consumer price index (annual % change)	1.2	5.6	8.5	1.5	2.4	3.4
Total trade at current prices (S$m)	7,554.8	12,289.6	92,797.1	167,278.0	183,980.2	205,011.6
Total trade (annual % change)	4.2	20.2	34.0	30.0	10.0	11.4
Imports (S$m)	4,077.7	7,533.8	51,344.8	88,226.7	96,863.7	109,805.8
Exports (S$m)	3,477.1	4,755.8	41,452.3	79,051.3	87,116.5	95,205.8
Domestic exports (S$m)	217.1	1,832.2	25,805.2	49,555.2	55,251.7	62,754.1
Re-exports	3,260.0	2,923.6	15,647.1	29,496.1	31,864.8	32,451.7
Official foreign reserves (S$m)	na	3,097.9	13,757.7	33,276.6	38,607.2	48,521.3
External debt (S$m)	na	173.8	937.0	240.8	138.7	67.9
Debt servicing ratio (%)	na	0.6	1.0	0.4	0.7	0.2

Source: Economic Survey of Singapore, 1990 (Singapore: Ministry of Trade and Industry, 1991).

Gross national savings as a percentage of GNP increased from 19 percent in 1970 to 34 percent in 1980 and further to 45 percent in 1990, arguably the highest in the world. But the rise in domestic savings did not reduce Singapore's dependence on multinational corporations (MNCs), which have continued to provide Singapore with the needed skills and entrepreneurship, as well as the export market connection. This also serves to explain why Singapore of all the NIEs has been so dependent on MNCs for its economic development.[16]

Compared with the other NIEs, Singapore's labor supply, in terms of both quantity and quality, was also in a less favorable position. As the smallest of the four NIEs, Singapore's labor force is also understandably the smallest. That is why the Singapore economy has, since the early 1970s, been dependent on the inflow of a substantial number of foreign workers. Even more critically, in terms of education and skill levels Singapore's human resource endowment has all along been inferior to that of the other NIEs. Even by 1980, 43.7 percent of Singapore's population aged twenty-five and over had no formal schooling, as compared to only 19.7 percent for South Korea, 23.1 percent for Taiwan, and 22.5 percent for Hong Kong.[17] Not surprisingly, manpower availability has remained the Achilles' heel of the Singapore economy to the present day.

In fact, the manpower constraint posed an even greater challenge to Singapore than the shortage of capital. Much of Singapore's early industrialization effort was therefore directed toward intensifying human resource development, which included revamping the colonial system of general education into one that emphasized science, technology, and skill training. Furthermore, in August 1968 the Industrial Relations (Amendment) Act was passed to ensure industrial peace by banning illegal strikes.

In this way Singapore's past progress toward industrialization can be captured and analyzed using conventional neoclassical economic theory, without any need to resort to cultural explanations such as the role played by Confucianism. As a matter of fact, Confucianism was not even a subject of public discussion prior to 1979. Apart from the underlying methodological difficulty of the contention as I have outlined it, to assert that Singapore's economic success is due to Confucianism would imply that the non-Chinese minorities played little or no part in that development. Such an explicitly cultural-deterministic argument would clearly be politically untenable in this multiracial and multireligious society. It would also damage Singapore's relations with those neighbors with historically rooted anti-Chinese feelings. Why, then, did the government start a campaign to promote Confucian ethics in the schools in the 1980s?

THE RISE AND DECLINE OF
THE CONFUCIAN MOVEMENT

In 1979, as the Singapore economy achieved self-sustained growth, the government launched the so-called Second Industrial Revolution, a development strategy that was aimed at accelerating economic restructuring from labor-intensive production to more capital-intensive and higher value-added activities. Productivity would now be the main springboard for further economic growth. But productivity growth depends on the quality of inputs, particularly good management, a good work attitude, and a strong urge to improve skills. In other words, even more intensive manpower development would be needed in the future for the new phase of industrial upgrading, and the success of manpower development would depend critically on the right social milieu.

In the early phase of Singapore's development, it was relatively easy for the government to mobilize maximum support from the people for economic development in order to attain the common goal of national survival. Now, with a stronger economy and growing prosperity, it had become more difficult to galvanize the national consensus for the same social purpose. There were increasing reports of "job-hopping" and incidents of declining work ethics among the younger Singaporean workers.

The government was even more concerned with the general erosion of traditional values among the younger generation, who, as children of affluence, had not grown up with the hardship that their parents had experienced. Many young people simply equated modernization with Westernization, with some even drawn to the permissive life-style and counterculture of the West. It should be noted that such problems are the inevitable by-products of modern industrialization everywhere; they have arisen in the other NIEs and are reported to be emerging even in mainland China today. But the conservative Singapore leadership has long been known to be unhappy with such undesirable social trends. For example, in the early 1970s the government was openly concerned about young men sporting long hair. The overall problem was perceived to be particularly serious for Singapore because many people use English as their first language and are therefore much more susceptible to Western values and thinking via direct Western media and television programs. In the other Asian societies, which are insulated by their national languages, only a small proportion of the population is so exposed.[18]

Thus, the government saw the need to inculcate in young people more traditional Asian values as a means of counteracting the Western cultural onslaught, starting with the majority Chinese race. This may be said to be the origin of the "Confucian movement," whose main objective was initially to introduce Confucian ethics into the school curriculum.

In January 1979 Deputy Prime Minister Goh Keng Swee took charge of the Ministry of Education, and three months later he released the "Goh Report" on education, which, among other things, recommended that "moral education" replace the existing "education for living and civics" course in the schools.[19] At first the moral education program was supposed to be purely ethical rather than religious in character, stressing universal values such as honesty and integrity. Since it would be difficult to teach Malay students ethical values in isolation from Islamic teachings, and since many mission schools already had elements of moral education in their religious instruction, eventually moral education and religious studies were linked up as a package, with the former being taught at primary and lower secondary school levels, and the latter at upper secondary levels. Beginning in 1984 a "religious knowledge" course in any of Singapore's four major religions—Islam, Christianity, Buddhism, and Hinduism—as well as a "world religions" alternative for the nonbelievers, was made compulsory for all third- and fourth-year secondary students.[20] Subsequently, Sikhism and then Confucian ethics were added as fifth and sixth options to the religious knowledge program.[21]

The Confucian ethics component of the religious knowledge program sparked intense publicity and debate in Singapore, in part because Confucian values are clearly identified with the Chinese race and hence touched off certain ethnic sensitivities. First, the government itself had to be convinced of the intrinsic social merits of Confucian ethics as applied to modern Singapore. Then it had to explain the program to the non-Chinese population (24 percent of the total) as well as to a large proportion of Chinese who were English-educated and who had never been formally exposed to the intricacies of Confucian philosophy.[22]

In 1989, when the first complete statistical information on the moral education program was made known, the results for the Confucian ethics option were plainly discouraging. As Table 14.3 shows, only 17.8 percent of students at the third-year secondary level opted for Confucian ethics, as compared to 44.4 percent for Buddhist studies, 21.4 percent for (Christian) Bible knowledge, and 13.4 percent for Islamic religious knowledge. Admittedly, those students who chose Confucian ethics were predominantly, if not exclusively, ethnic Chinese, as were those taking Buddhist studies. This works out to barely one quarter of the total ethnic Chinese student population opting for Confucian ethics, not even half as many as those who chose Buddhist studies. Such a poor response must have been disappointing to the

Table 14.3   Religious knowledge options at the third-year secondary level in Singapore schools, 1989

Subject	No. of students
Bible knowledge	7,874 (21.37%)
Buddhist studies	16,352 (44.37%)
Chinese	2,215
English	14,137
Confucian ethics	6,563 (17.81%)
Chinese	4,333
English	2,230
Hindu studies	1,008 (2.74%)
Islamic religious knowledge	4,921 (13.35%)
Malay	4,408
English	513
Sikh studies	136 (0.37%)
Total	36,854 (100.00%)

Source: Ministry of Education, Singapore (March 1989).
Note: Rounded to 100%.

promoters of the Confucian movement; certainly it did not do justice to all the efforts which the government had devoted to this movement.

In retrospect, there seems to have been a tactical mistake in implementing the Confucian ethics course as one of the options in the religious knowledge program. Right from the beginning, for a pluralistic society such as Singapore, a distinction should have been made between secular and religious morality. It was unfair to pit Confucianism, as a philosophy of life or as a body of ethical wisdom, in a head-on competition against the other religions, which had already established social support and developed institutional infrastructures such as temples, churches, rituals, and ceremonies.

It turned out that the Chinese students did not flock to the Confucian ethics class with ethnocentric enthusiasm, as was originally feared by the non-Chinese opponents of the Confucian movement. On the contrary, results have clearly shown that the Chinese segment of the population has been fast losing its "Chineseness." Over the years, as more parents sent their children to English schools to improve their career prospects, fewer and fewer young Chinese acquired a command of the Chinese language sufficient to take advantage of the Confucian option. In fact, by 1988, as shown in Table 14.4, Chinese-medium schools in Singapore had already become an extinct species, with all Chinese students learning Chinese only as a second language. Such a general dilution of Chinese language ability clearly led to a reduced demand for the Confucian ethics course.

Table 14.4   Enrollment of pupils in primary and secondary schools
by language medium, Singapore

Year	Chinese	English	Malay	Tamil	Total
1948	55,956	33,010	7,175	1,012	97,135
	57.6%	34.0%	7.4%	1.0%	100%
1953	76,295	69,569	9,236	1,293	156,399
	48.8%	44.5%	5.9%	0.8%	100%
1958	129,155	142,450	14,213	1,399	287,217
	45.0%	49.6%	4.9%	0.5%	100%
1963	159,693	229,347	29,409	1,632	420,081
	18.0%	54.6%	7.0%	0.4%	100%
1968	174,072	310,635	36,086	1,818	522,611
	33.3%	59.4%	6.9%	0.3%	100%
1973	155,210	344,040	17,961	1,182	518,393
	29.9%	66.4%	3.5%	0.2%	100%
1978	110,170	365,405	4,306	328	480,209
	22.9%	76.1%	0.9%	0.1%	100%
1983	34,708	435,909	417	38	471,072
	7.4%	92.5%	0.1%	0.0%	100%
1988	—	459,813	—	—	459,813
		100%			100%

Source: Ministry of Education, Singapore (March 1989).

In the meantime, the Confucian scheme was overtaken by other events associated with a strong religious revival. Probably as a result of too fast a pace of economic growth and social change, people in Singapore were increasingly turning to religion to cope with stress and competition in their modern urban lives.[23] Thus, there has been a significant increase in the number of Christians in Singapore, from 10.3 percent of the population in 1980 to 18.7 percent in 1988, with the growth in the number of evangelical charismatic denominations particularly pronounced.[24] There has also been a marked revival of Buddhism over the same period, with many formerly "self-proclaimed" Buddhists suddenly becoming organized and active. Under such circumstances Confucianism did not seem to stand up well against the established religions.

In October 1988 First Deputy Prime Minister Goh Chok Tong (now prime minister) brought up the idea of a national ideology, arguing that Singapore, as an open society constantly exposed to Western ideas and values, needed to formalize a set of core values in order to give Singaporeans a sense of direction so that they might develop a cultural ballast in determining their own future. Four sets of core values were accordingly identified: community over self, upholding the family as the basic building block of society, resolving major issues through consensus instead of contention, and stressing racial and religious tolerance and harmony.[25] These four sets of core values, fully compatible with Chinese, Malay, and Indian cultures, would provide the starting point for a national ideology. Furthermore, they would operate as a common framework within which the Chinese could interpret them in terms of Confucian teachings, the Malays in terms of Islamic teachings, and the Indians in terms of Hindu traditions. This would eventually evolve into shared values of some kind. The idea was endorsed in the president's address to the Seventh Parliament on January 9, 1989, and was subsequently debated.[26]

For two years the idea of core values was hammered out into "shared values," and then formally presented by the president on January 2, 1991, for parliamentary debate. Specifically for Confucianism the report stated:

> Initially, non-Chinese Singaporeans were concerned that the Shared Values might become a subterfuge for imposing Confucian values on them. This was never the Government's intention. The Government has never allowed the majority race to impose itself on the minority communities. It cannot force Confucianism on the non-Chinese, or let the Shared Values lead to Chinese chauvinism, narrowing the outlook of Chinese Singaporeans and making them less tolerant of the other communities.
>
> The Shared Values must be shared by all communities. Confucian ethics cannot be so shared. But the Chinese community can draw upon Confucian concepts which form part of their heritage, to elaborate the abstract Shared Values into concrete examples and vivid stories.
>
> Many Confucian ideals are relevant to Singapore. For example, the importance of human relationships and of placing society above self . . .
>
> But even for Chinese Singaporeans the Shared Values cannot just be Confucianism by another name. Precepts and practices which evolved in a rural, agricultural society have to be revised to fit an urban, industrial society. Confucianism has no monopoly of virtue. It needs to be brought up-to-date and reconciled with other ideas which are also essential parts of our ethos.[27]

With the official blessing of the shared values, the Confucian movement in Singapore can be said to have come to an end. In reality the movement had already met its foregone conclusion in October 1989 when the minister of education, Tony Tan, announced the government's decision to phase out

the teac[...] [...]bject in schools,
thereby [...] [...]olicy changes in
Singapor[...]

[handwritten note, Korean:]
상품에서 원료들이 법추르르
덕게 전가는 점.
한의 所 래버르 그걸로 있음
반성하는 위기 유효 비판
나 그다 유리자게는 한층이의
생화습심이 그래도 남아있음
위신검의 것이 아니라 거기
붕조의 그 우인.

[...]?

The Conf[...] d waned in response to [...] say that these
policy shi[...] to Singapore's
prevailing [...] unfair to view
the rise an[...] policy vicissi-
tudes. Few [...] question [...] serious [...] [...] government's
efforts to p[...] Confucian values [...] Singaporeans. The top
Singapore [...] genuinely believed in the merit of Confucian values as
applied to Singapore. Few at the beginning had actually anticipated the complexity of the movement and the immense difficulty of implementing it in
the context of a multiracial society, though all along the promoters had taken
care to moderate the movement in deference to the non-Chinese ethnic
groups.

When the response from the Chinese students in Singapore to the Confucian ethics course was less than enthusiastic, there was really little the
government could do. It was rather unfortunate that such a poor response
came at a time when Singapore was experiencing a rising religious fervor,
which, warned Minister of Education Tony Tan, "if carried to extremes,
could disrupt the traditional religious harmony and tolerance which are 'pre-
requisites' of life in Singapore."[28] That was the last straw.

It is not certain to what extent the introduction of the religious knowledge
program in the school curriculum contributed to any heightened consciousness of religious differences in Singapore. But the government of multiracial
Singapore certainly could not afford to take a chance. Religious conflict
could easily spark off communal violence, as is happening in India today.

In what way has the Singaporean case contributed to the continuing international debate on the issue of Confucian influence on East Asian economic development? Actually it has neither proved nor disproved this thesis,
which is, in any case, intellectually quite sterile. From the outset Singapore
approached the issue not by linking Confucian values to its past economic
success, but by treating them as the main cultural heritage of the Chinese
Singaporean population. Although these values should be fostered and encouraged so that the Chinese will not lose their bearings in the fast-changing
society of Singapore, many of these traditional values also happen to be
conducive to Singapore's further economic growth, inasmuch as they would

help maintain a vital and competitive economy.[29] This could be an instructive lesson for the other East Asian NIEs. Instead of continuing the intellectual debate on whether or not Confucianism contributed to their economic take-off, it would be more productive for them to identify and emphasize the positive aspects of Confucianism in order to strengthen their cultural identity and use it as a social bulwark against negative Western cultural inroads.

It would be a mistake to argue that the "Confucian movement" is a lost cause. Confucian values will still be promoted, albeit under the broad format of the shared values scheme. Admittedly, there is still a great deal of uncertainty as to how Singapore will eventually evolve its distinctive brand of values out of the interaction of the different value systems of its constituent ethnic groups—a kind of social melting pot. This is a long-term social challenge for Singapore. For the moment the government has realistically recognized that Confucian ethics cannot be shared by the Malays, just as Islamic teachings cannot be shared by the Chinese. At the starting point there is precious little common ground. But the present Singapore leadership is apparently undaunted. It is determined to ensure that Singapore's social structure and dominant values remain distinctly Asian as the economy rapidly develops into an integral part of the global economic structure dominated by the West.[30]

15

CONFUCIANISM AS POLITICAL DISCOURSE IN SINGAPORE

The Case of an Incomplete Revitalization Movement

Eddie C. Y. Kuo

In early 1982 the government of Singapore announced plans to introduce Confucian ethics as an option in the required religious knowledge (RK) course for secondary school students as a component of the new moral education program.[1] It was realized from the beginning that, to achieve the objectives of moral education, a Confucian ethic had to be promoted not only as a school subject but also as a moral system for the Chinese population in Singapore. In subsequent years what began as a program for moral education in the schools evolved to become a campaign to promote Confucianism among the general public, akin to a rudimentary form of a "revitalization movement."[2] As such, the campaign received strong support from the political leadership, spearheaded by then Deputy Prime Minister and Minister for Education Goh Keng Swee, with explicit endorsement from Prime Minister Lee Kuan Yew. The mass media, Chinese voluntary associations, and the Chinese community in general were duly mobilized in a concerted effort to promote Confucianism as a moral and cultural foundation for Singaporean society.

The campaign, however was not without its detractors. Given the multiethnic nature of Singaporean society, the campaign was soon entangled with issues of ethnicity and national identity, cultural roots, and nation building, as well as traditions and modernity. The public debate was also politicized when the new school subject and related activities were criticized as a conspiracy of political socialization and ideological indoctrination by the ruling party to legitimize an authoritarian system.

Meanwhile, a series of related events occurred during the late 1980s. A reversal of the policy on the religious knowledge course was announced in late 1989 after the release of a much-publicized and debated controversial study on the religious situation in Singapore.[3] All RK subjects, which had been implemented for between five and seven years, were to be phased out as compulsory after 1990. Confucian ethics, while secular and nonreligious in nature, had to go along with the rest since it had been packaged as one of the RK subjects in the beginning. Subsequently some institutional arrangements that were crucial to the promotion of Confucianism were modified or canceled.

In early 1991 the government announced a "White Paper for Shared Values,"[4] after two years of government-initiated debates on formulating a national ideology "to evolve and anchor a Singaporean identity."[5] While such values apparently implied well-recognized Confucian ideals, the White Paper made it clear in no uncertain terms that these were not Confucian. In what appeared to be an attempt to distance itself from Confucianism, the White Paper insisted that it was never the intention of the government to allow the shared values to become "a subterfuge for imposing Chinese Confucian values" on non-Chinese Singaporeans.[6]

It now appears that the Confucian movement has reached a stage of transition and hence faces some uncertainty. It is most revealing that the movement which began as a political discourse initiated by the political leadership also concluded, though tentatively, on a political note. This essay reviews and analyzes the rise and fall of Confucianism as political discourse as an incomplete revitalization movement.

FROM ECONOMIC PROSPERITY TO MORAL CRISIS

Formerly a British colony, Singapore gained self-government in 1959 and became an independent state in 1965. By the late 1970s, after almost two decades of nation building under the PAP (People's Action party) government, Singapore had sustained an impressive record of political stability and economic prosperity. With a per capita income second in Asia only to Japan's, Singapore ranked among the Four Mini-Dragons, together with South Korea, Taiwan, and Hong Kong. This level of economic prosperity and social development had been gained in part owing to successful implementation of a series of economic and social policies on industrialization, urban renewal, public housing, population control, and public education. This was a period of rapid social change.

Nation building in Singapore involved a massive scheme of urban renewal. Older communities (kampongs) had to be torn down to pave the way for new development projects; their residents were dispersed and relocated to new towns built by the Housing and Development Board (HDB). Also gone with the older communities were traditional neighborhoods and their networks, as well as many community-based traditions, customs, and folk practices. As a result of the very successful public housing scheme, more than 85 percent of the population in Singapore now live in (and most of them own) HDB flats. Being "young" communities, these densely populated new towns are not yet seasoned enough to become "urban villages." With this process of urbanization, social relations in Singapore have shifted toward becoming more impersonal, contractual, and "secondary."

The process of industrialization was equally disruptive of the existing social organization. The changing economic structure weakened the economic function of the family, providing job opportunities and conferring new economic and social status on the young and the female. This resulted in changes in family relations. Moreover, industrialization, being functionally compatible with individualism, utilitarianism, and instrumental rationality, also encouraged and facilitated the development of such values, which were seen as non-Asian and antitraditional.

By the late 1970s, when most of the basic needs of the population had been fulfilled, there came the time for soul-searching and reflection, and there emerged a new and increased concern over the nonmaterial (social and cultural) dimensions of nation building. Alarmed by increasing (or at least more visible) instances of crime, delinquency, drug abuse, abortion, and divorce (despite the fact that the rates of such social indicators were relatively low in Singapore compared to other equally urbanized societies), there emerged a collective sense of moral crisis and a call for collective action.

The concern over an incipient moral crisis was not new in Singapore. Public statements warning against the danger of Westernization had been heard since the early 1960s. During the early stage of nation building, however, there were more pressing political and economic crises to be attended to. By the late 1970s most of these problems had been tackled with success. There was now a surplus of energy and resources for taking on the issues of moral and cultural development. As a general pattern, the increased attention and proposed action had been initiated by the political leaders, who, in Singapore's political culture, invariably were the ones to set and define the agenda for social planning and social action.

In tracing the causes of the perceived moral crisis, the public discourse generally took a somewhat simple view that "the West" was the culprit, and "Westernization" became a convenient label for all the evils that eroded the foundation of a sound, noncorrupt Asian society. Westernization was seen to be a double-edged sword. To the extent that Singapore had to rely on the capital investment, the scientific knowledge, and the technological know-how of the West for its development, it had to face the danger and the consequences of the intrusion of undesirable, "decadent" Western values. It was further argued that Singaporean society could not effectively resist such Western intrusion precisely because its people had lost their cultural bearings and become rootless.

The perceived moral crisis at the societal level therefore reflected an identity crisis at the individual level. As is typical in a situation in which a society is confronted with "alien" threats, Singapore responded to the perceived crisis by calling on its own resources from various Asian traditions for self-defense. What needed to be done, it was argued, was to retain and revive traditional Asian values, to build up the confidence in one's own culture, and to strengthen a sense of identity. The situation was no different from other revitalization movements in the history of many other Asian countries, such as the New Life Movement in Nationalist China during the Second World War.

It was against this background that comprehensive reviews of the education policies were conducted in the late 1970s, leading to the release of the New Education Report, followed by the Report on Moral Education, both in 1979. The latter, in turn, was to lead to the implementation of the compulsory religious knowledge course, of which Confucian ethics was a component. It was more than coincidental that the same year saw the beginning of a number of long-term national campaigns, including the National Courtesy Campaign, Senior Citizens' Week Campaign, and, more significantly, the Speak Mandarin Campaign, which, in addition to being a language-planning campaign, was also intended for the promotion of Chinese culture and values, and hence Chinese identity.

Such was the social and political context within which the Confucian movement was initiated as part of a larger attempt, segmented but concerted, to revive traditional values to counter the intrusion of Western influence.

FROM CURRICULUM DEVELOPMENT TO SOCIETAL CAMPAIGN

When Deputy Prime Minister and Minister of Education Goh Keng Swee first announced the introduction of RK as a compulsory course under the moral education program in January 1982, only five religious subjects were mentioned: Christianity, Buddhism, Islam, Hinduism, and world religion. Confucianism, as a secular ethical system, could have no place among religious teachings. It was at the suggestion of Prime Minister Lee Kuan Yew, after spending "many of his wakeful hours and several sleepless nights," that two weeks later, in early February 1982, Goh announced that Confucian ethics was to be included as an additional subject for those Chinese who might not be religiously inclined, "to give young Singaporeans a cultural ballast against the less desirable aspects of Western culture."[7] A few days later, in his annual Chinese New Year reception speech, in which he stressed the urgent task of preserving the three-generation family, the prime minister referred to the importance of Confucian tradition and the introduction of Confucian ethics in the school curriculum: "Anyone brought up in the Confucianist tradition will be ashamed to let his or her old parents live by themselves in loneliness and desolation . . . Our task is to implant these traditional [Confucian] values into our children when their minds are young and receptive, so that when they grow out of their teenage years, these attitudes harden and are forged for a life-time."[8]

Through this political drama, Confucian ethics made its grand entrance and immediately claimed a legitimacy endorsed by two of the most influential political figures in Singapore. As one of the RK subjects, it was showered with a disproportionate share of resource allocation, media coverage, and public attention in comparison with other "ordinary" RK courses.

For all the other courses, curriculum development was to rely mostly on local expertise. In the case of Confucian ethics this was difficult, as there was simply no such local expertise available. (Significantly, this itself reflects the lack of an intellectual tradition of Confucianism in Singapore.) To consult the views of the experts, Goh Keng Swee visited the United States in May 1982 and met a number of Chinese American professors from leading American universities. These scholars were invited to present their views and make suggestions for the successful implementation of the course. Their written comments and suggestions were prominently reported in detail in major newspapers in Singapore. By careful synchronization and coordination, such reports invariably appeared on Sundays in consecutive weeks, apparently to maximize publicity.

This was followed by the visits of eight overseas "Confucian scholars," as they were labeled, in the summer of 1982, who were to help draw up a conceptual framework for the Confucian doctrines relevant to modern Singapore. During their visits the scholars gave public lectures, conducted seminars, met with cabinet members and MPs, and appeared on television forums, in an attempt to publicize Confucianism and to persuade unconvinced Singaporeans of its relevance. The newspapers, especially the Chinese papers, again duly and fully covered their activities and the content of their lectures and speeches. It was obvious that Confucian ethics were being promoted at the societal level, in a manner and following a format similar to those of numerous other campaigns in Singapore. Given the frequency and intensity of Confucian-related public events throughout the year, 1982 could be called the Year of Confucianism.

There indeed appeared to be an early decision that, to be successful as a moral education subject, Confucian ethics could not rely on its being taught in schools alone; it had to seek the support of the family, parents, and society in general. In the words of Goh Keng Swee, "Confucianism in Singapore will not be merely for the classroom. It will be reinterpreted as a code of personal conduct for modern Singapore and promoted in the form of public debate and discussion over the media."[9] In other words, Confucian ethics had to be promoted and accepted as a relevant ethical system in Singapore, among the Chinese at least. One of the Confucian consultants, Yale professor Yü Ying-shih (now at Princeton), had earlier suggested that the persuasion could be achieved through an "intellectual movement" born out of national debates and discussions. The movement had to be promoted at both the school and society levels, which are "like the two wings of a bird."[10]

Similarly, another overseas consultant, Tu Wei-ming of Harvard, also pointed out that "Confucian thoughts could not be realized in life without the coordinated effort of the society, the mass media and the family."[11] Tu's views were readily supported by an editorial in the *Nanyang Siang Pao* (Nanyang Business News) titled "The Beginning of the Promotion of Confucian Thoughts."[12]

Apparently this was a task willingly taken up by the Chinese-language press, itself a champion of Chinese culture and Chinese language, acting in the interests of the Chinese community. By contrast, the English-language press, with its predominantly English-educated readership, took a more cautious and detached position. The difference was understandable and indeed to be expected in Singapore's multiethnic and multilingual setting.

In addition to the Chinese press, other Chinese interest groups gave the movement ready support, among them the Singapore Chinese Chamber of Commerce and Industry, the Singapore Federation of Clan Associations, and academic groups such as the South Sea Society and the Association of Asian Studies. Like the Chinese press, these organizations represented the interests of the Chinese community and were avowed champions of Chinese culture and traditions. They were the major sponsors of numerous forums, seminars, public lectures, and conferences on Confucianism or related topics throughout the 1980s, which were in turn duly reported by the papers, generating still greater awareness among the public.

New organizations were also set up to provide institutional support for curriculum development, teachers' training, and the teaching of Confucian ethics in general. Within the Ministry of Education's Curriculum Development Institute of Singapore (CDIS), a new Confucian Ethics Project Team was set up to take charge of curriculum development. Consultants were drawn both locally from the university and overseas from Taiwan and the United States. The project team duly fulfilled its tasks in developing textbooks, supplementary teaching materials, and teaching aids, both in Chinese and in English. The project team also ran training sessions, seminars, and public lectures for teachers of Confucian ethics. In 1985 these teachers formed a new Association of Confucian Studies, which published a journal called *Confucian Studies* and cosponsored seminars and public speeches. Being teachers of Confucian ethics, and presumably convinced of its value in Singapore, they became active supporters of the movement.

The establishment of the Institute of East Asian Philosophy (IEAP) in 1983 was a particularly significant development. The institute was generously funded and received patronage at the highest level, with Goh Keng Swee (by then retired from politics) as its chairman and Deputy Prime Minister Ong Teng Cheong (who was responsible for the Moral Education Report in 1979) its vice chairman. As the name implies, the institute's major function was to promote the study of East Asian philosophies, initially focusing on Confucianism. It actualized what Goh had suggested a year earlier: "An academy could be established to reinterpret Confucianism in line with [the] changing times, with Singapore even developing into a center for the study of Confucianism."[13]

Sociologically, the establishment of IEAP signified a long-term commitment of Singapore and its leadership to the promotion of Confucian studies. If there had been any doubt about the sincerity and determination of the authorities in the promotion of Confucianism, it must have been dispelled by the high-profile presence of IEAP. At the functional level IEAP effectively provided an institutional base for Confucian studies and connected such research work in Singapore with an international network of Confucian scholars. It has been most effective in bringing in overseas Confucian scholars to attend conferences or as visiting fellows.[14] Such scholars helped promote and stimulate research work in Singapore. They also played an important role in publicizing the Confucian program and its related activities in Singapore to the international academic community. Through its conferences, seminars, and forums and its publication programs,[15] IEAP made a serious attempt to promote Confucian studies in Singapore. More important, these academic activities were duly reported as public events and hence contributed to public education in Confucian teachings. As far as the Confucian movement is concerned, during its active years, from 1983 to 1989, IEAP was no doubt the single most important institution helping to sustain high visibility (and hence continuity) of the movement.

FAVORABLE CONDITIONS

The promotion of Confucian ethics aroused much attention and interest among the general public, especially the Chinese. As I pointed out earlier, with the support and cooperation of government offices, the mass media, and Chinese voluntary organizations, Confucianism was extended from the school level to the societal level and was promoted as a form of revitalization movement. There were several sociological factors that facilitated the progress of the movement in Singapore.

Most important of all was perhaps that Confucianism remained a core component of Chinese tradition in a society dominated by a Chinese population. To most Chinese Confucianism was not alien but indigenous. Even though the early immigrants from China were mostly uneducated, Confucian moral teachings had been transmitted over generations through the family and "little traditions," if not through formal teaching. The Confucian ethos was also embodied in the values and relationships found in traditional Chinese organizations such as clan and dialect-based associations, temple organizations, business firms, and even secret societies. Confucian ideals were also a fundamental element in the Chinese educational tradition. As Lee Kuan Yew put it: "Confucianism was part of the Chinese school environment, the fables and the parables recounted over and over again in books and through the teachers and encapsuled in sparkling sayings and succinct epigrams . . . The doctrines and philosophy of Confucianism in the Chinese school syllabus are spread in textbooks on Chinese language, Chinese literature and Chinese history."[16]

It has often been pointed out that the Chinese in Singapore had always been Confucian to some extent in their thinking and behavior, even if only unconsciously, and that Singaporean society was Confucian in value orientation and organizational structure, perhaps latently. Such an unconscious and latent Confucian orientation reflected a collective perception and made the Chinese more receptive to the campaign. Such characterization or labeling also led many Chinese to a rediscovery of their Confucian roots and, among those convinced, converted them to "born-again" Confucians.

The characterization also reflected a public perception that Confucianism was fundamentally Chinese. To promote Confucianism was therefore to promote Chinese culture. In the 1950s and 1960s many Chinese-educated people had been discouraged from becoming involved in activities that were suspected of promoting Chinese culture and education, since such activities were equated to being pro-China, and hence procommunist. Now that the Confucian movement, together with the Speak Mandarin Campaign, were both being endorsed by the political leadership, the Chinese-educated population, including a small number of latent chauvinists, could safely jump on the bandwagon and promote Chinese culture by way of promoting Confucianism. To many Chinese and Chinese organizations, whether the movement was Confucian or not may have been secondary, for what was fundamentally important was that it served to promote Chinese culture, Chinese education, and hence Chinese identity. Confucianism hence served as a symbol of collective Chinese identity.

Still another element favorable to the promotion of Confucianism was that it was secular and this-worldly in nature; it was religiously neutral and not exclusive. Confucianism did not present a threat to other religions. It was thus possible for the government and community leaders to advocate the Confucian ethic without arousing strong objections from other religious and ethnic communities. It would have been unthinkable for the government to promote any of the traditional religions as it did Confucianism, for this would have been tantamount to making any such religion a state religion.

Another important source of support for the Confucian movement originated from overseas. In the late 1970s and early 1980s the economic "miracle" of several East Asian countries aroused great interest in the international academic community. The miracle was in part attributed to the common prodevelopment cultural ethos, believed to be Confucian in nature, of these East Asian societies. Confucianism (or Neo-Confucianism, according to some) thus gained new respectability. The irony is that such new respectability did not initially emerge from the works of Asian scholars themselves. It was through the writings of Western scholars such as Herman Kahn, Ezra Vogel, Roy Hofheinz, Jr., and Kent Calder,[17] that East Asians and East Asian societies (such as Singapore) gained a new awareness and a cultural confidence that the Confucian ethic would not only provide a new moral order needed to confront the perceived moral crisis, but also play an active role in social and economic development.

This was apparently one reason behind the decision to launch the Confucian movement. At the time he announced the introduction of Confucian ethics as an RK subject, Goh Keng Swee referred to the four newly industrializing economies (NIEs) and remarked that the Confucian tradition produced a people of a certain kind of character which made it possible for these countries to achieve spectacular economic growth. "So in this sense there is a direct relevance of the Confucian ethic as a code of personal conduct to a country that is trying to achieve fast economic growth in the 20th Century, using modern science and technology."[18]

Finally, it is obvious that Confucianism was compatible with the dominant political culture in Singapore, specifically in terms of paternalism, communitarianism, pragmatism, and secularism. (To these a critic would add authoritarianism.)[19] Indeed, the very manner in which the Confucian movement was initiated and promoted reflected a top-down pattern, similar to other "social engineering" programs designed for various nation-building objectives. Moreover, the Confucian movement was also compatible with other developmental goals. For instance, promotion of the three-generation family as a Confucian practice serves to reduce the pressure on the government to provide public housing and social welfare. Such instrumental functions of Confucianism, no doubt, also facilitated its promotion.

DILEMMAS AND PARADOXES

The promotion of the Confucian movement in Singapore faced some resistance and constraints. There were generally three types of people who resisted the campaign, but for different reasons.

Many of the Chinese-educated Singaporeans had been strongly influenced by the anti-Confucian sentiments of the May Fourth Movement tradition from their school years in the 1950s and 1960s. They were familiar with the works of Lu Xun and the slogan "Down with the Confucian Store" *(Dadao Kongjiadian)*. They criticized Confucianism as corrupt, feudalistic, and ultraconservative. These Chinese faced a dilemma as they were critical of Confucianism on the one hand, and yet they identified strongly with Chinese culture and identity on the other. Being ambivalent, they were never outspoken in their criticism and, in the end, generally shifted to supporting the movement as a campaign to boost the status of Chinese culture and language in Singapore.

The position of many of the English-educated Chinese was different. Having been influenced by modern educational values of liberalism, scientism, and rationalism, they tended to see Confucianism as oppressive, authoritarian, and antidemocratic, and they believed it had lost its meaning and relevance for modern times. They were most ready to point to the antidemocratic tendency of Confucian ideology, and were not convinced that this ideological component of Confucianism could be separated from its ethical doctrines. Many of them believed that the government had an ulterior motive and charged it with using Confucianism to justify its authoritarian rule. This was the group who politicized the public discourse on the Confucian movement.[20]

From the viewpoint of the non-Chinese, who accounted for less than a quarter of the population, the Confucian movement, just like the Speak Mandarin Campaign preceding it, was another government-sponsored program (or conspiracy, according to some) to boost Chinese culture and identity and to reinforce Chinese dominance. They naturally felt threatened and were duly concerned that such moves might lead to heightened sentiments of Chinese chauvinism. In multiethnic Singapore such feelings among the minorities had to be assuaged and contained.

At a fundamental level the difficulties and dilemmas in the promotion of Confucianism in Singapore can be attributed to some structural features or structural constraints of Singaporean society. In a multiethnic society which has proclaimed multiracialism (i.e., recognition and respect for all ethnic groups) as a state ideology, the promotion of Confucianism, a Chinese philosophy, had to be restricted to the Chinese community. In fact, it was due to the multicultural nature of Singaporean society that the revitalization movement could not take the form of a pan-Singaporean national movement, for there was no common cultural foundation to revive from. It had to appear in partial, segmented, and incremental forms as the National Courtesy Campaign and Senior Citizens' Week or to appeal to the cultural and religious traditions of respective ethnic communities, appearing in the form of various religious courses, the Speak Mandarin Campaign, and the present Confucian movement. These different campaigns and activities collectively formed a concerted effort to revive traditional values to counter the perceived evils of Westernization.

There had been attempts to interpret the Confucian ethic as a universalistic moral code, as Asian or at least East Asian, and hence relevant not only to the Chinese in Singapore but to the Malays and Indians as well. This was precisely the argument advocated by Tu Wei-ming.[21] In his words, "Confucian teachings have developed in countries such as Japan, Korea, and Vietnam. Therefore, Confucianism, like Christianity, cuts across ethnic lines and can be embraced by other peoples."[22]

While such a view is no doubt theoretically valid, it apparently did not appeal to the non-Chinese. The paradox, and indeed the irony, is that when Confucianism was promoted as a universal moral system relevant to all peoples in Singapore, it became, in the view of the non-Chinese, an expansionist conspiracy which threatened the legitimacy and relevance of their own ethnic, cultural, and religious values. This was so precisely because it was impossible to separate Confucianism and Chineseness in the perception of the general public, Chinese or otherwise. The Confucian movement was thus entangled, inevitably, with ethnic issues and had to walk a tightrope and maintain a delicate balance.

The relationship between the Confucian ethic and Confucian political ideology posed another paradox. Apparently aware of the sensitive nature of its political implications, Minister of Education Goh Keng Swee stressed from the beginning that the two, Confucianism as an ethical system and as a political ideology, had to be differentiated: "As a political ideology . . . Confucian doctrine was not relevant to Singapore today."[23] He thereby made it clear that the present campaign was strictly for the promotion of Confucian ethics, not an endorsement of Confucian political ideology. The same point had been repeated by practically all Confucian scholars consulted by the Singaporean government. The message was clear: Confucianism must not be politicized to serve political purposes. That was necessary to minimize resistance from those who suspected the campaign of an ulterior motive.

The repeated assurance from Goh himself, as well as other major figures involved in the campaign and in curriculum development, were, however, not enough.[24] Many of the critics, both local (represented by the opposition parties) and foreign (represented by some unsympathetic foreign journalists), conveniently pointed to the "match" between Confucian political ideology and the paternalistic political culture of Singapore and developed a conspiracy theory. The campaign was thus seen as having been designed to contain an emergent trend toward democratization, to reinforce an existing authoritarian system, or even (as one version had it) to prepare for and legitimize a forthcoming power succession following the family line.

Furthermore, as I mentioned earlier, the Confucian movement itself was a manifestation of the political culture of Singapore. The very manner in which Confucianism was launched and campaigned for reflected a top-down pattern. It was initiated by the government, which played a dominant role throughout. Whatever latent grass-roots support mobilized by the leadership, it still had to operate within tacitly understood political constraints (ethnicity, language, and religion being the "sensitive" political minefields). In this sense Confucian thought and practice had always been a part of the ideological system in contemporary Singapore.

POLICY REVIEWS AND REVERSALS

By 1988–89, seven years after the launching of the campaign and five years after the introduction of Confucian ethics as a subject for third- and fourth-year secondary students, the Confucian movement reached a stage of "routinization." Meanwhile, reviews on this and other related policies and programs were, as usual, being conducted continuously. Such reviews eventually led to reversals in policies and caused major setbacks to the movement, possibly irreversible.

At the school level preparation of textbooks and supplementary reading materials was completed. Teaching went on smoothly. Progress was carefully monitored. It must have been disappointing to the promoters of Confucianism that in 1989 only 17.8 percent of third-year students, practically all of them Chinese, chose Confucian ethics as their RK option. The figure, which was notably underpublicized, compared poorly with the enrollments in Buddhist studies (44.4 percent) and bible knowledge (21.4 percent).[25] This result hardly justified the enormous amount of resources and effort put into the course and the campaign, and suggested that the campaign had failed to persuade students and their parents to take up Confucian ethics as their option.

With the benefit of hindsight it became clear that this result was inevitable when Confucian ethics as a secular subject was made to compete with established and highly institutionalized religions. Few followers of a religion would "betray" their own faith and choose Confucian ethics instead, even if they were convinced of the relevance of Confucian teachings to themselves and to Singapore. In the end, Confucian ethics became a residual subject chosen mostly by those Chinese who were not strongly attached to any of the established religions, as had been the intent in the first place. From this point of view, one may actually argue that 17.8 percent enrollment in Confucian ethics was not such a failure after all.

The small student enrollment may have been disappointing, but that in itself did not affect the overall operation and the continuity of the course. All those involved in curriculum development and teaching apparently came to accept the reality and carried on with their duties routinely, though perhaps with reduced zest. Little did they expect to find a drastic reversal of policy coming their way, for reasons having nothing at all to do with Confucianism.

Meanwhile, at the societal level routine campaign activities continued. *Lianhe zaobao* (United Morning News), the leading Chinese newspaper, carried a regular Sunday column, "Culture and Life," publishing essays by scholars from the IEAP to promote Asian (especially Confucian) cultural and philosophical ideas. The Chinese press also occasionally reported stories on academic activities such as public lectures, seminars, forums, and conferences on Confucian topics by (mostly visiting) Confucian scholars. Political and community leaders also routinely made speeches supporting Confucian values on appropriate occasions such as Chinese New Year and Senior Citizens' Week.

At the same time, criticisms concerning the wisdom and relevance of Confucianism to Singaporean society persisted as the national debate continued in search of a common basis for nation building. Of all the thorny issues raised in the debate, religion became a particularly salient topic, which captured the attention of the whole nation in 1988–89 after the release of a series of six reports based on a government-commissioned study of religion in Singapore. The study found a strong upsurge of religious activities during the 1980s, especially Christianity and to a lesser extent Buddhism and Islam. With the trend toward fervent religious revivalism, the delicate religious equilibrium in multireligious Singapore was being disturbed. The authors warned of the potential danger of interreligious conflict and called for careful handling of this very sensitive situation.[26] Referring to the role of education, the researchers pointed out that "the introduction of religious courses has a significant impact on the present and future religious development in Singapore" and recommended that "a systematic study be conducted to assess the long-term effects of the Religious Knowledge programme on Singapore society."[27]

The observation and recommendation were taken seriously by the authorities. The Ministry of Education conducted a series of public forums and closed-door sessions to review the RK program. After six months of review and deliberation, the government decided to phase out the teaching of religious knowledge as a compulsory subject and to make it optional from 1990. To justify such a drastic policy reversal within a span of seven years, Minister of Education Tony Tan explained: "One fundamental change has taken place. Unlike 1982, there is today a heightened consciousness of religious differences and a new fervor in the propagation of religious beliefs."[28]

As the decision was based almost purely on a consideration of the changing and complex religious situation, the position of Confucian ethics as a secular subject was uncertain. Initially, during the period of public discussion some promoters of Confucianism had harbored a hope that this secular subject might be able to survive the onslaught. Attempts were made by the usual pro-Confucian groups and individuals, including some MPs and the minister of state for education, to appeal for the retention of Confucian ethics as a course in moral education. This, however, was rejected, as, according to the minister of education, it would have been unfair to the other religious courses in the RK program.[29] What had come in as a package had to go out as a package.

Now that Confucianism would no longer be taught as a part of the required RK course, the Confucian campaign had lost half of its battle, if not half of its battlefield. It remained to be seen whether and to what extent it could still attract secondary school students and survive as an optional, non-examination subject. This would be the real test of its appeal and popularity among the students and their parents.

In a related development in 1989, and equally significant as far as the Confucian movement was concerned, a major policy change in the research direction of the IEAP took place. With the retirement of Wu Teh Yao, a respected scholar, as IEAP director in November 1989, the board signaled its decision to make a drastic shift in its research direction by appointing an economist as the new director. Short of making a formal announcement, the IEAP in actual practice has since early 1990 phased out most projects on Confucian studies and concentrated on topics regarding contemporary economic and political issues in China.[30] Given the crucial role of the IEAP as a key promoter of Confucianism, this inflicted a serious, possibly fatal blow to the Confucian movement in Singapore.

SHARED VALUES AND CONFUCIANISM

At the societal and political levels the search for a solution to guard Singapore against the cultural onslaught from the West and to overcome the moral crisis continued throughout the 1980s. In October 1988 First Deputy Prime Minister Goh Chok Tong (who succeeded Lee Kuan Yew as prime minister in November 1990) suggested developing a "national ideology" which Singaporeans of all races and faiths could subscribe to and live by to evolve and anchor a Singaporean identity. After more than two years of government-initiated debates, the "White Paper for Shared Values" was announced in January 1990. While the identified Shared Values[31] are fully compatible with Confucianism (as with other Asian cultural traditions), the White Paper makes a few revealing remarks on Confucianism, suggesting an "official" position that was by now somewhat ambivalent and detached.

In a section titled "Relations with Confucianism," the White Paper insists that it was never the intention of the government to allow the shared values to become "a subterfuge for imposing Chinese Confucian values" on non-Chinese Singaporeans.[32] Furthermore, it stresses that Confucian "precepts and practices which evolved in a rural, agricultural society have to be revised to fit an urban, industrial society." Specifically, "hierarchical family relations" (where "sons owe an absolute duty of filial piety and unquestioning obedience to fathers") was singled out as one aspect of the Confucian concept of family ties that was undesirable and hence required "notable modification."[33]

Meanwhile, the White Paper praises the concept of government by "honorable men" (junzi) as a Confucian ideal that fits Singaporean society and its needs.[34] This was a reversal of the earlier position held by several leading champions of the movement, including Goh Keng Swee, that Confucianism as a political ideology must be distinguished from Confucianism as an ethical system that is to be promoted as the basis for moral growth and the building of character.[35]

•　　•　　•

From the perspective of the present, the reinterpretation of Confucianism in modern Singapore is finally and officially completed, its relevance redefined. The movement has served to arouse the awareness of the general public about Confucian and related Asian traditions and stimulated a lively debate in an exercise of soul-searching over values relevant to modern Singapore. To this extent the movement has not been futile.

Yet the irony is, in a Confucian political structure, and as a government-initiated campaign, the rise and fall of the Confucian movement is also politically defined. The movement cannot continue as it was, since the government has modified its policies on moral education and reinterpreted the relevance of Confucian ideals in modern Singapore. Given the strong policy-driven orientation and the multiethnic structure of Singaporean society, the circumstances are such that the Confucian movement will most likely remain incomplete. Meanwhile, at the national level the larger revitalization movement in Singapore continues, seeking other forms and formats (such as "national ideology" and "shared values") which better suit the political climate and needs of the time.

It remains to be seen whether we are reading the final chapter of the Confucian movement in Singapore. Its future status and development depend eventually on the spontaneous support it can generate from concerned organizations, communities, and the masses, as the government withdraws to play only a secondary role in its promotion. Such spontaneous support, however, may not be readily forthcoming, as Singapore has yet to evolve into a civil society and to develop its own strong intellectual tradition, Confucian or otherwise, to provide the necessary driving force behind a grassroots movement. This is a time when the vitality and viability of Confucianism in Singapore are subject to a stringent test.

Meanwhile, many of the Confucian ethics, though not necessarily labeled as such, are and will continue to be incorporated into the curriculum of moral education courses, whatever their titles. Similarly, elements of the Confucian political ideology persist to play a part in Singapore's political drama. The ultimate question is: Can Confucianism, or some of its elements, be packaged in a changing context and environment and remain relevant to the evolving new economic, political, and cultural order? In other words, can such selected and reinterpreted Confucian values be made compatible with an urban-industrial social structure and with the larger social system of Singaporean society? If they can, they will eventually be incorporated into the evolving value system of contemporary Singapore. When and if that happens, of course, it will become inconsequential to argue whether such values are Confucian, Singaporean, Asian, or universal.

16

SOCIETAL TRANSFORMATION AND THE CONTRIBUTION OF AUTHORITY RELATIONS AND COOPERATION NORMS IN OVERSEAS CHINESE BUSINESS

S. Gordon Redding

Four background assumptions run through this essay and should be specified at the outset. First, as the work of Peter Berger has established, there are "economic cultures," which display in economic structures and behavior the influence of deeper systems of values and of cognition in a society.[1] The second assumption is the crucial antecedent of such thinking, namely that of Max Weber, who proposed the need for a moral base to legitimize and sustain the behavior of the key actors known as entrepreneurs.[2] The third background idea comes from S. N. Eisenstadt, who proposed an amendment to Weber by arguing for an examination of the theoretical middle ground between determinants such as value systems and outcomes such as business structures and economic exchange behavior. He offered as a suggestion the idea of "transformative capacities" and thus brought to the forefront the question of how a society is changed during modernization and economic development, with certain kinds of transformation having positive results for progress, and with such tendency to change being either amplified or suppressed by cultural predispositions.[3] The fourth notion is that mechanisms for handling trust and cooperation lie at the heart of the problem of development. The successful meeting of this need for trust either by using institutional structures or by some widely accepted alternative, although not in itself a sufficient condition for progress, is nevertheless a crucially necessary one.

The specific arguments I propose are:

1. Certain values surrounding authority in Chinese culture foster the stability and adaptiveness of the organizational type favored by the overseas Chinese in business, namely, the family firm.
2. Chinese values also legitimize a distinct form of cooperation between organizations.
3. These values retain long-term legitimacy because of their grounding in Chinese ethics.
4. Economic exchange and the growth of economic activity at large are enhanced by intraorganizational stability and interorganizational cooperation, and in consequence certain societies have been substantially transformed.

Such an analysis, though concentrating on one significant chain of determinants and consequences, does *not* propose that this is the sole explanation of progress. It is not. This is simply one of the least understood sets of connections in a larger framework.

A further step with respect to understanding the development process is to refer to a more abstract level of analysis than can be reached if just the Confucian success stories of East Asia are considered. It is necessary, in other words, to come to terms with the universals of the development process if the Confucian dynamic is to be seen in context, and if comparisons with different historical processes reaching toward similar outcomes in other parts of the world are to be attempted. It is a significant step from discussing how Confucianism stabilizes authority relations to considering the function of a legitimate moral base for stabilizing vertical order. In the former instance descriptions can be offered ideographically. In the latter comparisons can be made nomothetically.

This chapter takes the case of the overseas Chinese family business and examines it as an example of an economic structure capable of contributing significantly to modernization and economic growth, and thus acting as a key part of the transformation process. Its capacity to do so is examined from three standpoints: Where does its formula come from? How does it work? How does it contribute to the larger growth process?

The societies to which this analysis applies are those of Pacific Asia, particularly Hong Kong and Taiwan. At the same time it is possible to extend the argument, with some adjustment, to the Philippines, Malaysia, Indonesia, and Thailand, all of which are strongholds of Chinese family business interests. China itself can be used to illustrate both the negative consequences of the undermining of core values, and the other features of the institutional fabric of society that need to be in place before such values can work their influences for the societal good.

THE IDEA OF TRANSFORMATIVE CAPACITIES

Eisenstadt's critique of Weber argued that the significance of religious values was to be found not in any direct effect on economic, political, or scientific activity, but in the contribution toward the restructuring of European society in general. The capacity of values to transform society is founded in their capacity to legitimize in religious or ideological terms the development of new motivations, activities, and institutions.

As an example of the application of this idea, and an illustration of how much more complex the European process was than Weber's explanation implies, Eisenstadt discusses:

the connection of values with political structures, evident in the reformulation of state and society;

the restructuring of central legal institutions based on the concepts of covenant and contract, and the freeing of business corporations from politics;

the development of new roles, including that of the economic entrepreneur, and a new type of labor;

the development of intense motivation for undertaking the new roles and adopting the goals associated with them;

the crucial emergence of states capable of decentralizing power to autonomous subunits.

In considering the Asian equivalent, R. N. Bellah notes the incompleteness in themselves of either the entrepreneurship-motivation model or the institutional explanation. The two are interdependent and make sense only when taken together. Japanese achievement-oriented groups had to wait for the Meiji reforms of institutional structures. Chinese merchants "who made an indifferent showing within the institutional limitations of Imperial China turned into a vigorous capitalist class under more favourable conditions in Southeast Asia."[4] A clear statement about the role of such institutional, political, and societal influences on the emergence of various successful business recipes in the Confucian domains of East Asia has been offered by R. D. Whitley, and it confirms the validity of warnings about preferred sets of causes which may be based on a single discipline.[5]

The reformation and transformation of the basic structure of society contains two strands: the economic process of development, and the sociocultural process of modernization. These are both matters of immense complexity. My aim here is to chart a pathway through this conceptual jungle (such a path being only one of many possible routes). This particular path will be for those interested in organization as the principal unit of analysis, but organization in the context of societal change and thus surrounded by other features and influences. I proceed by considering the four propositions already outlined, involving the values that induce stability and organizational adaptiveness; the legitimacy of cooperation; the ethical base; and transformation via unit growth and interunit exchange.

VALUES SURROUNDING AUTHORITY AND THE CHINESE FAMILY BUSINESS

The proposition to be argued here is that certain values surrounding authority in Chinese culture foster the stability and adaptiveness of the organizational type favored by the overseas Chinese, namely, the family business.

The importance of stability and adaptiveness as contributors to the health of an organization and its capacity to grow is well established in the literature on organizations. The argument, in simple terms, is that business organizations in free societies rely for their internal efficiency on the intensity of cooperation within the structure and especially the identity of members with the organization's core purposes. This internal stability derives largely from the legitimacy of the leadership as perceived by the members. Organizations also rely, no less critically, on their ability to adapt to external circumstances and thus to change what they are doing without disturbing the basic equilibrium. These core concerns of cooperation and adaptiveness, first clarified by Chester Barnard,[6] are the central dilemmas to which organization theorists consistently return.[7]

If we turn first to the question of cooperation inside the vertical structure of the organization, and thus to the issue of the legitimacy of leadership, it becomes clear that in Asian societies the set of predispositions that governs the process is different from the set that surrounds legitimacy of leadership in the Western bureaucratic form of organization. Societal norms about the allocation of power are a prime distinguishing feature of culture and a major variable. The work of Geert Hofstede on power distance indicates the naturally hierarchical nature of many Asian cultures.[8] The implications of an established vertical social order are well analyzed by Lucian Pye, whose study of the special nature of Asia's modernization process concludes that paternalism and its corollary dependency are the universally accepted pre-scriptions for the structuring of authority relations, and that they do not stand in the way of modernization. They simply provide it with a different format.[9]

The legitimizing force behind paternalism and dependence in the overseas Chinese case is Confucianism, for the Chinese derived from its secular trans-mission the ideals necessary for the maintenance of family, identity, and wel-fare. A social structure based on Confucian ideals begins with the father figure and prescribes role behavior for that figure as well as for others in the attendant structure. These role prescriptions then serve to produce a high degree of order in society, visible in what appears as largely programmed behavior.

The adoption of family business as the normal structure for economic coordination and control in overseas Chinese society is a natural outcome. Authority rests most naturally with the paterfamilias, and is legitimized by two forces in particular: ownership of assets needed for the business, and properly paternalistic behavior within the Confucian code. The latter in-cludes a benevolent concern for the welfare of subordinates. Reinforcing the stability of the patrimonial type of organization is the psychological depen-dence that is part of the Confucian social order. In Pye's view Asian depen-dence has positive features: it can build cooperation and strong bonds for teamwork; it can encourage supportive, sympathetic leadership without sac-rificing strength; strong leadership is favored because of its ability to create durable institutions; and in exchange for concrete materialistic rewards, sub-ordinates owe positive sentiments of loyalty and obedience.[10]

The end result of the operation of these forces is that, in the case of the Chinese family business, a structure emerges which has strong leadership able to exercise a very large amount of decision-making power without con-sultation as well as direct the organization toward change if need be. The organization is staffed in all the key positions, and throughout much of the work force, by people who are loyal and obedient. The requirements for both stability and adaptiveness are therefore supported by the values sur-rounding the issue of authority."

An illustration of the workings of this value system, derived empirically from a study of seventy-two overseas Chinese chief executives, is given in Figure 16.1.[11] This provides a more complex analysis of the determinants of behavior in the Chinese family business. Figures 16.2 and 16.3 trace the connections into organization structure and ways of managing. These are given here for reference rather than detailed analysis, but they serve to illus-trate the core supposition that an organizational type as distinct as this is embedded in a cultural matrix in complex but discernible ways.

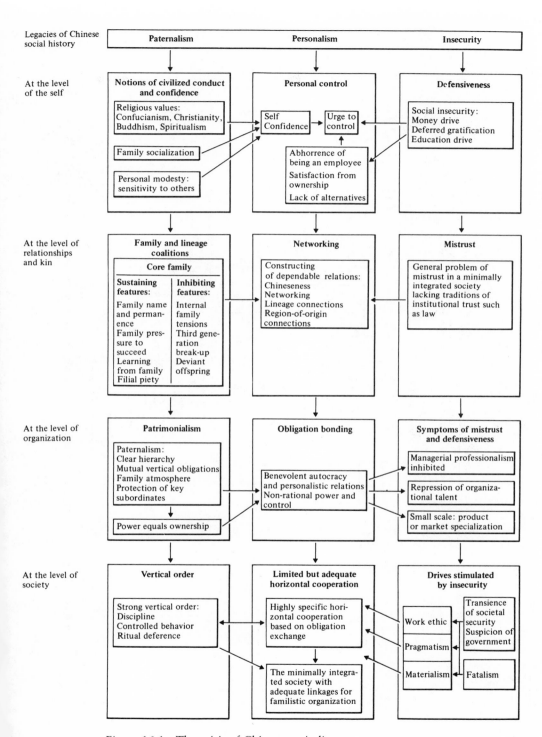

Figure 16.1 The spirit of Chinese capitalism

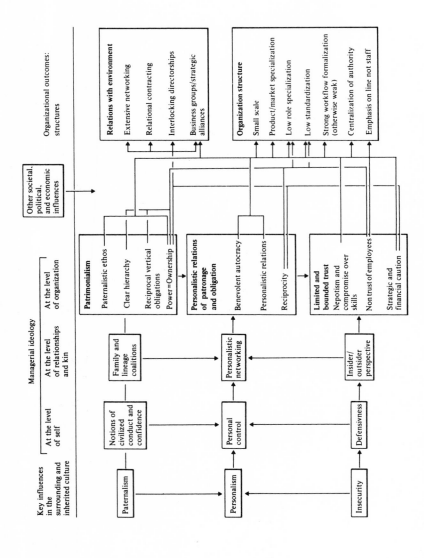

Figure 16.2 The Chinese family business: Ideological determinants of organization structure

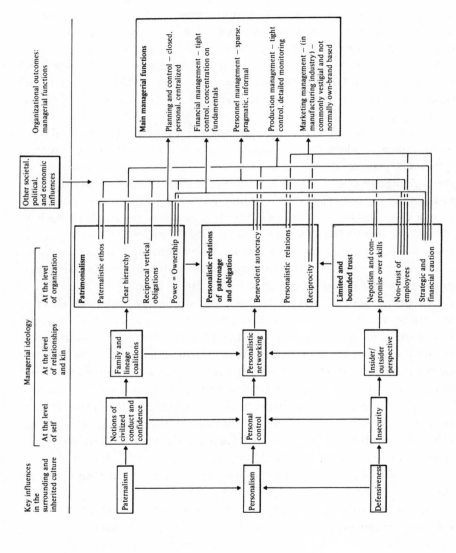

Figure 16.3 The Chinese family business: Ideological determinants of managerial functioning

COOPERATION BETWEEN ORGANIZATIONS

The Chinese family business is usually small. Examples of large ones do exist but are atypical and relatively unstable if family domination remains. The norm is more likely fifty to one hundred employees, key positions in family hands, a dominant owner and/or chief executive, and a limited amount of internal complexity. Such organizations are inevitably constrained in what they can do. They may well be very efficient at making to order, say, a certain kind of knitwear, but they would not create the design, dye the wool, or market the goods. For these necessary activities they would need to rely on other companies, and they thus depend on a network of stable business relationships.

They do, in fact, achieve this requirement to a point where the total economic system to which they contribute is successful and competitive in world terms. The essence of the system's efficiency is the low transaction costs of the exchange processes within it. This means that transactions are reliable, fast, and easily available. This systemic efficiency rests on two social elements: first, the large amount of controlling power in the hands of the key actors, the owner-managers; and second, the Chinese ethics surrounding trust. There are clearly other factors in the background, such as access to information, but power and trust are especially imbued with Chinese values in the particular business context of concern to us here.

The power derives from the fact that Chinese family businesses are centralized power structures in which all important decisions (and often many unimportant decisions) are made by the owner-manager. This is attributed by S. G. Redding to the obsession with control which typifies the Chinese owner-manager and which largely derives from the societal insecurity from which the Chinese have suffered endemically and historically.[12] A practical outcome is that contracting between organizations can take place among people who can decide on behalf of an organization without reference to others. It can therefore happen fast. Moreover, the implementation of decisions is rarely slowed down by the need to persuade subordinates. Finally, the financing of a company can be done on the basis of backing of an individual.

The selected focusing of decision-making power in the hands of dominant owner-managers in turn means that they deal with people like themselves in conducting the majority of the key transactions in the economy. This both encourages and reinforces the reliance on interpersonal obligation as the guarantee of reliability in exchanges. Studies of overseas Chinese business practices consistently report that trustworthiness (a combination of *hsin-*

yung, or trust, and *kan-ch'ing,* or rapport) is a central component of the system of ethics which controls behavior.[13]

The reputation for trustworthiness is a crucial asset with strong economic implications, especially for mutual financial assistance in fund-raising or credit allowance. It also affects the exchange of information. By combining these two advantages, Chinese business networks in host economies such as the Philippines or Indonesia can perform substantially better than their local equivalents. Thus, Richard Robison estimates that 75 percent of private capital in Indonesia is in the control of ethnic Chinese, who make up only 4 percent of the population.[14] Similar startling disparities emerge in descriptions of Thailand, Malaysia, and the Philippines.[15]

TRUST AND CHINESE ETHICS

The crucial nature of trust as a facilitator of development is perhaps best seen by considering societies where it is absent. Diego Gambetta has analyzed the constant diffraction and aggression of Mafia society in southern Italy as a result of endemic mistrust.[16] In a study of what he sees as the relative economic failure of South American countries, L. E. Harrison has argued that economic cooperation at the base level of the economy is severely hampered by the lack of ethics to promote it. Arguing that the Hispanic version of individualism stresses dignity and honor and destroys the possibility of stable cooperative communities, he further argues that there is a tendency to take advantage of others and to exploit rather than change society.[17] He quotes Samuel Huntington, who wrote:

> The absence of trust in the culture of the society provides formidable obstacles to the creation of public institutions. Those societies deficient in stable and effective government are also deficient in mutual trust among their citizens, in national and public loyalties, and in organization skills and capacity. Their political cultures are often said to be marked by suspicion, jealousy, and latent or actual hostility toward everyone who is not a member of the family, the village, or, perhaps, the tribe. These characteristics are found in many cultures, their most extensive manifestation perhaps being in the Arab world and in Latin America.[18]

In an analysis of the workings of trust as a commodity, Partha Dasgupta has offered seven propositions, which will serve, in turn, as a framework for considering the overseas Chinese form of trust bonding. These are:

1. There has to be suitable punishment for breaking agreements before people will enter transactions.

2. The enforcement agency itself must be trustworthy; that is, it must do what it says and only what it says (this may be society at large, using, for example, social ostracism).
3. Trust between persons and agencies is interconnected. If you lose trust in the system, your trust in its members is weakened.
4. The other person's promise must be credible, that is, you must believe that he will *choose* to fulfill it.
5. Entering an agreement includes understanding the other person's perspective when he is fulfilling his part.
6. Trust can be seen as a commodity, like information or knowledge, in that it has value or worth which cannot easily be quantified.
7. Trust is an expectation about the *actions* of other people, bearing on one's own field, but before the other's action can be monitored.[19]

In overseas Chinese business communities the principal sanction for breaking an agreement is loss of face, an important commodity in such a collectivist society. Face has two aspects for the Chinese, *lien* and *mien-tzu,* the former referring to moral authority, and the latter roughly based on accomplishments.[20] Loss of face, and particularly of moral authority, is deeply threatening, and through long processes of socialization Chinese people are taught to build and protect it. Because of its salience as social currency, it is a matter for open discussion, comment, and comparison, and an important part of the system of status ascription.

A related and pragmatic threat is the destruction of creditworthiness which comes from defaulting on an agreement. In such tightly networked communities word travels fast, and a reputation can be demolished overnight, leaving a businessman severely handicapped. In a society where responsibility for extended family welfare is deeply ingrained in the business owner, the loss of revenue-earning ability is a powerful threat.

The reliability of the controlling agency in imposing sanctions is a matter of the predictability of the societal reaction. Here the power of Confucian socialization comes into play, as well as the remarkable self-reproducing nature of this secular ideology. Here is a set of rules for social conduct, role prescriptions, and moral principles, which are passed on from generation to generation, so far without obvious dilution. The function of this belief system for stabilizing society, and perhaps more particularly its function for perpetuating internal family welfare (especially of the elderly) in societal contexts with few welfare alternatives, ensures that it continues to dominate. This domination of overseas Chinese consciousness is the guarantee that societal reaction to the breaking of Confucian ideals will remain predictable.

The agencies of trust control for the overseas Chinese are, of course, not entirely ideological. Societal institutions, many of them the result of Western borrowing, have been added to supplement the system of Confucian ethics. Accounting systems, legal infrastructures, securities commissions, and anti-corruption bodies, as well as independent professions, have all been added to the mixture, and appear to act not as alternatives to the ethics but as a means for greatly enlarging their scope and applicability. These additions of unaccustomed structures and institutions are taken as powerful weapons, and the opportunities they present are seized with both hands. It is arguably this combination of indigenous trust ethics plus Western institutional trust supports which gives Hong Kong most of its business dynamism, and the same argument applies, in varying degrees and in different contexts, throughout the diaspora.

The empathy which is required for a trust system to be effective is clearly best achieved among people who can predict one another's behavior because they share characteristics such as ethnicity (and preferably subethnicity), language, cultural traditions, family experiences, education, and reference groups. These are common for the majority of Chinese entrepreneurs transacting with one another, and they thus strengthen the likelihood that the credibility of promises can be accurately judged and the other's perspective understood. There is also a hard edge to this mutual understanding. In a society in which the most fundamentally right thing to pursue is one's own family's welfare, no assumptions can be made about the goodwill of others until the obligation bonds have been built.

ORGANIZATIONAL STABILITY, ECONOMIC COOPERATION, AND THE QUESTION OF TRANSFORMATION

In what ways have the societies, or at least the economies, in which the overseas Chinese flourish been transformed by particularly Confucian ways of organizing economic cooperation? Hong Kong and Taiwan are characterized by social stability, increasing wealth, technical sophistication, capital availability, extensive education, increasing regulation, and a large stock of creative entrepreneurs. In other Chinese business communities in Pacific Asia where they are part of a host society, such as in Indonesia, Malaysia, Thailand, and the Philippines, they have succeeded in securing a strong position by virtue of extensive political cooptation, and many of the previously mentioned characteristics still apply in that part of the economy which they control.

It is possible to identify a number of transformation processes that may be traced to Chinese norms surrounding authority and cooperation. They are illustrated in Figure 16.4. A brief examination of these processes follows.

Acceptance of Hierarchy.   The essential problem for management in many countries is the justification of its authority. This is challenged ideologically in many countries and practically by organized labor. Among the overseas Chinese the legitimacy of an owner's power is not a matter for debate. Paternalism is accepted as normal, and so long as behavior is responsible and benevolent, cooperation is a natural reaction. This force serves to stabilize organizations and reduce the difficulty of coping with change.

Large Companies.   A number of large indigenous companies are visible in the overseas Chinese economies, and although there is much variety here, they commonly display a mixture of paternalism based on local ownership and systems of organization and technology brought in from the West. Examples are Wharf Holdings, Hutchison Whampoa, the Charoen Pokphand Group, the Bangkok Bank group, Formosa Plastics, and so on. Their significance is partly due to their dominance in certain industries, but also they act as symbols of what smaller organizations may aspire to.

The Entrepreneur as Hero.   It must be remembered that for many overseas Chinese, traditional routes to social status are closed. Political careers were not generally possible under colonialism or in host societies, military careers even less so, and education was not easily available, so aspirations could most easily be met in the open world of business. The society's values appear to have shifted from those of traditional China in order to accommodate this,[21] and now the popular heroes in Hong Kong and Taiwan are the successful entrepreneurs. Their stories are almost exclusively about building their own companies. Such values then serve to build up the stock of family businesses.

Hybrid Organizations.   Although not completely Chinese in terms of business behavior, the large *hongs* which have played such a significant part in transforming Hong Kong (such as the Swire Group, Jardine Matheson, and the Hongkong and Shanghai Bank) are all Western structures which were designed to match Chinese expectations about authority. They have been, until very recently, essentially paternalist in corporate culture and structure. As such they have "fitted" the local culture and flourished.

Education.   The acquisition of education and training is driven partly by individuals' acceptance of responsibility to contribute to family welfare by

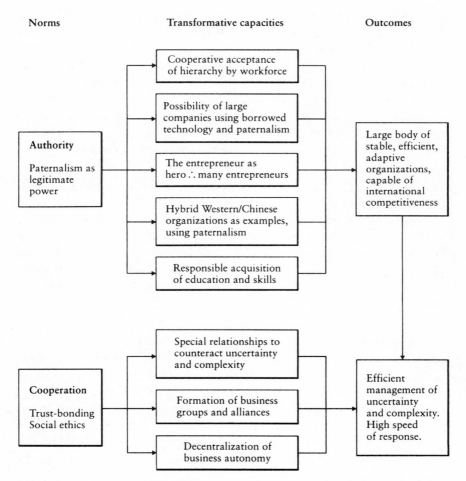

Norms | Transformative capacities | Outcomes

Authority

Paternalism as legitimate power

Cooperative acceptance of hierarchy by workforce

Possibility of large companies using borrowed technology and paternalism

The entrepreneur as hero ∴ many entrepreneurs

Hybrid Western/Chinese organizations as examples, using paternalism

Responsible acquisition of education and skills

Large body of stable, efficient, adaptive organizations, capable of international competitiveness

Cooperation

Trust-bonding Social ethics

Special relationships to counteract uncertainty and complexity

Formation of business groups and alliances

Decentralization of business autonomy

Efficient management of uncertainty and complexity. High speed of response.

Figure 16.4   Influence of Chinese cultural norms on societal transformation

career progress. It is heavily imbued with Confucian notions of duty, and contributes greatly to the societal accumulation of skill.

Trust as Response to Uncertainty.   Many of the contexts in which Chinese business is conducted are uncertain and complex. Societies that are developed respond to such challenges by codifying and diffusing information through, for example, accounting systems, market research, and a financial press. If these are only minimally available, then trust bonding will extend people's capacity to capture informal, unstructured information, and to use it to make business judgments. They will be able to reduce complexity to manageable proportions where information is scarce and unreliable,[22] and this becomes an important strategic asset in the world of business.

Business Groups.   Chinese business groups are significant actors now in the East Asian economies.[23] They have come about as a result of the value of strategic alliances and the consequent exchanges of capital, information, markets, and supplies. They are formulated in the Chinese case on grounds of mutual trust and often on social grounds, such as common region of origin, as well. Such alliances are loose affiliations rather than integrated corporations,[24] but their concerted behavior is capable of large economic impact.

Decentralization.   For a government to pursue a laissez-faire policy, it is easier if a basic set of business ethics facilitates the self-government of many business transactions at the base of the economy. In these circumstances the decentralization of power can be allowed without destabilizing society. I contend that the success of such policies is founded in the overseas Chinese norms for the maintenance of long-term stable relations, in the ethics surrounding trust, and in the long-standing tradition of centralized government responsible for societal order in nonbusiness fields. Such forces are clearly visible in Taiwan and Hong Kong.

These various processes of business evolution, supported and to a large extent determined by Confucian values, have contributed significantly to the transformation of overseas Chinese societies. Perhaps the most crucial contribution has been the encouragement of decentralization. Without the ethics supporting pragmatic and selective cooperation, laissez-faire government could have led to the anarchy typical of many South American economies. This same pragmatic cooperativeness has also allowed the small organizations of the Chinese to transcend the limitations of size by creating loose but adequately coordinated strategic alliances and business networks. These have fostered the capacity for large-scale investment and thus supported the development of industry.

A more subtle contribution of the strong ethics and sanctions surrounding trust (in this fundamentally wary and insecure society) is the reduction of transaction costs. Eliminating much legal formality and dispensing with much information backup produces a leanness and efficiency in doing business which remains impossible to quantify but is assessable in the inspiring statistics of national performance.

These economies are thus decentralized, stable, adaptive, well-coordinated, and self-sustaining. They have emerged from the chronically overcentralized despotism of China, through the somewhat more benevolent subordination of colonialism, to flourish as emerging industrial states with foreign reserves that are the envy of the developed world. In this transformation there has been much borrowing, but the Confucian ideals of authority and cooperation have ensured that while the borrowed ideas have been inordinately well used, the end product remains essentially Confucian in structure.

THE PROBLEM OF BUILDING A MORE GENERAL THEORY

It has been noted that an occasional venture into more abstract and more generally universal theory building can be salutary, and other observers have attempted to outline what seemed to be key components of a more universal model. Such thoughts were initially provoked by Edward Shils's discussion of the way in which Confucianism extends its hand toward a doctrine of civil society by defining the way as a means of judging government, even though the actual development of civil society was historically crippled by the exclusion of the mass of the people from contributing to the formation of institutions. This point was extended by Thomas Gold, who questioned the applicability of the term *civil society* to non-Western countries, and thus introduced the question of what its functional equivalent might be in the Confucian case, or more accurately the Confucian cases. S. N. Eisenstadt has pointed to the disappearance of institutional Confucianism and its present manifestation in combinations of transformed and repackaged components, all of which tend away from civil society, in that they are not founded in the notion of *public* good.

Discussions of this nature inevitably raise questions about the underlying components at work in the kinds of societal transformations being debated, given that the Confucian ethic is manifest in a variety of responses in modern economic life. Three abstract and universal components have been proposed, all of which could vary substantially in the ways they arise in daily life from one society to another, but which are necessary (though not sufficient) conditions for economic development to proceed.

The first of these is a moral basis for the legitimization of authority at the level of the firm. This serves to stabilize the primary economic units, and does so by fostering the cooperation needed within them. It works differently in Japan, Korea, and for the overseas Chinese, each of which expresses distinctly the Confucian ethics about authority, but the end product of cooperation is equally well achieved.[25] It could be argued that the Western equivalent is the rational pursuit of efficiency, traceable also to moral precepts in the society's ethical system, and serving in that case to legitimize performance-based authority structures.[26]

The second universal is the moral basis for the facilitation of reliable transactions. This brings into account the ethics of trust, and underlies the rules governing networking behavior and economic exchange. It underpins the construction of ties of mutual obligation, it provides a rationale for the system of sanctions which protect the day-to-day displays of trustworthiness, and it defines much of the structure of the economic system.

The third component is not a moral basis but an institutional structure. It is the provision of a state infrastructure which allows stable decentralization. This is, however, still traceable to deep-seated ethical principles about the role of government, the provision of societal order, and the importance of role compliance in support of such order. The "strong states" of the Confucian world all rest on clear notions of order and government responsibility, but they do not all interpret this role the same way in practice. If decentralization of power is included in its implementation, then economic development is fostered, as in Japan, Taiwan, and Korea. If not, it is stifled, as in China.

It is in this latter context that the notion of civil society can reenter the debate, as it is the Western form of response to societal decentralization, which works by providing intermediating institutions that bridge the state elite and the mass of society. In elaboration of his questioning of the relevance of the notion of civil society in the Confucian state, Thomas Gold has argued that the functional equivalent of Western civil society was, in the Confucian case, the set of stable, prosperous families, together with their supporting institutions. These latter (e.g., clan associations, guilds, hospital committees) provide security rather than public good but also foster trust and exchange. The addition to this set of Western-inspired institutions such as stock exchanges, a regulated banking system, and commercial law simply increases the power of gearing within the trust system without radically altering its essential nature.

It is, of course, necessary to acknowledge that there are many other elements in the equation. Economic progress, in Confucian conditions or otherwise, cannot be explained solely by the three universals just outlined. World trade patterns, technological learning, political events and philosophies, social history, and so on must also be allowed for. They are, however, appropriate when comparisons are being attempted, for the variables are being used at a conceptual level which allows them to be transported to another context and then reinterpreted on that ground. Until this is common practice, the refinement of general theory will remain slow.

17

OVERSEAS CHINESE
CAPITALISM

Gary G. Hamilton

In the last decade or so a substantial literature has emerged that attempts to explain the post–World War II industrialization of East Asia. A large part of this literature focuses on what might be called country studies. East Asian specialists examine the country of their expertise and advance a thesis accounting for that country's industrialization. A few of these country studies emphasize the role of culture, a larger number the role of unfettered market economies, and a still larger number—the clear majority—the role of the East Asian states themselves in creating the Asian miracles.[1] Most end with a pronouncement that the favored thesis may be generalizable to other East Asian cases and possibly to cases throughout the developing world as well.[2]

A smaller though still significant part of the literature may be called comparative studies. The standard approach, common to at least nine out of ten of these studies, is to test the generalizability of a favored thesis by examining several countries, one or more of which is East Asian. The same three perspectives—culture, economy, and politics—predominate in comparative studies as in the case of country studies, and in roughly the same proportion.[3] The usual conclusion of these comparative studies is to announce that the thesis is indeed generalizable—that, for instance, the state is important in all cases of successful industrialization.[4]

As informative as both types of studies often are, they rest on fundamental errors in logic for the generation and testing of explanatory hypotheses. Although one could point out several errors, such as generalizations based on a one-shot case study,[5] the key error made by such scholars is the assumption that each country constitutes one independent case.[6] Like individuals lined up in row—some big, some small, but all autonomous and self-contained—Japan, Taiwan, South Korea, Hong Kong, and Singapore, as well as all the other countries of Southeast Asia, are assumed to be independent cases, each requiring a separate explanation for its successful industrialization.

Using this line of reasoning, proponents of both approaches begin with the presumption that national boundaries constitute autonomous units and that the causes for something that occurs within a given set of boundaries in a given time frame are necessarily endogenous (i.e., they are bounded by specific spatial and temporal dimensions). Thus, the following logic results: in Country X at Time 1 there is no industrialization, but in the same country at Time 2 industrialization is present; the causes for this case of industrialization must have occurred internally and after Time 1. Using this logic, writers examine the interval between "no industrialization" and "successful industrialization" to discover what new factors were introduced that would account for the success of development.

It is, therefore, no slip in logical thinking that so many writers should credit the Asian states for the Asian miracles. In the interval between the Second World War and the present, one of the most apparent new features of the East Asian region is its new and distinct governments. These new Asian states are modeled after strong Western states; they have constitutions, legislative bodies, court systems, leaders chosen through prescribed procedures, and a clearly delineated administrative structure that contains at least one ministry devoted to economic planning and implementation. Examining these states, many writers observe that they use strong-arm tactics to eliminate internal opposition and do not always obey the constitutionally prescribed procedures for maintaining and transferring power.[7] They conclude that the states are authoritarian, and that authoritarianism can move entire societies toward economic policy goals. The label Bureaucratic-Authoritarian Industrializing Regimes (BAIR)—which was originally applied to Latin American states—is thought to fit the Asian cases best.[8] The more authoritarian the state, the more likely that industrialization will occur. Because Asian states are more industrialized than Latin American states, then, ipso facto, they must also be more authoritarian.[9]

Assuming that national boundaries do define the units and that exact temporal dimensions bracket the topic to be explained, then one can muster a lot of support for the strong-state thesis. The same argument, though not with the same persuasiveness, can be made for the effects of strong cultures, or for the strength of free markets. All these factors, singly or in combination, work endogenously to produce the industrial transformation.

States, markets, and cultures are indeed important in explaining Asia's economic transformations, but the assumptions that states are autonomous, that they are the most appropriate units of analysis, and that the post–World War II period is the correct time frame within which to explain Asian industrialization do not hold up under close analysis. In this essay I argue that Chinese capitalism is not confined to precisely defined temporal and geographic boundaries, and that Chinese and Japanese capitalism differ in nearly every respect.

I start by locating geographically what I mean by overseas Chinese capitalism, and then in each subsequent section I contrast a dimension of Chinese capitalism with that found in Japan. I define overseas Chinese as all Chinese who do not live within the People's Republic of China. The topic of investigation in this chapter is economic activity undertaken by the overseas Chinese in those locations where they live in the greatest concentration, such as Hong Kong, Singapore, and Taiwan, as well as the overseas Chinese communities that are spread throughout the Pacific rim, particularly in Southeast Asia.

By every measure the geographic areas of Hong Kong, Singapore, and Taiwan can be defined as industrial and capitalistic. Hong Kong and Singapore are world-class cities second to none in their modernity and profit orientation, and Taipei is approaching the same level, if a bit more slowly. The hinterlands of these cities—South China, Malaysia, and Thailand, and the rest of Taiwan, respectively—are filled with factories; they bubble with industry. Extrapolating from the 1989 GATT report, I would calculate that the three places most heavily dominated by the overseas Chinese—Hong Kong, Singapore, and Taiwan—contribute almost 6 percent of the world's total trade but contain only one half of 1 percent of the world's population.[10] These countries produce clothes, radios, television sets, shoes, computers, bicycles—so many items that one can hardly enumerate them.

Although these areas have industrialized, are they the product of Chinese capitalism? To answer this question is the purpose of this essay. The answer, however, is not an obvious one. On the world map Hong Kong, Singapore, and Taiwan are easy to locate, but Chinese capitalism is, I believe, less so, because it is not readily confined to a time in history, to a place in the world, or even to what we might think of as a capitalist mode of production. In this chapter I discuss these ambiguities by outlining the temporal, spatial, and organizational dimensions of Chinese capitalism. In the course of my discussion, I show the weaknesses of what I have labeled the country studies and comparative studies approaches, and I suggest a more historically grounded alternative.

CHINESE CAPITALISM IN HISTORY

Most people would date the development of modern Chinese capitalism from the post–World War II period. Certainly it is from this period that the three Chinese newly industrializing countries (NICs)—Hong Kong, Singapore, and Taiwan—began their industrial development. But the assignment of this beginning point ignores two facts. The first is the fact that the groundwork for this development had been laid long in advance. The Chinese were already "capitalistic"—that is, profit-oriented in the private sector—well before the skylines of Hong Kong, Singapore, and Taipei were dotted with skyscrapers; these cities are the outcomes, not the causes, of Chinese capitalism. Second, the actual industrialization of these countries was not an isolated phenomenon, occurring only in that corner of South China and Southeast Asia, but rather was set in a rapidly developing capitalist world economy that produced economic changes in many other societies. As I shall demonstrate, the formation of Chinese capitalism cannot be understood apart from the dynamics of the global economy because—and I want to emphasize this point—Chinese capitalism is *not* a domestic capitalism (i.e., the product of indigenous economic growth), but rather is integral to world capitalism itself.

It is this lack of a pattern of indigenous growth that makes Chinese capitalism such an elusive phenomenon. Many interpreters of East Asia's recent history have argued that there was no capitalistic development in late nineteenth- and early twentieth-century China, thereby giving the post–World War II date substantial credence. In fact, it is conventional to argue that, whereas Japan industrialized in the late nineteenth and early twentieth centuries, China remained economically backward. This is a standard thesis that many scholars have offered, including Marion Levy, Norman Jacobs, Immanuel Wallerstein, and Frances Moulder.[11]

The Japanese-Chinese contrast is central to the entire interpretation of modern Asian industrial development. In economic terms it always dwells on the obvious and early industrial capacity of the Japanese, particularly in heavy industries such as iron and steel, and in the products that derive from these industries, such as ships, trains, and automobiles, and the lack of these industries in China. With these industries, so the interpretation goes, the Japanese developed modern armies and navies that won wars against the Chinese in 1895 and against the Russians in 1905. By contrast, the Chinese did not do so well in these areas. While it is true that the Chinese developed some state-owned and merchant-run heavy industry in the nineteenth century, these industries were not particularly successful.[12] Besides, the Chinese lost every war they fought with an outside power from the time of the Opium Wars in the 1840s until the Second World War, and even then it was the outside powers that defeated the Japanese.[13] Based on these obvious comparisons, the conclusion is drawn that the Japanese industrialized and the Chinese did not.

But if we take another look at these "obvious" comparisons, we may find that they are not very persuasive. The time frame is too short and the definition of capitalism too narrow. If we were to make exactly the same comparisons today, weighing industrial capacity based on heavy industry, we would reach nearly the same conclusions: Japan is an industrial power, whereas Hong Kong, Singapore, and Taiwan, which do not have much in the way of heavy industry, are relatively undeveloped. But does this mean that they are not industrialized or capitalistic? Such a conclusion is, of course, nonsense. Today, Hong Kong, Singapore, and Taiwan lead the world with the highest ratio of manufactured exports to total output. Even so, it is still true that none of these countries makes a car for export.[14] Chinese-dominated areas of the world economy are not characterized by heavy industry; rather, the Chinese specialize in relatively small and medium-sized industries. These modest-sized factories make consumer nondurables—products such as clothes, shoes, television sets, calculators, computers—manufactured items that fill houses throughout the United States and Europe. Economists know that one cannot compute a country's rate of economic growth and its GNP based only on developments in one or two industrial sectors. Why, then, should historians and sociologists, in their comparisons between the Japanese and Chinese economies, implicitly do this for the nineteenth and early twentieth centuries?

Even if we were to take all of the sectors into account, the historical comparison between Japan and China would still be clouded by the political dimension. China neither won its wars nor developed a successful political economy; therefore it failed, so the judgment goes, as an industrializing society. Is political power, in the form of a strong state in war and peace, necessary for or even synonymous with capitalist development? As I mentioned earlier, in the literature on economic development most writers confidently conclude that centralized political power and capitalistic success are causally interrelated.[15] Indeed, one can list numerous examples where the two are in fact interrelated. But can one not also envision successful forms of capitalism without a state structure and without an integrated political economy? Let me submit that Chinese capitalism is such a case.

Consider again the two Asian cases—Japan and China in the late nine-teenth and early twentieth centuries. What we see in this contrast is not the presence of capitalism in the one and the absence of capitalism in the other. Rather, we see two different versions of capitalism that emerge more or less simultaneously with the opening of these economies to global economic and political influences. These same two versions of capitalism have become very important in the late twentieth century.

Japanese capitalism was largely an indigenous economic development—a product of political economy—that the Japanese consciously created by borrowing industrial technology and economic organization from the West and adapting and refining these social and scientific inventions to the social and economic conditions existing in Japan.[16] Recent research in Japan sug-gests that Japanese officials selected this course of action by recognizing their own limitations vis-à-vis their chief opponents in Asia, the Chinese.[17] The Japanese determined that they could not beat the Chinese at their own game of being Asia's chief merchants, and so they began to develop internally, by promoting industry. The Japanese elite had sufficient control over the other groups within society to mobilize and then channel the rapidly changing economy in the late Tokugawa and Meiji periods.[18]

The Japanese elite also had the support of both the Tokugawa and Meiji regimes. These regimes, however, did not serve as strong, authoritarian states.[19] The Japanese emperor was a powerful symbol but a weak political force. The imperial presence provided a point of unity, a source of legitimacy, but not a center of authority. So apparent is Japan's centerlessness that Karel van Wolferen calls Japan a "stateless nation" and governmental power "elu-sive."[20] Staffed by upper-class bureaucrats, the state apparatus became a site for resolving disputes among different segments of society, including the various factions within the elite. As Richard J. Samuels puts it, the Japanese state "does not dominate, it negotiates."[21] The combination of state and elite forces promoted a consciously designed and well-implemented political economy that was created to achieve industrialization through a strategy of decentralized political control and sponsored development of the productive forces within the domestic economy.

In Japan during the nineteenth and early twentieth centuries, the primary carriers of capitalist development came to be cooperating coalitions of po-litical and economic elites. Japanese capitalism was not a creation of the merchant class, although a few merchants participated in the elite coalition. Nor was Japanese capitalism a creation of the peasants, although peasants certainly changed their productive and labor outputs drastically. By com-parison with the Chinese case, Japanese capitalism was a creation of political economy, of a mutually reinforcing system of governmental controls and elite privileges. In a very short period the Japanese were able to shift from small-scale production of handicraft goods to large-scale production of industrial products, and from small factories to a hierarchy of bureaucratic corporations organized into conglomerate networks known as *zaibatsu*.[22]

There was a rapid turnover of the elite in the early period of industrialization, as well as considerable changes in the nature of social mobility into the elite groups, moving from privilege based on heredity to privilege based on educational achievement; nonetheless, Japanese society was and continues to be fundamentally a society dominated by such elite groups. The economy is also elitist. Even today sixteen conglomerate business networks—including Mitsubishi, Mitsui, Sanwa, and Toyota—have a ratio of total nonfinancial sales to GNP of 82 percent They employ over 20 percent of the total work force.[23] From the outset Japanese capitalism was a powerful, indigenously developed, and politically bounded form of capitalism, and remains so today.

Chinese capitalism historically, as well as in the present, was nothing like this. Chinese capitalism rests on very different political, economic, and social foundations. It was not, and is not today, an elite-based capitalism, and it does not rest on an explicit political system. The carriers of Chinese capitalism have been heads of households. These people were peasants, merchants, artisans, and occasionally scholars; they were not organized as distinct classes of people but rather were family heads who moved into and out of these ambiguously defined political and economic roles. Chinese capitalism rests largely on family enterprises and uses consanguineous relationships as the organizational medium for the economy.[24] In other words, it is not an economy organized through institutions controlled directly by the state.

This household-based economy nurtured a distinctive form of enterprise structure. Because Chinese kinship relationships cannot mobilize many people for very long, Chinese enterprises have usually been small and without a separation between family and firm.[25] If the family businesses were really successful, the firms, like the households of prominent scholars, grew larger as more relatives and employees were included in the expanding circle of household members. Huge businesses, however, were the exception, because most wealthy businessmen did not try to create larger and larger horizontally or vertically integrated firms. If they remained economically active at all and did not retire to the countryside, as so many wealthy businessmen did, they invested in extensive networks of small and middle-sized firms, often covering several areas of business.

The reasons for this strategy are several. The first reason is the effect of kinship systems on shaping business practices.[26] Japanese kinship rests on the centrality of the stem family *(ie)* and on the practice of primogeniture. In contrast, Chinese kinship rests on the importance of the patrilineage and on partible inheritance, with each son receiving an equal share of his father's estate. If the father worked to create a single large business, it would almost certainly be broken up and the assets divided *(fenjia)* after his death. A more reasonable strategy would be to start multiple small businesses that would be divided intact among the sons after the father's death.[27] This inheritance pattern is reinforced by an institutionalized system that creates economies of scale not from individual firms but rather from networks that interconnect firms. Businesspeople use these networks, based on reciprocal relationships (*guanxi* networks), to raise investment capital, secure the necessary labor, manufacture products, and distribute commodities.[28]

This form of economy, composed largely of small and medium-sized family firms linked together through various types of social relationships, is not conducive to developing heavy industry. Nor does this form of economy have an affinity for firms that produce world-famous products known by their brand names. Instead, from the outset this household-based economy produces a type of petty capitalism.[29] It is a nonpolitically based form of capitalism that is very flexible and readily adaptable to external economic opportunities, such as those offered with the expansion of Western capitalism in Asia. The Chinese integrated themselves into the expanding world economy; they followed the currents of Western capitalism and, using their flexible networks, quickly monopolized selected economic niches in many countries throughout the world. In contemporary terminology we would say that they monopolized segments of the service sector in the world economy in the nineteenth and early twentieth centuries. They were retailers, wholesalers, and financiers; they were the world's most prominent capitalist merchant group.

I have space to give only two brief examples of integration of Chinese capitalism in the world economy. Beginning shortly after the Opium War in 1842, when China opened to the West, the Chinese began to migrate around the world in search of their fortunes. This migration was extremely large and was widely dispersed throughout the world. The migration was also, from a comparative perspective, quite unusual. The only other country in Asia that produced many migrants in these years was the British colony of India, whose people migrated to other parts of the British empire. The Chinese, however, migrated wherever money was to be made.

They searched for gold in California and in Australia in the 1850s and 1860s, and when the digging produced little, they turned to other pursuits, usually to become paid laborers building canals and railways. The majority, however, migrated to Southeast Asia. Some Chinese had lived in Thailand for a long time, serving the royal household as privileged merchants and tax farmers. In the last half of the nineteenth century, these Chinese were joined by thousands of other Chinese, who began to organize networks to collect primary products such as timber and rice and distribute sundry goods throughout the countryside. Chinese also poured into the Malay Peninsula, Indochina, and the Philippines, as well as Java and the other Indonesian islands—into every spot in Southeast Asia where they could make money. By the turn of the century the Chinese dominated the service and manufacturing sectors of the local economies throughout the entire region and were major figures in trade between Asian countries and the West.[30]

The second example occurred on the coast of China. By the turn of the century, Chinese merchants and small-scale manufacturers largely dominated the Chinese economy.[31] In every sector of the economy except heavy industry, local Chinese were able to outcompete Westerners in the production and sale of products that the Chinese would buy. The Chinese bought very few cars, tractors, and trains, but they did buy a lot of textiles, cigarettes, opium, and small household items. Moreover, with a few exceptions the Chinese controlled banking, retailing, and wholesaling, and when department stores became important in the 1920s, the Chinese controlled them too.[32]

All of this occurred in both China and Southeast Asia without the support and coordination of a strong state. In Japan the state legitimized capitalism, coordinated elite interests, and resolved conflicts among the elite. During the same period in China, the state collapsed. That, however, did not hinder Chinese entrepreneurs as much as it freed them to create networks that spanned political boundaries and that worked despite, not because of, politics. The weakening and ultimate defeat of the Chinese state opened up commerce and industry on the coast of China and connected the Chinese with capitalist developments elsewhere. Chinese migration ensued. Moreover, with the decline, collapse, and disintegration of the Chinese political order, the real forces of Chinese capitalism moved to where money could be made—to safe havens on the coast such as Shanghai, Canton, and other treaty ports, as well as overseas to Southeast Asia, Hawaii, and the American West Coast.

To summarize, then, we have on the one hand the Chinese peasants who rode the waves of capitalism around the world—from Shanghai to California, Australia, England, the Caribbean, and Southeast Asia. Wherever they worked, they typically occupied service sector niches; they began as laborers and merchants and only later became bankers and industrialists. Being so responsive to market demands, this household-based form of capitalism became integrated into and dependent on the world economy, but it was in-

dependent of any one political order. In the post–World War II period political stability in Asia led to the creation of three politically stable areas
dominated by the Chinese—Hong Kong, Singapore, and Taiwan. Previous
accumulations of wealth and capitalistic know-how allowed the Chinese in
these locations to industrialize the societies quickly in response to burgeoning consumer demands in the West, mainly in the United States. These three
societies, however, are not three separate instances of capitalism, but rather
are so interconnected with one another and similarly integrated into the
world economy that they are, in truth, part of the same case of overseas
Chinese capitalism.

On the other hand, the Japanese elite initially resisted becoming dependent on the demand structures of Western consumerism. Instead, they created their own internal markets and built their own version of a strong
corporate-oriented political economy. They started as industrialists
producing for local and regional markets, and from there expanded into the
service sectors by organizing their own banks and trading companies; then
and only then did they begin to integrate themselves into the world economy.
They created products and then created markets for those products. The
Japanese and Chinese responses are separate reactions to the spread of Western imperialism; both are equally capitalistic, and both have led historically
to distinct trajectories of economic development.

CHINESE CAPITALISM CONSIDERED SPATIALLY

Keeping the historical dimension in mind, let us now consider the spatial
element of Chinese capitalism. This dimension is very important because
Chinese capitalism is not confined to a political space the way many other
forms of capitalism have been. Rather, Chinese capitalism fills an economic
space. The distinction here is significant.

The formation of Japanese capitalism was tightly linked to an integrated
social and political system that purposefully constructed the conditions for
capitalist development. In the early period of Japanese industrialization, political and economic space were coterminous; in fact, the Coprosperity
Sphere was a logical outcome of the tight linkages between the political and
economic orders. In the postwar era, as Japanese businesses became successful again, they developed techniques to extend industrial organization
beyond the political boundaries without actually disrupting the integration
between politics and economics.[33] Japanese economic and political spaces
are still linked, but they are no longer coterminous.

By contrast, Chinese capitalism—consisting of household-based firms
linked together into investment, production, and distribution networks—

was neither tied to nor reliant on a political order for the stability of its own institutional patterns. Chinese economic institutions were extensions of relational networks. The Chinese state did not guarantee the economic order; local, regional, and occupational groups, not the state, promoted such standardization and predictability as existed in economic transactions.[34] In fact, not only were economic institutions quite separate from the Chinese state, but also political officials preyed on the economy more than they supported it, and this parasitic behavior widened the gap between family enterprises and state officials. Therefore, when Western expansion created economic opportunities in the nineteenth century, Chinese households, detached from Chinese political controls, were well positioned to take advantage of the new opportunities. The Chinese expanded their networks of relatives and fellow regionals to follow opportunities wherever they went and in whatever sectors they happened to occur.

Because Chinese networks are so demand-responsive, Chinese capitalism fills an economic but not a political space. Politicians and even political regimes have tried to constrain Chinese entrepreneurs and to channel their energies; though sometimes successful in the short run, they have ultimately failed. For example, although many analysts have claimed that Taiwan's government was instrumental in creating Taiwan's economic development, there is more than sufficient evidence to show that state actions complemented the private sector but were not directly responsible for its industrialization.[35] Moreover, now that the private sector has industrialized, state officials are incapable of containing the expansion of Taiwan's enterprises within the political boundaries of Taiwan. Following previous routes of overseas Chinese involvement, Taiwan's Chinese have become one of the two largest groups of investors in Southeast Asia and in the People's Republic of China, even though investments in the latter had been outlawed until recently.

Unlike the Taiwan government, the Hong Kong government has never tried to limit the expansion of its Chinese capitalists. Now, with a change in sovereignty in 1997, the expansion of local Chinese entrepreneurs beyond Hong Kong has been particularly rapid and far-reaching.

On the surface the Singapore government seems to have been the most successful in constraining local Chinese capitalism, but that is more illusion than fact. The Singaporean Chinese are among the largest international investors in Southeast Asia, but most of their investment is in neighboring countries.[36] The Chinese of Southeast Asia are so interlinked that it is impossible to put political boundaries on Chinese economic endeavors. Chinese capitalism may be territorial, but that territory is economically and not politically defined.

THE ORGANIZATION OF CHINESE CAPITALISM

In order to understand Chinese capitalism, one must understand its organizational dimensions. Here, again, I need to emphasize the distinction between the political economy of an economic system, on the one hand, and the underlying organizational principles of capitalism, on the other. In many instances of capitalist economic development, political economy and business organization are closely linked. In the West, for example, key economic institutions such as property rights, contracts, standardization of weights and measures, banking, and insurance are maintained by the state regulatory apparatus. The list of such institutions is long, but most important, Western states rest on a legal system which has created the conditions for and established the legitimacy of the economic order that spawned capitalism. In a somewhat different way, the Japanese political system created the institutional environment that nurtured its industrialization. In the case of Chinese capitalism, however, the tight linkage between a set of state-supported institutions and the organizational principles of business does not exist as it does in the West and in Japan.

Overseas Chinese have been among the most prominent groups encouraging the economic development of East and Southeast Asia. Aside from the People's Republic of China, in each location where Chinese entrepreneurs control the economy—Hong Kong, Singapore, Taiwan, Thailand, Malaysia, and to a lesser extent Indonesia and the Philippines—the Chinese were historically in a position to mobilize economic resources quickly and early in the industrializing period, and have largely carried the forces of domestic capitalism throughout the region. In doing so they have created complex business networks spanning political boundaries. The linkages among the Chinese in each location are similar in character. Because of differences in the Chinese states in the region, however, the configurations of Chinese business networks also differ somewhat from place to place.

The Chinese method of organization is based on utilizing fixed patterns of social relationships and relies particularly on two sets of relationships. First, at the center of Chinese business networks, in terms of ownership and control of businesses, are kinship relationships. In Suehiro Akira's report on Thailand he concludes that, "regarding their capital ownership and corporate structure, most of the [Chinese] industrial groups are owned and operated by a single family . . . Only three or four groups can be identified as multiple family–owned."[37] The same conclusion—that Chinese business conglomerates are family-owned—applies to the other locations in Southeast Asia and to Taiwan as well.[38]

Family ownership in a Chinese context, however, means something quite different from family ownership in the West. Whereas a "family" for Westerners is an organization with set members and fixed boundaries, for Chinese the family is a rather flexible network that can be extended to include a great number of people, not all of whom need be related by blood.[39] Kinship relationships typically underlie the ownership and control of the core firms in Chinese business networks. Although most firms in a Chinese business network are small or medium in size, the family-owned network of firms can include many firms, and can even incorporate some very large individual firms.[40]

The second set of relationships consists of the regional or subethnic ties *(tongxiang guanxi)* that link people who come from the same general area in China. These people share dialects, cuisines, perhaps even surnames, but these commonalties merely add to the force of complying with the normative requirements of being a fellow regional.[41] These and other forms of relational ties *(guanxi),* such as graduating from the same school, represent important types of linkages that can be used to build extensive networks connecting core family-owned firms to other sets of firms controlled by other families. Chinese *guanxi* networks can serve as the basis for creating production, distribution, or investment networks.

These two sets of relationships are used to construct business networks that span political boundaries. The Chinese family and the Chinese firm have remained institutionally linked, and therefore the stability of Chinese business organization does not depend on a set of externally developed political and legal institutions. Continuity and predictability—both of which are required for ongoing businesses—is generated internally from relational principles in society and are not legitimated by or imposed through political means from the outside.

If we trace the development of Chinese business networks in Hong Kong, Singapore, and Taiwan, we find some distinct differences in the early periods of industrialization that remain important in understanding the development of these economies. But we also find many important similarities. In each location the state structure remained distinct from the business sector, so that industrialization was largely controlled by people independent of national politics. In Hong Kong the British controlled the government and let the Chinese create the industrial sector of the economy largely independent of their control. In Taiwan most of the successful businessmen have been Taiwanese rooted in local *guanxi* networks; the political structure, however, was controlled by Mandarian-speaking Chinese who migrated with Chiang Kai-shek in 1948 and 1949. In Singapore Lee Kuan Yew established a centralized regime that created privileges for the state-run industries and for multinational firms but disadvantages for local businesses, including the local Chinese. Their expansion occurred despite the state, not because of it. In each case the formation of Chinese business networks was linked neither to government patronage nor to government planning and supervision.

The differences in the political economy in these three cases, however, did create variations in network configurations. In Hong Kong the colony's economic policies allowed the large British firms to dominate the financial and service sectors, thereby blocking Chinese firms from increasing their share. Chinese entrepreneurs expanded instead into petty manufacturing and later into property, where they gained a substantial foothold. Subsequently Chinese entrepreneurs bought out some of the British businesses and have expanded their business networks into the Pearl River delta and Southeast Asia, as well as into North America.[42] In Singapore, because the state favored its own infrastructure businesses and foreign manufacturing firms, local Chinese entrepreneurs became prominent in adjacent economies such as those of Malaysia, Indonesia, Thailand, and even Hong Kong.[43] Since Taiwan is a country rather than a city-state, manufacturers became successful locally before they expanded their networks outside the country. Therefore, the network formations inside Taiwan were denser, but less international, than was the case in Hong Kong and Singapore. Since the late 1980s, however, this situation has greatly changed. After Taiwan's currency appreciated against the U.S. dollar, thereby driving up labor costs, Taiwanese entrepreneurs started offshore production units in Southeast Asia and in mainland China. This soon became a mass movement, and Taiwanese investments have surpassed even Japanese and American investments in several locations in Southeast Asia.

In sum, Chinese capitalism rests on a form of social organization that is legitimated through kinship principles and is not dependent on a system of political economy. These principles nurture the formation of business networks that are extremely flexible and that give Chinese entrepreneurs a comparative advantage in demand-responsive settings. Utilizing these principles, however, Chinese entrepreneurs do not normally engage in businesses requiring high overhead or large factories. There is no affinity between heavy industry and Chinese business organization, and for this reason large infrastructure projects have usually been undertaken by the Chinese states themselves. The preference for small and medium-sized businesses, however, does not make the Chinese less capitalistic or less oriented toward profit and expansion. Instead, the preference for family firms and networked business structures leads to the formation of a different type of capitalist development and a different type of market structure than that found in Japan or in the West.

To understand Chinese capitalism is to understand that not all cases of capitalism start historically with large factories, are confined to a particular political space, or require a particular type of industrial organization. Instead, it is necessary to see that economic action, wherever it occurs, is embedded in a historically situated, socially constructed institutional environment.[44] Social institutions, ranging from family to state, are conditioned by their historical past, and in the present these same institutions serve as the medium within which people plan their strategies of action for the future. Economic goals, such as starting a factory or looking for a job, build from the prescribed strategies (recipes, as one writer calls them) for achieving success that are current in a society at any given time.[45] These strategies are shaped by people's power, status, and sociability as these are defined historically within an institutional environment. That the Chinese should differ from the Japanese in these respects, and that both should differ from the people of the United States, attests to the very different historical trajectories that each of these societies has followed. They will surely have different futures as well.

EPILOGUE

In this volume our explorations of Confucian traditions in East Asian modernity complicate, if not refute, the common impression that modernity is either a conscious rejection or an unintended departure from tradition. The continuous presence of Confucian ideas and practices in Japan and the Four Mini-Dragons as unreflected habits of the heart or as a deliberate reappropriation of cultural values for social development calls into question the thesis that the advent of modernity entails the passing of traditional society. We authors are enjoined by the findings of our venture to appreciate the vitality of the Confucian tradition, the dynamism of East Asian modernity, and the complex interaction between indigenous cultural resources and the models of economic, political, and social transformation imported from the modern West. Indeed, the industrial East Asian case raises challenging questions about the modernization process as it historically originated from the unique Western European experience. The emergence of an East Asian form of modernity, while deeply rooted in the Enlightenment mentality of the modern West, exhibiting a style of life significantly different from that of Western Europe and North America, impels us to consider the possibility that the modernizing process may assume different cultural forms and to reexamine the idea of modernity as a norm, a standard of inspiration, or an emergent global phenomenon.

If we assume, as the East Asian example dictates, that traditions shape the modernization process and, in a substantial way, define the meaning of being modern, what is the status of the claim that modernity must be conceived in terms of three inseparable dimensions: market economy, democratic polity, and individualism? Surely the case at hand enhances the conviction that a market economy, as a powerful engine of modernization, is a constitutive part of modernity. In light of the political change and social transformation as a result of the marketization of the economy in virtually all communist countries in recent years, we must acknowledge the enormous influence of market forces in a fundamental and irreversible restructuring of the industrial East Asian societies since the end of the Second World War. Indeed, the single most important variable differentiating *industrial* East Asia from *communist* East Asia has been the adoption of the market as a mechanism for integration into the global economy. The relative success of the People's Republic of China, as compared with the difficulties in the former Soviet Union, to revitalize its economy through the market mechanism further shows that the wisdom of Adam Smith, while historically and culturally specific, does have global appeal.

It is worth noting, however, that the market economy, as it has been practiced in East Asia, is not at all incompatible with strong and comprehensive government participation. Often, political leadership provides necessary guidance for a functioning market. In both domestic coordination and foreign competition, economically sophisticated government officials are often instrumental in allowing for the smooth functioning of the system and for creating an environment for healthy growth. Collaboration between officialdom and the business community is the norm in East Asian societies, and the pervasive and fruitful interaction between polity and economy is a defining characteristic of East Asian political economy. The idea that, from the economic point of view, government intervention is always unwelcome and, at best, a necessary evil is alien to East Asian thinking; the well-established practice of official involvement in private enterprises is shown even in negative examples of collusion between bureaucrats and entrepreneurs. The authority of the government in adjudicating economic matters may take different forms—direct management (Singapore), active leadership (South Korea), informed guidance (Japan), passive interference (Taiwan), or positive noninterference (Hong Kong)—but the presence of the government in all weighty economic decisions is not only expected but desired by the business community as well as the general public.

Similarly, Japan and the Four Mini-Dragons all embrace democratic aspirations defined in terms of the electoral process. Democratic polity as a salient feature of modernity is fully recognized in industrial East Asia not merely as an imported Western institution but also as a universal aspiration for realizing values derived from the Enlightenment, such as liberty, equality, human rights, rationality, and due process of law. The vibrancy of the East Asian economy may not be a direct consequence of political liberalization, but the close affinity between market economy and democratic polity is undeniable. It is not at all farfetched to suggest that even if democratization did not produce the East Asian economic miracles, it provided an essential favorable condition for sustaining the vibrant economies. The question of the linkage between market economy and democratic polity in terms of temporal priority and logical sequence may be controversial, but, beyond doubt, there is an interdependence, mutuality, and complementarity between them. The industrial East Asian case solidly confirms that modernization as well as democratization, while originating in the modern West, is universally applicable. It is possible that a market economy may not lead directly to a democratic polity, but it is inconceivable that economic strength can be sustained without substantial progress in democratizing the overall political structure.

The universal applicability of democratic polity notwithstanding, the East Asian manifestations of the democratic idea strongly suggest that democratization as a process is not necessarily incompatible with bureaucratic meritocracy, educational elitism, and particularistic social networking. The Western democratic experience itself has been significantly shaped by traditions of pragmatism, empiricism, skepticism, and gradualism as in the English case; anticlericalism, rationalism, culturalism, and the revolutionary spirit as in the French case; and romanticism, nationalism, and ethnic pride as in the German case. The Confucian faith in the betterment of the human condition through individual effort; commitment to family as the basic unit of society and to family ethics as the foundation of social stability; trust in the intrinsic value of moral education; belief in self-reliance, the work ethic, and mutual aid; and a sense of an organic unity with an ever-extending network of relationships all provide rich cultural resources for East Asian democracies to develop their own distinctive features.

It is true that Confucian rhetoric, as in a discussion of Asian values, may be used as a strategy for criticizing the indiscriminate imposition of Western ideas on the rest of the world. The new agenda for broadening human rights—from the exclusive emphasis on political and civil rights to the inclusion of economic, social, and cultural rights—may very well be perceived as a strategic maneuver engineered by Asian leaders to divert attention from blatant human rights violations by authoritarian regimes. While the need for East Asian societies under the influence of Confucian culture to free themselves from nepotism, authoritarianism, and male chauvinism is obvious, democracy with Confucian characteristics is not only imaginable but also practicable. The strong thesis that Confucian democracy is an oxymoron seems simplistic. Although authoritarian equality, like cruel kindness, is a contradiction in terms, a democracy supported by a trustworthy source of power and informed by an ever-present moral authority is certainly conceivable and, under certain conditions, may even be highly desirable.

In the modern liberal-democratic perspective, the Confucian tradition clearly suffers from manifold shortcomings. Yet, what is lacking may not necessarily be required for growth into a mature democracy *if* complementary ideas can be generated and comparable structures developed. In its overall spiritual orientation, the Confucian tradition lacks a strong commitment to individualism. The issue of individualism as a reflection of the modern ethos is complex. But, undeniably, the dignity, autonomy, and independence of the person are greatly valued in all modern societies. If a Confucian society, based on its cherished value of "learning for the sake of oneself" and the moral imperative of continuous self-realization, can generate concepts of basic liberties and rights and develop a legal system to protect the privacy of its citizenry, its belief in the person as a center of relationships rather than as an isolated individual may be conducive to stable democracy.

In its basic beliefs the Confucian tradition lacks ideas of radical transcendence, positive evil, and transcendental rationality. As a result, Confucian societies may not have rich resources for checking abuses of power by autocratic or paternalistic regimes. Modern Confucian societies must learn to appreciate the psychology of suspicion in conceptualizing the proper relationship between the government and the governed. Lord Acton's liberal dictum that "power tends to corrupt and absolute power corrupts absolutely" is particularly instructive to East Asian intellectuals, who have been too much seasoned in the Confucian scholar-official mentality to cultivate a critical spirit against the dictatorial tendency of strong rulership. The idea of God as the Absolute has been, by and large, effective in rendering all worldly structures of power relative in the West. The unintended healthy consequence of subsuming political authority under a more transcendent framework of meaning is eminently suited as a prescription to the East Asian vulnerability to authoritarianism. Yet the Confucian theory of the Mandate of Heaven, based on the ethic of responsibility of the elite, is more congenial to democratic polity than, say, the divine right of kings. The Confucian ideas of benevolent government, the duty-consciousness of the elite, and the right of the people to revolution are all consistent with democratic demands for civility, impartiality, and public accountability. Actually the Confucians are noted for their commitment to cultivating the value of reasonableness in ordinary daily human interaction for they believe that true social harmony is attainable only through communication and negotiation.

In its political philosophy the Confucian tradition lacks concepts of liberty, human rights, privacy, and due process of law. The Confucian predilection for distributive justice, duty, public-spiritedness, and ritual may have undermined the East Asian capacity fully to integrate freedoms of individual expression, inalienable political and civil rights, respect for the private sphere, and an independent judiciary. In a complex modern society, however, we can no longer afford to underscore the value of liberties without considering adequate political measures for protecting the economically disadvantaged. The ills of an inefficient welfare system notwithstanding, the government must ensure that vicious competitiveness enhanced by market forces does not lead to unbearable inequalities. This requires the cultivation of a strong sense of culpability and responsibility of business and government to the well-being of society at large. The Confucian concern for duty is not at variance with the demand for rights. Actually, for a discourse on self-interest and privacy to have the salience it deserves, the development of a public sphere, where the spirit of impartiality is respected, is both desirable and necessary. Paradoxically, the formation of a civilized mode of conduct (a fiduciary commitment to the public good) by legal professionals may still be the most effective way to curtail concern for self-interest.

In its institutional structure, the Confucian tradition lacks a mechanism of checks and balances against autocracy, an adversarial division of labor within a constitutional framework, loyal opposition, and total political participation. Authoritarianism, whether harsh or lenient, continues to haunt East Asian democracies. The penchant for consensus formation undermines the dynamism, engendered by a creative tension inherent in an adversarial system, of East Asian political culture. The patient tolerance and informed understanding of the role and function of the loyal opposition characterized by most Western democracies is yet to have a presence in East Asia. Multiparty elections have already become a reality of life for all of industrialized East Asia. Even the people of Singapore and Hong Kong are experienced in voting. Nonetheless, while the political process within a constitutional framework is being worked out in most industrial East Asian societies, it will take years to create an ethos of civility and openness in intraparty communication. The idea of government of, by, and for the people is no longer wishful thinking in Japan and the Four Mini-Dragons. But democratic polity, far from being fully integrated into the ordinary way of life, remains contentious, disruptive, and even explosive.

In interpersonal praxis the Confucian tradition lacks the concepts of social contract, civil society, and public sphere. Still, the fruitful human interaction involved in "network capitalism," which has successfully extended to virtually all corners of the global community, suggests that the ethical requirements of complex business transactions, such as trust, reliability, responsibility, and obligation, are rooted in Confucian culture. Although, without a well-developed legal system, this way of generating wealth is hardly universalizable, it has already created a unique style of economic and social development with far-reaching implications for the rest of the world. The emergence of public institutions in business, mass media, academia, religion, and the professions, independent of the political center and yet instrumental in shaping its long-term policies, has enabled industrial East Asia gradually to develop full-fledged civil societies. While it is difficult to predict the course of action of these emerging institutions which have made the idea of civil society intelligible to East Asian intellectuals, the increasing pluralism inevitably leads to new constellations of thought, religion, ethics, aesthetics, and worldviews. Whether or not a truly functioning public sphere adjudicated by communicative rationality will come into being in each of these newly industrial countries, the density of the human network and the complexity of the cultural texture have made them a remarkably modern exemplification of "organic solidarity," in Emile Durkheim's conception of division of labor as a necessary condition for modernity.

The foregoing discussion of the limitations of the Confucian tradition in the liberal-democratic perspective and the possible Confucian responses to the Enlightenment mentality suggest a new ethical-political horizon. Its uniqueness can be revealed only in sharp contrast to an old and still influential interpretive position:

> The verdict that Confucianism is incompatible with science and democracy, the two defining characteristics of the modern West, renders it inconsequential or irrelevant to China's modernization (that is Westernization) has been the consensus of the Chinese intelligentsia, representing a variety of [ethical-]political persuasions (such as pragmatism, liberalism, anarchism, socialism and constitutional monarchism) since the May Fourth Movement in 1919. Understandably, Levenson, in his classical trilogy on Confucian China concludes that its modern fate was sealed.[1]

East Asian intellectuals are actively involved in probing the Confucian tradition as a spiritual resource for economic development, nation-building, social stability, and cultural identity. But the echoes of the iconoclastic attacks on Confucius and Sons still reverberate in the halls of academia and in the corridors of government throughout Japan and the Four Mini-Dragons. Paradoxically, the Confucian personality ideals (the authentic person, the worthy, or the sage) can be realized more fully in a liberal democratic society than in either a traditional imperial dictatorship or a modern authoritarian regime. East Asian Confucian ethics must creatively transform itself in light of Enlightenment values before it can serve as an effective critique of the excessive individualism, pernicious competitiveness, and vicious litigiousness of the modern West.

Another challenge to Confucian self-reflexivity is the gender issue. The time is ripe for feminist critiques of the Confucian tradition and possible Confucian answers to such a mode of inquiry. The absence in this volume of focused investigations by scholars, especially feminist scholars, on gender (with the notable exception of Robert Smith's chapter) does not at all indicate our lack of effort or enthusiasm to engage feminists in this joint intellectual enterprise; we are critically aware that, without special attention to the gender issue, our views, divergent as they are, remain one-sided. This is particularly regrettable because the Confucian conversation can be greatly enriched by feminist discourse with its emphasis on relationship, context, history, sympathy, and holism.

As East Asian societies have begun conscientiously tapping their indigenous cultural resources to shape their own versions of modernity in response to the challenges of capitalism, science, and democracy from the modern West, they may discover that the feminist philosophy of life presents the most daunting challenge to their Confucian habits of the heart. Indeed, the vitality of the Confucian traditions in East Asian modernity in large measure depends on their transvaluation of male-centered dispositions into an inclusive, humanistic project embodying the perspectives of both women and men. It is not enough for the Confucian traditions to adapt themselves to capitalist economy and democratic polity; they must also adapt to and help create a new vision of the lifeworld: family, workplace, power, authority, social intercourse, and self-understanding.

NOTES

Preface

1. Tu Wei-ming, Milan Hejtmanek, and Alan Wachman, eds., *The Confucian World Observed: A Contemporary Discussion of Confucian Humanism in East Asia* (Honolulu: Institute of Culture and Communication, East-West Center, 1992).
2. See Tu Wei-ming, ed., *The Triadic Chord: Confucian Ethics, Industrial East Asia, and Max Weber* (Singapore: Institute of East Asian Philosophies, 1991).
3. They include Wm. T. de Bary, Shmuel Eisenstadt, Gary Hamilton, Hao Chang, Ambrose King, Koh Byong-ik, Eddie Kuo, Shu-hsien Liu, Roderick MacFarquhar, S. G. Redding, Edward Shils, Tu Wei-ming, Ezra Vogel, and John Wong.
4. Christine C. Schnusenberg, "In Memoriam: A Narrative Account of the Last Phase of Professor Edward Shils' Life" (manuscript), p. 13.

Introduction

1. Edwin Reischauer, "The Sinic World in Perspective," *Foreign Affairs,* 52, no. 2 (January 1974): 341–348.
2. Salient features include the creation myth, ethnic homogeneity, a history of full-fledged feudalism, a martial spirit, and the imperial system. These make Japan distinct among Asian nations. In addition, its exceptional performance as a competitive modern state

since the Meiji Restoration of 1868 enabled it to play the role of an awesome "Western" power on the world stage for decades.

3. This is commonly understood as the "Confucian hypothesis." See Peter L. Berger and Hsin-Huang Michael Hsiao, eds., *In Search of an East Asian Development Model* (New Brunswick, N.J.: Transaction Books, 1988), p. 7.

4. Max Weber, *The Protestant Ethic and the Spirit of Capitalism,* trans. Talcott Parsons (New York: Scribner's, 1976), p. 183.

5. Weber, *The Protestant Ethic,* pp. 182–183.

6. Max Weber, *The Religion of China,* trans. Hans H. Gerth (New York: Free Press, 1968), pp. 248–249. Ironically, in the same passage the deletion reads, "probably more capable than the Japanese."

7. Wolfgang Schluchter, "Weber's Sociology of Rationalism and Typology of Religious Rejections of the World," in *Max Weber, Rationality, and Modernity,* ed. Scott Lasch and Sam Whimster (London: Allen & Unwin, 1987), pp. 109–113.

8. Peter L. Berger, *The Capitalist Revolution: Fifty Propositions about Prosperity, Equality, and Liberty* (New York: Basic Books, 1986).

9. Max Weber, *The Sociology of Religion,* trans. Ephraim Fischoff (Boston: Beacon Press, 1963), p. 269.

10. Herman Kahn and Thomas Pepper, *The Japanese Challenge* (New York: William Morrow, 1980), p. 27.

1. Confucian Education in Premodern East Asia

1. See Wm. Theodore de Bary, *The Trouble with Confucianism* (Cambridge, Mass.: Harvard University Press, 1991), pp. 74–86.

2. Wm. Theodore de Bary, *East Asian Civilizations: A Dialogue in Five Stages* (Cambridge, Mass.: Harvard University Press, 1988), p. 91.

3. See Ch'iu Chün, *Ta-hsüeh yen-i pu* (A supplement to the developed meaning of the *Great Learning*), chaps. 54–55 ("General Discussion of Rites").

4. See Wm. Theodore de Bary and John W. Chaffee, *Neo-Confucian Education: The Formative Stage* (Berkeley: University of California Press, 1989), pp. 212–218.

5. See Huang Tsung-hsi, *Huang Tsung-hsi ch'üan-chi* (The complete works of Huang Tsung-hsi) (Hangchou: Chekiang ku-chi ch'u-pan-she, 1985), *Ming-i tai-fang lu,* pp. 10–19.

2. Reflections on Civil Society and Civility in the Chinese Intellectual Tradition

1. I refer to Lenin's description of bourgeois society as that in which the state is the executive committee of the bourgeoisie.

2. D. C. Lau, trans., *The Analects: Confucius* (Harmondsworth: Penguin Books, 1979), 15.5, p. 132.

3. *Analects,* 1.12, p. 61.

4. *Analects,* 1.7, p. 60.

5. D. C. Lau, trans., *Mencius* (Harmondsworth: Penguin Books, 1970), 2B:10, pp. 92–93.

6. *Analects,* 9.24, p. 109.

7. Ibid.

8. *Analects,* 8.13, p. 94.

9. *Analects,* 18.7, p. 151.

10. *Analects,* 14.21, pp. 127–128.

11. *Analects,* 2.21, p. 66.

12. *Analects,* 14.42, p. 131.

13. A note on the Confucian view of rationalization and bureaucracy seems in order here. Bureaucracy is, in the first place, compatible with autocratic oligarchy or even totalitarianism. It is, however, necessary for civil society, although its powers must be kept in check if the sphere of civil society is to avoid infringement and diminution. This is not a danger in the Confucian view. There are boundaries to government activities prescribed by the Way; Confucian scholars would not encroach on those boundaries. The Confucian recommendation that scholars become officials was prompted by the awareness that the ruler needed knowledge of the Way in order to rule properly. Propriety and probity were the qualities that Confucian scholars would bring to their task, in addition to their knowledge of the Way. There was never any reference to the greater efficiency of administration by highly educated persons as compared with administration by officials selected on the basis of their connection with the great landowning families.

14. *Analects,* 8.14, p. 94, and 14.26, p. 128.

15. *Analects,* 5.26, p. 80.

16. *Analects,* 5.28, p. 80.

17. *Analects,* 7.16, p. 88.

18. *Analects,* 8.13, p. 94.

19. *Book of Lord Shang: A Classic of the Chinese School of Law,* trans., J. J. L. Duyvendak (London: A. Probsthain, 1928), p. 169.

20. *Analects,* 14.21, pp. 127–128.

21. The legalists were well aware of the potential for conflicts of interests, and they had clear ideas about how such conflicts should be dealt with: they must be suppressed by the ruler.

22. *Analects,* 8.14, p. 94; see also 14.26, p. 128.

23. *Book of Lord Shang,* p. 188.

24. *Book of Lord Shang,* p. 190.

25. *Analects,* 2.14, p. 65.

26. It is difficult to know why the idea of public discussion of political issues was able to emerge in Greece at around this time. Perhaps the small size of the Greek polis rendered feasible arrangements that the vast territory and huge population of China could not permit.

27. *Mencius*, 3A:3, p. 99.
28. Mencius envisaged more mutual sympathy between the ruler and the ruled than Confucius, who thought that the first duty of the ruled was self-cultivation. See *Mencius*, 3A:3, p. 100.
29. *Analects*, 4.16, p. 74.
30. *Analects*, 16.l, pp. 138–139. See Lau's note to this passage on p. 138.
31. *Analects*, 17.16, p. 146.
32. See *Analects*, 19.19, p. 155.
33. *Analects*, 6.5, p. 81.
34. *Analects*, 7.16, p. 115.
35. Ibid.
36. *Analects*, 12.17, p. 115.
37. *Analects*, 12.18, p. 115.
38. *Analects*, 8.2, p. 92.
39. *Analects*, 14.41, p. 131.
40. *Analects*, 12.19, pp. 115–116.
41. *Analects*, 8.9, p. 93.
42. *Analects*, 12.20, p. 116.
43. *Analects*, 12.22, p. 117.
44. *Analects*, 13.l, p. 118.
45. See *Analects*, 12.17, p. 115.
46. *Analects*, 13.3, p. 118.
47. *Analects*, 13.4, p. 119.
48. *Analects*, 12.7, p. 113.
49. *Analects*, 15.2, p. 132.
50. *Analects*, 1.9, p. 60.
51. *Analects*, 12.17, p. 115.
52. *Analects*, 2.20, p. 65.
53. *Analects*, 13.l, p. 118.
54. *Analects*, 8.2, p. 92.
55. See *Analects*, 15.35, pp. 136–137.
56. *Analects*, 8.9, p. 93.
57. *Analects*, 16.9, p. 140.
58. Mencius has a more symmetrical conception of the relations between the ruler and the common people. He said, "The people will delight in the joy of him who delights in their joy, and will worry over the troubles of him who worries over their troubles. He who delights and worries on account of the Empire is certain to become a true King" (*Mencius*, 1B:4, p. 63). Also, "Practice benevolent government and the people will be sure to love their superiors and die for them" (*Mencius*, 1.B.12, p. 71).
59. *Analects*, 1.6, p. 59.
60. *Analects*, 12.22, p. 116.
61. *Analects*, 13.18, p.121.
62. *Analects*, 1.1, p. 59.

63. *Analects,* 1.4–8, pp. 59–60.
64. *Analects,* 1.8, p. 60.
65. *Analects,* 2.12, p. 64.
66. *Analects,* 20.l, p. 159.
67. Mencius holds that the egocentric philosophy of Yang Chu "amounts to a denial of one's prince," and that Mo Ti's advocacy of universal love is the same as "a denial of one's father" (*Mencius,* 3B:9, p. 114). These heresies deceive the people, and so are regarded by Mencius as dangerous to society, a sign of decline in the empire. For this reason he wishes "to banish excessive views" (*Mencius,* 3B:9, p. 115). He says they should be prevented, although the mode of prevention is not specified.
68. See *Analects,* 5.28, p. 80; 13.18, p. 121; 13.24, p. 122; 17.13, p. 145. There is also one reference to "local community" (*Analects,* 10.l, p. 101).
69. *Analects,* 14.2, p. 124.
70. Mencius seems to be more sensitive to the attachment to territory: "This is the land of our forebears. It is not a matter for us to decide. Let us defend it to the death" (1B:15, p. 72).

3. The Intellectual Heritage of the Confucian Ideal of Ching-shih

1. Tseng Kuo-fan, *Tseng Ti-sheng chih tzu-wo chiao-yü* (Tseng Kuo-fan's self-education) (Chungking: Commercial Press, 1943), pp. 1–2.
2. Benjamin Schwartz, "Some Polarities in Confucian Thought," in *Confucianism in Action,* ed. David S. Nivison and Arthur Wright (Stanford: Stanford University Press, 1959), pp. 54–58.
3. See Wm. Theodore de Bary, *Learning for One's Self: Essays on the Individual in Neo-Confucian Thought* (New York: Columbia University Press, 1991), pp. 4, 8, 23, 95, 182. Yü Ying-shih, *Ts'ung chia-chih hsi-t'ung k'an Chung-kuo wen-hua te hsien-tai i-i* (Modernization of Chinese culture: a discussion from the standpoint of the traditional value system) (Taipei: Shih-pao wen-hua ch'u-pan shih-yeh yu-hsien kung-ssu, 1984), p. 5.
4. Hsiao Kung-ch'üan, *Chung-kuo cheng-chih ssu-hsiang shih* (A history of Chinese political thought) (Taipei: Chung-hua wen-hua ch'u-pan shih-yeh wei-yüan hui, 1961), pp. 297–298.
5. Chang Po-hsing, *Chin-ssu-lu chi-chieh* (Commentaries on Chu Hsi's reflections on things at hand) (Taipei: Shih-chieh ch'u-pan-she, 1967), 8:236.
6. *Hsin-i ssu-shu tu-pen* (A newly translated primer of the Four Books) (Taipei: San-min shu-chü, 1957), p. 1.
7. Hao Chang, "Some Reflections on the Problems of the Axial Age Breakthrough in Relation to Classical Confucianism," in *Ideas across Cultures: Essays on Chinese Thought in Honor of Benjamin I. Schwartz,* ed. Paul A. Cohen and Merle Goldman (Cambridge, Mass.: Council on East Asian Studies, Harvard University, 1990), pp. 17–31.

8. Ibid. For Voegelin's concept of "the order of soul," see Eric Voegelin, *The New Science of Politics* (Chicago: University of Chicago Press, 1952), pp. 52–106.

9. Hao Chang, "Ch'ao-yüeh i-shih yü yu-an i-shih" (The sense of transcendence and the sense of darkness), in *Yu-an i-shih yü min-chu ch'uan-t'ung* (Sense of darkness and the democratic tradition), ed. Hao Chang (Taipei: Lien-ching ch'u-pan shih-yeh kung-ssu, 1990), pp. 54–55.

10. Hao Chang, "Confucian Cosmological Myth and Neo-Confucian Transcendence," in *Cosmology, Ontology, and Human Efficacy*, ed. Richard J. Smith and D. W. Y. Kwok (Honolulu: University of Hawaii Press, 1993), pp. 11–33.

11. Ibid.

12. Hao Chang, "Ch'ao-yüeh i-shih yü yu-an i-shih," pp. 35–56.

13. Chen Teh-hsiu, *Chen wen-cheng kung ch'üan-chi* (The collected writings of Chen Teh-hsiu) (Taipei: Wen-yu Book Company, 1968), preface, 2b–3a. See also Wm. Theodore de Bary, *Neo-Confucian Orthodoxy and the Learning of the Mind-and-Heart* (New York: Columbia University Press, 1981), pp. 79–83.

14. *Ta-hsüeh* (Great Learning), in *Hsin-i ssu-shu tu-pen*, p. 1.

15. Thomas A. Metzger, *Escape from Predicament: Neo-Confucianism and China's Evolving Political Culture* (New York: Columbia University Press, 1977), pp. 49–166.

16. For a concise summary of this debate, see Tao Hsi-sheng, *Chung-kuo cheng-chih ssu-hsiang shih* (A history of Chinese political thought) (Taipei: Chüan-min Publishing Company, 1954), 2:159–171.

17. Chang Po-hsing, *Chin-ssu-lu chi-chieh*, 8:236.

18. Ch'iu Chün, *Ta-hsüeh yen-i pu* (A supplement to the developed meaning of the *Great Learning*), in Ch'en Hung-mou, *Ta-hsüeh yen-i pu chi-yao* (The essential selections from the Great Learning), yüan-hsü (preface), and tsung-mu (table of contents). See also Chu Hung-lam, *Ch'iu Chün (1421–1495) and the Ta-hsüeh yen-i pu: Statecraft Thought in Fifteenth-Century China* (Ann Arbor: University Microfilms International, 1990), pp. 1–284.

19. Ibid.

20. That subbureaucrats were held in low regard is indicated by the fact that in traditional China the word for "subbureaucrat," *li*, was often lumped together with two of its homonyms, "precedent" and "greed." The implication is that the subbureaucrat is invariably precedent-oriented in a slavish way and greedy.

21. For a brief review of this debate, see Lien-sheng Yang, "Ming Local Administration," in *Chinese Government in Ming Times*, ed. Charles O. Hucker (New York: Columbia University Press, 1969), pp. 1–10.

22. Schwartz, "Some Polarities in Confucian Thought," pp. 54–58.

23. Ch'ien Mu, *Chung-kuo chin san-pai-nien hsüeh-shu shih* (An intellectual

history of China during the past three hundred years) (Taiwan: Commercial Press, 1964), 1:317, 628.

24. This was the unstated assumption of both the Ch'eng-Chu and Lu-Wang persuasions, as reflected in their commentaries on the Four Books.

25. Hsiao Kung-ch'üan, *Chung-kuo cheng-chih ssu-hsiang shih,* pp. 449–469; see also Yang P'ei-chih, *Yen Hsi-chai yü Li Shu-ku* (Yen Yüan and Li Kung) (Wuhan: Hu-pei jen-min ch'u-pan-she, 1956), pp. 63–91.

26. Chou Fu-ch'eng, *Lun Tung Chung-shu ssu-hsiang* (On Tung Chung-shu's thought) (Shanghai: Jen-min ch'u-pan-she, 1962), p. 28.

27. Such an unvarnished utilitarianism belonged only to the legalist school, which was universally denounced by all Confucians.

28. Hsiao Kung-ch'üan, *Chung-kuo cheng-chih ssu-hsiang shih,* pp. 449–469.

29. Hou Wai-lu, *Chung-kuo ssu-hsiang tung-shih* (A general history of Chinese thought) (Peking: Jen-min ch'u-pan-she, 1958), 5:240–241.

30. Huang Tsung-hsi, *Ming-i tai-fang lu* (A plan for the future prince) (Shanghai: Chung-hua shu-chu, 1957), p. 2. See also Kao Chun, *Huang Li-chou cheng-chih ssu-hsiang yen-chiu* (A study of Huang Tsung-hsi's political thought) (Taipei: Ta-han ch'u-pan-she, 1967), pp. 52–85; Wm. Theodore de Bary, "Chinese Despotism and the Confucian Ideal: A Seventeenth-Century View," in *Chinese Thought and Institutions,* ed. John K. Fairbank (Chicago: University of Chicago Press, 1957), pp. 163–203; and de Bary, "Ming Neo-Confucianism and the Liberal Thought of Huang Tsung-hsi," in *The Liberal Tradition in China* (Hong Kong: Chinese University Press, 1983), pp. 67–90.

31. Hsiao Kung-ch'üan, *Chung-kuo cheng-chih ssu-hsiang shih,* pp. 101–120, 408–409, 466–467, 611–617. For Huang Tsung-hsi's thinking in this regard, see Huang Tsung-hsi, *Ming-i tai-fang lu,* p. 5.

32. Hsiao Kung-ch'üan, *Chung-kuo cheng-chih ssu-hsiang shih,* pp. 461–481.

33. Ibid.

34. Kao Chun, *Huang Li-chou cheng-chih ssu-hsiang yen-chiu,* pp. 83–86.

35. Lin Ts'un, *T'ing-lin ssu-hsiang shu-yao* (Ku Yen-wu's thought: a summary) (Taipei: Lo-t'ien Publishing Company, 1969), pp. 109–111.

36. Hsiao Kung-ch'üan, *Chung-kuo cheng-chih ssu-hsiang shih,* p. 615; Kung Tzu-chen, "Nung tsung" (On the peasant kinship system), in *Chung-kuo che-hsüeh-shih tzu-liao hsüan-chi, chin-tai chih-pu* (A selection of materials on the history of Chinese philosophy: the modern part) (Peking: Chung-hua ch'u-pan-she, 1959), 1:13–22; Feng Kuei-feng, *Chiao-pin-lu k'ang-i* (Personal proposal from the Studio of Chiao-pin) (Taipei: Hsüeh-hai ch'u-pan-she, 1967), pp. 111–117; and Ch'en Ch'iu, *Chih-p'ing t'ung-i* (A general discussion on setting the state and world in order) (n.p., 1893), pp. 1a–4a.

37. Hsiao Kung-ch'üan *Chung-kuo cheng-chih ssu-hsiang shih,* p. 615.

38. Chang Hao, "Sung Ming i-lai Ju-chia ching-shih ssu-hsiang shih-shih" (A tentative interpretation of the *ching-shih* thought since the Ming-Ch'ing Con-

fucian tradition), in *Chin-shih Chung-kuo ching-shih ssu-hsiang yen-t'ao-hui lun-wen chi* (Symposium on *ching-shih* thought in modern China) (Taipei: Institute of Modern History, Academia Sinica, 1984), pp. 16–19.

39. For Pao Shih-ch'en's blueprint for comprehensive institutional reform of the bureaucracy, see Pao Shih-ch'en, *Pao Sheng-po shuo-ch'u* (Pao Shih-ch'en on preparation for the future) (Shanghai, 1906).

4. Confucian Ideals and the Real World

1. Wing-tsit Chan, trans. and comp., *A Source Book in Chinese Philosophy* (Princeton: Princeton University Press, 1963), p. 33.
2. D. C. Lau, trans., *The Analects* (Hong Kong: Chinese University Press, 1983), p. 65; quoted with slight modification.
3. Ibid., p. 177.
4. Ibid., p. 73.
5. Ibid., p. 149.
6. "Tzu-kung said, 'We can hear our Master's [views] on culture and its manifestation, but we cannot hear his views on human nature and the Way of Heaven' " (Wing-tsit Chan, *Source Book*, p. 28).
7. "Confucius said: 'The gentleman stands in awe of three things. He is in awe of the Decree of Heaven. He is in awe of great men. He is in awe of the words of the sages. The small man, being ignorant of the Decree of Heaven, does not stand in awe of it. He treats great men with insolence and the words of the sages with derision' " (Lau, *Analects*, p. 165). It is precisely because Heaven operates in an unobtrusive way and does not seem to interfere with natural and human affairs that small men totally ignore its existence. Obviously Confucius' Heaven cannot be understood as a personal God imposing its will on the course of human history and creating miracles in the world. Rather, the Chinese conception of Heaven is well expressed in a statement from the "Declaration of Ch'in" in the *Book of History* as cited by Mencius: "Heaven sees as my people see; Heaven hears as my people hear" (Wing-tsit Chan, *Source Book*, p. 78).
8. "The Master said, 'At fifteen I set my heart on learning; at thirty I took my stand; at forty I came to be free from doubts; at fifty I understood the Decree of Heaven; at sixty my ear was attuned; at seventy I followed my heart's desire without overstepping the line' " (Lau, *Analects*, p. 11). Wing-tsit Chan renders *t'ien-ming* as the Mandate of Heaven (*Source Book*, p. 22).
9. "What Heaven [*t'ien*] imparts to man is called human nature. To follow our nature is called the Way [*Tao*]. Cultivating the Way is called education" (Wing-tsit Chan, *Source Book*, p. 98).
10. Mencius said: "The Emperor can recommend a man to Heaven but he cannot make Heaven give this man the Empire . . . In antiquity, Yao recommended Shun to Heaven and Heaven accepted him; he presented him to the people and the people accepted him . . . If Heaven wished to give the Empire to a

good and wise man, then it should be given to a good and wise man. But if Heaven wished to give it to the son, then it should be given to the son . . . When a thing is done though by no one, then it is the work of Heaven; when a thing comes about though no one brings it about, then it is decreed . . . A common man who comes to possess the Empire must not only have the virtue of a Yao or Shun but also the recommendation of an Emperor. That is why Confucius never possessed the Empire." D. C. Lau, trans., *Mencius* (Hong Kong: Chinese University Press, 1984), 2:189–193.

11. Wing-tsit Chan, *Source Book*, p. 43.

12. Ibid., p. 56.

13. See Edwin O. Reischauer and John K. Fairbank, *East Asia: The Great Tradition* (London: George Allen & Unwin, 1960), pp. 293–294.

14. See Yü Ying-shih, *Li-shih yü ssu-hsiang* (History and thought) (Taipei: Lien-ching shih-yeh ch'u-pan kung-ssu, 1976), pp. 43–44.

15. See Shu-hsien Liu, "The Problem of Orthodoxy in Chu Hsi's Philosophy," in *Chu Hsi and Neo-Confucianism*, ed. Wing-tsit Chan (Honolulu: University of Hawaii Press, 1986), pp. 437–460. See also Wm. Theodore de Bary, "Human Renewal and the Repossession of the Way," in *The Liberal Tradition in China* (Hong Kong: Chinese University Press, 1983), pp. 11–20.

16. See Liu Shu-hsien, *Chu Tzu che-hsüeh ssu-hsiang te fa-chan yü wan-ch'eng* (The development and completion of Master Chu's philosophical thought) (Taipei: Hsüeh-sheng shu-chu, 1982), pp. 367–393.

17. See Huang Chin-hsing, "An Investigation of Early Ch'ing Political Attitudes: the Politicization of Confucian Orthodoxy," *Bulletin of the Institute of History and Philology, Academia Sinica,* 57, pt. 1 (1987):105–131.

18. See Liu Shu-hsien, "Postwar Neo-Confucian Philosophy: Its Development and Issues," in *Religious Issues and Interreligious Dialogues*, ed. Charles W. H. Fu and Gerhard E. Spiegler (New York: Greenwood Press, 1989), pp. 277–302.

19. See Benjamin A. Elman, *From Philosophy to Philology* (Cambridge, Mass.: Council on East Asian Studies, Harvard University, 1984), pp. 14–53.

20. See Liu Shu-hsien, "Postwar Neo-Confucian Philosophy," pp. 277–302.

21. Liu Shu-hsien, "The Contemporary Significance of Chinese Philosophy," *Journal of Chinese Philosophy,* 13 (1986): 204; quoted with slight modifications.

22. See Joseph R. Levenson, *Modern China and Its Confucian Past* (New York: Doubleday, 1964), pp. 83–85.

23. See Chow Tse-tsung, *The May Fourth Movement* (Stanford: Stanford University Press, 1967), p. 332.

24. "A Manifesto for a Reappraisal of Sinology and Reconstruction of Chinese Culture," in Carsun Chang, *The Development of Neo-Confucian Thought* (New York: Bookman Associates, 1957–62), 2:461. The manifesto was first published in Chinese in *Democratic Review* in Hong Kong on New Year's Day 1958. The translation cannot quite express the subtlety of thought in

the original. For a discussion of the implications of the article, see Hao Chang, "New Confucianism and the Intellectual Crisis of Contemporary China," in *The Limits of Change,* ed. Charlotte Furth (Cambridge, Mass.: Harvard University Press, 1976), pp. 276–302.

25. "A Manifesto for a Reappraisal," pp. 476–481.

26. See Joseph Levenson, "Part Two: Chinese Culture in Its Modern Metamorphosis: The Tensions of Intellectual Choice," in *Modern China and Its Confucian Past.*

27. I borrow the term "depth of reason" from Paul Tillich, but use it here in a totally different sense. Since Tillich's "depth of reason" points to faith in God, only the Chinese have been able to find the true "depth of reason" in man. See Shu-hsien Liu, "The Contemporary Development of a Neo-Confucian Epistemology," *Inquiry,* 14 (1971):19–40; republished as Chapter 2 of *Invitation to Chinese Philosophy,* ed. Arne Naess and Alstair Hannay (Oslo-Bergen-Tromsö: Universitetsforlaget, 1972), pp. 19–40.

28. See Shu-hsien Liu, "The Religious Import of Confucian Philosophy: Its Traditional Outlook and Contemporary Significance," *Philosophy East and West,* 21, no. 2 (April 1971):157–175.

29. See Shu-hsien Liu, "The Confucian Approach to the Problem of Transcendence and Immanence," *Philosophy East and West,* 22, no. 1 (January 1972):45–52.

30. Ibid.

31. For example, see Mou Tsung-san, *Hsin-t'i yü hsing-t'i* (The substance of the mind and the substance of nature) (Taipei: Cheng-chung Book Company, 1968–69), 1:115–189.

32. See Wing-tsit Chan, *Source Book,* pp. 498–500.

33. Ibid., pp. 65–66.

34. See Shu-hsien Liu, "Sinological Torque: An Observation," *Philosophy East and West,* 28, no. 2 (April 1978): 204–205.

35. Wing-tsit Chan, *Source Book,* p. 549.

36. See Ying-shih Yü, "On Confucian Thought and Economical Development," *Chinese Intellectual,* 2, no. 2 (Winter 1986):29.

37. Ibid., pp. 28–43.

38. See Mou Tsung-san, *Chung-kuo wen-hua te hsing-ch'a* (Reflections on Chinese culture) (Taipei: Lien-ching shih-yeh ch'u-pan kung-ssu, 1983), pp. 67–69.

5. "They Are Almost the Same as the
Ancient Three Dynasties"

1. See Peter L. Berger and Hsin-Huang Michael Hsiao, eds., *In Search of an East Asian Development Model* (New Brunswick, N.J.: Transaction Publishers, 1988).

2. See table in *Shisō,* no. 792 (June 1990):10–12.

3. "Nihon no kazoku—shinzoku kankei to sosensuhai" (Japanese family—from parental relationship to ancestral veneration), in *Nihonjin no shakai* (Japanese society), ed. Masuda Giro, *Koza hikaku bunka*, (Comparative Culture Lecture Series), no. 6 (Tokyo: Kenkyusha Publishers, 1977), p. 126.

4. *Ishida Baigan zenshū* (Complete works of Ishida Baigan), ed. Shibata Minoru (Osaka: Seibundo, 1972), p. 251.

5. Mori Arinori, "Saishoron" (On wives and concubines), in *Mori Arinori zenshū* (Complete works of Mori Arinori), ed. Okubo Toshiaki (Tokyo: Jimbutsuhen, 1972), 1:242.

6. Ronald P. Dore, *Will the Twenty-first Century Be the Age of Individualism?* (Tokyo: Simul Press, 1990), p. 71.

7. Ibid.

8. For another reason, see Watanabe Hiroshi, " 'Taihei' to 'Kokoku,' "(Great peace or imperial nation), in *Koka to shimin* (Nation and the citizen), vol. 2 of the Centenary of the Kokka Scholarly Society (Tokyo: Yubika, 1987).

9. Shuzuki Tadao, "Sakokuron" (On national seclusion), in *Shonen histsudoku bunko* (Library of required readings for the young) ed. Shizuku Misao (Tokyo: Hirofumi, 1891), 5:359–360.

10. Watanabe Kazan, "Shinkilun" (On being vigilant of opportunities) in *Nihon shisō taikei*, vol. 55, ed. Sato Shosuke (Tokyo: Iwanami Book Shoten, 1971), p. 70.

11. Takano Choei, "Bojutsu yumei monogatari" (The story of the dream of 1838), in *Nihon shisō taikei*, 55:167.

12. See *Dai Nihon komonjo, bakumatsu gaikoku kankeimonjo* (Ancient texts of Great Japan—documents concerning foreign relations toward the end of Bakufu) (Tokyo: Humanities College, Tokyo Imperial University, 1910–), p. 1.

13. Ibid., pp. 269–270.

14. J. Gallagher and R. Robinson, "The Imperialism of Free Trade," *Economic History Review,* 2d ser., 6, no. 1 (1953).

15. Sakuma Shōzan, "Harisu-tono seitshoan ni kansuru bakufu wansho shoko" (The manuscript of the Bakufu Ejo concerning the case of Harris's confrontation), in *Nihon shisō taikei*, 55:296.

16. Ibid.

17. *Yokoi Shonan iko* (Posthumous works of Yokoi Shonan), ed. Yamazaki Masatada (Tokyo: Nishin shoen, 1942), p. 11.

18. Ibid., pp. 39–40.

19. Ibid.

20. Shiba Kokan, "Wa-Ran doba," (Japanese-Dutch maritime trade), in *Nihon shisō taikei*, vol. 64, ed. Numato Jiro (Tokyo: Iwanami Shoten, 1976), p. 504.

21. Ibid., p. 485.

22. Watanabe, "Shinkilun," 55:70.

23. Yokoi Shonan, "Kokuze sanron" (Three essays on national policy), in *Nihon shisō taikei,* 55:39–40.

24. Kato Hiroyuki, "Rinso" (Neighboring grass), in *Meiji bunka zenshū* (Complete works of the Meiji era) (Tokyo: Meiji bunka kenkyūkai, 1955–56), pp. 5–6.

25. Jean-Jacques Rousseau wrote, "If Sparta and Rome perished, what state can hope to last forever?" See "The Death of the Body Politic," in *The Social Contract,* bk. 3, trans. Maurice Cranston (London: Penguin Books, 1968), p. 134.

26. Fukuda Sataro, "Eikoku tansaku" (Exploring England), in *Nihon shisō taikei,* vol. 66, ed. Numata Jiro (Tokyo: Iwanami Shoten, 1974), p. 490.

27. Fukuzawa Yukichi, *Seijōjijō* (Conditions of the West), in *Fukuzawa Yukichi zenshū* (The complete works of Fukuzawa Yukichi) (Tokyo: Iwanami Shoten, 1959), pp. 161–63.

28. Fukuzawa Yukichi, *Gakumon no susume* (Invitation to learning), in *Fukuzawa Yukichi zenshū,* vol. 3.

29. On this subject, also see Albert Craig, "Fukuzawa Yukichi: The Philosophical Foundations of Meiji Nationalism," in *Political Development in Modern Japan,* ed. Robert E. Ward (Princeton: Princeton University Press, 1968).

30. Fukuzawa, *Gakumon no susume,* vol. 1.

31. Ibid., vol. 13.

32. Fukuzawa Yukichi, "Fukuo hyakugo" (One hundred statements by elderly Fukuzawa), in *Fukuzawa Yukichi zenshū,* 6:217.

6. Confucianism and the Japanese State, 1904–1945

I thank Dorinne Kondo, Lynne Miyake, and Stefan Tanaka for their comments on and criticisms of an early draft of this essay.

1. For a general account of Confucianism in modern Japan, see Warren W. Smith, *Confucianism in Modern Japan: A Study of Conservatism in Japanese Intellectual History* (Tokyo: Hokuseido Press, 1959). The best published studies of prewar Japanese textbooks are those by Harry Wray, "A Study in Contrasts: Japanese School Textbooks of 1903 and 1941–1945," *Monumenta Nipponica* 28 (1973): 70–86; and E. Patricia Tsurumi, "Meiji Primary School Language and Ethics Textbooks: Old Values for a New Society?" *Modern Asian Studies* 8 (1974): 247–261.

2. See Michel de Certeau, *The Practice of Everyday Life,* trans. Steve Rendell (Berkeley: University of California Press, 1988), p. 167.

3. See Kaigo Tokiomi, "Shūshin kyōkasho sōkaisetsu" (A comprehensive commentary on the ethics textbooks), in *Nihon kyōkasho taikei: kindaihen* (Collection of Japanese textbooks: modern editions), ed. Kaigo Tokiomi (Tokyo: Kōdansha, 1962), 3:616–617; hereafter cited as *NKT.*

4. Tsunoda Ryūsaku et al., comps., *Sources of Japanese Tradition* (New York: Columbia University Press, 1958), pp. 646–647.

5. See Carol Gluck, *Japan's Modern Myths: Ideology in the Late Meiji Period* (Princeton: Princeton University Press, 1985), pp. 103–120; and *NKT,* 3:616–617.

6. *NKT,* 3: 616–617.

7. Ibid., pp. 618–619.

8. Ibid., p. 620.

9. Kaigo Tokiomi, "Shoshū kyōkasho kaidai," in *NKT,* 3:494–501.

10. See *NKT,* 3:63, 68, 75, 84, 95, 109.

11. Ibid., p. 14.

12. Ibid., pp. 140–141.

13. Ibid., pp. 10–21, 31, 57–58, 63, 81, 88–89, 119, 128, 135, 152, 162, 175–176, 219, 229–230, 257–258, 276–277, 300–301, 366.

14. For entries on "diligence," see ibid., pp. 18, 29, 69, 127, 145, 163–164, 179–180, 208–209, 250–251, 303–304; for those on "industriousness," see ibid., pp. 39, 46, 86–87; for "independence and initiative," see ibid., pp. 18–19, 44–45, 115, 162, 199, 279–280, 335–336.

15. The entries on "enterprise" are found in ibid., pp. 39, 101, 178–179, 198, 307–308; for those on "starting industries," see ibid., pp. 43, 58–59, 100, 117, 177, 306.

16. For entries on "honesty," see ibid., pp. 13, 20, 40, 55, 65, 66, 72, 77, 129, 130, 137–138, 146, 221, 256–257; for those on "obeying rules and laws," see ibid., pp. 78, 93, 115–116, 142, 148, 160–161, 168, 237, 260, 273–276; for those on "universal love," see ibid., pp. 48, 92, 106–107, 166–167, 189, 286–287, 317–319; for those on "keeping promises," see ibid., pp. 12, 73, 139, 243–244; for those on "not inconveniencing others," see ibid., pp. 15, 67, 131, 222; and for those on "being orderly," see ibid., pp. 11, 45, 64, 70, 134, 146, 221, 252, 365.

17. See ibid., pp. 43, 99–100, 147, 176–177, 248–249, 304–306.

18. See ibid., pp. 27–28, 97, 112–113, 171–172, 195–196, 330–333.

19. For entries on Katō Kiyomasa, see ibid., pp. 97–98, 187–188; for those on Nakae Tōju, see ibid., pp. 50, 104, 188–189, 324–326; for those on Kaibara Ekken, see ibid., pp. 81, 152, 281–282; for those on Arai Hakuseki, see ibid., pp. 103–104, 184–185, 313–315; for those on Ogyū Sorai, see ibid., pp. 94, 169, 291–292; for those on Ninomiya Sontoku, see ibid., pp. 68–69, 144–145, 250–252; and for those on Yoshida Shōin, see ibid., pp. 21, 183–184, 320–321.

20. For entries on Florence Nightingale, see ibid., pp. 47–48, 92, 166–167, 317–319; for those on Abraham Lincoln, see ibid., pp. 54–55; for those on Benjamin Franklin, see ibid., pp. 45–46, 116–117, 199–200, 336–340; for the one on George Washington, see ibid., pp. 46–47; for those on Christopher Columbus, see ibid., pp. 46–47, 102, 182–183; for those on William Jenner,

see ibid., pp. 163, 274–275, 308–310; and for those on Socrates, see ibid., pp. 30, 168, 277–278.

21. Gluck, *Japan's Modern Myths,* p. 102.

22. Ibid.

23. See *NKT,* 3:39, 85–86, 111–112, 144, 138, 263.

24. Ibid., pp. 14–15.

25. See ibid., pp. 18, 68, 145–146, 180–181, 251–252, 310–311.

26. See ibid., pp. 54, 103.

27. Ibid., p. 34.

28. Ibid., p. 9.

29. For entries on Kusunoki Masashige, see ibid., pp. 27–28, 97, 112–113, 171–172, 195–196, 320–321; and for those on other historical figures, see ibid., pp. 17, 53, 85–86, 114–115, 144, 149, 348–350.

30. See ibid., pp. 19, 75.

31. See ibid., pp. 15, 73, 112–113, 138, 242–243, 263.

32. See ibid., pp. 111–112, 195, 263, 320–321.

33. Ibid., pp. 10–11.

34. Ibid., p. 68.

35. See ibid., pp. 101, 178, 321–322.

36. Ibid., p. 71.

37. See ibid., pp. 249–250.

38. See ibid., pp. 35–36, 107–108, 120–121, 184, 207–208, 322–323.

39. For the impact of Confucianism on Meiji intellectuals, see Smith, *Confucianism in Modern Japan;* Matsumoto Sannosuke, "Nakae Chōmin and Confucianism," in *Confucianism and Tokugawa Culture,* ed. Peter Nosco (Princeton: Princeton University Press, 1984); Donald Shively, "Motoda Eifū: Confucian Lecturer to the Meiji Emperor," in *Confucianism in Action,* ed. Arthur Wright and David Nivison (Stanford: Stanford University Press, 1958); and Shively, "Nishimura Shigeki: A Confucian View of Modernization," in *Changing Japanese Attitudes Toward Modernization,* ed. Marius Jansen (Princeton: Princeton University Press, 1965).

40. *NKT,* 3:620.

41. Ibid., p. 34.

42. Ibid., p. 620.

43. Ibid., pp. 355–356.

44. Ibid., p. 621.

45. For a discussion of Chinese moral biography, see Dennis Twitchett, "Problems of Chinese Biography," in *Confucian Personalities,* ed. Arthur Wright and David Nivison (Stanford: Stanford University Press, 1962), pp. 24–39.

46. *NKT,* 3:248, 436, 440.

47. Michel Foucault, "The Subject and Power," in *Michel Foucault: Beyond Structuralism and Hermeneutics,* ed. Hubert Dreyfus and Paul Rabinow (Chicago: University of Chicago Press, 1982), p. 7.

48. Catherine Belsey, *Critical Practice* (London: Methuen, 1980), pp. 61–62;

Louis Althusser, *Lenin and Philosophy and Other Essays,* trans. Ben Brewster (New York: Monthly Review Press, 1971), pp. 128–186.

49. *NKT,* 3:18.

50. Ibid., p. 68.

51. Ibid., pp. 133–134.

52. Ibid., p. 75.

53. Ibid., p. 144.

54. Ibid., p. 15.

55. Ibid., p. 131.

56. Ibid., p. 331.

57. See ibid., pp. 121–123, 210–212.

58. See ibid., pp. 76–78, 80–81, 85–90, 93–94, 96–97, 101–106, 114–115, 117–119.

59. Ibid., p. 635.

60. Foucault, "The Subject and Power," p. 7.

61. *NKT,* 3:248.

62. Ibid., p. 320.

63. Ibid., pp. 35, 94.

64. Mikiso Hane, *Reflections on the Way to the Gallows: Rebel Women in Prewar Japan* (Berkeley: University of California Press, 1988), p. 27.

65. Maruyama Masao, *Thought and Behaviour in Modern Japanese Politics* (London: Oxford University Press, 1963), pp. 2–19.

66. *NKT,* 3:227.

67. Ibid., pp. 226–227; emphasis added.

68. Ibid., p. 248.

69. Ibid., p. 640.

70. Ibid., p. 629. Three sets of textbooks were published: *Yoi kodomo* (Good children) for first- and second-year primary school students; *Shotōka shūshin* (An elementary course in ethics) for older primary school students; and *Kōtōka shūshin* (A higher course in ethics) for middle school students. Only one of the projected two volumes of the last of these texts was published before the end of the Second World War. *NKT,* 3:502.

71. See *NKT,* 3:367, 370–371, 382, 385–386, 389–390, 399–401, 403–404, 409–416, 420.

72. For the entry on the rising sun, see ibid., p. 382; for those on the flag, see ibid., pp. 367, 380, 403–404, 416, 446–447; for those on the imperial house, see ibid., pp. 363, 382, 386, 389–392, 407–410, 413–414, 419–423, 425, 429–432; for the one on the national anthem, see ibid., pp. 409–410; and for those on shrines, see ibid., pp. 396–397.

73. Ibid., pp. 413–414.

74. Ibid., p. 420.

75. Ibid., p. 386.

76. Ibid., pp. 389–390.

77. See ibid., pp. 374, 381–382, 402–403.

78. See ibid., pp. 370–380, 398–400, 403–404, 407–410.
79. Edward Said, *Culture and Imperialism* (New York: Knopf, 1993), p. 62.
80. See *NKT,* 3:367–368, 370–371, 374–375, 378–380.
81. See ibid., pp. 371, 373–374, 379–382.
82. See ibid., pp. 373, 386.
83. See ibid., pp. 385, 374.
84. Ibid., p. 645.
85. Ibid., p. 373.
86. Ibid., pp. 403–404.
87. Ibid., p. 640.
88. *Kokutai no Hongi: Cardinal Principles of the National Entity of Japan,* trans., John Owen Gauntlet and ed. with an intro. Robert King Hall (Cambridge, Mass.: Harvard University Press, 1949), p. 91.
89. Ibid., p. 87.
90. Ibid., p. 91.
91. Ibid., p. 645.
92. Ibid.
93. Ibid.
94. Matsumoto, "Nakae Chōmin and Confucianism," in Nosco, *Confucianism and Tokugawa Culture,* pp. 251–266.

7. The Japanese (Confucian) Family

1. Roderick MacFarquhar, quoted in *The Confucian World Observed: A Contemporary Discussion of Confucian Humanism in East Asia,* ed. Tu Weiming, Milan Hejtmanek, and Alan Wachman (Honolulu: Institute of Culture and Communication, East-West Center, 1992), p. 12.
2. I thank Jan Zeserson for many stimulating discussions that touched on most of the issues dealt with in this essay. The usual disclaimers apply.
3. Never mind Vietnam, the war that we have been told repeatedly "we fought with one hand tied behind our backs" but, in any event, "now have put behind us" by virtue of the stunning execution of the Desert Storm military campaign.
4. Actually, in recent years the term "Judaeo-Christian tradition" has been used with increasing frequency, apparently the result of an outburst of ecumenical fervor. One Jewish friend told me that he finds the new usage, with regard to his being incorporated into some larger entity, more threatening to his identity than reassuring.
5. Particularly so since the resurgence of fundamentalist Islam in Iran and the extraordinary events in eastern Europe and the former Soviet Union. Among many other revelations is the clear demonstration that the passing of even two or three generations will not guarantee the eradication of commitment to ethnic group and religious faith, despite the dedication of the authorities

to the destruction of both. There are lessons to be learned, however, about the correlation between chronological age and commitment.

6. I set aside for the moment the vexing question whether or not the ancestral rites in Japan have anything to do with Confucianism. I am persuaded, however, that the low estate to which women fell during the Tokugawa period had a great deal to do with the Japanese construal of Neo-Confucian doctrine. For example, there are five curiously structured chapters in Kaibara Ekken's *Teachings for Children*. The first two address the importance of learning, the third deals with what to teach children between the ages of six and twenty, the fourth with calligraphy as a reflection of *kokoro*, and the fifth "with the manner of teaching women." Throughout, the root of learning is said to be in moral training that develops a sense of humaneness and duty, among children and women alike. See Mary Evelyn Tucker, *Moral and Spiritual Cultivation in Japanese Neo-Confucianism: The Life and Thought of Kaibara Ekken (1630–1714)* (Albany: State University of New York Press, 1989), pp. 114–115.

7. I cite English-language sources throughout so that readers who do not know Japanese may pursue the arguments advanced on their own. As it happens, many of these sources are translations, and others are based on original and secondary sources in Japanese.

8. Julia Ching, *Confucianism and Christianity: A Comparative Study* (Tokyo: Kodansha International, 1977), pp. 7–8.

9. Warren W. Smith, Jr., *Confucianism in Modern Japan: A Study of Conservatism in Japanese Intellectual History* (Tokyo: Hokuseido, 1959), p. 232.

10. Byung Tai Hwang, "Confucianism in Modernization: Comparative Study of China, Japan and Korea" (Ph.D. diss., University of California, Berkeley, 1979), p. 18.

11. John O. Haley, "The Role of Law in Japan," *Kobe University Law Review: International Edition,* 18 (1984):6–7.

12. Ronald P. Dore, "The Ethics of the New Japan," *Pacific Affairs,* 25, no. 2 (1952):315.

13. Wm. Theodore de Bary, "Some Common Tendencies in Neo-Confucianism," in *Confucianism in Action,* ed. David S. Nivison and Arthur F. Wright (Stanford: Stanford University Press, 1959), pp. 25–49.

14. Tetsuo Najita, *Visions of Virtue in Tokugawa Japan: The Kaitokudo Merchant Academy of Osaka* (Chicago: University of Chicago Press, 1987), p. 23.

15. Ryusaku Tsunoda, Wm. Theodore de Bary, and Donald Keene, comps., *Sources of Japanese Tradition* (New York: Columbia University Press, 1958), pp. 330–331, citing Daidō-ji Yūzan, *Iwabuchi Yawa-besshū,* in *Dai-Nihon shiryō,* pt. 12, 24:438–439. The Japanese reads, "Ada o hōzuru ni on o motte suru." The maxim is from *Lao Tzu,* 63.

16. Peter Nosco, "Introduction: Neo-Confucianism and Tokugawa Discourse,"

in *Confucianism and Tokugawa Culture,* ed. Peter Nosco (Princeton: Princeton University Press, 1984), p. 5.

17. Ibid., p. 12.

18. Still, no less a personage than Ogyū Sorai had written: "It is not necessary that the common people should be taught anything apart from the virtues of filial piety, brotherly submission, loyalty, and trustworthiness. Their reading should not extend beyond the Classic of Filial Piety and the Lives of Famous Women, and other improving biographical collections which deal with the relationships between sovereign and subject, father and child, man and wife. The study of other works will merely increase their cunning and will lead to disruption." See J. R. McEwan, *The Political Writings of Ogyū Sorai* (Cambridge: Cambridge University Press, 1962), p. 132. The passage illustrates perfectly Hwang's comment concerning the social utilitarianism of Tokugawa intellectuals (see no. 10).

19. Richard Rubinger, "Education: From One Room to One System," in *Japan in Transition, from Tokugawa to Meiji,* ed. Marius B. Jansen and Gilbert Rozman (Princeton: Princeton University Press, 1986), p. 198.

20. Najita, *Visions of Virtue,* p. 60. While a reader of the Kabuki plays of the late Tokugawa might conclude that Confucian ideals were moribund, "even when they were most conspicuously ridiculed in the theater, they continued to affect the lives of most Japanese. The theater is a mirror of society, but it may magnify, diminish, or hopelessly distort. The one thing one can say with certainty is that as long as something appears in the mirror, no matter how crooked or warped, it still exists in society and has compelled the attention of the makers of mirrors." Donald Keene, "Characteristic Responses to Confucianism in Tokugawa Literature," in Nosco, *Confucianism and Tokugawa Culture,* p. 137.

21. Nobuyoshi Okumura, "Foreword," in Kōjin Shimomura, *A Book of Heaven and the Earth: Stories from the Confucian Analects* (Tokyo: University of Tokyo Press, 1973), p. xii.

22. Evidently not including women.

23. Nobuo K. Shimahara, *Adaptation and Education in Japan* (New York: Praeger, 1979), pp. 53–55.

24. Martin Collcutt, "Buddhism: The Threat of Eradication," in Jansen and Rozman, *Japan in Transition,* pp. 144–145.

25. Cited in Un Sun Song, "A Sociological Analysis of the Value System of Pre-War Japan as Revealed in the Japanese Government Elementary School Textbooks, 1933–1941" (Ph.D. diss., University of Maryland, 1958), p. 214; emphasis added.

26. He was in good company. A few years before, the Baron K. Suyematsu offered what I think of as a typical "Meiji man's" point of view: "I am acquainted to some extent with the Greek ethics of the Platonian school, and also with the moral teaching of the Gospel. Our moral notions, as it seems to me, do not materially differ from either in essence and purport, though

in classification of the different virtues, and in the prominence given to one or another of these virtues above the rest, all these systems in some respect diverge." He goes on to say that during the Tokugawa period, the Japanese founded their ethical system on Confucian dicta, "but in such a manner as to conform to our own ideas and characteristics." For the new age the Imperial Rescript on Education was promulgated; it embodied the cardinal points of what he calls "Oriental ethics"—loyalty and filial piety. In China the latter takes precedence, in Japan the former. See K. Suyematsu, "Moral Teaching in Japan," *The Nineteenth Century,* 57 (1905):198.

27. In his exhaustive treatment of the fate of institutional Confucianism *(jukyō)* in Japan from 1868 to 1945, Warren W. Smith, Jr., points out that "because the Imperial line was considered as one of the cornerstones of Japan's *kokutai,* to the extent that Confucianism was associated with the Imperial system it also became an integral part of the Japanese *kokutai*" (Smith, *Confucianism in Modern Japan,* p. 139).

28. E. Patricia Tsurumi, "Meiji Primary School Language and Ethics Textbooks: Old Values for a New Society?" *Modern Asian Studies,* 8, no. 2 (1974):247–261. Because pupils devoted so much more time to the study of language than to morals and ethics, Tsurumi assigns greater importance to the former, noting that the language textbooks contain a great deal of material that in effect offers moral and ethical instruction.

29. Ibid., pp. 248–249.

30. Ibid., p. 250.

31. Ibid., p. 258.

32. Ibid., p. 260. By far the best and most detailed account of the quite similar mix of ideas and concepts—Confucian, Japanese, and Western—that went into the Meiji definition of striving and success is Earl H. Kinmonth, *The Self-Made Man in Meiji Japanese Thought: From Samurai to Salary Man* (Berkeley: University of California Press, 1981).

33. Song, "A Sociological Analysis."

34. Robert King Hall, *Shūshin: The Ethics of a Defeated Nation* (New York: Bureau of Publications, Teachers College, Columbia University, 1949), p. 124.

35. Ibid., p. 132. This volume contains an invaluable annotated translation of the textbook. It deserves close reading by anyone interested in the weights assigned various concepts, ideas, and ideologies. Of great interest are the people used to illustrate the different principles; they include Columbus, Franklin, Japanese emperors and heroes, and several very ordinary folk.

36. Dore, "Ethics," pp. 150–152.

37. Betty B. Lanham, "Ethics and Moral Precepts Taught in Schools of Japan and the United States," *Ethos,* 7, no. 1 (1979):1–18.

38. Dore, "Ethics," p. 154.

39. Lanham, "Ethics and Moral Precepts." Because I cannot do justice to the complicated comparisons Lanham makes, I urge readers who are interested

in the U.S. "ethics curriculum" to consult this article for insight into how it differs from the Japanese. They are likely to be surprised by her findings.

40. Fernando M. Basabe, *Religion in the Japanese Textbooks of Ethics and Society,* vol. 1 of *Religion in the Japanese Textbooks,* ed. Vincente M. Bonet (Tokyo: Enderle Book Company, 1973), pp. 98–99.

41. Ibid., p. 100.

42. Robert Epp, "The Challenge from Tradition: Attempts to Compile a Civil Code in Japan, 1866–78," *Monumenta Nipponica,* 22, nos. 1–2 (1967):16.

43. "Nobody puts new wine into old wineskins. If he does, the new wine bursts the skins, the wine is spilled and the skins are ruined. No, new wine must go into new wineskins" (Mark 2:2).

44. Eric Hobsbawm, "Mass-Producing Traditions: Europe, 1870–1914," in *The Invention of Tradition,* ed. Eric Hobsbawm and Terence Ranger (Cambridge: Cambridge University Press, 1983), p. 265.

45. Munroe Smith, "The Japanese Code and the Family," *Law Quarterly Review,* 23 (1907):46–47.

46. Hiroshi Wagatsuma, "Some Aspects of the Contemporary Japanese Family: Once Confucian, Now Fatherless?" *Daedalus,* 106, no. 2 (1977):181–182. The point was stressed by Tu Wei-ming in the workshop leading up to the conference that gave rise to this volume. Although the hierarchical aspects of Confucianism often are strongly criticized, the dyads such as father/son have mutual social obligations that guide correct, harmonious, and humane relations. See Tu, Hejtmanek, and Wachman, *Confucian World,* p. 7.

47. John C. Pelzel, "Japanese Kinship: A Comparison," in *Family and Kinship in Chinese Society,* ed. Maurice Freedman (Stanford: Stanford University Press, 1970), p. 240.

48. Ibid., pp. 240–241.

49. Interestingly enough, in an insider's invaluable detailed account of the revision of the code during the Allied Occupation, there is not one mention of Confucianism. See Kurt Steiner, "The Occupation and the Reform of the Japanese Civil Code," in *Democratizing Japan: The Allied Occupation,* ed. Robert E. Ward and Yoshikazu Sakamoto (Honolulu: University of Hawaii Press, 1987). Nonetheless, there are some tantalizing survivals from the earlier code touching on the ancestral rites. One is article 897, which reads in part: "The ownership of genealogical records, of utensils of religious rites, and of tombs and burial grounds is succeeded to the person who is, according to custom, to hold as a president the worship of the ancestors." See Ministry of Justice (Japan), *The Civil Code of Japan* (Tokyo: Eibun hōrei sha, 1966), p. 521.

50. Wagatsuma, "Some Aspects," p. 205.

51. Toshio Fueto, "Revision of the New Civil Code," *American Journal of Comparative Law,* 6 (1957): 560.

52. Robert J. Smith and Ella Lury Wiswell, *The Women of Suye Mura* (Chicago: University of Chicago Press, 1982), pp. 61–84.

53. Nobuyuki Kaji, "Confucianism, the Forgotten Religion," *Japan Quarterly,* 38, no. 1 (1991):60.

54. Ibid., p. 62; emphasis added.

55. Michio Ozaki, "Introduction and Summary to the Survey of the Family," in *Summary of the National Opinion Survey of the Family in Japan,* University Research Center (Tokyo: Nihon University, 1989), pp. 17–18.

56. Ibid., pp. 18–19. A commentator on the results of this survey assigns more fundamental importance to the strong attachment to the ancestral grave, regardless of the age, stage in the life cycle, and type of family to which the respondent belongs. "What does the tomb mean for the Japanese? In this case it is a symbol for the continuity of the family." Kiyohide Seki, "Summary and Conclusion," *Summary of National Opinion Survey,* p. 121. See also Clark B. Offner, "Continuing Concern for the Departed," *Japanese Religions,* 11, no. 1 (1979):1–16, where it is reported that among some eighty-five households in Aichi Prefecture, the primary motivation for conducting the ancestral rites was to comfort and cheer the spirits of the dead and to express gratitude toward them. Far down on the list of reasons were fulfilling responsibility and showing respect.

57. Robert S. Ellwood and Richard Pilgrim, *Japanese Religion: A Cultural Perspective* (Englewood Cliffs, N.J.: Prentice-Hall, 1985), pp. 130–131. For further discussion, see Kunio Yanagita, *About Our Ancestors* (Tokyo: Japan Society for the Promotion of Science, 1970), a translation of *Senzo no hanashi* (1946) by Fanny Hagin Mayer. Various aspects of the problem are considered in Helen Hardacre, *Kurozumikyō and the New Religions of Japan* (Princeton: Princeton University Press, 1986), and Robert J. Smith, *Ancestor Worship in Contemporary Japan* (Stanford: Stanford University Press, 1974), pp. 1–38.

58. I am indebted to Jan Zeserson for providing the first two illustrations. The original texts of letters written to her by Japanese women friends have been edited.

59. Apropos of only one aspect of the problem of the translatability of terms having to do with the domestic ancestral rites in Japan, for example, see Clark B. Offner, " 'Worship' in the Bible and in Japan," *Japanese Missionary Bulletin,* 35 (1981):93–99. As a missionary, he frequently faced the problem of how to deal with the apparently inconsistent behavior of Japanese Christians who "worshiped" both God and their ancestors. Concluding that the two acts were not the same, he went to the Old and New Testaments for help in finding what "worship" meant. He discovered that there is no single biblical concept of worship at all, but rather a surprisingly large number of terms that reflect everything from attitudes of respect to adoration. A further complication is that there are several Japanese words—*ogamu, sūhai suru, matsuru*—that are used to describe the act of venerating the ancestral spirits.

8. Some Observations on the Transformation of
Confucianism (and Buddhism) in Japan

1. See three works by Max Weber: *The Religion of China* (New York: Free Press, 1951); *Ancient Judaism* (New York: Free Press, 1952); and *The Religion of India* (New York: Free Press, 1956); also S. N. Eisenstadt, "Innerweltiche Transzendenz und die Strukturierung der Welt. Max Webers Studie ueber China und die Gestalt der chinesischen Zivilization," in *Max Webers Studie ueber Konfuzianismus und Taoismus. Interpretation und Kritik,* ed. Wolfgang Schluchter (Frankfurt am Main: Suhrkamp, 1983), pp. 363–412.

2. See James B. Palais, *Politics and Policy in Traditional Korea* (Cambridge, Mass.: Harvard University Press, 1975); André Schonberg, *Social Structure and Political Order in Traditional Vietnam* (London: Sage Publications, 1970); Alexander Woodside, "History, Structure, and Revolution in Vietnam," *International Political Science Review,* 10, no. 2 (April 1989): 143–159, and Martina Deuchler, *The Confucian Transformation of Korea: A Study of Society and Ideology* (Cambridge, Mass.: Harvard University Press, 1992).

3. See Palais, *Politics and Policy in Traditional Korea.*

4. See Woodside, "History, Structure, and Revolution in Vietnam"; and Ngoc Huy Nguyen and Ta Van Tai, *The Le Code: Law in Traditional Vietnam* (Athens: Ohio University Press, 1982).

5. See Edwin O. Reischauer and John King Fairbank, *A History of East Asian Civilization,* vol. 1, *The Great Tradition* (Boston: Houghton Mifflin, 1960); and H. P. Varley, *Japanese Culture: A Short History* (Tokyo: Tuttle, 1973).

6. See Peter Nosco, ed., *Confucianism and Tokugawa Culture* (Princeton: Princeton University Press, 1988).

7. See Joseph Kitagawa, *On Understanding Japanese Religion* (Princeton: Princeton University Press, 1987).

8. Shigeru Matsumoto, *Motoori Norinaga, 1730–1801,* Harvard East Asian Series, no. 44 (Cambridge, Mass.: Harvard University Press, 1970), p. 180.

9. See, for instance, Takeshi Umehara, "Shinto and Buddhism in Japanese Culture," *Japanese Foundation Newsletter,* 15, no. 1 (1987): 1–7; and Hajime Nakamura, *Ways of Thinking of Eastern People: India, China, Tibet, Japan* (Honolulu: East-West Center Press, 1964), pp. 345–588.

10. See Joseph Kitagawa, "The Japanese Kokutai (National Community): History and Myth," *History of Religions,* 13, no. 3 (1974): 214–225.

11. M. Wahida, "Sacred Kingship in Early Japan: A Historical Introduction," *History of Religions,* 4, no. 4 (May 1976): 335–340.

12. Kitagawa, *On Understanding Japanese Religion,* pp. ii–iv.

13. See Minoru Sonoda, "The Religious Situation in Japan in Relation to Shinto," *Acta Asiatica,* 51 (1987): 1–21; Shoji Okada, "The Development of State Ritual in Ancient Japan," *Acta Asiatica,* 51 (1987): 22–41; and C. Blacker, "Two Shinto Myths: The Golden Age and the Chosen People," in

Themes and Theories in Japanese History: Essays in Memory of Richard Storry, ed. Sue Henny and Jean-Pierre Lehmann (Atlantic Highlands, N.J.: Athlone Press, 1988), pp. 64–78.

14. See Ryūsaku Tsunoda, Wm. Theodore de Bary, and Donald Keene, comps., *Sources of the Japanese Tradition* (New York: Columbia University Press, 1958).

15. See David S. Nivison and Arthur Wright, eds., *Confucianism in Action* (Stanford: Stanford University Press, 1959); and Arthur Wright, *Buddhism in Chinese History* (Stanford: Stanford University Press, 1959).

16. See Nosco, *Confucianism and Tokugawa Culture,* especially the introduction, "Neo-Confucianism and Tokugawa Discourse," pp. 3–26.

17. See I. F. Silber, "Opting Out in Theravada Buddhism and in Medieval Christianity: A Comparative Study of Monasticism as Alternative Structure," *Religion,* 15, no. 3 (1985): 251–278.

18. See S. C. Malik, ed., *Dissent, Protest, and Reform in Indian Civilization* (Simla: Indian Institute of Advanced Study, 1977); and M. S. A. Rao, ed., *Social Movements in India* (New Delhi: Mahonar, 1978–79).

19. See S. J. Tambiah, *World Conqueror and World Renouncer* (Cambridge: Cambridge University Press, 1976).

20. See C. Gaillat, "Jainism," in *The Encyclopedia of Religion* (New York: Macmillan and Free Press, 1987), 7:507–514; John B. Carman and Frederique A. Marglin, eds., *Purity and Auspiciousness in Indian Society* (Leiden: E. J. Brill, 1985); John B. Carman, "Bhakti," in *Encyclopedia of Religion,* 2:130–134; and Jayant Lele, ed., *Tradition and Modernity in Bhakti Movements* (Leiden: E. J. Brill, 1981).

21. See Paul Mus, "La Sociologie de George Gurvitch et l'Asie," *Cahiers internationaux de sociologie,* 43 (1967): 1–21; and Paul Mus, "Traditions anciennes et bouddhisme moderne," *Eranos Jahrbuch,* 32 (1968): 161–275.

22. See Thomas A. Metzger, *Escape from Predicament: Neo-Confucianism and China's Evolving Political Culture* (New York: Columbia University Press, 1977).

23. See Erik Zürcher, *The Buddhist Conquest of China* (Leiden: E. J. Brill, 1959); and Wright, *Buddhism in Chinese History.*

24. See Kwang-ching Liu, ed., *Orthodoxy in Late Imperial China* (Berkeley: University of California Press, 1990).

25. See Metzger, *Escape from Predicament;* and Wm. Theodore de Bary, *Neo-Confucian Orthodoxy and the Learning of the Mind-and-Heart* (New York: Columbia University Press, 1981).

26. See Kitagawa, *On Understanding Japanese Religion,* esp. chaps. 12, 13, and 15.

27. See J. H. Foard, "In Search of a Lost Reformation," *Japanese Journal of Religious Studies,* 7, no. 4 (1980): 284–286.

28. See Nosco, *Confucianism and Tokugawa Culture,* pp. 3–26.

29. See S. N. Eisenstadt, *Revolution and the Transformation of Societies* (New

York: Free Press, 1978); and Marius B. Jansen, "The Meiji Restoration," in *The Cambridge History of Japan,* vol. 5, *The Nineteenth Century* (Cambridge: Cambridge University Press, 1989), pp. 308–360.

9. *Confucianism in Contemporary Korea*

1. For modern studies of Korean Neo-Confucianism in English, see Wm. Theodore de Bary and JaHyun Kim Haboush, eds. *The Rise of Neo-Confucianism in Korea* (New York: Columbia University Press, 1985); Michael C. Kalton, *To Become a Sage* (New York: Columbia University Press, 1988); and Martina Deuchler, *The Confucian Transformation of Korea* (Cambridge, Mass.: Harvard University Press, 1992).
2. See *Chu Hsi's Family Rituals: A Twelfth-Century Chinese Manual for the Performance of Cappings, Weddings, Funerals, and Ancestral Rites,* trans., Patricia B. Ebrey (Princeton: Princeton University Press, 1991).
3. Shim Jae Hoon, "Confucianist South Korea Rapidly Converts to Christianity," *Far Eastern Economic Review,* April 19, 1984, p. 45. The statement is quoted from Rev. K. C. Suh, a former theology professor at Erwha Women's University.
4. *Lao Tzu (Tao-te Ching),* chap. 1, in *A Source Book in Chinese Philosophy,* trans. and comp. Wing-tsit Chan (Princeton: Princeton University Press, 1963), p. 139.

10. *The Reproduction of Confucian Culture in Contemporary Korea*

This essay is based on research carried out from 1986 to 1991, supported by a grant from the ASAN Foundation for the year 1986–87. A shorter version was presented at the Workshop on Confucian Dimensions of the Dynamics of Industrial East Asia, sponsored by the American Academy of Arts and Sciences, May 1991. I thank Tu Wei-ming for his kind comments and encouragement.

1. See Kwang-ok Kim, "A Study on the Political Manipulation of Elite Culture: Confucian Tradition in Local-Level Politics," in *Korean Studies, Its Tasks and Perspectives: Papers of the Fifth International Conference on Korean Studies* (Seongnam: Academy of Korean Studies, 1988).
2. See Yi-hum Yoon, "Social Change and Religious Response in Korea," in *Social Transformation and Korean Religions* (Seongnam: Academy of Korean Studies, 1987), p. 6.
3. See Kwang-ok Kim, "Sociopolitical Implications of the Resurgence of Ancestor Worship in Contemoporary Korea," in *Home Bound: Studies in East Asian Society,* ed. Chie Nakane and Chiao Chien (Tokyo: Center for East Asian Cultural Studies, 1992).
4. Yi-hum Yoon, "Social Change and Religious Response in Korea," p. 6.

5. See Kwang-ok Kim, "Sociopolitical Implications of the Resurgence of Ancestor Worship in Contemporary Korea."

6. In 1591, King Seonjo dispatched Kim Seong-il and Hwang Yun-kil to Japan in order to judge the recently emerged Toyotomi Hideyoshi. Hwang warned the king of the possibility of Japanese invasion, while Kim reported that Toyotomi was nothing but a barbarous leader of hooligans, and there was no reason to alarm the whole nation by preparing for military action against a possible invasion. Kim's report was accepted by the king, but the Japanese invaded Korea the following year. Park reminded people of this historical fact and used it as a rationale to criticize the literati tradition and to advocate the superiority of military elitism. He highly praised military leaders such as Admiral Yi Soonshin, General Kwon Yul, and General Kim Shimin, because they had sacrificed their lives to save the nation from the Japanese invasion.

7. Tu Wei-ming, *Way, Learning, and Politics: Essays on the Confucian Intellectual* (Singapore: Institute of East Asian Philosophies, 1989), p. 171.

11. State Confucianism and Its Transformation

1. Pye writes: "This new challenge is that of analyzing and explaining the crisis of authoritarianism that during the last decade has been sweeping the world, bringing into question both the legitimacy and the competence of all manner of authoritarian systems." Lucian W. Pye, "Political Science and the Crisis of Authoritarianism," *American Political Science Review,* 84, no. 1 (March 1990): 3.

2. Ernest Gellner, "Democracy and Industrialization," in *Readings in Social Evolution and Development,* ed. S. N. Eisenstadt (New York: Pergamon Press, 1970), p. 247.

3. John Dunn, *Western Political Theory in the Face of the Future* (Cambridge: Cambridge University Press, 1979), p. 2.

4. Ibid., p. 11.

5. For a detailed analysis of institutional Confucianism, see Ambrose Y. C. King, "The Role of Political Tradition in the Evolution of Democracy in China: Continuity and Change," paper presented at the International Conference on the Evolution of Democracy in China, jointly sponsored by the Pacific Cultural Foundation and the Carnegie Council on Ethics and International Affairs, New York, December 13–15, 1989.

6. Benjamin I. Schwartz, "The Primacy of Political Order in East Asian Societies: Some Preliminary Generalizations," in *Foundations and Limits of State Power in China,* ed. Stuart R. Schram (Hong Kong: Chinese University Press, 1987), p. 1.

7. Ibid., p. 2.

8. Max Weber, *The Religion of China,* trans. H. H. Gerth (New York: Free Press, 1964), p. 31.

9. Schwartz, "The Primacy of Political Order," p. 3.

10. Weber, *The Religion of China*, p. 31.
11. See Leon Vandermeesch, "An Enquiry into the Chinese Conception of the Law," in *The Scope of State Power in China*, ed. Stuart R. Schram (Hong Kong: Chinese University Press, 1985), pp. 3–25.
12. Lucian Pye, *Asian Power and Politics: The Cultural Dynamics of Authority* (Cambridge, Mass.: Harvard University Press, 1985), p. 27.
13. Tilemann Grimm, "State and Power in Juxtaposition: An Assessment of Ming Despotism," in Schram, *The Scope of State Power in China*, p. 39.
14. Hsü Fu-kuan, *Liang-Han ssu-hsiang shih* (The thought of two Han dynasties) (Taipei: Hsüeh-sheng shu-tien, 1978), pp. 257–258.
15. Jacques Gernet, "Introduction," in Schram, *The Scope of State Power in China*, p. xxxii.
16. Ch'ien Mu, *Kuo-shih hsin-lun* (New treatise on Chinese history) (Hong Kong: privately printed, 1953), p. 34.
17. Tu Wei-ming, "A Confucian Perspective on the Rise of Industrial East Asia," *Bulletin of the American Academy of Arts and Sciences,* 43, no. 6 (March 1990): 41.
18. Karl Bunger, "Concluding Remarks on Two Aspects of the Chinese Unitary State as Compared with the European State System," in Schram, *Foundations and Limits of State Power in China*, p. 316.
19. Chang Hao, "Neo-Confucian Moral Thought and Its Modern Legacy," *Journal of Asian Studies,* 39, no. 2 (February 1980): 260.
20. See Michael Loewe, "Attempts at Economic Co-ordination during the Western Han Dynasty," in Schram, *The Scope of State Power in China*, pp. 239–242.
21. Ibid.
22. See S. N. Eisenstadt, *The Political System of Empires* (New York: Free Press, 1969), pp. 365–368, 370.
23. See A. Doak Barnett, *Cadres, Bureaucracy, and Political Power in Communist China* (New York: Columbia University Press, 1967), pp. 428–429.
24. Weber, *The Religion of China*, pp. 95–96.
25. Ibid., p. 16.
26. Ibid., p. 13.
27. Thomas Metzger argues that the "political center" in imperial China was rather an "inhibited" one. See Thomas A. Metzger, "The Ideological Context of Modernization in the Republic of China," paper presented at the Eighteenth Sino-American Conference, Hoover Institution, Stanford University, June 8–11, 1989.
28. Neil H. Jacoby, *U.S. Aid to Taiwan: A Study of Foreign Aid, Self-Help, and Development* (New York: Frederick A. Praeger, 1966), p. 11.
29. See Hung-chao Tai, "The Kuomintang and Modernization in Taiwan," in *Authoritarian Politics in Modern Society: The Dynamics of Established One-Party Systems*, ed. S. P. Huntington and C. H. Moore (New York: Basic Books, 1970), pp. 424–433.

30. See Ambrose Y. C. King, *Chung-kuo min-tsu te k'un-ch'ing yü fa-chan* (The predicament and development of Chinese democracy) (Taipei: China Times Publishing Company, 1984), p. 2066.

31. Roy Hofheinz, Jr., and Kent E. Calder, *The Eastasia Edge* (New York: Basic Books, 1982), p. viii.

32. Talcott Parsons, *Structure and Process in Modern Societies* (New York: Free Press, 1960), p. 116.

33. Alice H. Amsden, "The State and Taiwan's Economic Development," in *Bringing the State Back In,* ed. Peter B. Evans, Dietrich Rueschemeyer, and Theda Skocpol (Cambridge: Cambridge University Press, 1985), p. 99.

34. See Ying-shih Yü, "Sun Yat-sen's Doctrine and Traditional Chinese Culture," in *Sun Yat-sen's Doctrine in the Modern World,* ed. Chu-yüan Cheng (Boulder, Colo.: Westview Press, 1989), pp. 79–102.

35. See A. James Gregor and Maria Hsia Chang, "The Thought of Sun Yat-sen in Comparative Perspective," in Cheng, *Sun Yat-sen's Doctrine in the Modern World,* pp. 130–131.

36. See Herbert H. Ma, "Republic of China," in *Constitutionalism in Asia,* ed. L. W. Beer (Berkeley: University of California Press, 1979), pp. 39–49.

37. Chu-yüan Cheng, "The Doctrine of People's Welfare: The Taiwan Experiment and Its Implications for the Third World," in Cheng, *Sun Yat-sen's Doctrine in the Modern World,* p. 253.

38. See John C. H. Fei, Gustor Ranis, and Shirley Kuo, *Growth with Equity: The Taiwan Case* (New York: Oxford University Press, 1979).

39. Schwartz, "The Primacy of Political Order," p. 7.

40. Lo Fang-chi, *Lun ssu hsiao-lung* (On the Four Mini-Dragons) (Hong Kong: Wide Angle Press, 1988), p. 32.

41. K. T. Li and M. C. Chen, *Chung-hua min-kuo ching-chi fa-chan ts'e-lüeh de ch'uan-mien fen-hsi* (A complete analysis of the developmental strategies of the economy of the Republic of China) (Taipei: Lien-ching ch'u-pan shih-yeh kung-ssu, 1987), p. 156.

42. Chiang Kai-shek, *Statement to All Members of the Kuomintang, September 1949* (Taipei: Chinese Cultural Services, 1954), pp. 22–23.

43. The development policies of the modernizing technocrats have been criticized for being based on instrumental rationality and neglecting other normative value issues. See C. S. Chen, *Kuo-chia cheng-ts'e chi-ch'i p'i-p'an te kung-lun* (Public discourse on national policies and its critique) (Taipei: Center of National Policy Studies, 1988).

44. See Samuel P. S. Ho, *Economic Development of Taiwan* (New Haven: Yale University Press, 1978), pp. 116–120.

45. *Kuo-fu ch'üan-chi* (The collected works of Sun Yat-sen), rev. ed. (Taipei: Kuomintang Central Executive Committee, 1981), 1:517.

46. Hung-chao Tai, "The Kuomintang and Modernization in Taiwan," p. 431.

47. U.S. Comptroller General, "Report to the Congress of the United States: Examination of Economic and Technical Assistance Program for the Gov-

ernment of Republic of China (Taiwan), Fiscal Years 1955–1957," mimeographed (August 1958), p. 22; quoted ibid.

48. Jacoby, *U.S. Aid to Taiwan*, pp. 137–138.

49. Chu-yüan Cheng, "The Doctrine of People's Welfare: The Taiwan Experiment and Its Implication for the Third World," in Cheng, *Sun Yat-sen's Doctrine in the Modern World*, p. 252.

50. The relationship between type of political system and economic growth is discussed in Stephan Haggard, *Pathways from the Periphery: The Politics of Growth in the Newly Industrializing Countries* (Ithaca, N.Y.: Cornell University Press, 1990), pp. 254–270.

51. John Mingsien Lee, "Political Change in Taiwan, 1949–1974: A Study of the Processes of Democratic and Integrative Change with Focus on the Role of Government" (Ph.D. diss., University of Tennessee, 1975), p. 211.

52. Amsden, "The State and Taiwan's Economic Development," p. 101.

53. Ibid.

54. See Wei Yung, *Hsiang wen-ting ho-hsieh chi ch'uang-chien te she-hui mai-ching* (March toward a stable, harmonious, and innovative society: an analysis of the trend of political development based on the results of six public opinion surveys), Republic of China, government publication, May 5, 1986.

55. Thomas Gold, *State and Society in the Taiwan Miracle* (New York: M. E. Sharpe, 1986), p. 90.

56. Hsiao Hsin-huang, "Development, Class Transformation, Social Movements and the Changing State-Society Relations in Taiwan," paper presented at the "Eighteenth Sino-American Conference," Hoover Institute, Stanford University, June 8–11, 1989.

57. Alfred Stepan, "State Power and the Strength of Civil Society in the Southern Cone of Latin America," in Evans, Rueschemeyer, and Skocpol, *Bringing the State Back In*, p. 337.

58. Thomas Gold writes: "In retrospect, the Chung-li Incident offers a unique key to understanding both the success and the shortcomings of Taiwan's development strategy wherein a strong authoritarian state guides and participates in rapid economic growth while suppressing the political activities of the social forces it has generated in the process." Gold, *State and Society in the Taiwan Miracle*, p. 3.

59. Ramon H. Myers, "Political Theory and Recent Political Developments in the Republic of China," *Asian Survey*, 27, no. 9 (1987): 1003–22.

60. A comprehensive discussion of the reasons for these social movements can be found in Mau-kuai Michael Chang, *She-hui yün-tung chi cheng-chih chuan-hua* (Social movements and political transformation) (Taipei: Center of National Policy Studies, 1989), pp. 20–45.

61. *Chung-yang jih-pao* (The Central Daily), November 12, 1986, p. 2; translated in Myers, "Political Theory," p. 1007.

62. Hu Fu and You Ying-long, "Hsüan-min te t'ou-p'iao tung-chi" (The voting

motives of the electorate), *Journal of Social Science* (Taipei), 33 (October 1985): 1–34.

63. Hu Fu, "Min-chung cheng-chih ts'an-yü ti t'ai-tu" (The people's attitudes toward political participation), paper presented at the Symposium on Basic Research on Taiwan's Social Change, organized by Academia Sinica and National Taiwan University, Taipei, August 28–30, 1987.

64. Metzger, "The Ideological Context of Modernization," p. 15.

65. Ibid. Also consult, Thomas Metzger, "The Chinese Reconciliation of Moral-Sacred Values with Modern Pluralism: Political Discourse in the ROC, 1949–1989," in *Two Societies in Opposition: The Republic of China and the People's Republic of China after Forty Years,* ed. Ramon H. Myers (Stanford: Hoover Institution Press, 1991), p. 10.

66. Pye, *Asian Power and Politics,* pp. 245–246.

67. Daniel Bell, "American Exceptionalism Revisited: The Role of a Civil Society," *Dialogue,* 1 (1990): 9–14. Bertrand Badie and Pierre Birnbaum consider the United States together with Great Britain as prime examples of "government by civil society," characterized by "the relative weakness of the state and the relatively low level of state autonomy." Bertrand Badie and Pierre Birnbaum, *The Sociology of the State,* trans. A. Goldhammer (Chicago: University of Chicago Press, 1983), p. 129.

68. Gernet, "Introduction," p. xxxii.

69. Bunger, "Concluding Remarks on Two Aspects of the Chinese Unitary State," p. 319.

70. Schram, *Foundations and Limits of State Power in China,* pp. 322–323.

71. See Ambrose Y. C. King, "Max Weber and the Question of Development of the Modern State in China," paper presented at the International Conference on Max Weber and the Modernization of China, sponsored by the Institut für Soziologie der Universität Heidelberg, Bad Homburg, Germany, July 23–27, 1990.

72. Metzger and Myers, *Two Societies,* p. xxiv.

12. Civil Society in Taiwan

1. Tu Wei-ming, "The Confucian Dimension of the East Asian Development Model," paper presented at the Conference on Democracy in China, Syracuse, N.Y., April 27–29, 1990. These habits, which may not be conscious, include learning for the sake of the self, which (the self) is at the center of relationships; society as a fiduciary community predicated on internal cohesiveness; the harmonizing of private interest and the public good; duty consciousness, which increases with one's responsibility; the expectation that leaders will act as moral exemplars; social responsibility of the cultural elite; and meritocratic hierarchy.

2. Shlomo Avineri, *Hegel's Theory of the Modern State* (Cambridge: Cambridge University Press, 1972), p. 147.

3. Karl Marx and Friedrich Engels, *The German Ideology* (New York: International Publishers, 1970), p. 57.

4. See Jacques Texier, "Gramsci, Theoretician of the Superstructures," in *Gramsci and Marxist Theory,* ed. Chantal Mouffe (London: Routledge and Kegan Paul, 1979), pp. 48–79, esp. p. 71.

5. Antonio Gramsci, *Selections from the Prison Notebooks,* ed. and trans. Quintin Hoare and Geoffrey Nowell Smith (New York: International Publishers, 1971), p. 12.

6. David Forgass, ed., *An Antonio Gramsci Reader* (New York: Schocken Books, 1988), p. 224.

7. Gramsci, *Selections from the Prison Notebooks,* pp. 229–239.

8. Jerome Karabel, "Revolutionary Contradictions: Antonio Gramsci and the Problem of Intellectuals," *Politics and Society,* 6 (1976): 123–172.

9. Jürgen Habermas, *The Structural Transformation of the Public Sphere* (Cambridge, Mass.: The MIT Press, 1989), p. 27.

10. Guillermo O'Donnell and Philippe C. Schmitter, *Transitions from Authoritarian Rule: Tentative Conclusions about Uncertain Democracies* (Baltimore: Johns Hopkins University Press, 1986), pp. 48–56.

11. Ibid., p. 49.

12. John Keane, "Introduction," in *Civil Society and the State,* ed. John Keane (London: Verso, 1988), pp. 13–29.

13. See the special issue of *Modern China,* 19, no. 2 (April 1993), a symposium titled " 'Public Sphere'/'Civil Society' in China?" See also two survey articles, William T. Rowe, "The Public Sphere in Modern China," *Modern China,* 16, no. 3 (July 1990): 309–329; and David Strand, "Protest in Beijing: Civil Society and Public Sphere in China," *Problems of Communism,* 39, no. 3 (May–June 1990): 1–19. Three monographs are Mary Backus Rankin, *Elite Activism and Political Transformation in China: Zhejiang Province, 1865–1911* (Stanford: Stanford University Press, 1986); William T. Rowe, *Hankow: Commerce and Society in a Chinese City, 1796–1889* (Stanford: Stanford University Press, 1984); and David Strand, *Rickshaw Beijing* (Berkeley: University of California Press, 1989).

14. Mayfair Mei-hui Yang, "Between State and Society: The Construction of Corporateness in a Chinese Socialist Factory," *Australian Journal of Chinese Affairs,* 22 (July 1989): 35–36. Hegel saw civil society as coming between the family and the state. But in traditional China clans and lineages, with their strong corporate identity, should be included as constituent elements of latent civil society. This would accord with the Chinese term *minjian shehui,* but not *shimin shehui,* with its connotation of market and *civis,* the latter more akin to the Hegel-Marx usage of civil society. In Taiwan *minjian shehui* has been used most commonly in discussions about civil society. See Shi Yuankang, "Teshuxing yuanze yu xiandaixing: Heigeer lun shimin shehui" (The principle of particularity and modernity: Hegel on civil society), *Dangdai* (Contemporary), March 1, 1990, pp. 20–28; and He Fang, "Cong

'minjian shehui' lun renmin minzhu" (From 'civil society,' discuss people's democracy), ibid., pp. 39–52. These are part of a special issue on civil society. See also a special issue of *Zhongguo luntan* (China Tribune), September 25, 1989, pp. 6–47. A less frequently used translation is *gongmin shehui,* which connotes "citizen."

15. Gary G. Hamilton, "Regional Associations and the Chinese City: A Comparative Perspective," *Comparative Studies in Society and History,* 21, no. 3 (July 1979): 346–361. See also Rowe, *Hankow;* and Strand, *Rickshaw Beijing.*

16. Wm. Theodore de Bary, *The Trouble with Confucianism* (Cambridge, Mass.: Harvard University Press, 1991), p. 95.

17. This discussion draws on Charles O. Hucker, "Confucianism and the Chinese Censorial System," in *Confucianism in Action,* ed. David S. Nivison and Arthur F. Wright (Stanford: Stanford University Press, 1959), pp. 182–208, esp. pp. 193–199.

18. Elizabeth J. Perry and Ellen V. Fuller, "China's Long March to Democracy," *World Policy Journal* (Fall 1991): 666.

19. Ibid., p. 667.

20. Lin Hengdao, ed., *Taiwanshi* (History of Taiwan) (Taipei: Zhongwen Tushu, 1977).

21. Wen-hsiung Hsü, "Frontier Social Organization and Social Disorder in Ch'ing Taiwan," in *China's Island Frontier,* ed. Ronald G. Knapp (Honolulu: University Press of Hawaii and the Research Corporation of the University of Hawaii, 1980), p. 89.

22. Alexander Chien-chung Yin, "Voluntary Associations and Rural-Urban Migration," in *The Anthropology of Taiwanese Society,* ed. Emily Martin Ahern and Hill Gates (Stanford: Stanford University Press, 1981), pp. 319–337.

23. Harry J. Lamley, "Private Conflict: The Hsieh-tou Phenomenon in Taiwan and South China," paper prepared for the Conference on Taiwan in Chinese History, Asilomar, Calif., 1972.

24. Huang Fusan, *Wufeng linjia de xingqi* (The rise of the Wufeng Lin family) (Taipei: Zili Wanbao, 1987); Johanna Menzel Meskill, *A Chinese Pioneer Family* (Princeton: Princeton University Press, 1979).

25. Chen Ch'ing-chih, "Japanese Socio-Political Control in Taiwan, 1895–1945" (Ph.D. diss., Harvard University, 1973); Edward I-te Chen, "Japanese Colonialism in Korea and Formosa: A Comparison of the Systems of Political Control," *Harvard Journal of Asiatic Studies,* 30 (1970): 126–158.

26. Thomas B. Gold, "Colonial Origins of Taiwanese Capitalism," in *Contending Approaches to the Political Economy of Taiwan,* ed. Edwin A. Winckler and Susan Greenhalgh (Armonk: M. E. Sharpe, 1988), pp. 101–117.

27. Lin Hengdao, *Taiwanshi;* Edward I-te Chen, "Formosan Political Movements under Japanese Colonial Rule, 1914–1937," *Journal of Asian Studies,* 31, no. 3 (May 1972): 477–497; Hsu Shikai, *Nihon tochika no Taiwan* (Taiwan under Japanese rule) (Tokyo: Tokyo University Press, 1972).

28. For details, see Hung-mao Tien, *The Great Transition: Political and Social Change in the Republic of China* (Stanford: Hoover Institution Press, 1989), esp. chaps. 4–5.

29. Ralph Clough, *Island China* (Cambridge, Mass.: Harvard University Press, 1978), pp. 102–103.

30. Hung-mao Tien, *The Great Transition*, chap. 3. Also, Wen Chongyi, "Shequ quanli jiegou de bianqian" (Change in the structure of community power), in *Woguo shehui de bianqian yu fazhan* (Our nation's social change and development), ed. Zhu Cenlou (Taipei: Dongda Books), pp. 289–355. Missionaries—who fostered civil society in some other countries—tended to be very close to the regime, headed by the avowedly Christian Chiangs. The Presbyterians were an exception, having a long-term concern for human rights and a proindependence tilt. See Marc J. Cohen, *Taiwan at the Crossroads* (Washington, D.C.: Asia Resource Center, 1988), pp. 190–206.

31. Fan Heyan, "Liangge shinian he wushuge shinian" (Two decades and countless decades), in *Gongshang xiejin ershinian* (Twenty years of promoting industry and commerce) (Taipei: Chinese Association for the Promotion of Industry and Commerce, 1971), pp. 12–19.

32. Hung-mao Tien, *The Great Transition*, chap. 8.

33. Chantal Mouffe, "Hegemony and Ideology in Gramsci," in Mouffe, *Gramsci and Marxist Theory*, pp. 194–195.

34. Ts'ai Ling and Ramon H. Myers, "Out of the Ashes of Defeat: Revitalizing the Kuomintang in Taiwan, 1950–1952," Working Papers in International Studies, I-91–6, Hoover Institution, 1991.

35. See C. L. Chiou, "Politics of Alienation and Polarization: Taiwan's *Tangwai* in the 1980s," *Bulletin of Concerned Asian Scholars*, 18, no. 3 (July–September 1986): 16–28; George H. Kerr, *Formosa Betrayed* (Boston: Houghton Mifflin, 1965); Douglas Mendel, *The Politics of Formosan Nationalism* (Berkeley: University of California Press, 1970).

36. Chen Guuying, "The Reform Movement among Intellectuals in Taiwan since 1970," *Bulletin of Concerned Asian Scholars*, 14, no. 3 (July–September 1982): 32–47; Mab Huang, *Intellectual Ferment for Political Reforms in Taiwan, 1971–1973*, Michigan Papers in Chinese Studies, no. 28 (Ann Arbor: Center for Chinese Studies, University of Michigan, 1976).

37. Ch'ien Tuan-sheng, *The Government and Politics of China* (Cambridge, Mass.: Harvard University Press, 1961).

38. See Joseph Bosco, "Faction versus Ideology: Mobilization Strategies in Taiwan's Elections," *China Quarterly*, no. 137 (March 1994): 28–62.

39. Cohen, *Taiwan at the Crossroads*, chap. 14. Members of many of these groups returned to the island after the end of martial law. Gordon Chang, leader of WUFI, was arrested on charges of having advocated independence in 1970 when he landed in Taipei on December 6, 1991.

40. See Zhu Cenlou, *Woguo shehui de bianqian*; and Hsin-Huang Michael Hsiao, Wei-Yuan Cheng, and Hou-Sheng Chan, eds., *Taiwan: A Newly In-*

dustrialized State (Taipei: Department of Sociology, National Taiwan University, 1989), for empirical data.

41. Thomas B. Gold, "Taiwan in 1988: The Transition to a Post-Chiang World," in *China Briefing, 1989,* ed. Anthony J. Kane (Boulder, Colo.: Westview Press, 1980), pp. 87–108.

42. For more details, consult Tun-jen Cheng, "Democratizing the Quasi-Leninist Regime in Taiwan," *World Politics,* 41, no. 4 (July 1989): 471–499; Tun-jen Cheng and Stephan Haggard, eds., *Political Change in Taiwan* (Boulder, Colo.: Lynne Rienner Publishers, 1992); Kuo Tai-chün and Ramon H. Myers, "The Great Transition: Political Change and the Prospects for Democracy in the Republic of China on Taiwan," *Asian Affairs,* 15, no. 3 (Fall 1988): 115–133; Hung-Mao Tien, *The Great Transition;* and Yu-shan Wu, "Marketization of Politics: The Taiwan Experience," *Asian Survey,* 29, no. 4 (April 1989): 382–400.

43. On the rise of the private sector, see Karl James Fields, "Developmental Capitalism and Industrial Organization: Business Groups and the State in Korea and Taiwan" (Ph.D. diss., University of California, Berkeley, 1990); Thomas B. Gold, "Entrepreneurs, Multinationals, and the State," in Winckler and Greenhalgh, *Contending Approaches to the Political Economy of Taiwan,* pp. 175–205; Susan Greenhalgh, "Families and Networks in Taiwan's Economic Development," ibid., pp. 224–245; and Ichiro Numazaki, "Networks of Taiwanese Big Business," *Modern China,* 12, no. 4 (October 1986): 487–534.

44. Council for Economic Planning and Development, Republic of China, *Taiwan Statistical Data Book, 1991* (Taipei, 1991), pp. 86, 89.

45. Contrast the situation in the 1960s with that in the mid-1980s. See Allan B. Cole, "Political Roles of Taiwanese Enterprisers," *Asian Survey,* 7, no. 9 (September 1967): 645–653; Karl Fields, "The Anatomy of a Financial Scandal: The Rise and Fall of the Cathay Business Group," paper presented at the Center for Chinese Studies Regional Seminar, University of California, Berkeley, April 27, 1991; cited with permission. Scions of capitalist families (mainlanders and Taiwanese) ran on the KMT ticket in the 1992 Legislative Yüan elections as part of Chairman Lee Teng-hui's strategy of seeking support from the business community. This, however, split the party, driving some members, mostly mainlanders, to establish their own party, the New party, in August 1993.

46. Hung-mao Tien, *Brothers in Arms: Political Struggle and Party Competition in Taiwan's Evolving Democracy* (New York: Asia Society, 1991), p. 5.

47. On two competitive campaigns, see Ramon H. Myers, "Political Theory and Recent Political Developments in the Republic of China," *Asian Survey,* 27, no. 9 (September 1987): 1003–22; and John F. Copper, "Taiwan's 1989 National Election," *Journal of Northeast Asian Studies,* 9, no. 1 (Spring 1990): 22–40.

48. Two notable think tanks are the Twenty-First Century Foundation and the Institute for National Policy Research.

49. There is an expanding literature on these movements. For overviews, see Chang Mau-kuei, *Shehui yundong yu zhengzhi zhuanhua* (Social movements and political transformation) (Taipei: Guojia zhengce ziliao zhongxin, 1989); Mau-kuei Michael Chang, "Social Movements and the Transformation of State-Society Relations: Taiwan in the Late Eighties," paper presented at the Annual Meeting of the American Sociological Association, Washington, D.C., August 5–10, 1990; and Hsin-huang Michael Hsiao, "Emerging Social Movements and the Rise of a Demanding Civil Society in Taiwan," *Australian Journal of Chinese Affairs*, 24 (July 1990): 163–179. For detailed studies of specific movements, see Gwo-Shyong Shieh, "Public Interest Groups, Corporatism, and the State: The Consumerism Movement in Taiwan" (M.A. thesis, University of Hawaii, 1986); Hsü Mu-tsu, *Wuerling shijian diaocha baogaoshu* (Investigative report on the May Twentieth incident) (Taipei: Shehui yundong guancha xiaozu, 1988); on farmers' protests, Hsin-Huang Michael Hsiao, "Political Liberalization and the Farmer's Movement in Taiwan," paper presented at the Conference on Democracy, Peace, and Development in East Asia, Kauai, August 19–21, 1990; James Reardon-Anderson, *Pollution, Politics, and Foreign Investment in Taiwan: The Lukang Rebellion* (Armonk, N.Y.: M. E. Sharpe, 1992); and Ku Yen-lin, "The Feminist Movement in Taiwan, 1972–87," *Bulletin of Concerned Asian Scholars*, 21, no. 1 (January–March 1989): 12–22.

50. On this date KMT troops liquidated the Taiwanese elite and thousands of others. See Lai Tse-han, Ramon H. Myers, and Wei Wou, *A Tragic Beginning: The Taiwan Uprising of February 28, 1947* (Stanford: Stanford University Press, 1991).

51. An exhaustive study on the buildup to this conference has been done by Ts'ai Ling and Ramon H. Myers, "Manichaean Suspicions and the Spirit of Reconciliation: Currents of Public Opinion in Taiwan on the Eve of the 1990 Conference on the Republic of China's Destiny," *American Asian Review*, 9, no. 2 (Summer 1991): 1–41.

52. For discussions of the "inhibited political center," see Thomas A. Metzger and Ramon H. Myers, "Introduction," in *Two Societies in Opposition: The Republic of China and the People's Republic of China after Forty Years*, ed. Ramon H. Myers (Stanford: Hoover Institution Press, 1991), pp. xiii–xiv; and Lü Ya-li, "Political Modernization in the ROC: The Kuomintang and the Inhibited Political Center," ibid., pp. 111–126.

53. Such civility did not characterize behavior in the newly constituted National Assembly and Legislative Yüan, where fistfights, furniture smashing, and other outbursts have occurred frequently, and receive wide publicity. In fact, some opposition politicians argue that they engage in such shenanigans to some extent to raise their profile with the public.

54. Ann Swidler, "Culture in Action: Symbols and Strategies," *American Sociological Review,* 51, no. 2 (April 1986): 273–286.

13. The Transformation of Confucianism in the Post-Confucian Era

1. See Peter L. Berger, "Secularity—West and East," paper presented at the Kokugakuin University Centennial Symposium on Cultural Identity and Modernization in Asian Countries, September 11–13, 1983.
2. See Edward A. Tiryakian, ed., *The Global Crisis: Sociological Analyses and Responses* (Leiden: E. J. Brill, 1984).
3. See Ezra Vogel, *Japan as Number One* (Cambridge, Mass.: Harvard University Press, 1979); Roy Hofheinz, Jr., and Kent E. Calder, *The Eastasia Edge* (New York: Basic Books, 1982).
4. Vogel, *Japan as Number One;* Hofheinz and Calder, *The Eastasia Edge.*
5. See Herman Kahn, *World Economic Development: 1979 and Beyond* (London: Croom Helm, 1979); S. G. Redding and G. L. Hicks, "The Story of the East-Asia Economic Miracle: Part II: The Culture Connection," *Euro-Asia Business Review,* 2, no. 4 (1983): 18–22; S. G. Redding and G. L. Hicks, *Culture, Causation, and Chinese Management* (Hong Kong: Department of Management Studies, University of Hong Kong, 1983).
6. Thomas A. Metzger, *Escape from Predicament* (New York: Columbia University Press, 1977), p. 235.
7. Talcott Parsons, "Some Reflections on the Institutional Framework of Economic Development," in *Structure and Process in Modern Societies,* ed. Talcott Parsons (New York: Free Press, 1960), p. 99.
8. Ibid., pp. 102ff.; Robert Bellah, "Reflection on the Protestant Ethic and Modernization," in *The Protestant Ethic and Modernization: A Comparative View,* ed. S. N. Eisenstadt (New York: Basic Books, 1968), pp. 245–247.
9. See Yu-sheng Lin, *The Crisis of Chinese Consciousness: Radical Anti-Traditionalism in the May Fourth Era* (Madison: University of Wisconsin Press, 1979).
10. Lucian W. Pye, *Asian Power and Politics: The Cultural Dimension of Authority* (Cambridge, Mass.: Harvard University Press, 1985), p. 56.
11. See C. K. Yang, "Introduction," in Max Weber, *The Religion of China: Confucianism and Taoism* (New York: Free Press, 1968), pp. xiii–xliii.
12. See S. N. Eisenstadt, "The Protestant Ethic Thesis in an Analytical and Comparative Framework," in Eisenstadt, *The Protestant Ethic and Modernization,* pp. 7–8.
13. Ibid., p. 8.
14. Stephen Boyden et al., *The Ecology of a City and Its People* (Canberra: Australian National University Press, 1981), pp. 123–125.
15. See M. H. Bond and A. Y. C. King, "Coping with the Threat of Westerni-

zation in Hong Kong," *International Journal of Intercultural Relations,* 9 (1986): 351–364.

16. See Robert J. Lifton, "Cultural Perspectives: The Fate of Filial Piety," in *Thought Reform and the Psychology of Totalism* (New York: Penguin Books, 1961), chap. 19, pp. 410–422.

17. See R. E. Mitchell, *Family Life in Urban Hong Kong,* 2 vols. (Taipei: Orient Cultural Service, 1972).

18. S. K. Lau, "Utilitarianistic Familism: The Basis of Political Stability," in *Social Life and Development in Hong Kong,* ed. Y. C. King and Rance P. L. Lee (Hong Kong: Chinese University of Hong Kong Press, 1981), p. 204.

19. Marion J. Levy, *The Family Revolution in Modern China* (Cambridge, Mass.: Harvard University Press, 1949), p. 345.

20. Ambrose Y. C. King and Peter J. Man, "The Role of Small Factory in Economic Development," in *Hong Kong: Economic, Social, and Political Studies in Development,* ed. Tzong-biau Lin, Rance P. L. Lee, and Udo-Ernst Simonis (White Plains, N.Y.: M. E. Sharpe, 1979), pp. 31–63.

21. V. F. S. Sit, S. L. Wong, and T. S. Kiang, *Small Industry in a Laissez-Faire Economy: A Hong Kong Case Study* (Hong Kong: Centre of Asian Studies, University of Hong Kong, 1979), p. 353.

22. Victor Mok, *The Organization and Management in Kwun Tong* (Hong Kong: Social Research Centre, Chinese University of Hong Kong Press, 1974), p. 48.

23. J. L. Espy, "The Strategy of Chinese Industrial Enterprise in Hong Kong" (B.A. thesis, Harvard University, 1970), p. 174.

24. Weber, *The Religion of China,* p. 236.

25. Ibid., pp. 236–237.

26. C. K. Yang, "Introduction," in Weber, *The Religion of China,* p. xxvi.

27. S. N. Eisenstadt, "This Worldly Transcendentalism and the Structuring of the World: Weber's 'Religion of China' and the Format of Chinese History and Civilization," in *Max Weber in Asian Studies,* ed. Andreas E. Buss (Leiden: E. J. Brill, 1985), p. 48.

28. Boyden et al., *The Ecology of a City and Its People,* p. 47.

29. Weber, *The Religion of China,* p. 242.

30. James Hayes, "Hong Kong: Tale of Two Cities," in *Hong Kong: The Interaction of Tradition and Life in the Towns,* ed. Marjorie Topley (Hong Kong: Hong Kong Branch of the Royal Asiatic Society, 1975), p. 3.

31. Maurice Freedman, "The Family in China, Past and Present," in *The Study of Chinese Society: Essays by Maurice Freedman,* ed. G. W. Skinner (Stanford: Stanford University Press, 1979), p. 250.

32. E. J. Ryan, "The Value System of a Chinese Community in Java" (Ph.D. diss., Harvard University, 1961); quoted in Gordon Redding and Gilbert Y. Y. Wong, "The Psychology of Chinese Organizational Behaviour," in *The Psychology of the Chinese People,* ed. Michael H. Bond (Hong Kong: Oxford University Press, 1986), pp. 267–295.

33. Weber, *The Religion of China,* pp. 245–246.

34. Boyden et al., *The Ecology of a City and Its People,* p. 284.

35. See W. L. Chau and W. K. Chan, "A Study of Job Satisfaction of Workers in Local Factories of Chinese, Western, and Japanese Ownership," *Hong Kong Manager,* 20 (1984): 9–14.

36. Reinhard Bendix, *Max Weber: An Intellectual Portrait* (New York: Anchor Books, 1962), pp. 116–119.

37. Weber, *The Religion of China,* p. 135.

38. See D. C. McClellend, "Motivational Patterns in Southeast Asia with Special Reference to the Chinese Case," *Journal of Social Issues,* 19 (1963): 6–19.

39. David Y. F. Ho, "Chinese Patterns of Socialization: A Critical Review," in Bond, *The Psychology of the Chinese People,* p. 25.

40. Boyden et al., *The Ecology of a City and Its People,* p. 295.

41. In his small-scale study of occupational prestige in Hong Kong, R. L. Moore finds that "shipping magnate" and "commercial manager" top the list, ahead of "colonial secretary" and "professor." See R. L. Moore, "Modernization and Westernization in Hong Kong: Patterns of Cultural Change in an Urban Setting" (Ph.D. diss., University of California, Riverside, 1981); quoted in Wong Siu-lun, "Modernization and Sinic Tradition: Reflections on the Case of Hong Kong," paper presented at the Twenty-fifth Annual Meeting of the American Association for Chinese Studies, Santa Barbara, November 4–6, 1983.

42. S. L. Alatas, "Religion and Modernization in Southeast Asia," in *Modernization in South-East Asia,* ed. Hans-Dieter Evers (London: Oxford University Press, 1973), p. 163.

43. By "withdrawal of status respect" Hagen means that in a transition from a traditional state to one of continuing economic development, an important factor initiating change is a historical shift that causes some groups that previously had a respected place in the social hierarchy to feel that they are no longer valued. See Everett E. Hagen, *On the Theory of Social Change* (Homewood, Ill.: Dorsey Press, 1962).

44. Boyden et al., *The Ecology of a City and Its People,* p. 57.

45. King and Man, "The Role of Small Factory in Economic Development," p. 54.

46. S. K. Lau, "Employment Relations in Hong Kong: Traditional Modern?," in Lin et al., *Hong Kong: Economic, Social, and Political Studies in Development,* p. 77.

47. Wong Siu-lun, "Modernization and Sinic Tradition," pp. 5–15.

48. Freedman, "The Family in China, Past and Present," p. 242.

49. B. F. Hoselitz, "Economic Growth and Development: Non-Economic Factors in Economic Development," in *Political Development and Social Change,* ed. Jason L. Findle and Richard W. Goble (New York: John Wiley and Sons, 1966), pp. 190–191.

50. See Bond and King, "Coping with the Threat of Westernization in Hong Kong," p. 362.

51. Marjorie Topley, "Some Basic Conceptions and Their Traditional Relationship to Society," in *Some Traditional Chinese Ideas and Conceptions in Hong Kong Social Life Today*, ed. Marjorie Topley (Hong Kong: Hong Kong Branch of the Royal Asiatic Society, 1966), p. 19.

52. Lau, "Utilitarianistic Familism: The Basis of Political Stability," p. 201.

53. S. K. Lau, "Chinese Familism in an Urban-Industrial Setting: The Case of Hong Kong," *Journal of Marriage and the Family*, 43, no. 4 (November 1981): 990.

54. The new familial utilitarian values presented in this essay existed mainly among distant relatives. The relationships among close family members are based more on affective bonds than on instrumental considerations.

14. Promoting Confucianism for Socioeconomic Development

1. See Benjamin Higgins, *Economic Development: Principles, Problems, and Policies* (London: Constable, 1968), chap. 12.

2. A clear example is the study by the eminent development economist P. T. Bauer, *The Rubber Industry* (Cambridge, Mass.: Harvard University Press, 1948), which is a classic on the subject. In retracing his experience, Bauer in the early 1980s repeated what has been largely taboo in the literature: "Many rubber estates kept records . . . The output of the Chinese was usually more than double that of the Indians, with all of them using the same simple equipment of tapping knife, latex cup, and the bucket. There were similar or even wider differences between Chinese, Indian, and Malay small-holders . . . The differences in their performance could not be explained in terms of differences in human capital formation." Gerald M. Meier and Dudley Seers, eds., *Pioneers in Development* (New York: Oxford University Press, 1984), p. 32.

3. Herman Kahn, *World Economic Development: 1979 and Beyond* (London: Croom Helm, 1979), p. 2.

4. See Michio Morishima, *Why Has Japan Succeeded? Western Technology and Japanese Ethos* (London: Cambridge University Press, 1982); and Harry T. Oshima, *Economic Growth in Monsoon Asia: A Comparative Survey* (Tokyo: Tokyo University Press, 1987).

5. Roderick MacFarquhar, "The Post-Confucian Challenge," *Economist*, February 9, 1980.

6. See Lawrence J. Lau, "A Comparative Analysis of Economic Development Experience in Chinese Societies," paper presented at the International Symposium on Economic Development in Chinese Societies: Models and Experiences, organized by the Hong Kong Economic Association, December 18–20, 1986.

7. See, for example, Roy Hofheinz, Jr., and Kent E. Calder, *The Eastasia Edge* (New York: Basic Books, 1982).

8. See, for example, Hung-chao Tai, ed., *Confucianism and Economic Development: An Oriental Alternative?* (Washington, D.C.: Washington Institute Press, 1989).

9. Peter L. Berger and Hsin-Huang Michael Hsiao, *In Search of an East Asian Development Model* (New Brunswick, N.J.: Transaction Books, 1988), p. 19.

10. The Singapore government does not believe in publicizing its high GNP, which would lead to the forced graduation of the Singapore economy into developed country status with a loss of some trade concession benefits. Thus, Singapore introduced an unconventional concept of "indigenous GNP," on the grounds that part of its GNP has been generated by foreign multinational corporations, which should be separated from that part of the GNP created by the resident population. Thus, the per capita indigenous GNP in 1990 worked out to be S$18,437, or U.S. $10,535, which is still quite high.

11. See *Economic Survey of Singapore, 1990* (Singapore: Ministry of Trade and Industry, 1991).

12. Ibid., p. 142.

13. Thus, the Oxford economist I. M. D. Little, in drawing lessons from the successful East Asian development experiences, crisply concludes that "everything can be attributed to good policies and the people." I. M. D. Little, "The Experience and Causes of Rapid Labor-Intensive Development in Korea, Taiwan Province, Hong Kong, and Singapore and the Possibilities of Emulation," in *Export-Led Industrialisation and Development,* ed. A. R. Kahn (Geneva: ILO, 1981), p. 43.

14. Thus, it was admitted by Dr. Goh Keng Swee, commonly regarded as the chief architect of Singapore's economic success, that "the policies to induce the growth of manufacturing industries in Singapore excited much comment, in Singapore, when they were introduced. Later they attracted international attention. But our policies were not novel, innovative, or path-breaking . . . The general policy line follows what had already been attempted in many developing countries. What was different was perhaps that our policies produced results. This could be because they were implemented more thoroughly, and with a high standard of integrity." Goh Keng Swee, *The Economics of Modernization and Other Essays* (Singapore: Asia Pacific Press, 1972), p. 101.

15. This has been candidly conceded by Dr. Goh Keng Swee: "But more important than what *we* did was the generally favorable background of the world economy." Goh Keng Swee, *The Practice of Economic Growth* (Singapore: Federal Publications, 1977), p. 99.

16. In 1990, of Singapore's total net investment commitments in manufacturing, 89 percent was considered foreign and only 11 percent local. Furthermore, foreign investment accounted for 55 percent of total industrial employment,

68 percent of total industrial output, and 81 percent of total manufactured exports. *Economic Development Board Annual Report, 1989–90* (Singapore, 1991).

17. Lim Chong Yah et al., *Policy Options for the Singapore Economy* (Singapore: McGraw-Hill, 1988), p. 162.

18. In an interview with a Taiwanese journalist in 1989, former Prime Minister Lee Kuan Yew expressed his concern: "I think we will face a serious problem because of the constant assault on our core values, like attitudes between men and women, husband and wife, father and children, attitudes between citizens and the government. Singaporeans watch so much of Western, especially American television, that they may begin to feel that is the norm, that is the standard. And we may move into that standard unconsciously." *Straits Times,* January 3, 1989. Mr. Lee spoke much like a Confucian moralist.

19. The report stated: "One of the dangers of secular education in a foreign tongue is the risk of losing the traditional values of one's own people and the acquisition of the more spurious fashions of the west . . . We recommend that formal instruction in moral education be given in all classes and all streams . . . While moral education would help to give school children a set of values which could guide them in their adult life, this may not be sufficient to provide the cultural ballast to withstand the stresses of living in a fast changing society exposed to influences, good and bad of an open society such as ours . . . With the large scale movement to education in English, the risk of deculturisation cannot be ignored. One way of overcoming the dangers of deculturisation is to teach children the historical origins of their culture." Goh Keng Swee, *Report on the Ministry of Education, 1978* (Singapore, 1979), pp. 1–5. About three months later, another report was released, spelling out the content of moral education from the Moral Education Committee headed by Ong Teng Cheong. See *Report on Moral Education, 1979* (Singapore, 1979).

20. The world religions course was never offered for lack of suitable teaching materials and competent teachers.

21. For a further discussion of the evolution of the moral education program, see Ong Jin Hui, "Future of Religion and Education in the Asia-Pacific Age: A Report from a Modern Multicultural Industrial Nation, Singapore," in *Asia-Pacific Culture: History and Outlook* (Tokyo: Tenri Yamato Culture Bureau, 1985).

22. In May 1982 Dr. Goh Keng Swee went to New York to consult a group of Chinese-American scholars, including Tu Wei-ming of Harvard and Yü Ying-shih of Yale (now at Princeton), for a general briefing on what aspect of Confucian ethics should be introduced to the schools in Singapore and how it should be taught. See *Straits Times,* June 13, 1982. Subsequently eight of these scholars were engaged as consultants to help devise the conceptual framework and syllabus for teaching the Confucian ethics course. They were

also invited to Singapore to conduct public talks and hold open forums to explain and popularize the subject to the general public. See Tu Wei-ming, *Confucian Ethics Today: The Singapore Challenge* (Singapore: Curriculum Development Institute of Singapore and Federal Publications, 1984).

23. See Eddie C. Y. Kuo, Jon S. T. Quah, and Tong Chee Kiong, *Religion and Religious Revivalism in Singapore* (Singapore: Report for the Ministry of Community Development, 1988).

24. "Religious Trends 'Need Careful Handling,'" *Straits Times*, February 19, 1989.

25. "Will a National Ideology Help Build a Singaporean Identity?," *Mirror* (Singapore, Ministry of Communications and Information), April 1, 1989.

26. "B. G. Lee Zeroes on the Core Issues," *Straits Times*, January 12, 1989.

27. "Shared Values," presented to Parliament by command of the President of the Republic of Singapore, January 2, 1991.

28. "RK to be replaced with Civics," *Straits Times*, October 7, 1989.

29. In a 1991 public lecture in Singapore, George Lodge of Harvard attributed the competitiveness of the East Asian economies to their communitarian social values. Hence, he said, "there are economic winners in the world to-day—for example, Singapore, other Asian countries . . . and there are economic losers—for example, the United States. The winners derive their comparative advantage from a particular brand of an ideology which I call communitarian and the United States owes much of its difficulty to the lingering effects of an eroding individualism. The challenge for Singapore is to retain the vitality of its communitarian ideology." George C. Lodge, "Social Values and Economic Competitiveness," public lectures at the National University of Singapore, January 3–10, 1991, p. 3.

30. Thus, the concluding paragraph of "Shared Values" states: "Through careful guidance and patient consensus building, we can influence, even if we cannot completely determine, the values which future generations of Singaporeans will share, and thus improve their chances of thriving and prospering together. This is a key responsibility of the present generation."

15. Confucianism as Political Discourse in Singapore

I am indebted to the comments made by Chua Beng-Huat and Kwok Kian-Woon on an earlier draft of this chapter.

1. In the final implementation six subjects were offered under the religious knowledge course. These are (in order of student enrollment numbers): Buddhist studies, Bible knowledge, Confucian ethics, Hindu studies, Islamic religious knowledge, and Sikh studies. All third- and fourth-year secondary students had to choose one of the six as an examination subject.

2. See Anthony Wallace, "Revitalization Movements," *American Anthropolo-*

gist, 58 (1956): 264–281; and Anthony Wallace, "Nativism and Revolution," *International Encyclopedia of the Social Sciences,* 11 (1968): 75–80.

3. The project was conducted by three social scientists from the National University of Singapore. A total of six reports were prepared and released. For a summary of the findings and recommendations, see Eddie Kuo, Jon Quah, and Tong Chee Kiong, *Religion and Religious Revivalism in Singapore: Report to the Ministry of Community Development* (Singapore, 1988).

4. The five "shared values" adopted by Parliament were (1) nation before community and society above self; (2) family as the basic unit of society; (3) community support and respect for the individual; (4) consensus, not conflict; and (5) racial and religious harmony. *Straits Times,* January 16, 1991, p. 1.

5. *Sunday Times* (Singapore), January 6, 1991, p. 16.

6. Ibid.

7. *Straits Times,* February 4, 1982, p. 1; February 8, 1982, p. 1.

8. Ibid., February 8, 1982, p. 36. Lee Kuan Yew also referred to the proposed Confucian ethics course and revealed: "Dr. Goh Keng Swee agreed with me that for most Chinese students, Confucianism not Buddhism will be what parents would prefer their children to study," p. 36.

9. *New Nation,* June 13, 1982, p. 2.

10. *Sinchew Jit Poh* (Sinchew Daily), May 9, 1982, p. 3.

11. Ibid., September 9, 1982, p. 7.

12. *Nanyang Siang Pao* (Nanyang Business News), September 10, 1982, p. 29.

13. *New Nation,* June 13, 1982, p. 2.

14. IEAP visiting fellows included Wm. Theodore de Bary, A. C. Graham, Li Zhehou, Lin Yü-sheng, Liu Shu-hsien, and Liu Ts'un-yan. Tu Wei-ming and Yü Ying-shih served as directors of the board and consultants in its curriculum development.

15. From 1985 to 1990 IEAP organized three major international conferences in Singapore: the International Conference on Confucian Ethics, July–August 1985; the Conference on Confucian Ethics and the Modernization of Industrial East Asia, January 1987; and the International Conference on the Development of Confucian Learning: Problems and Prospects, August–September 1988. The proceedings of the 1987 conference have been published as Tu Wei-ming, ed., *The Triadic Chord: Confucian Ethics, Industrial East Asia, and Max Weber* (Singapore: Institute of East Asian Philosophy, 1991). The institute also published an occasional paper and monograph series (twelve titles published by 1989) and sponsored a public lecture series (ten titles).

16. *Straits Times,* February 8, 1982, p. 14.

17. Herman Kahn, *World Economic Development: 1979 and Beyond* (London: Croom Helm, 1979); Ezra Vogel, *Japan as Number One* (Cambridge, Mass.: Harvard University Press, 1979); Roy Hofheinz, Jr., and Kent E. Calder, *The Eastasia Edge* (New York: Basic Books, 1982).

18. Quoted in *Straits Times,* February 4, 1982, p. 32.

19. In an article on Singapore, Ezra Vogel observes: "The willingness of the populace ... to allow more leeway to leaders than is common in Western democracies is *rooted in Confucian patterns* of relationships between subjects unaccustomed to exercising political power and their rulers." Ezra Vogel, "A Little Dragon Tamed," in *Management of Success: The Moulding of Modern Singapore,* ed. Kernial Singh Sandhu and Paul Wheatley (Singapore: Institute of Southeast Asian Studies, 1989), p. 1051; emphasis added.

20. See, for example, Chua Beng-Huat, "Confucianization in Modernizing Singapore," paper presented at the Beyond the Culture? The Social Sciences and the Problem of Cross Cultural Comparison conference, Evangelical Academy at Loccum, Germany, October 22–25, 1990.

21. Tu is commonly recognized as the scholar who has contributed the most to the promotion of Confucianism in Singapore, at both the societal and the intellectual levels.

22. Tu Wei-ming, *Confucian Ethics Today: The Singapore Challenge* (Singapore: Federal Publications and CDIS, 1984), p. 135.

23. *Straits Times,* February 4, 1982, p. 32.

24. Lee Kuan Yew has, on more than one occasion, praised the wisdom of the Confucian precept on the relationships between the government and the people. See, for example, *Straits Times,* January 8, 1987, p. 1.

25. Ministry of Education statistics, quoted in John Wong and Aline Wong, "Confucian Values as a Social Framework for Singapore's Economic Development," paper presented at the Conference on Confucianism and Economic Development in East Asia, Taipei, May 29–31, 1989. See also John Wong, "Promoting Confucianism for Socioeconomic Development," Chapter 14 of this volume. The prediction of Lee Kuan Yew was thus proven too optimistic (see note 8).

26. Kuo, Quah, and Tong, *Religion and Religious Revivalism in Singapore.*

27. Ibid., p. 41.

28. *Straits Times,* October 7, 1989, p. 1.

29. *Lianhe Zaobao* (United Morning News), October 7, 1989, p. 1.

30. The institute was subsequently renamed the Institute of East Asian Political Economy (IEAPE) in 1992. Although it cannot be documented, there are reasons to believe that this turn of research direction might have been influenced by the T'ien-an-men crackdown in 1989. First, the bloody crackdown may have caused some rethinking of the relations between Confucian ideology and an autocratic regime such as China's. Second, and more directly, the event and the outcome may have surprised and alarmed the authorities, as it revealed a lack of understanding of Chinese affairs. It is noted that IEAP chairman Goh Keng Swee was for several years an adviser to the Chinese government on the Special Economic Zones.

31. See note 4.

32. *Sunday Times,* January 6, 1991, p. 16.

33. Ibid.

34. It is thus most revealing that Lee Kuan Yew was praised by his successor Goh Chok Tong as a "modern Confucius." *Straits Times,* April 24, 1990, p. 3.

35. It should be noted that the position of the "shared values" as a political or ideological statement is rather ambiguous. The White Paper was adopted by Parliament in January 1991 but has no formal legal status. It has seldom been mentioned since its adoption, even during the 1991 general election. I am grateful to Chua Beng-Huat for pointing this out to me.

16. Societal Transformation and the Contribution of Authority Relations and Cooperation Norms in Overseas Chinese Business

1. See Peter L. Berger, *The Capitalist Revolution* (New York: Basic Books, 1986).

2. See Max Weber, *The Protestant Ethic and the Spirit of Capitalism* (New York: Scribner's, 1958).

3. See S. N. Eisenstadt, "The Protestant Ethic in an Analytical and Comparative Framework," in *The Protestant Ethic and Modernization: A Comparative View,* ed. S. N. Eisenstadt (New York: Basic Books, 1968), pp. 3–45.

4. R. N. Bellah, "Reflections on the Protestant Analogy in Asia," in Eisenstadt, *The Protestant Ethic and Modernization,* p. 244.

5. See R. D. Whitley, "The Social Construction of Business Systems in East Asia," *Organization Studies,* 12, no. 1 (1991): 1–28.

6. See Chester I. Barnard, *The Functions of the Executive* (Cambridge, Mass.: Harvard University Press, 1938).

7. See, for example, John P. Kotter, *Organizational Dynamics: Diagnosis and Intervention* (Reading, Mass.: Addison-Wesley, 1978); Henry Mintzberg, *The Stucturing of Organization* (Englewood Cliffs, N.J.: Prentice-Hall, 1979); Rosabeth M. Kanter, *The Change Masters* (London: Unwin, 1983); and Thomas J. Peters and Robert H. Waterman, Jr., *In Search of Excellence* (New York: Harper and Row, 1982).

8. See Geert Hofstede, *Culture's Consequences* (Beverly Hills: Sage Publications, 1980).

9. See Lucian Pye, *Asian Power and Politics* (Cambridge, Mass.: Harvard University Press, 1985).

10. Ibid., p. 334.

11. For an illustration of the workings of this value system, derived empirically from a study of seventy-two overseas Chinese chief executives, see S. G. Redding, *The Spirit of Chinese Capitalism* (New York: de Gruyter, 1990).

12. Ibid.

13. See Robert F. Silin, *Leadership and Values* (Cambridge, Mass.: Harvard University Press, 1976); Norbert Dannhaueser, "Evolution and Devolution of

Downward Channel Integration in the Philippines," *Economic Development and Cultural Change*, 29, no. 3 (1981): 577–595; C. A. Barton, "Trust and Credit: Some Observations Regarding Business Strategies of Overseas Chinese Traders in Vietnam," in *The Chinese in Southeast Asia*, vol. 1, *Ethnicity and Economic Activity*, ed. Linda Y. L. Lim and L. A. Peter Gosling (Singapore: Maruzen Asia, 1983), pp. 46–64; Redding, *The Spirit of Chinese Capitalism*; and Siu-lun Wong, *Emigrant Entrepreneurs: Shanghai Industrialists in Hong Kong* (Hong Kong: Oxford University Press, 1988).

14. Richard Robison, *Indonesia: The Rise of Capital* (Sydney: Allen and Unwin, 1986).

15. See, respectively, Kevin Hewison, "The Structure of Banking Capital in Thailand," presented at the symposium Changing Identities of the S.E. Asian Chinese since World War II, Australia National University, Canberra, 1985; James V. Jesudason, *Ethnicity and the Economy: The State, Chinese Business, and Multinationals in Malaysia* (Singapore: Oxford University Press, 1989); G. L. Hicks and S. G. Redding, "Culture and Corporate Performance in the Philippines: The Chinese Puzzle," in *Essays in Development Economics in Honor of Harry T. Oshima* (Manila: Philippine Institute for Development Studies, 1982), pp. 199–215; and Kunio Yoshihara, *The Rise of Ersatz Capitalism in South-East Asia* (Singapore: Oxford University Press, 1988).

16. Diego Gambetta, ed., *Trust: Making and Breaking Cooperative Relations* (Oxford: Blackwell, 1988).

17. Lawrence E. Harrison, *Underdevelopment Is a State of Mind* (Cambridge, Mass.: Harvard University, Center for International Affairs, 1985).

18. Samuel P. Huntington, *Political Order in Changing Societies* (New Haven: Yale University Press, 1968), p. 28.

19. Partha Dasgupta, "Trust as a Commodity," in Gambetta, *Trust: Making and Breaking Cooperative Relations*, pp. 49–72.

20. S. G. Redding and Michael Ng, "The Role of 'Face' in the Organizational Perceptions of Chinese Managers," *Organization Studies*, 3, no. 3 (1982): 201–219.

21. Gungwu Wang, "The Culture of Chinese Merchants," Working Paper Series no. 57, University of Toronto/York University Joint Centre for Asia Pacific Studies, 1990.

22. Niklas Luhmann, *Trust and Power* (New York: Wiley, 1979).

23. Gary G. Hamilton, ed., *Business Networks and Economic Development in East and Southeast Asia* (Hong Kong: Centre of Asian Studies, University of Hong Kong, 1991).

24. Ichiro Numazaki, "The Role of Personal Networks in the Making of Taiwan's *Guanxiqiye* (Related Enterprises)," in Hamilton, *Business Networks and Economic Development in East and Southeast Asia*, pp. 77–93.

25. Jon P. Alston, "*Wa, Guanxi* and *Inhwa*: Managerial Principles in Japan, China and Korea," *Business Horizons*, (March–April 1989): 26–31.

26. See Ernest Gellner, *Reason and Culture: The Historic Role of Rationality and Rationalism* (Oxford: Basil Blackwell, 1992).

17. Overseas Chinese Capitalism

1. The best of the country studies can be very good indeed. For examples of those emphasizing the role of the state, see, by Alice H. Amsden, *Asia's Next Giant: South Korea and Late Industrialization* (New York: Oxford University Press, 1989), and "The State and Taiwan's Economic Development," in *Bringing the State Back In,* ed. Peter B. Evans, Dietrich Rueschemeyer, and Theda Skocpol (Cambridge: Cambridge University Press, 1985), pp. 778–106; Thomas B. Gold, *State and Society in the Taiwan Miracle* (Armonk, N.Y.: M. E. Sharpe, 1986); Stephan Haggard and Chung-in Moon, "The South Korean State in the International Economy: Liberal, Dependent, or Mercantile?," in *The Antinomies of Interdependence: National Welfare and the International Division of Labor,* ed. John G. Ruggie (New York: Columbia University Press, 1983), pp. 131–189. Chalmers Johnson, *MITI and the Japanese Miracle: The Growth of Industrial Policy, 1925–1975* (Stanford: Stanford University Press, 1982); Edwin Winckler and Susan Greenhalgh, eds., *Contending Approaches to the Political Economy of Taiwan* (Armonk, N.Y.: M. E. Sharpe, 1988). For examples of those studies emphasizing the roles of markets and firms, see Masahiko Aoki, *Information, Incentives, and Bargaining in the Japanese Economy* (Cambridge: Cambridge University Press, 1988); Walter Galenson, *Economic Growth and Structural Change in Taiwan* (Ithaca, N.Y.: Cornell University Press, 1979); Samuel P. S. Ho, *Economic Development of Taiwan, 1860–1970* (New Haven: Yale University Press, 1978); Lawrence B. Krause, Koh Ai Tee, and Lee Yuan, *The Singapore Economy Reconsidered* (Singapore: Institute of Southeast Asian Studies, 1987); Shirley W. Y. Kuo, Gustav Ranis, and John C. H. Fei, *The Taiwan Success Story* (Boulder, Colo.: Westview Press, 1981). For examples of those studies emphasizing culture, see Peter Berger and Hsin-Huang Michael Hsiao, eds., *In Search of an East Asian Development Model* (New Brunswick, N.J.: Transaction Books, 1988); Michio Morishima, *Why Has Japan "Succeeded"?* (Cambridge: Cambridge University Press, 1982); William Ouchi, *Theory Z* (Reading, Mass.: Addison-Wesley, 1981); Hung-chao Tai, ed., *Confucianism and Economic Development: An Oriental Alternative?* (Washington, D.C.: Washington Institute Press, 1989).

2. For instance, Amsden's study *Asia's Next Giant* concludes with the generalization that all late-industrializing countries can successfully follow South Korea's example of a strong state and big corporations.

3. For examples of comparative studies that emphasize the state, see Frederic C. Deyo, ed., *The Political Economy of the New Asian Industrialism* (Ithaca, N.Y.: Cornell University Press, 1987); Gary Gereffi and Donald Wyman,

eds., *Manufacturing Miracles* (Princeton: Princeton University Press, 1990); Robert Wade, *Governing the Market* (Princeton: Princeton University Press, 1990); Gordon White, ed., *Developmental States in East Asia* (London: Macmillan, 1988). For examples of studies that emphasize the role of markets, see Bela Balassa, *Development Strategies in Semi-Industrial Economies* (Baltimore: Johns Hopkins University Press, 1982); Jagdish Bhagwati, *Anatomy and Consequences of Exchange Control Regimes* (Cambridge, Mass.: Ballinger, 1978); Edward K. Y. Chen, *Hyper-Growth in Asian Economies: A Comparative Study of Hong Kong, Japan, Korea, Singapore, and Taiwan* (London: Macmillan, 1979); Lawrence Lau, ed., *Models of Development: A Comparative Study of Economic Growth in South Korea and Taiwan* (San Francisco: Institute for Contemporary Studies, 1986). For one of the few successful comparative studies on economic development emphasizing a cultural point of view, see S. G. Redding, *The Spirit of Chinese Capitalism* (Berlin: de Gruyter, 1990).

4. For example, Wade, in *Governing the Market* (pp. 345–381), concludes with "lessons from East Asia," in which he recommends that industrial and industrializing countries need to improve the "effectiveness" of the state in order for it to play the same role it does in East Asia.

5. For a discussion of the one-shot case study, see Thomas Cook and Donald T. Campbell, *Quasi-Experimentation* (Chicago: Rand McNally, 1979), pp. 95–98.

6. In the literature on comparative methodology, the issue of determining independent units for a proper comparative analysis is called Galton's Problem, after Sir Francis Galton, who first showed that a lack of independence among the units of analysis hopelessly confuses the issue of diffusion versus independent causation. For a discussion of Galton's Problem, see Adam Przeworski and Henry Teune, *The Logic of Comparative Social Inquiry* (New York: Wiley-Interscience, 1970), pp. 51–57.

7. For some examples of this interpretation, see Amsden, *Asia's Next Giant;* Gold, *State and Society in the Taiwan Miracle;* Deyo, *The Political Economy of the New Asian Industrialism;* and Winckler and Greenhalgh, *Contending Approaches to the Political Economy of Taiwan.*

8. Bruce Cummings, "The Origins and Development of the Northeast Asian Political Economy," *International Organization,* 38 (1984): 1–40.

9. Peter Evans, "Class, State, and Dependence in East Asia: Lessons for Latin Americanists," in Deyo, *The Political Economy of the New Asian Industrialism,* pp. 203–226.

10. General Agreement on Tariffs and Trade (GATT), 1989.

11. Marion Levy, "Contrasting Factors in the Modernization of China and Japan," *Economic Development and Cultural Change,* 2, no. 3 (October 1953): 161–197; Norman Jacobs, *The Origin of Modern Capitalism and Eastern Asia* (Hong Kong: Hong Kong University Press, 1958); Immanuel Wallerstein, *The Modern World-System* (New York: Academic Press, 1974);

Frances V. Moulder, *Japan, China, and the Modern World Economy* (New York: Cambridge University Press, 1977).

12. See, for instance, Kwang-ching Liu, *Anglo-American Steamship Rivalry in China, 1862–1874* (Cambridge, Mass.: Harvard University Press, 1962); and Albert Feuerwerker, *China's Early Industrialization* (Cambridge, Mass.: Harvard University Press, 1958).

13. I should perhaps qualify this statement by noting that while China lost all of its wars with outside powers, it continued to have some success against those of inner Asia.

14. Taiwan's government has tried to create automobile exports but to date has had no success, even though there are a number of automobile-producing firms in Taiwan. On Taiwan's automobile industry, see Gregory Noble, "Contending Forces in Taiwan's Economic Policymaking," *Asian Survey,* 27, no. 6 (June 1987): 683–704.

15. One of the first statements of this point was made by Alexander Gerschenkron, *Economic Backwardness in Historical Perspective* (Cambridge, Mass.: Harvard University Press, 1962), and one of the more recent by Amsden, *Asia's Next Giant.*

16. One of the finest analyses of Japanese borrowing of Western technology is D. Eleanor Westney, *Imitation and Innovation: The Transfer of Western Organizational Patterns to Meiji Japan* (Cambridge, Mass.: Harvard University Press, 1987).

17. For this very innovative thesis, see Takeshi Hamashita, "The Tribute Trade System and Modern Asia," in *Memoirs of the Research Department at the Toyo Bunko,* 46 (1988): 1–25.

18. See, for example, Sheldon Garon, *The State and Labor in Modern Japan* (Berkeley: University of California Press, 1987); Richard J. Samuels, *The Business of the Japanese State* (Ithaca, N.Y.: Cornell University Press, 1987); Thomas C. Smith, *The Agrarian Origins of Modern Japan* (Stanford: Stanford University Press, 1959); and Westney, *Imitation and Innovation.*

19. For a full discussion of this phenomenon in modern times, see Karel van Wolferen, *The Enigma of Japanese Power* (New York: Vintage, 1990).

20. Ibid., pp. 25–49.

21. Samuels, *The Business of the Japanese State,* p. 260.

22. For some material on the origins of the *zaibatsu,* see Eleanor Hadley, *Antitrust in Japan* (Princeton: Princeton University Press, 1970), pp. 20–60.

23. Gary Hamilton, William Zeile, and Wan-jin Kim, "The Network Structures of East Asian Economies," in *Capitalism in Contrasting Cultures,* ed. Steward R. Clegg and S. Gordon Redding (Berlin: de Gruyter, 1990), pp. 111–117.

24. A classic statement of the relationship between enterprise and family is found in Fei Xiaotong, *From the Soil: The Foundations of Chinese Society* (Berkeley: University of California Press, 1992), chap. 12; see also references in Gary G. Hamilton and Wang Zheng's introduction to Fei's book.

25. Wong Siu-lun, "The Chinese Family Firm: A Model," *British Journal of Sociology*, 36, no. 1 (1981): 58–72; Redding, *The Spirit of Chinese Capitalism*.

26. Redding, *The Spirit of Chinese Capitalism*. pp. 143–182.

27. Gary Hamilton and Cheng-shu Kao, "The Institutional Foundations of Chinese Business: The Family Firm in Taiwan," *Comparative Social Research*, 12 (1990): 107–108.

28. For more on the importance of *guanxi* in business, see relevant chapters in Gary Hamilton, ed., *Business Networks and Economic Development in East and Southeast Asia* (Hong Kong: Centre of Asian Studies, University of Hong Kong, 1991).

29. Yen-p'ing Hao, *The Commercial Revolution in Nineteenth-Century China* (Berkeley: University of California Press, 1986), characterizes the late imperial economy as "commercial capitalism." The term is adequate for the nineteenth century because a great deal of the economic expansion that occurred then in China was indeed commercial and not industrial. But the term is inadequate now because the same family principles and the same type of networks are still being used, but this time to put together small firms that manufacture industrial products—garments in Hong Kong and bicycles in Taiwan.

30. The literature on the overseas Chinese in Southeast Asia is substantial. A basic text, though quite old, is still Victor Purcell, *The Chinese in Southeast Asia* (London: Oxford University Press, 1965). See also G. William Skinner, *Chinese Society in Thailand* (Ithaca, N.Y.: Cornell University Press, 1957); Edgar Wickberg, *The Overseas Chinese in the Philippines* (New Haven: Yale University Press, 1965); Linda Lim and L. A. Peter Gosling, *The Chinese in Southeast Asia*, 2 vols. (Singapore: Maruzen Asia, 1983); and Wang Gungwu, *China and the Chinese Overseas* (Singapore: Times Academic Press, 1991).

31. Kerrie L. MacPherson and Cliffon K. Yearley, "The 2 1/2 Margin: Britain's Shanghai Traders and China's Resilience in the Face of Commercial Penetration," *Journal of Oriental Studies*, 25, no. 2 (1987): 202–234.

32. Wellington K. K. Chan, "The Organizational Structure of the Traditional Chinese Firm and Its Modern Reform," *Business History Review*, 56, no. 2 (Summer 1982): 218–235.

33. On government-business cooperation, see Johnson, *MITI and the Japanese Miracle;* and for some insights on the outward expansion of Japanese businesses, see Terutomo Ozawa, *Multinationalism, Japanese Style* (Princeton: Princeton University Press, 1979).

34. These points are discussed more fully in Gary G. Hamilton, "Why No Capitalism in China?," in *Max Weber in Asian Studies,* ed. Andreas E. Buss (Leiden: E. J. Brill, 1985), pp. 65–89.

35. This point has been discussed at length in Gary G. Hamilton and Nicole Woolsey Biggart, "The Organization of Business in Taiwan," *American Journal of Sociology*, 96, no. 4 (January 1991): 999–1006.

36. Lim Ma-hui and Teoh Kit Fong, "Singapore Corporations Go Transnational," *Journal of Southeast Asian Studies,* 17, no. 2 (September 1986): 336–365.

37. Suehiro Akira, *Capital Accumulation in Thailand, 1855–1985* (Tokyo: Centre for East Asian Cultural Studies, 1989), p. 224.

38. For example, Peng Hwai-jen, "Taiwan qiye yezhu de 'guanxi' qi zhuanbian" (Relationships among Taiwan business owners and their changes: a sociological analysis) (Ph.D. diss., Department of Sociology, Tunghai University, 1989), demonstrates the overwhelming predominance of family ownership for the largest business groups in Taiwan.

39. Fei Xiaotong, *From the Soil,* chap. 6. See also Hamilton and Kao, "The Institutional Foundations of Chinese Business."

40. See Hamilton and Kao, "The Institutional Foundations of Chinese Business," for their discussion of family-owned networks in Taiwan.

41. For Taiwan, the best analyses are found in Peng Hwai-jen, "Taiwan qiye yezhu de 'guanxi' qi zhuanbian"; Ichiro Numazaki, "Networks and Partnerships: The Social Organization of the Chinese Business Elite in Taiwan" (Ph.D. diss., Michigan State University, 1991); and Hamilton, *Business Networks and Economic Development in East and Southeast Asia.*

42. For an analysis of the changing composition of Hong Kong's business structure, see Gilbert Wong, "Business Groups in a Dynamic Environment: Hong Kong, 1976–1986," in Hamilton, *Business Networks and Economic Development in East and Southeast Asia,* pp. 126–154.

43. Lim and Teoh, "Singapore Corporations Go Transnational."

44. The perspective advocated in this essay is congruent with what is being called the new economic sociology. For a clear statement on this perspective, see Richard Swedberg, "Major Traditions of Economic Sociology," *Annual Review of Sociology,* 17 (1991): 251–276. The key theoretical statement of this perspective is presented in Mark Granovetter, "Economic Action and Social Structure: The Problem of Embeddedness," *American Journal of Sociology,* 91, no. 3 (November 1985): 481–510.

45. Richard D. Whitley, *Business Systems in East Asia* (London: Sage, 1992). See also Whitley, "East Asian Enterprise Structures and the Comparative Analysis of Forms of Business Organization," *Organization Studies,* 11, no. 1 (1990): 47–74.

Epilogue

1. Tu Wei-ming, "Historical Significance of the Confucian Discourse," *China Quarterly,* no. 140 (December 1994): 1140.

GLOSSARY

Amano Teiyū　天野貞祐
Andong　安東
Andong Hyangkyo　安東鄉校
Arai Hakuseki　新井白石

Bak-yak-hoe　博約會
Bakufu　幕府
Buk-in　北人
bulch'eonwi　不遷位
bunmei　文明
Bunmeiron gaiyaku　文明概略
Bushido　武士道
Byoungsan Seowon　屏山書院

Chang Chih-tung　張之洞
Chang Hao　張灝
Chang Tsai　張載
Chen Te-hsiu　眞德秀
Ch'en Ch'iu　陳虯
Ch'en Liang　陳亮
Cheng Chu-yüan　鄭竹園
Ch'eng-Chu　程朱
Ch'eng I　程頤
Ch'eng-shih chia-shu tu-shu
　fen-nien jih-ch'eng　程氏家
　塾讀書分年日程

Ch'eng Tuan-li　程端禮
ch'eong-baek-ni　清白吏
ch'eongbin hobak　清貧好學
ch'i　氣
chia　家
Chia-yi　嘉義
Chiang Ching-kuo　蔣經國
chiang-hsüeh　講學
Chiang Kai-shek　蔣介石
Ch'ien Mu　錢穆
Ch'ien-tzu wen　千字文
chih　治
chih-fa　治法
chih-luan　治亂
chih-shan　至善
chih-tao　治道
chih-t'i　治體
chih-t'ung　治統
ching-shih　經世
ching-shih chih hsüeh
　經世之學
Ch'iu Chün　丘濬
chokopo. See *tsu-p'u*
Chosŏn　朝鮮
Chu Hsi　朱熹

Chu-tzu chia-li 朱子家禮
Chu-yüan Cheng. *See* Cheng Chu-
　yüan
Chuang Tzu 莊子
chukun aikoku 忠君愛國
chün 君
chün-hsien 郡縣
chün-tzu 君子
Chung-li 中壢
ch'ung 忠
ch'ung-hyo 忠孝

Dadao Kongjiadian 打倒孔家店
daimyō 大名
Dajōkan 太政官
Dam-soo-hee 淡水會
danka 檀家
Diaoyutai 釣魚台
do-jip-le 都執禮
dōgi 道義
Dong-in 東人
dori 道理
dōtoku 道德
dōtoku no jissen o shido suru
　道德の實踐を指導する

Edo 江戶
Eifu 永孚

fan-chen 藩鎮
Fan Chung-yen 范仲淹
Fang Tung-shu 方東樹
Fei Hsiao-t'ung 費孝通
feng-chien 封建
Feng Kuei-fen 馮桂芬
fengshui 風水
fenjia 分家
Fueto Toshio 不破勝敏夫
fūfu no wa 夫婦の和
fujin 不仁
Fukuzawa Yukichi 福澤喻吉

Gakumon no Susume
　學問のすすめ
gi 義

giri 義理
Go-daigo Tenno 後醍醐天皇
Goh Chok Tong 吳作棟
Goh Keng Swee 吳慶瑞
guanxi 關係
gui 鬼

Hakka 客家
Han-hsüeh 漢學
Han-shu 漢書
Hayashi Razan 林羅山
Hideo Yamashita. *See* Yamashita
　Hideo
Hiroshi Wagatsuma. *See* Wagatsuma
　Hiroshi
Hōjō Takatoki 北條高時
hsiang-lung fu-hu 降龍伏虎
Hsiao-ching 孝經
Hsiao Hsin-huang 蕭新煌
Hsiao-hsüeh 小學
hsin-hsing 心性
hsin wai-wang 新外王
hsin-yung 信用
hsiu-chi chih-jen 修己治人
hsiu-shen ch'i-chia 修身齊家
Hsiung Shih-li 熊十力
Hsü Fu-kuan 徐復觀
Hsüan 宣
Hsün Tzu 荀子
Hu Fu 胡佛
Hu Shih 胡適
Hu Yüan 胡瑗
Huang-Ch'ing ching-shih wen-p'ien
　皇清經世文編
Huang-Ming ching-shih wen-p'ien
　皇明經世文編
Huang Tsung-hsi 黃宗羲
hyang-eum-le 鄉飲禮
hyanggo. See hyangkyo
hyangkyo 鄉校

i 義
i-ch'ieh fang-hsia 一切放下
i-hsüeh 義學

i-li chih-hsüeh 義禮之學
ie 家
Ieyasu 家康
in 仁
Ise 伊勢
Itō Jinsai 伊藤仁齋
Izumo 出雲

jen 仁
jen-i-li-chih 仁義禮智
Jeong Yak-yong 丁若鏞
ji 慈
Jiang Zemin 江澤民
jigō-jitoku 自業自得
jin 仁
jingi 仁義
Jin Guantao 金觀濤
Jinjō shogaku shūshinso
　尋常小學修身書
jinrin no kanke 人倫の關係
jiri ninjo 義理人情
jitsugaku 實學
jiyū 自由
jukyo 儒教

kagyo 家業
Kaibara Ekken 貝原益軒
Kaji Nobuyuki 加地伸行
kajok 家族 (긔)
kan-ch'ing 感情
K'ang-hsi 康熙
K'ang Yu-wei 康有爲
kao iro 顔色
k'ao-cheng 考證
Kaohsiung 高雄
Katō Hiroyuki 加藤弘之
Katō Kiyomasa 加藤清正
Kiho 畿湖
Kim Kwang-ok 金光億
Kim Kyehaeng 金係行
Kim Seong-il 金誠一
ko (fairness) 公
ko (filial piety) 孝
Kōdai 神代

Koh Byong-ik 高炳翊
kokai 公會
kokoro 心
kokugaku 國學
kokugo 國語
kokumin dōtoku 國民道德
kokutai no hongi 國體の本義
kokyo no do 公共の道
kokyo wahei 公共和平
komei seidai 光明正大
kong-li-kong-ron 空理空論
koron 公論
kosei no ninfu 好生の仁風
Kōtō shogaku shūshinso
　高等小學修身書
Ku Yen-wu 顧炎武
kuan 官
Kumazawa Banzan 熊澤蕃山
kung (public) 公
kung (utility) 功
Kung Tzu-chen 龔自珍
kunja 君子
Kuomintang 國民黨
Kusunoki Masashige 楠木正成
kwan-le 冠禮
kyōgaku taishi 教學大旨
kyōiku chokugo 教育敕語
kyoung 敬

Lao Tzu 老子
le-hyang 禮鄉
le-i 禮義
Lee Kuan Yew 李光耀
Lee Syngman 李承晚
Lee Teng-hui 李登輝
Lei Chen 雷震
li (ritual) 禮
li (profit) 利
li (moral reason) 理
li (establish) 立
Li Kou 李覯
Li Kung 李塨
li-ming 立命
Li Zhehou 李哲厚

Liang Ch'i-ch'ao　梁啓超

liang-hsin　良心

Liang Sou-ming　梁漱溟

Lianhe Zaobao　聯合早報

lieh-chuan　列傳

lien　臉

Liu Shu-hsien　劉述先

Liu Tsung-yüan　柳宗元

Lu Xun　魯迅

Mao Tse-tung　毛澤東

Maruyama Masao　丸山眞男

Matsumoto Shigeru　松本茂

Matsumoto Sonnosuke　松本三之助

mei　命

Meiji　明治

meue no hito　目上の人

mien-tzu　面子

min　民

ming　命

minjung munhwa woondong
　民眾文化運動

minpō　民法

Mito　水戸

Mo Tzu　墨子

Motoda Nagazane　元田永眞

Mou Tsung-san　牟宗三

munmin jeongch'i　文民政治

munmyo　文廟

Nakae Tōju　中江藤樹

Nam-in　南人

Nanyang Siang Pao　南洋商報

Natsume Soseki　夏目漱石

Nimomiya Kinjiro　二宮金次郎

nin　仁

ningi　仁義

ninji　仁慈

ninjō　人情

Ninomioya Sontoku　二宮尊德

Nobuyuki Kaji. *See* Kaji Nobuyuki

Noron　老論

o-haka-mairi　お墓參り

Ogyū Sorai　荻生徂徠

Ong Teng Cheong　王鼎昌

oya-ko　親子

pa　霸

Pao Shih-chen　包世臣

Park Chung-hee　朴正熙

Peng Ming-min　彭明敏

ppurich'atki woondong　뿌리찾기 (探
　根) 運動

ri (principle)　理

ri (ritual)　禮

rinri　倫理

ritsu　立

ritsumei　立命

Ritsumeikan　立命館

ritsuryo　律令

Rongo no Kōshi　論語の孔子

Ryoo Seong-ryong　柳成龍

ryoshin　良心

Saaek seowon　賜額書院

Saemaul Undong　새마을 運動

Saionji Kimmochi　西園寺公望

Sakuma Shōzan　佐久間象山

san-kang　三綱

san-kang wu-lun　三綱五倫

san-min-chu-i　三民主義

san-tai　三代

San-tzu ching　三字經

sawoo　祠宇

Seijo jijo　西洋事情

seodo　書道

Seo-in　西人

seon-bi-jeong-shin　선비(讀書人) 精神

seong　誠

Seongkyunkwan　成均館

Seonjo　世宗

seowon　書院

seoye　書藝

Shang　商

she-hsüeh　社學

shen　神

sheng　生

Shiba Kokan　司馬江漢

shiei no sei　私營の政

Shigeru Matsumoto. *See* Matsumoto
　Shigeru

shih　師

Shih-chi　史記

Shi Huang Ti　始皇帝

shimin no michi　臣民の道

Shingaku　心學

Shingi-kan　神祇官

shinjinrui　新人類

Shinran　親鸞

Shinto　神道

Shisō　思想

Shizuki Tadao　志筑忠雄

Shoggakkōrei　小學校令

shogun　將軍

shu-yüan　書院

Shun　舜

Shushigaku　朱子學

shūshin　修身

sirhak　實學

Sorai-gaku　徂徠學

Soron　少論

sŏwon. See *seowon*

ssu　私

Ssu-shu　四書

Ssu-shu wu-ching　四書五經

su-ki ch'i-in　修己治人

Sun Yat-sen　孫逸仙

Suruga　駿河

Ta-hsüeh　大學

Ta-hsüeh yen-i　大學衍義

Ta-hsüeh yen-i pu　大學衍義補

Taewon-gun　大院君

Taido　大道

Takano Choei　高野長英

tang-hsia chi-shih　當下即是

Tang Junyi. *See* T'ang Chün-i

tang-wai　黨外

T'ang Chün-i　唐君毅

tao　道

tao-t'ung　道統

ten　天

Tenchi kokyo no dōri
　天地公共の道理

Tenchi ningi no taidō
　天地仁義の大道

Tenchi no kodō　天地の公道

Tenchi no shin　天地の心

Tendō　天道

Teni　天意

Tenri　天理

t'i　體

t'ien　天

T'ien-an-men　天安門

t'ien-hsia　天下

t'ien-jen ho-i　天人合一

t'ien-ming　天命

t'ien-tao　天道

Tokugawa　德川

tokusei o kan'yo suru
　德性を涵養する

tongxiang guanxi　同鄉關係

Tosan Seowon　陶山書院

Toshio Fueto. *See* Fueto Toshio

Tseng Ching　曾靜

Tseng Kuo-fan　曾國藩

tsu-p'u　族譜

tsung-fa　宗法

tsung-fa chih-tu　宗法制度

Tu Wei-ming　杜維明

Tung Chung-shu　董仲舒

Tunghai　東海

Tzu-kung　子貢

Tzu-lu　子路

Uesugi Yozan　上杉鷹山

wa　和

Wagatsuma Hiroshi　我妻洋

wang　王

Wang An-shih　王安石

wang-pa ping-yung i-li shuang-hsing
　王霸並用義利雙行

Wang Yang-ming　王陽明

watakushi　私

watakushitachi　私達

Watanabe Hiroshi　渡邊浩
Watanabe Kazan　渡邊華山
wei　位
Wen-hsüan　文選
Wong Siu-lun　黃紹倫
Wu　武
Wu Teh Yao　吳德耀
wu-wei　無爲

xiangtu wenxue　鄉土文學

Yamashita Hideo　山下秀雄
Yamazaki Anzai　山崎闇齋
yangban　兩班
Yao　堯
Yasukuni　靖國
ye-hyang　藝鄉
Yean Hyangkyo　禮安鄉校
Yeh Shih　葉適
Yen Yüan　顏元
yi. See i
Yi Eonjeok　李彥迪
Yi Soonshin　李舜臣
Yi T'oegye　李退溪
Yi Yulgok　李栗谷
yin-ssu　淫祀

Yin-yang　陰陽
Yoi Nihonjin　よい日本人
Yokoi Sonan　橫井小楠
Yoshida Shoin　吉田松陰
Yoshihisa Shinno　能久新王
Yoshikawa Akimasa　芳川顯正
Yoshikawa Koretaru　吉川惟足
Youngnam　嶺南
yü　欲
yü feng-chien yü chün-hsien　寓封建於郡縣
yü feng-chien yü shih-ta-fu　寓封建於士大夫
Yü Ying-shih　余英時
Yüan　院
Yüan Shih-k'ai　袁世凱
yudohoe　儒道會
yuitsu　唯一
yung　用
Yung-cheng　雍正
Yuri kosei　由利公正
yurim　儒林

zaibatsu　財閥
zhi　治
Zhu Xi. *See* Chu Hsi

CONTRIBUTORS

CHANG HAO is Professor of History at Ohio State University and a member of the Academia Sinica in Taiwan. He is the author of *Liang Ch'i-ch'ao and Intellectual Transition in China, 1890–1907* (1975) and *Chinese Intellectuals in Crisis: The Search for Order and Meaning, 1890–1919* (1987). His research interests are the intellectual history of modern China and the Neo-Confucian tradition.

WM. THEODORE DE BARY is John Mitchell Mason Professor and Provost Emeritus of Columbia University and a fellow of the American Academy of Arts and Sciences. Among his many works in East Asian thought, and especially Neo-Confucianism, are *The Trouble with Confucianism* (Harvard, 1991) and *Waiting for the Dawn* (1993).

S. N. EISENSTADT is Rose Issacs Professor Emeritus of Sociology at the Hebrew University of Jerusalem, where he has been a faculty member since 1946. He has served as visiting professor at numerous universities, including Harvard, Stanford, Chicago, Zürich, and Vienna. He is a member of the Israeli Academy of Sciences and Humanities, Foreign Honorary Fellow of the American Academy of Arts and Sciences, and Honorary Fellow of the London School of Economics. He is the recipient of the International Balzan Prize in Sociology, the McIver award of the American Sociological Association, and the Israel Prize. His publications include *The Political System of Empires* (1963), *From Generation to Generation* (1971), *Revolutions and the Transformation of Societies* (1978), *Order and Transcendence: The Role of Utopias in the Dynamics of Civilizations* (ed., with E. Ben-Ari, 1990), and *Martin Buber on Intersubjectivity and Cultural Creativity* (ed., 1992).

THOMAS B. GOLD is Associate Professor of Sociology at the University of California, Berkeley, where he has taught since receiving his Ph.D. from Harvard in 1981. From 1990 to 1994 he was chair of Berkeley's Center for Chinese Studies. He has written *State and Society in the Taiwan Miracle* (1986) and numerous articles on aspects of Taiwan's society and Chinese youth, civil society, and popular culture. He is currently writing a book on the fate of private business in China since 1949 as a way of examining the fate of privacy and individual autonomy.

GARY G. HAMILTON is Professor of Sociology at the University of Washington. His major areas of interest are East Asian business networks, Chinese societies, economic sociology, and historical-comparative sociology with an emphasis on East Asia. He is the editor of *Business Networks and Economic Development in East and Southeast Asia* (1991), with Wang Zheng; translator of Fei Xiaotong's *From the Soil: The Foundation of Chinese Society* (1992); and author of "Civilizations and the Organization of Economics" (in *Handbook of Economic Sociology,* ed. Neil Smelser and Richard Swedberg, 1994). He has been awarded a Fulbright Fellowship, a Guggenheim Fellowship, and a fellowship to attend The Advanced Center for the Behavioral Sciences in Palo Alto.

KIM KWANG-OK, D. Phil. in Social Anthropology (Oxford, U.K.), is currently Professor of Anthropology at Seoul National University. He has written many books and articles, including studies on politics of religion and ritual in Korea, elite culture and local level politics in contemporary Korea, and a Chinese peasant community in socialism. Having carried out field researches in China since 1990, Professor Kim's scholarly interests are comparative studies of Chinese and Korean cultures with particular emphasis on politics and culture in state and society.

AMBROSE Y. C. KING is Pro-Vice-Chancellor and Chair Professor of Sociology at the Chinese University of Hong Kong. He received his B.A. from National Taiwan University, his M.A. from National Cheng-chi University (Taiwan), and his Ph.D. from the University of Pittsburgh. He has been Visiting Fellow at the Center for International Studies, Massachusetts Institute of Technology, and Visiting Professor at the University of Wisconsin and the University of Heidelberg. His publications in Chinese include *From Tradition to Modernity: An Analysis of Chinese Society and Its Transformation, the Politics of Three Chinese Societies,* and *Salient Issues of Chinese Society and Culture.* He has been an editorial board member of the *Journal of Applied Behavioral Science* and *The China Quarterly.* He is a member of the Academia Sinica and has held several advisory positions to the Hong Kong government, including the Independent Commission against corruption and the Law Reform Commission.

KOH BYONG-IK is currently chairman of Humanities and Social Sciences at the Korean National Academy of Sciences. He has served as President of Seoul National University and the Academy for Korean Studies. Educated at Tokyo University, Seoul National University, and the University of Munich, where he earned a doctoral degree in history, Professor Koh has taught at Seoul National University and the University of Washington in Seattle. He was a research fellow at the Woodrow Wilson Center for Scholars. His scholarly interests include the history of historiography, Confucianism, and interrelations in East Asia, and he has published several books in Korean on those subjects.

EDDIE C. Y. KUO (Ph.D., University of Minnesota) is the founding Dean of the School of Communication Studies at Nanyang Technological University in Singapore. He is currently Professor of Sociology and Director of the Mass Communication Programme at the National University of Singapore. Dr. Kuo's research interests include the sociology of communication, the sociology of language, and cultural policy and national integration. He is co-author or co-editor of *The Contemporary Family in Singapore, Language and Society in Singapore, Communication Policy and Planning in Singapore,* and *Mirror on the Wall: Media in a Singapore Election.*

LIU SHU-HSIEN is Professor of Philosophy and Director of Research Institute for the Humanities at the Chinese University of Hong Kong. He has published more than a dozen books in Chinese, including *The Development and Completion of Chu Hsi's Philosophical Thought* (1982), *A Study of Huang Tsung-hsi's Philosophy of Mind* (1986), *Confucian Thought and Modernization* (1992), and has written numerous papers in English and Chinese. Professor Liu's research is focused on Chinese philosophy in general and Sung-Ming and Contemporary Neo-Confucian Philosophy in particular. His research interests include comparative philosophy and the philosophy of culture.

S. GORDON REDDING, the author *The Spirit of Chinese Capitalism,* is Professor of Management Studies and Director of the University of Hong Kong Business School. He has published extensively on the role of culture in the marketing process, research models in comparative management, participative management, and organizational behavior in the overseas Chinese communities.

EDWARD SHILS, a leading American sociologist and a major Western thinker of the twentieth century, was Distinguished Service Professor of the Committee on Social Thought and the Department of Sociology at the University of Chicago. He was the editor of *Minerva* and author of *Tradition, Intellectual and Powers, Torment of Secrecy,* and six volumes of collected papers. He was working on *The Movements of Knowledge* in the last days of his life.

ROBERT J. SMITH is Goldwin Smith Professor of Anthropology and Asian Studies at Cornell University, where he has taught since 1953. Among his publications are *Ancestor Worship in Contemporary Japan* (1974) and, with Ella Lury Wiswell, *The Women of Suye Mura*. He continues his long-term pursuit of research in Japanese popular religion. In 1993 the government of Japan conferred on him the Order of the Rising Sun in recognition of his contributions to the study of Japanese society and culture.

TU WEI-MING is Professor of Chinese History and Philosophy at Harvard University and a fellow of the American Academy of Arts and Sciences. He has taught at Princeton University and the University of California at Berkeley and has lectured at Peking University, Taiwan University, The Chinese University of Hong Kong, and the University of Paris. His research interests are Confucian thought, Chinese intellectual history, Asian philosophy, and comparative religion. He is the author of *Confucian Thought: Selfhood as Creative Transformation* (1985) and *Way, Learning, and Politics: Essays on the Chinese Intellectual* (1989) and editor of *China in Transformation* (1994) and *The Living Tree: Changing Meaning of Being Chinese Today* (1995).

WATANABE HIROSHI is Professor of the Graduate School of Law and Politics at the University of Tokyo and the author of *Early Modern Japanese Society and Sung Learning*. His research interests are Japanese intellectual history and the comparative study of East Asian Confucianism.

JOHN WONG is Professor and Director of The Institute of East Asian Political Economy in Singapore. He was formerly with the Economics Department of the National University of Singapore. He has been a Fullbright Visiting Professor at Florida State University and has held visiting positions at Harvard, Yale, Stanford, Toronto, and Oxford. He has written twelve books and numerous articles and papers on the Chinese economy, ASEAN (Association of Southeast Asian Nations) economies, and Asian NIEs (newly industrialized economies) for regional and international journals. His books include *Land Reform in the People's Republic of China* (1973), *ASEAN Economies in Perspective* (1979), and *Understanding China's Socialist Market Economy* (1993).

SAMUEL HIDEO YAMASHITA received his Ph.D. in history from the University of Michigan in 1981 and is Associate Professor of History at Pomona College. He was a postdoctoral fellow at the Edwin O. Reischauer Institute of Japanese Studies and a senior tutor in East Asian Studies at Harvard University. Professor Yamashita has written several articles on the ancient learning movement in Japan and recently published *Master Sorai's Responsals,* a translation of Ogyū Sorai's *Sorai sensei tōmonsho.* His research interests include Confucian academies in the early modern period, warrior vendettas, the modern Japanese state's appropriation of Confucian and warrior discourses, and the response of Asians to the Pacific War.

INDEX

activism, 73–74, 89
Acton, Lord, 346
Amano Teiyū, 164–165
American exceptionalism, 241
Americanization, 9
Amsden, Alice, 233, 237
Andong, 203–209, 212–217, 219, 226
antiforeignism, 123, 126
antitraditionalism, 266
Arai Hakuseki, 140–141, 153
asceticism, 3, 10, 73–74, 88–89
ASEAN (Association of East Asian Nations), 119
authentic person, 348. *See also* gentleman; noble man; superior man
authoritarianism, 122, 159, 190, 228–229, 233–239 *passim*, 244–246, 252–253, 257, 262, 295, 303–305 *passim*, 329, 345–349 *passim*
Avineri, Shlomo, 245

BAIR (Bureaucratic-Authoritarian Industrializing Regimes), 329
Barnard, Chester, 313

Bell, Daniel, 241
Bellah, R. N., 312
benevolence, 53, 56–57, 61–67, 159, 165, 346
Berger, Peter, 4, 265, 281, 310
Bhakti movement, 180
bourgeois class, 14, 39, 245–246, 254
Boyden, Stephen, 270
Buddhism, 98, 103, 117–118, 158–162, 165, 172; Japanese, 175–184
Bunger, Karl, 231
bureaucracy, 16, 69, 81, 85–90, 177, 181, 230, 232, 241, 313
Bushido, 159

Calder, Kent, 232, 302
capitalism, 3–10 *passim*, 118, 236, 254, 260, 264–270 *passim*, 275, 280, 283; Confucian, 119, 121–122; Chinese, 330–331, 334–342, 348; Japanese, 333–334, 336–337
Cassirer, Ernest, 187
centralization, 86